Dateline: Canada

Bob Bowman

VANCOUVER CITY COLLEGE

Holt, Rinehart and Winston of Canada, Limited
Toronto   Montreal

Robert T. Bowman, educated at Ashbury College, Ottawa, and at McGill University, served as a BBC broadcaster, and then with the CBC as a Canadian war correspondent. He was the Washington correspondent for Southam Newspapers. He now freelances for radio and newspapers, writes a column "Canada's Story" and lectures frequently.

ISBN 0-03-925262-0 (Paperback)

Library of Congress Catalog Number: 72-9493

Cover design by Barry Rubin

HOLT, RINEHART AND WINSTON OF CANADA, LIMITED

Printed in Canada
73 74 75 76   4 3 2 1

Preface

My main purpose in writing this book is to illustrate that Canadian history can be interesting. Our history has the unfortunate—and in my opinion, unjust—reputation of being dull. To me it is fascinating mainly because of the men and women who, by their energy and spirit, have left us the best of tradition, and the roots for a prosperous future. Many of these people are relatively unknown. Have you ever heard of James Mowat's desperate ride during the Northwest Rebellion? It was more dangerous and exciting than Paul Revere's famous ride. Sitting Bull was perhaps the most feared Indian in American history. How many Canadians know that he came to Canada with 4,000 of his fierce warriors and spent four years on the Prairies?

These 366 short stories are "teasers." It is my sincere hope that they, and the lists of other events which occurred on the same days, will lead you to read more detailed accounts in the many new and excellent history books in our libraries and book stores.

While compiling my calendar of events, I have become indebted to people from coast to coast. I am most grateful for the assistance given by the Vancouver Public Library, Saint John Public Library, Toronto Central Library, Oakville Memorial Library, Halifax Memorial Library, and the Department of Canadian History, New Brunswick Museum.

For their guidance, I would also like to thank Dr. W. G. Black of Vancouver; W. K. Lamb, Director of the National Archives of Canada; Dr. M. Ormsby, Director of the Department of History, University of British Columbia; and Miss M. W. Hagerman, head of the history section of the Vancouver Public Library.

Finally, my heartfelt thanks to one of Canada's best broadcasters, Marita McNulty of Saint John, who first interested me in Canadian history, and helped along the way.

BOB BOWMAN

Picture Credits

AIR CANADA, Oct. 17

ALBERTA GOVERNMENT, May 22, Sept. 22, Nov. 20, Dec. 27

ALBERTA GOVERNMENT, ERNEST BROWN COLLECTION, Feb. 4, 19; Aug. 14

APPLEBY, BARRIE, Jan. 18, April 2

ANDERSON, MAJOR C. WARREN, Dec. 5

ATLANTIC FILMS AND ELECTRONICS LTD., March 31

ARAU PHOTO, Oct. 1

BRITISH COLUMBIA ARCHIVES, Feb. 7, March 7, 11, 15; May 23, 29; June 13, July 6, 7, 20; Sept. 20, Oct. 25, Nov. 19

BRITISH COLUMBIA GOVERNMENT, July 31–Aug. 1

CAMPBELL, RALPH G., March 22

CANADIANA COMPANY LIMITED, March 18

Canadian Expeditionary Force 1914-1919, BY COL. G. W. L. NICHOLSON, C.D. REPRODUCED WITH PERMISSION OF THE QUEEN'S PRINTER, OTTAWA, May 25

CANADIAN GOVERNMENT TRAVEL BUREAU, Dec. 9

CANADIAN NATIONAL RAILWAYS, Aug. 29

CAPITAL PRESS SERVICE, Feb. 29–March 1

CENTRAL PRESS PHOTOS LTD., Nov. 11

CONFEDERATION LIFE ASSOCIATION, March 8, April 20, Sept. 3

CONFEDERATION LIFE COLLECTION, PAINTED BY J. D. KELLY AFTER C. HUOT, Dec. 17

CONFEDERATION LIFE COLLECTION, PAINTED BY REX WOODS, Nov. 18

CROSBY PHOTO STUDIOS, LTD., March 26

DEPARTMENT OF NATIONAL DEFENCE, Aug. 19

EXPO '67, Oct. 31–Nov. 1

IMPERIAL OIL COLLECTION, C. W. JEFFERYS DRAWINGS, Jan. 6, 8; Feb. 1, 11; March 13, 16, 19; May 5, 7, 17, 21; June 5, July 15, 24, 28; Aug. 15, 16, 23; Oct. 15, 22, 26; Dec. 8, 11, 26

IMPERIAL OIL LIMITED, Feb. 28

KARSH, OTTAWA, Feb. 29–March 1, March 31–April 1

MACKINAC ISLAND STATE PARK COMMISSION, July 17

MANITOBA ARCHIVES, April 12, May 2, 31; June 21, 28; July 29, Dec. 2, 28

MANITOBA DEPARTMENT OF INDUSTRY AND COMMERCE, May 31–June 1

NATIONAL FILM BOARD, Jan. 31–Feb. 1

NATIONAL MUSEUM OF CANADA, May 28

NEW BRUNSWICK MUSEUM, Feb. 15, May 13, Aug. 7, Oct. 7, Nov. 6, 23

NEW BRUNSWICK MUSEUM, WEBSTER CANADIANA COLLECTION, Jan. 2, 4, 7, 9, 11, 13, 15, 17, 24, 28, 30, 31; Feb. 3, 4, 5, 13, 14, 21, 26; March 3, 6, 10, 12, 14, 17, 28; April 1, 3, 7, 9, 13, 16, 17, 21, 26, 28, 29; May 3, 9, 11, 18, 19, 20, 24, 27; June 2, 7, 9, 11, 12, 14, 15, 16, 17, 20, 23, 27; June 30–July 1; July 1, 2, 4, 5, 16, 22, 23, 26, 27, 30; Aug. 2, 6, 12, 17, 18, 21, 26, 27, 31; Sept. 1, 4, 5, 6, 8, 9, 11, 13, 14, 15, 19, 21, 25, 27, 29; Oct. 2, 3, 5, 6, 10, 12, 16, 18, 19, 24, 27, 31; Nov. 2, 3, 5, 7, 9, 13, 15, 22, 26, 30; Dec. 7, 16, 18, 20, 22, 29, 30, 31

NEWFOUNDLAND ARCHIVES, Dec. 12

NEWFOUNDLAND MUSEUM, Aug. 3

NOVA SCOTIA INFORMATION SERVICE, Jan. 16

ONTARIO ARCHIVES, Jan. 27, 29; Feb. 5, 6, 10, 12, 16, 17; March 27, 29, 30; April 5, 24; May 4, June 1, 8, 22; Aug. 8, Oct. 30

ONTARIO DEPARTMENT OF TOURISM AND INFORMATION, Oct. 13

PROVINCE OF QUEBEC DEPARTMENT OF TOURISM, FISH AND GAME, July 31–Aug. 1

PROVINCE OF QUEBEC FILM BUREAU, Jan. 23, 25; Feb. 24, March 2, April 25, May 26, July 3, Aug. 31–Sept. 1

PROVINCE OF QUEBEC FILM BUREAU, PHOTO BY TUROFSKY, Aug. 31–Sept. 1

PROVINCIAL OFFICE OF PUBLICITY OF QUEBEC, PHOTO DISCOLL, May 31–June 1

PUBLIC ARCHIVES OF CANADA, Jan. 1, 3, 5, 10, 21, 24; Feb. 27, 29; April 4, 18, 27; May 15, 30; June 4, July 21, Aug. 13, 25; Sept. 26, Nov. 27, 28; Dec. 6

QUEBEC ARCHIVES, Nov. 16

ROYAL CANADIAN MOUNTED POLICE, May 6, July 9, Oct. 14

SASKATCHEWAN ARCHIVES, Jan. 20, April 10, June 30, Dec. 10

TORONTO PUBLIC LIBRARIES, Jan. 19, Feb. 8, 25; April 15, Nov. 12, Dec. 4

TORONTO STAR SYNDICATE, Feb. 23, July 11, Aug. 31–Sept. 1

UNIVERSITY OF NEW BRUNSWICK, Nov. 29

UNIVERSITY OF TORONTO, DEPARTMENT OF INFORMATION, March 31–April 1

WIDE WORLD PHOTO, Aug. 1, 11

Howe, "Not Guilty"

Poetry was the maiden I loved, but politics was the harridan I married.

—JOSEPH HOWE

Over the years many important events have taken place in Canada on January 1. One that happened in 1835 helped to establish the principle of freedom of the press in Canada, and for that reason it is outstanding.

Joseph Howe, son of the King's Printer in Halifax, worked as a "printer's devil" from the time he was fifteen years old, and managed to buy a newspaper called *The Nova Scotian*. He paid the equivalent of $5,000 for it, in instalments of $1,000 a year.

On January 1, 1835, *The Nova Scotian* printed a letter to the editor which accused the magistrates of Halifax of imposing excessive fines so that they could line their own pockets. The writer said he was prepared to prove his charges.

The magistrates had Howe arrested on a charge of libel, and no lawyer would defend him. Howe decided to fight his own case, although he had little education except for what he had learned through reading. In preparation he studied the laws of libel for two weeks before appearing in court.

When the magistrate asked him, "Are you a devil?" Howe replied, "Yes, but only a printer's devil." That got the jury on his side. He spoke for six hours in his defense, and parts of his address to the jury rank with the most eloquent statements in the English language.

The judge practically ordered the jury to declare Howe guilty, but it brought in a verdict of "not guilty" after deliberating for only ten minutes. Howe was carried out of the court on the shoulders of the people, and there were celebrations in Halifax for two days, with bands marching in the streets. It was a significant victory for freedom of the press.

Joseph Howe eventually became one of Canada's greatest statesmen.

Hon. Joseph Howe, c. 1871

Other Events on January 1:

1743   Sons of Pierre de la Verendrye were the first white men to see the Rockies.

1748   François Bigot, perhaps Canada's top ranking criminal, was appointed Intendant of Quebec.

1776   United States forces under Montgomery and Arnold attacked Quebec.

1823   Nova Scotia became the first province to issue coinage.

1833   Newfoundland's first representative assembly met at St. John's.

1855   Ottawa was incorporated as a city.

1894   Ontario voted for prohibition.

1922   British Columbia changed to driving on the right-hand side of the road.

1947   Canadians became "Canadian citizens" rather than "British citizens."

1952   Old Age Security Act took effect.

1958   British Columbia celebrated its Centennial.

1964   A new electoral act became law in Quebec; the minimum age for voting in provincial elections was reduced to eighteen.

William Lyon Mackenzie (1795-1861)

Mackenzie Re-elected

I am incapable of moderating the spirit of party—I am hot and fiery and age has not yet tempered as much as I could wish my political conduct and opinions.

—W. L. MACKENZIE, 1835

Anyone can make good in Canada regardless of his background. Take William Lyon Mackenzie King, who was prime minister for most of the years between 1921 and 1948, longer than any other leader in the British Commonwealth. Yet his grandfather, William Lyon Mackenzie, probably caused more trouble than any other man in the history of the country.

Like Joseph Howe, Mackenzie was a reformer and a newspaper editor. In his paper, the *Colonial Advocate*, he kept bombarding the governor and his advisers with criticisms. He made the ruling classes so angry that a group of gay sparks from the "best families"

raided his office, and threw his type into Toronto Bay. Mackenzie sued them and used the $3,000 he received in damages to pay off his debts and make a fresh start.

The raid helped him more than financially. In 1828 he was elected to the Upper Canada Assembly as one of two members for York. During his parliamentary career he was expelled five times, but was always re-elected! On January 2, 1832, he won a by-election by 119 votes to 1 and was presented with a gold medal. In 1835, the year after York was renamed Toronto, Mackenzie became its first mayor.

Gradually Mackenzie's emotions overcame his commonsense, and in 1837 he led an armed revolt against the government of Upper Canada. It was easily crushed, and he fled to the United States. He established a base on Navy Island above Niagara Falls, proclaimed a provisional government, and even attacked a military establishment at Chippawa. Canadian militia led by Allan MacNab, who later became prime minister, set his supply ship *Caroline* on fire and sent it over the falls. One American was killed in the fighting.

This caused so much indignation that war almost broke out between Britain and the United States. Cooler heads prevailed, and Mackenzie was put in jail for a while. Soon after, he was allowed to return to Canada.

William Lyon Mackenzie King, his grandson, was always proud of his rebel ancestor.

Other Events on January 2:

1826   The Supreme Court of Newfoundland was established by Royal Charter.

1895   The Privy Council reversed a Supreme Court decision on Manitoba separate schools.

1908   The Royal Mint opened at Ottawa.

1929   Canada and the United States signed an agreement to preserve Niagara Falls.

1942   Canada promised to use its full resources against the Axis Powers.

Slavery Ends in Canada

On this day in 1802 the Niagara *Herald* carried the following advertisement:"For sale, a negro slave eighteen years of age, stout and healthy; has had the small-pox and is capable of service either in the house or out-of-doors. The terms will be made easy to the purchaser, and cash or new lands received in payment. Enquire of the publisher."

Although the advertisement seems cruel today, we should remember that Canada ended slavery long before the United States Congress passed anti-slavery legislation in 1862. Upper Canada prohibited the importing of slaves in 1793, mainly because Governor Simcoe was an abolitionist. However, many of the United Empire Loyalists had brought slaves with them and were allowed to keep them. Legislation provided that children of slaves would be freed when they became twenty-five years of age. The boy in the advertisement would therefore have been freed seven years later.

During the War of 1812 many American slaves discovered that there was freedom in Canada, and an underground system was developed to transport them across the border. By 1850 it was estimated that as many as 40,000 slaves had settled in the communities along the border, chiefly between Windsor and Niagara Falls. An Anti-Slavery Society was formed in Toronto and helped to find jobs for them.

Reverend Josiah Henson, whose experiences inspired Harriet Beecher Stowe to write *Uncle Tom's Cabin*, settled in Dresden, Ontario, where there is now a memorial to him. John Brown, immortalized in the song about his body lying "a-mouldering in the grave", held a big convention at Chatham in 1858 and in the following year used the "underground" to smuggle twelve negro slaves to Windsor.

Lower Canada and the Maritimes did not pass anti-slavery legislation, but their courts refused to recognize the rights of masters over slaves, and this had the same effect.

Chap. VII. 33rd GEORGE III. A.D. 1793.—Second Session

AN ACT to prevent the further introduction of Slaves, and to limit the term of contracts for servitude within this Province.

[Passed 9th July, 1793.]

WHEREAS it is unjust that a people who enjoy freedom by law should encourage the introduction of Slaves ; *And whereas* it is highly expedient to abolish Slavery in this Province, so far as the same may gradually be done without violating private property : *Be it enacted* by the King's most Excellent Majesty, by and with the advice and consent of the Legislative Council and Assembly of the Province of Upper Canada, constituted and assembled by virtue of and under the authority of an Act passed in the Parliament of Great Britain, intituled, "An Act to repeal certain parts of an Act passed in the fourteenth year of His Majesty's reign, intituled, 'An Act for making more effectual provision for the Government of the Province of Quebec, in North America,' and to make further provision for the Government of the said Province," and by the authority of the same, That from and after the passing of this Act, so much of a certain Act of the Parliament of Great Britain, passed in the thirtieth year of His present Majesty, intituled, "An Act for encouraging new Settlers in His Majesty's Colonies and Plantations in America," as may enable the Governor or Lieutenant Governor of this Province, heretofore parcel of His Majesty's Province of Quebec, to grant a license for importing into the same any Negro or Negroes, shall be, and the same is hereby repealed ; and that from and after the passing of this Act, it shall not be lawful for the Governor, Lieutenant Governor, or person administering the Government of this Province, to grant a license for the importation of any Negro or other person to be subjected to the condition of a Slave, or to a bounden involuntary service for life, into any part of this Province ; nor shall any Negro, or other person, who shall come or be brought into this Province after the passing of this Act, be subject to the condition of a Slave, or to such service as aforesaid, within this Province, nor shall any voluntary contract of service or indentures that may be entered into by any parties within this Province, after the passing of this Act, be binding on them, or either of them, for a longer time than a term of nine years, from the day of the date of such contract.

II. *Provided always,* That nothing herein contained shall extend, or be construed to extend, to liberate any Negro, or other person subjected to such service as aforesaid, or to discharge them, or any of them, from the possession of the owner thereof, his or her executors, administrators or assigns, who shall have come or been brought into this Province, in conformity to the conditions prescribed by any authority for that purpose exercised, or by any ordinance or law of the Province of Quebec, or by proclamation of any of His Majesty's Governors of the said Province, for

Anti-slavery legislation, 1793

Other Events on January 3:

1800   Attorney-General John White of Upper Canada was killed in a duel by John Small, Clerk of the Council.

1802   Three hundred Highlanders from Scotland settled in Sydney, Nova Scotia.

1862   Eight hundred and fifty officers and men of the Rifle Brigade of Britain landed at Saint John, New Brunswick and were transported to Quebec in sleighs. There was danger of war between Britain and the United States and a total of 3,000 troops was sent to defend Canada.

1863   The first covered skating rink in Canada opened at Halifax, Nova Scotia. It is claimed that the first ice hockey was played on the Dartmouth Lakes. Kingston, Ontario, disputes this claim.

Captain Vancouver exploring Nootka Sound Territory

Spain and Britain Approaching War

Nootka is a quiet harbor on the west coast of Vancouver Island. It does not get into the news often now, but in 1790 Nootka nearly caused a war that could have involved Britain, Spain, France, Holland, and Prussia.

Captains Cook and Vancouver, while exploring the coast looking for the Northwest Passage, had visited the beautiful ice-free harbor of Nootka Sound. The Indians were friendly and had bountiful supplies of sea-otter skins which they were willing to trade. Soon other British ships began to arrive and a profitable fur trade with China developed.

In those days Spain claimed most of the Pacific coast of North America, and had an important base at San Francisco. When the Spanish authorities became aware of what was going on, they sent a naval squadron to Nootka which destroyed the base and took possession of the British ships. On January 4, 1790, the British chargé d'affaires at Madrid heard what had happened and sent word to London. Spain added fuel to the fire by presenting a stiff note to Britain ordering British ships to keep out of the area.

Spain felt confident about challenging Britain at this time because she had an alliance with France. Britain had a similar alliance with Holland which immediately offered ships to strengthen the British navy in case of war. Prussia offered to send troops, providing Britain would join Prussia in an attack on Russia. This offer was refused.

The Spanish actions infuriated the British Government, and Parliament voted two million pounds to send a fleet under the dreaded Admiral Howe to attack Spain. Just at this time the French Revolution broke out, and France was lost to Spain as an ally. Spain then backed down quickly, and offered to pay reparations for the ships that had been taken, and to share Vancouver Island equally with Britain. Strangely enough, the United States missed this agreement when she later bought Spanish possessions in North America. If she hadn't, half of Vancouver Island might belong to the United States today (see March 23).

Other Events on January 4:

1817   Stagecoach service began between Kingston and York, Ontario; the fare was $18.

1830   Upper Canada College was opened at York.

Battle of Windmill Point, below Prescott, Nov., 1838

Americans Defy President – Land at Prescott, Ont.

Canada has been fortunate in escaping serious civil wars such as have taken place in the United States, Britain, France, Russia, and many other countries. Nevertheless, there were rebellions in which people were killed in Upper and Lower Canada in 1837-1838, and in what is now Saskatchewan in 1885.

The rebellions in Upper and Lower Canada might have been far more serious if it had not been for President Van Buren of the United States who, on January 5, 1838, issued a proclamation forbidding Americans to take any part in the fighting. The governors of New York and Vermont, the States most closely affected, took similar action. This took the wind out of the sails of the Canadian rebel leaders who had been counting on receiving aid from across the border.

Robert Nelson was one of the most active leaders. He had the brilliant idea of forming an organization called "Hunters' Lodges", which capitalized on the American weakness for joining secret organizations. The Hunters had "cells" all along the border. Each local group was commanded by a Snowshoe, who was in charge of nine Hunters. A Beaver directed five Snowshoes; an Eagle commanded the Beavers, and so on until the chain of authority reached the Grand Eagle, or supreme commander.

Sir John Colborne, Commander-in-Chief of the British forces in Canada, estimated that the Hunters had 200,000 members. They held a convention in Cleveland and proclaimed a "Republican Government" of Canada. Plans included an invasion of Canada all along the border from Detroit to Montreal. One quite serious battle occurred when a force from Ogdensburg, N.Y. landed at Prescott, Ontario with the idea of dividing Upper and Lower Canada. The battle lasted four days and by then the raiders had either been killed or captured. Although their leaders were defended by John A. Macdonald, then a young lawyer in Kingston, they were found guilty and hanged.

Other Events on January 5:

1680   La Salle built Fort Crèvecoeur on the Illinois River.

1805   The first issue of the Quebec *Mercury* was published.

1870   The first issue of Ottawa's *Le Courier* went on sale.

1874   Winnipeg held its first civic election; 331 votes were cast, although there were only 308 on the voters' list!

Maisonneuve at Mount Royal, 1643

Maisonneuve Erects Cross To Celebrate Epiphany

At night, when its lights can be seen for many miles, the huge cross on Mount Royal is one of the most impressive sights in Montreal. The original cross was planted near there on January 6, 1643, by Sieur de Maisonneuve, the founder and first governor of Ville Marie, now Montreal.

The occasion was the Feast of the Epiphany, and Maisonneuve had a path cleared through the snow so that he and his party could carry a wooden cross to the top of the mountain. It stood there for many years until it was replaced by its modern counterpart.

Montreal had only been founded the previous May and was the crossroads of a number of routes used by the fierce Iroquois. During the summer Maisonneuve's men had built a habitation for sixty people, protected by a strong wooden palisade. It was always dangerous to go outside the walls because the Iroquois lurked in the woods looking for opportunities to kill the white settlers. The party that climbed the mountain on January 6 was no doubt well-armed and kept a sharp lookout.

Among the company were two remarkable women, Jeanne Mance and Madame de La Peltrie, who respectively founded a hospital at Montreal and the Ursuline convent at Quebec. More about these courageous women will be heard in later stories.

Other Events on January 6:

1685   La Salle reached the mouth of the Mississippi River.

1789   Lord Dorchester (formerly Sir Guy Carleton) established the first agricultural college at Quebec.

1807   Reine Lajimonière was the first white child born in Western Canada.

1877   Canada's first flour mill (McLean's) was established in Manitoba.

1915   Princess Patricia's Canadian Light Infantry went into action in France.

Bowell Loses Ministers

This is the anniversary of an amazing event in Canadian political history. A Canadian prime minister found himself unable to fill all the positions in his cabinet because his colleagues had formed a picket line.

The Government of Manitoba, supported by a strong mandate of the people, had passed an act making public schools nonsectarian. Roman Catholics felt they were entitled to separate schools and appealed the act through a series of courts, with varying results. Finally, the Privy Council in London ruled that the federal government had the right to force Manitoba to provide separate schools.

The political situation became so confused that Conservative Prime Minister Sir Mackenzie Bowell, a leading Orangeman, found himself supporting the Roman Catholic position while the Liberal Leader of the Opposition, Sir Wilfrid Laurier, a Roman Catholic, supported the Protestant side.

Prime Minister Bowell's policy supporting separate schools was so unpopular with many members of his party that on January 7, 1896, seven cabinet ministers resigned. When Bowell tried to find replacements for them, the "rebels" picketed the government offices to stop him from recruiting new ministers.

The bill to force Manitoba to restore separate schools was filibustered in Parliament. On one occasion the House of Commons was in session for one hundred hours while members discussed everything from the Bible to *Alice in Wonderland*. Finally, the bill was withdrawn.

The Liberals under Wilfrid Laurier won the election that followed. Laurier won most of the seats in Quebec even though he had opposed his church. On the other hand, Manitoba returned four Conservatives to three Liberals, even though the Conservatives had favoured the return of separate schools. It was all very confusing, but Sir Wilfrid Laurier worked out a compromise which allowed for religious instruction and bilingual teaching in schools where ten or more students spoke a language other than English.

Sir Mackenzie Bowell (1823-1917)

Other Events on January 7:

1608   Henry IV of France renewed de Mont's fur trade monopoly and temporarily saved the colony at Port Royal, N.S.

1691   A second issue of money was made from playing cards in order to finance a garrison at Quebec (see April 18).

1765   French-speaking citizens appealed to King George to change the legal system.

1859   Canadian silver coinage was first issued. (Nova Scotia had issued coins earlier but was not then a part of Canada.)

1955   The opening ceremonies of Parliament were broadcast on television for the first time.

1960   Antonio Barrette became Premier of Quebec.

1963   Contracts for flood prevention in the Red River area were let. This was the largest earth moving job in Canadian history.

La Salle watching for the Griffon

La Salle Loses *Griffon*

This was a sad day for Robert Cavelier, Sieur de La Salle, one of the great early explorers of Canada. He and his colleagues had built the *Griffon*, which was the first ship to sail the Great Lakes above Niagara Falls. In September, 1679, after the *Griffon* had taken them through Lake Erie and Lake Huron, they arrived at what is now the home of the famous Green Bay Packers football team in Wisconsin.

There La Salle loaded the *Griffon* with furs which were to be transported to Montreal to pay his bills, while he explored the Illinois River. La Salle was always looking for the great river that might prove to be the short route to China. He talked about this so much that his men jokingly called the rapids above Montreal *La Chine* meaning China, and they are still called the Lachine Rapids today.

It was on January 8, 1680, that La Salle heard the news that the *Griffon* had disappeared with all hands and its valuable cargo. The loss of the ship remained a mystery for two hundred years until the wreckage of an old ship was found off Manitoulin Island, Lake Huron. Later six skeletons were found in a cave not far away. The wreckage is believed to be the *Griffon*, and the skeletons, the remains of the members of its crew.

The ship may have been sabotaged since La Salle had many enemies. Often, when he was on his trips, his men would desert him, and La Salle would have to continue alone. Fortunately, the Indians were friendly and he was frequently helped by them.

Eventually, La Salle did manage to lead a large group of men down the Mississippi to claim Louisiana for France. He was murdered by one of his own men while on a campaign to establish a colony on the Gulf of Mexico.

Other Events on January 8:

1801 The Lower Canada Assembly began the session that ordered walls around Montreal to be demolished. It also licensed billiard tables.

1814 Selkirk settlers put an embargo on supplies leaving the Red River.

1830 The Upper Canada Assembly began the session that rejected an act legalizing marriages by Methodist ministers.

1879 The first issue of *La Gazette d'Ottawa* was published.

1948 W. L. Mackenzie King established a record for being prime minister longer than any other government leader in the British Commonwealth.
General A. G. L. McNaughton was appointed permanent delegate from Canada to the United Nations and Representative of Canada on the Security Council.

1954 The world's longest pipeline flow of crude oil, starting from Alberta, reached Sarnia, Ontario—1,770 miles.

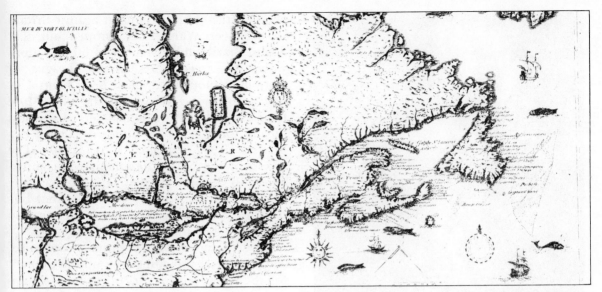

Champlain's map of Canada

Champlain Publishes *Voyages*

On January 9, 1613, Champlain published his *Voyages*, describing his adventures from 1604 to 1612. Around this time he also published several maps. (The map shown above was published in 1632.) Champlain showed great skill as a cartographer and these maps are still fascinating. King Henry IV was so impressed with Champlain's maps of Mexico that he appointed him royal cartographer.

When Champlain explored Canada from Nova Scotia to Lake Huron, he not only acquired a remarkably accurate impression of the terrain, but a good knowledge of the Indians as well. In 1615 he was forced to spend the winter in a Huron village after being wounded in an attack on the Iroquois. This enabled him to learn a great deal of lore the Indians normally would not tell a white man. He discovered that they were afraid to talk during the summer because they believed their gods roamed the woods, sat on their shoulders, and listened to everything they said. In the winter they were more willing to talk because they believed these same gods were frozen in blocks of ice!

The late Thomas B. Costain, in his book *The White and the Gold,* says there was one secret that Champlain did not learn: the Indians' conviction that there was one God greater than the gods they feared. Recent research into Indian legends, expressed in pictures on blocks of wood, has revealed their understanding of the creation of the world to be remarkably like the first chapter of Genesis: "At first there were great waters above all the land, and above the waters were thick clouds, and there was God the Creator."

Other Events on January 9:

1666 Courcelle led an expedition from Quebec to attack the Mohawks.

1760 Nova Scotia Micmac Indians made peace with settlers.

1786 The first legislature of New Brunswick opened at Saint John.

1862 The Grenadier Guards landed at Halifax because of the possibility of a war with the United States of America.

1885 An international bridge was opened at Sault Ste. Marie, Ontario.

Sir Robert Borden (1854-1937)

Canada Joins League

It was on January 10, 1920, that Canada became one of the founding members of the League of Nations, the organization set up to preserve peace after World War I. It was replaced by the United Nations after World War II.

The fact that Canada and other Dominions of the British Commonwealth could speak for themselves in the League of Nations showed the rest of the world that they had come of age. They would make their own decisions in international affairs from now on, and no longer would Britain speak for them.

It was a step not easily achieved. Other leading nations, including the United States, opposed the Dominions' joining the League of Nations as separate members. They felt that the effect would be to give Britain five votes instead of one. Subsequent events proved that this was far from being the case.

The leaders in the battle to give the British Dominions independence in the League were Sir Robert Borden, Prime Minister of Canada, and General Jan Christiaan Smuts of South Africa, who had fought against Britain in the Boer War. They pointed out that Spain, Brazil, and a number of other nations would be given votes in the League of Nations, although they had been neutral or had taken no active part in the war. More than 422,000 Canadians had served overseas during the war. They suffered 218,000 casualties, 50,000 of whom were killed. The record of the other Dominions was comparable. Sir Robert Borden said emphatically that, since Canada had been in the front line of battle, she deserved at least a back seat on the Council of the League of Nations.

Borden and Smuts eventually prevailed, and the article providing seats on the Council for the self-governing British Dominions was signed by President Clemenceau of France, President Wilson of the United States, and Prime Minister Lloyd George of Britain.

Other Events on January 10:

1811 Explorer David Thompson crossed the Rocky Mountains via the Athabaska Pass.

1815 Britain prohibited American citizens from settling in Canada.

1817 Selkirk's forces recaptured Fort Douglas on the Red River.

1831 The King of the Netherlands announced his decision on the boundary between New Brunswick and Maine. The United States rejected it immediately and Britain did the same later.

1842 Sir Charles Bagot arrived in Canada to take up his post as Governor-General of Canada.

1876 The British Columbia Legislature petitioned Queen Victoria about its grievances.

1910 Henri Bourassa published *Le Devoir* in Montreal.

1950 Prime Minister St. Laurent met the premiers of the ten provinces in Ottawa to discuss constitutional amendments.

French Begin Offensive

In his great book on early Canadian history, *The White and the Gold*, the late Thomas B. Costain wrote: "Some men are born for emergencies. They are not particularly successful when life flows easily and placidly. They are prone to display faulty judgment and almost certain to get at odds with their fellows; but when a crisis arises and courageous leadership is needed, they come into their own."

It might be thought that Costain was writing about Sir Winston Churchill, who was the man of the hour in World War II. Actually, he was referring to Count Frontenac who was twice governor of New France. During his first term from 1672 to 1682 he was involved in so many quarrels with the Bishop of Quebec and other officials of the garrison that he had to be recalled.

Frontenac spent seven years living in retirement in France, during which time the situation in New France deteriorated seriously. British settlers in New York and the New England States were making good progress, and their friends, the Iroquois, were attacking French settlements almost at will. They even forced Governor Denonville to dismantle the fort that Frontenac had built at Kingston. Other Indian tribes began to get the impression that France was finished as a power, and that they had better side with the British.

King Louis XIV then asked Frontenac to return to New France. In words almost humble for a king, he said, "I send you back to New France where I expect you will serve me as well as you did before. I ask for nothing more."

Frontenac returned to Quebec in October, 1689, and put New France on the attack. On January 11, 1690, he organized a three-pronged offensive against British settlements in New York, New Hampshire, and Maine. His aggressive policies soon impressed the wavering Indian tribes and probably enabled France to retain Canada fifty years longer than what might have otherwise been the case.

Frontenac Statue by Hébert, Quebec City

Other Events on January 11:

1726   The Marquis de Beauharnois was appointed Governor of New France.

1815   Sir John A. Macdonald was born in Glasgow, Scotland.

1905   The Tenth Parliament opened; members' sessional indemnities were increased to $2,500.

1909   Canada and the United States formed an International Joint Commission.

1914   Arctic explorer Stefansson's ship *Karluk* was crushed by ice.

1952   British Prime Minister Winston Churchill visited Ottawa until January 15.

1956   Mrs. Ann Shipley was the first woman to move the address in reply to the Speech from the Throne in the House of Commons.

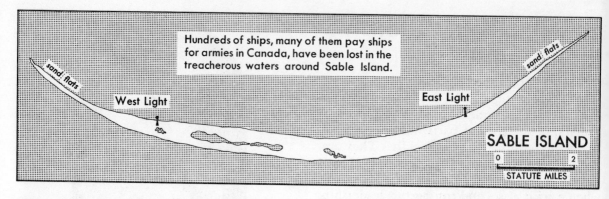

Hundreds of ships, many of them pay ships for armies in Canada, have been lost in the treacherous waters around Sable Island.

West Light

East Light

SABLE ISLAND

0   2

STATUTE MILES

De La Roche Abandons Convicts on Sable Island

In the development of a nation there is often conflict about whether certain work should be done by the government or by private enterprise. The theory is that private enterprise will work more quickly and economically because it wants to make money. Modern examples are the C.P.R. and Trans-Canada Pipeline. On the other hand, the development of air travel was entrusted to government-sponsored Trans-Canada Airlines, or Air Canada as it is now called.

This conflict has existed since the earliest days of Canada. King Henry IV of France would not spend money on colonial development, but gave men like de Monts and La Roche rights to the fur trade if they would finance their own enterprises. It was de Monts who made Champlain's explorations possible.

After the Treaty of Utrecht in 1713, the development of Canada was left to private enterprise in the form of the Hudson's Bay Company, or "The Merchant Adventurers of England trading into Hudson's Bay" as it was called. This company made money, but some earlier capitalists lost their shirts. One of them was the Marquis de La Roche, who was given a fur trading monopoly on January 12, 1598. He outfitted an expedition to Nova Scotia. His colonists consisted of forty convicts whom he landed on Sable Island, often called "the graveyard of the Atlantic" because so many ships have been wrecked there.

After La Roche put his men on shore, he sailed away to explore the coast of Nova Scotia, but his ship was damaged in a bad storm and he had to run before the wind to France. There his creditors put him in prison, and he died a pauper.

It was five years before another ship got to Sable Island, and only eleven of the forty convicts were still alive. They looked like Robinson Crusoes, dressed in shaggy skins, with beards to their waists. They were pardoned and allowed to go into the fur trade themselves, many of them doing quite well in their new careers.

Other Events on January 12:

1700   The death of Marguerite Bourgeoys was announced. She was one of the women pioneers of Montreal who founded a school for girls there.

1819   St. Boniface College was founded at Red River.

1842   The first issue of Prince Edward Island's *The Islander* was published under the editorship of John Inge.

1885   A Supreme Court decision vested liquor licensing in the federal government.

1916   An Order-in-Council increased the number of troops fighting in World War I to 500,000.

1961   A federal-provincial conference agreed to changes in the B.N.A. Act.

Vancouver Island Leased

Yesterday's story mentioned that Britain and France sometimes entrusted the development of Canada to private enterprise rather than doing it themselves. An example of such enterprise was the company called "The Merchant Adventurers of England trading into Hudson's Bay", formed in 1670.

The Hudson's Bay Company concluded a big deal on January 13, 1849 when it leased Vancouver Island from the British Government for seven shillings a year. In those days, seven shillings was worth about $1.75!

The reason the Hudson's Bay Company made such a bargain was that Britain was in the throes of a depression, including a famine in Ireland. In addition, the United States had in the year before bought California from Mexico and now controlled the Pacific to the 49th parallel. Britain needed a naval base on the Pacific coast, and Vancouver Island was the logical place for it.

The Hudson's Bay Company had exclusive trading rights on the island, but in return agreed to pay for the cost of defense and to bring in settlers. The agreement was supposed to last until 1859, but was kept in effect until 1866 when Vancouver Island was united with the mainland, and the whole area became British Columbia.

Some of the early settlers were quickly disenchanted. The first governor, Richard Blanshard, was sent out by the British Government. He agreed to serve without pay because he hoped the post would be the first step in a diplomatic career. However, he also expected that he would have a mansion and an estate of extensive lawns as in England. Not finding them, he lasted only a few months before asking to be recalled.

Other settlers arrived with coaches and horses, only to find that there were no roads. Some brought equipment for playing cricket, but, alas, it takes a long time to convert a forest into a cricket pitch! Still, they were no

HBC's coat-of-arms and motto, Skin for Skin

more badly informed than American tourists almost one hundred years later, who often arrived in Canada in July bringing skis and winter clothing.

Other Events on January 13:

1825 The legislative session opened in Upper Canada; amongst other measures, it set the price of bread.

1837 Fire destroyed a large part of Saint John, N.B.

1838 W. L. Mackenzie abandoned the base on Navy Island from which he had proclaimed a provisional government of Canada.

1865 Joseph Howe began daily attacks on Confederation in a Halifax paper.

1947 The British Privy Council agreed that the Supreme Court of Canada was to be the court of final appeal.

1951 The first group of Royal Air Force aircrew trainees arrived at Dorval, Quebec.

Winter Finally Arrives

Official weather records have only been kept in Canada for about a hundred years, and so it is impossible to know for certain whether or not the winter of 1671 was the shortest ever experienced. It probably was. In that year Quebec got its first real sign of winter on January 14, and the ice and snow had almost melted away by the middle of March.

If this happened today it would be pleasant for most people. In 1671, however, the short winter was a hardship. The early inhabitants of New France depended on cold weather to keep their food supplies from spoiling. They usually harvested their grain and vegetables in October and stored them in cool places. In November they killed and preserved as much wild game as they could: moose, deer, ducks, partridges, and fish. These were their supplies until fresh food became available. Unfortunately, the winter of 1671 was so mild and so brief that a great deal of food spoiled, and many people starved.

Even today many people have their own peculiar methods of weather-forecasting. If dewdrops lace the grass some people say,

"The fairies are hanging out their washing," and so they predict hot weather. It is possible to predict changes in the weather quite accurately by looking into a large barrel of sauerkraut! It helps to add a few quarts of brine. The sauerkraut juice acts like a barometer; when the weather is going to be good, the sauerkraut will be quite dry on the surface; if the weather is deteriorating, then more and more liquid will appear, depending on the intensity of the disturbance.

About the time of the short winter in 1671, a popular method of weather-forecasting was to keep a leech in a bottle of water. When the weather was about to change the leech would move around actively, agitating the water. If there was going to be a high windstorm the leech would be even more active, and before a thunderstorm it would have convulsions! Cats were also weather guides. If a cat sneezed, or sat on a doorstep combing its fur and whiskers, the old Canadians said that it was going to rain.

Other Events on January 14:

1645   The Company of New France transferred its trading rights to the Community of Habitants, which consisted of colonists in Canada.

1875   Serious riots at Caraquet, N.B., over an act providing for free, nonsectarian schools lasted until January 28, and militia had to be sent to restore order.

          The first issue of the Halifax *Herald* was published.

1898   Canada was asked to contribute one third of the cost of the Pacific cable.

1902   The Prince Edward Island Prohibition Act was declared valid by the Supreme Court.

1947   Canada was elected to the Economic and Social Council of the United Nations.

Roberval Chosen Viceroy

Canada's first mining venture was a great disappointment. King Francis I grew quite excited after Cartier's visits to Canada in 1534 and 1535 and got the idea that it was a land in which flowed "rivers of gold." He decided to equip an expedition that would be bigger and better than the ones which Spain and Portugal had sent to Central America.

Francis made one bad mistake. He felt that a sea captain like Jacques Cartier was not worthy to represent him in the new land, and so on January 15, 1540 he appointed the Sieur de Roberval as Viceroy of New France and leader of the expedition.

Roberval and Cartier did not get along together, and eventually Cartier sailed alone in May, 1541. Things went badly from the start. The first time Cartier crossed the Atlantic he made the trip in three weeks. This time his five ships took three months to reach Stadacona, or Quebec.

Cartier decided to establish his colony at Cap Rouge, where Quebec bridge now stands. His men took pigs and goats on shore and cleared an acre and a half of forest in one day. Although it was August, they planted lettuce, cabbage, and turnips.

Before winter came there was great excitement when Cartier's men found what they thought were diamonds, and rocks with veins of gold. In spite of this great discovery, it was a dreadful winter, and when June came they were glad to sail back to France with their special cargo.

When they arrived at St. John's, Newfoundland, they found Roberval and his expedition on its way to Canada. Roberval tried to force Cartier to go back to Quebec with him, but Cartier slipped away in the night to report to King Francis. Roberval stayed in Quebec for a winter and his men gathered more of the diamonds before returning to France.

Cartier kneeling before King Francis I

Unfortunately, the diamonds turned out to be rock crystal, and there was too little gold in the rocks to make mining worthwhile. For many years the expression "a Canadian diamond" was a term of derision in France, meaning something worthless. The colonization of Canada was set back more than fifty years, until de Monts obtained his charter from King Henry IV and sent Champlain to Quebec.

Other Events on January 15:

1634 Robert Giffard secured the seigniory at Beauport, Quebec, the first in Canada.

1635 Charles de La Tour was granted land at Saint John, N.B.

1852 Trinity College, Toronto, was opened.

1878 The Conservative convention adopted "the National Policy".

1901 The Northern Pacific Railway obtained a 999-year lease on a railway line in Manitoba. The lease was transferred to the Canadian Northern Railway on February 11.

1915 The Canadian Northern Railway between Quebec and Vancouver was completed. The last spike was driven at Basque, B.C.

1962 The R.C.M.P. musical ride was placed on a full-time basis.

A Naval Review in Halifax Harbour, 1967

Ottawa Acquires Bases

The people, who will be prepared for a Canadian navy when it will be necessary, do not wish to have a navy which is Canadian in time of peace and Imperial in time of war; that is, to say, a navy which will be Canadian when it is to be paid for, in order to be Imperial when it is required for use.

—F. D. MONK, 1910

It might be said that Canada came of military age on January 16, 1906. It was on that day that Britain relinquished her military bases at Halifax and Esquimalt, and transferred control to Ottawa. They are still the most important bases of the Royal Canadian Navy.

Halifax had been a British military base since 1749, the year after Britain traded Louisburg, N.S., to France for Madras, India. A strong fortress was needed to counteract Louisburg, and the deep harbor of Chebucto was chosen for its location. Wolfe assembled a large part of his forces there in 1759. In subsequent years it was commanded by Edward, Duke of Kent, who became the father of Queen Victoria. It was also the

scene of some wild visits by Prince William as a naval officer before he became King William IV.

Esquimalt became the most important British naval base on the Pacific coast in 1849, exactly one hundred years after the beginning of Halifax. When the Hudson's Bay Company leased Vancouver Island from the British Government for seven shillings a year, Esquimalt was included in the deal.

The withdrawal of British troops made a big difference to Canada's expenditure on national defense. In 1904 the Militia Act had fixed the strength of the permanent force at 2,000 men. This was raised to 5,000 men later, but when war broke out in 1914 there were only 3,000 in the permanent force. The national defense expenditure in 1906 was $6,000,000. By 1914, it had rocketed to $11,000,000. It is $1,600,000,000 today.

Although Britain gave up her bases in Canada in 1906, actual control of Canada's forces remained in London until the end of World War I. The Commonwealth armed forces were branches of the Imperial General Staff, although each branch was responsible to its own government. Even today, the senior soldier in Britain is called Chief of the Imperial General Staff, although he no longer exerts any control over the Canadian forces or those of any other Dominion.

Other Events on January 16:

1642   French settlers were given land in Acadia (Nova Scotia).

1694   Canadians and Indians massacred one hundred British settlers at Oyster River, Maine.

1869   The first issue of the Montreal *Star* was published.

1908   The Government of Manitoba took over the telephone system.

1958   Lester B. Pearson succeeded Louis St. Laurent as leader of the Liberal Party.

1961   The Canadian Nuclear Plant, a gift from Canada to India, was opened.

Verrazano Sets Sail

The first human beings to come to North America were probably Mongols from northern Asia. They crossed the Bering Strait and gradually made their way south to a warmer climate. The North American Indians descended from them.

There are conflicting stories about the first humans to land on the east coast. One version is that they were monks from the west coast of Ireland who went first to Iceland, and then landed in Nova Scotia about 875 A.D. Other evidence gradually being collected is expected to prove that Norsemen landed on the coasts of Labrador and Nova Scotia about 1000 A.D.

Strangely enough, the next great explorers were the Italians. Christopher Columbus, employed by Spain, John Cabot, working for England, and Giovanni da Verrazano, sent by France, were all Italians.

Verrazano's exploits are not as well known as those of Columbus and Cabot, but he sailed from the Azores on January 17, 1524. He was engaged by King Francis I of France who had finally decided to join the contest between Charles V, the Holy Roman Emperor, and King Henry VIII of England, to find the interoceanic passage between the Atlantic and the Pacific.

Verrazano actually sailed from Dieppe with four ships, but had to leave three of them at Madeira because they were not seaworthy. He then sailed for North America in the *Dauphine,* arriving at the coast which is now North and South Carolina.

From there he sailed north and entered the Hudson River which he noted would make a good harbor. It is now the port of New York, and the new Verrazano bridge has been erected there in his honor. It has the longest centre span in the world. Gradually Verrazano worked his way north and is believed to have circled Newfoundland.

His great feat had an unhappy ending. When Verrazano returned home, Francis I was engaged in war with Charles V and was defeated. Then Verrazano himself, who had

Bust of Verrazano, N.Y. History Collection

been a pirate and looted ships on the Spanish Main, is believed to have been captured by the Spanish and hanged in chains. Another version is that he was killed and eaten by cannibals in one of the lesser Antilles during his second voyage to America in 1528.

Other Events on January 17:

1651   Jean de Lauzon was appointed Governor of New France.

1694   Bishop St. Valier denounced theatrical performances staged at Quebec by Frontenac and Cadillac.

1839   Sir John Colborne took the oath of office as governor-general.

1861   A mass meeting in Montreal protested the return of slaves to the United States.

1881   An interprovincial bridge was opened between Ottawa and Hull.

1933   Newfoundland asked Britain to appoint a Royal Commission to investigate its financial problems.

1961   Canada returned Polish treasures stored for safe-keeping during the war.

Income Tax Introduced

The promises of yesterday are the taxes of today.

—W. L. MACKENZIE KING, 1931

This is the time of year when people start thinking about paying their income tax, and those who are expecting refunds waste little time submitting their returns! Income tax was introduced in 1917 as "a temporary wartime measure"!

It was only one of a number of important bills passed by the seventh session of the Twelfth Parliament that opened on January 18, 1917. Other legislation included measures giving the vote to women who had close relatives in the armed forces; the right to vote to every British subject in war service; the Soldiers Settlements Act, designed to help soldiers settle on the land when they returned from the war; the Military-Service Act, making every British subject between the ages of twenty-five and forty-five liable for active military service, with certain exceptions; a Public Service Loan of $100 million. The government also bought 600,000 shares in the Canadian Northern Railway.

There was little hint of any of these important measures in the Speech from the Throne, read for the first time by the Duke of Devonshire, who had been appointed governor-general in 1916. It pointed out that Parliament should end in October, but the government would ask for an extension of a year owing to the war situation. This would require special legislation to be passed by the British Parliament. As Prime Minister Sir Robert Borden reviewed the war situation, he was heckled by his former Minister of Militia, Sir Sam Hughes, who was seated in the private members' benches with his arms folded (see February 14).

Income tax and votes for women seemed of little importance at the time because the big issue was conscription for military service. It was the most difficult problem Canada had ever faced. Prime Minister Borden realized that he would have to form a union government with the Liberals in order to get it through, and invited Opposition Leader Sir Wilfrid Laurier to join him (see May 25). Sir Wilfrid refused, but enough Liberals joined Sir Robert to enable him to form a union government in October.

Other Events on January 18:

1820 An expedition under Captain John Franklin left Cumberland House to explore the Arctic by land (see June 11).

1839 Rebels were hanged at Montreal following the Lower Canada Rebellion.

1849 Parliament met at Montreal. This session included measures dealing with the Rebellion Losses Bill, dual language, and reciprocity with the United States.

1910 A French-Canadian Congress was opened in Ottawa.

Smith Offers Settlement

Can you identify Donald A. Smith? The chances are that you are stumped, although Donald Smith was one of the most colorful and successful Canadians of all time. One of the greatest roles he played was on January 19, 1870, when he stood on the balcony of a Winnipeg prison and spoke for five hours to a gathering of 1,000 people below. The temperature was 20 below zero, and they stood huddled in brightly-colored blankets, hoods over their heads, and icicles forming on their beards.

The meeting was arranged to announce proposals by the federal government for settling the uprising which Louis Riel was leading in Red River. Canada had taken over Rupert's Land from the Hudson's Bay Company on December 1, 1869, but the transfer had been badly arranged. The settlers of the area, most of them Métis, thought their lands were being taken from them. Riel, who had been elected president of a provisional government, seized Fort Garry and put a number of Canadian supporters in prison. He was considering making a deal with the United States to take over the Northwest.

Sir John A. Macdonald had asked Donald Smith, Montreal director of the Hudson's Bay Company, to go to Red River and present the government's proposals. The colorful meeting on the night of January 19 was successful, although it was necessary to send troops from the east in August to keep order. Louis Riel had to leave Canada and live in the U.S.A. until 1884, when he returned to lead another rebellion in Saskatchewan.

The name Donald A. Smith is hardly remembered today because in 1897 Smith became Lord Strathcona. A man of great wealth, he eventually became the resident governor of the Hudson's Bay Company and was also an important member of the group which built the C.P.R. One of the most famous regiments in Canada is the Lord Strathcona Horse, which he raised and financed to fight for Britain in the Boer War.

Lord Strathcona (1920-1914)

Other Events on January 19:

1824 The Welland Canal Company was incorporated.

1843 Mount Allison Wesleyan Academy was opened at Sackville, N.B.

1857 The *Lord Ashburton* was wrecked on Grand Manan Island en route from France to Saint John, N.B., with a loss of twenty-one lives. Two men saved themselves by climbing an icy cliff, a difficult feat even in summer.

1865 Parliament met at Quebec and adopted proposals for Confederation. The New Brunswick Legislature dissolved to hold an election on the Confederation issue, which was defeated.

1960 The announcement was made that Canada's second nuclear research centre, to be known as the Whiteshell Nuclear Research Establishment, would be built on the east bank of the Winnipeg River—60 miles northeast of Winnipeg.

Doukhobors in the West, 1899

Doukhobors Arrive

Some of Canada's most colorful and certainly most controversial immigrants landed at Halifax on January 20, 1899. They were the Sons of Freedom Doukhobors, members of a Russian religious sect, whose coming to Canada was arranged by the famous author Tolstoy and financed by Quakers in Britain and the United States. By the end of June more than 7,000 had arrived and were encouraged to settle in Saskatchewan. Each male was given 160 acres of land for $10.

They made a good impression at first, cultivating their land, tending their horses and cattle carefully, and building good homes and barns. About July, 1902, the Doukhobors in the Yorkton area began to behave strangely. It is now known that an agitator from New York was circulating among them, teaching that it was a sin to wear the skin of any animal. The Doukhobors already were vegetarians, but now they stopped eating eggs, butter, and milk. They said that by drinking milk they were robbing the calves of their food.

On August 21, 1902, they turned their horses, cattle, and sheep loose on the prairies, saying they were "giving them to the Lord".

The animals had to be rounded up by government officials before they froze to death or were destroyed by wild animals.

The situation became progressively worse, especially with the arrival of Peter Verigin, a spiritual leader, on December 1, 1902. When efforts were made to force the Doukhobors to send their children to school and to abide by other laws of the land, they began staging their famous nude parades in the Yorkton area. They made winter pilgrimages to Winnipeg and other centres, carrying their sick on stretchers, and singing hymns. If they had not been rounded up by government officials and sent home on trains, many would have died. In January, 1908, they got as far as Fort William and paraded naked through the streets.

One mountie worked out an ingenious method of discouraging nude parades in the summer. He enticed the marchers into a house, and nailed the doors open. When evening came and lamps were turned on, thousands of mosquitoes came in for the feast! The Doukhobors soon put on their clothes.

Other Events on January 20:

1783   Britain and the United States signed an armistice. Fighting stopped on February 4.

1831   The United States rejected the New Brunswick-Maine boundary award mediated by the King of the Netherlands.

1850   Captain McClure sailed to search for the Franklin expedition; he discovered the Northwest Passage.

1904   The federal government disallowed a British Columbia act restricting immigration.

1936   The death of King George V was announced.

Troops Sail to S. Africa

Canadian troops embark for the Boer War

One of the great paradoxes in Canadian political history was brought about by Britain's calls to Canada for military aid in 1884 and 1899. In 1884 Britain's General "Chinese" Gordon was besieged at Khartoum. Canada was asked to send troops but Prime Minister Sir John A. Macdonald, whose election battle-cry was, "A British subject I was born; a British subject I will die," refused. He would only allow Britain to recruit troops in Canada by paying them, with the result that only 400 French-Canadian voyageurs helped paddle Wolseley's expedition up the Nile (see December 21).

Late in 1899 Britain was in trouble again, this time in South Africa. German-Dutch leaders trying to win independence for the Transvaal and Orange Free State had besieged British-held Mafeking, Ladysmith and Kimberley. The Boer War had begun.

This time when Britain asked Canada for help, Sir Wilfrid Laurier, a French-Canadian, was Prime Minister. Despite the fact that French-Canadians have always objected to fighting outside their own country, Sir Wilfrid's government authorized the sending of troops within three days. One contingent sailed from Halifax on January 21, 1900, but the first had sailed from Quebec only three weeks after the war had been declared! Altogether more than 7,000 Canadians fought in the Boer War.

One of the Canadian units was the Lord Strathcona Horse, recruited and financed by Donald A. Smith (Lord Strathcona), who had made a fortune in the building of the C.P.R. The Canadians were better suited to the South African type of warfare than British "Regulars". They understood the guerilla type of fighting needed in that terrain. After the battle of Paardeberg, Lord Roberts, British Commander-in-Chief, said: "A most dashing advance made by the Canadian regiment and some engineers . . . apparently clinched matters."

Many Canadian place names commemorate the part played in the Boer War by Canadians. Kimberley and Ladysmith, British Columbia, are among them.

Why did Sir Wilfrid Laurier, a French-Canadian, do what Sir John A. Macdonald was not willing to do? Recognizing that French Canadians were opposed to going to war, but that most other Canadians wanted to help Britain, Laurier decided that the majority should rule.

Other Events on January 21:

1757 A French-Canadian force defeated the British at Ticonderoga, New York.

1796 General Robert Prescott became Governor of Lower Canada.

1807 A Jewish member of the Lower Canada Assembly was not allowed to take his seat.

1826 A Session of the Lower Canada Assembly opened. Measures included one which enabled courts to abstain from imposing the death penalty for certain crimes.

1839 Acadia College was opened at Wolfville, Nova Scotia.

1914 The death of Lord Strathcona in London, England, was announced.

1960 Prime Minister Kishi of Japan visited Canada.

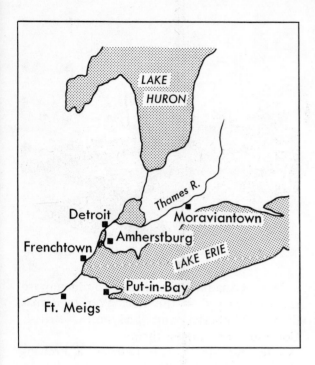

up and hid in the woods. It was a cold night, and the American sentries guarding the post at Frenchtown were sheltering from an icy wind. Procter led a bayonet attack on the village, and after a sharp fight, the Americans retreated into the woods not knowing that the Indians were waiting there. It was one of the worst defeats in the war for the Americans. Of the force of 966 men who had been stationed in Frenchtown, only 33 escaped. The British took about 540 prisoners, and the rest were killed in the bayonet attack or by the Indians in the woods. The latter had 400 scalps to show, and Chief Round Head put on an American officer's uniform in which he proudly paraded through the village. The British lost 182 killed and wounded.

Other Events on January 22:

1690   The Iroquois signed a peace treaty with the British and the Great Lakes tribes.

1699   Bishop St. Valier established an elementary school at Quebec which opened in October of that year.

1864   The first session of the Legislative Council of British Columbia opened at Sapperton.

1873   The Liberals under Alexander Mackenzie won a general election following the resignation of the Macdonald government owing to the C.P.R. scandal.

1878   Canada was given the right to decide whether or not she wanted to be included in British treaties.

1901   Queen Victoria died.

1906   The United States steamer *Valencia* was lost off Vancouver Island with 126 lives.

1951   H.M.C.S. *Huron* was placed under United Nations command.

1962   Federal grants to universities were increased by one-third.

1964   Canada and the United States signed the Columbia River agreement.

British Take Frenchtown

Although the War of 1812 was between Britain and the United States, the American objective was to capture Canada. In January, 1813, it looked as though this might be achieved.

The American General Harrison had 3,000 troops near the western end of Lake Erie, with an advance base at Monroe, Michigan. His plan was to cross the frozen Detroit River and attack the British army and naval base at Amherstburg. Then he would move up the river and recapture Detroit, which had been taken in 1812.

The commander of the British force at Amherstburg was twenty-six-year-old Colonel Henry Procter, who had only 500 British and Canadian soldiers, plus 450 Indians under Tecumseh. Procter and Tecumseh, both daring leaders, decided to surprise the Americans before they could cross the river.

On the night of January 22, Procter and his 500 men advanced across the ice unseen by the enemy, while the Indians crossed farther

A drawing of Château Saint-Louis before the Fire

Fire Destroys Famous Château Saint-Louis

When the old Château St. Louis in Quebec was destroyed by fire on January 23, 1834, it was said that Champlain, Montmagny and Frontenac watched from Heaven. The Château was started by Champlain, and had been the home of the governors of Canada ever since. Lord Aylmer was governor of Lower Canada in 1834, but he and Lady Aylmer happened to be away on the day of the fire.

The blaze started at noon in the apartment of Captain McKinnon, an aide to the governor. The alarm was sounded by the beating of drums and the blowing of bugles in the Citadel. Soon the top floor was lost in smoke as the fire spread down, and the entire building was enveloped in flames.

The temperature was 22 below zero and fire-fighting equipment became frozen. The famous old Château was soon reduced to ruin and rubble, but fortunately valuable papers and some of its furniture were saved. **Lord** and Lady Aylmer moved to **the** Château Haldimand le Vieux, built **in 1784.**

Actually, the old Château was badly in need of repairs. It was said that the British kept it that way, because they liked to preserve ruins. However, it is only fair to report that not long before the fire, the Assembly had voted the equivalent of $10,000 for repairs.

Quebec itself had been fortified in 1823 on a plan drawn up by the Duke of Wellington. It was the only walled city in North America at that time. The walls and citadel had cost the equivalent of $35,000,000.

Other Events on January 23:

1831   The Lower Canada Assembly voted legal rights for Jews.

1883   The first ice palace carnival was held in Montreal.

1888   Natural gas was found at Kingsville, Ontario.

1962   Old age and disability pensions were increased by $10 a month.

Robert Baldwin (1804-1858)

Sir Louis-Hippolyte Lafontaine (1807-1864)

Baldwin, Lafontaine Lead Reform Party to Victory

The first story in this book tells how Joseph Howe, Nova Scotian newspaper editor, fought and won a battle for freedom of the press. On January 24, 1848, "the Tribune," as he was called, played a part in the development that brought responsible government to Canada.

When Lord John Russell was British Colonial Secretary, Howe wrote letters to him which are now famous. He contended that the British Empire could hold together only if the colonies had their own responsible governments. In 1846 Lord Russell became prime minister and announced Britain's new colonial policy: "It is neither possible nor desirable to carry on the government of any of the British provinces in North America in opposition to the opinion of its inhabitants." Lord Elgin was sent to Canada as governor-general with that principle as part of his instructions. It had already been relayed to Sir John Harvey, Lieutenant-Governor of Nova Scotia, where Howe was leader of the Reform Party.

On January 24, 1848, the Reform Party led by Baldwin and Lafontaine won the general election in Canada. Thomas Raddall in his book *The Path of Destiny* says, "Baldwin and Lafontaine rode into power on a tide of Liberal votes—for there were no Reform votes any more: Reform had come."

Henceforth, the parliaments of Canada and the other British colonies would conduct their own affairs through the members elected by the voters. No longer would the governor interfere in political matters as Sir Charles Metcalfe had done only four years previously.

Other Events on January 24:

1797 The first session of the Assembly of Lower Canada opened and dealt with agreements with Upper Canada.

1885 The C.P.R. telegraph was completed from the Atlantic to the Pacific.

1903 Britain and the United States referred the Alaska boundary dispute to a committee of "impartial" judges. In October it made a decision which was unfavorable to Canada (see March 25).

1923 George H. Murray resigned as Premier of Nova Scotia after twenty-seven years in office.

1946 The Atomic Energy Commission of Canada was established and officially recognized.

1955 A plan was announced to build the first Canadian atomic energy power plant at Rapides des Joachims, Ontario.

Louis Hébert Dies

Canada's first doctor is often credited with being Canada's first farmer as well. He was Louis Hébert, who died at Quebec on January 25, 1627, greatly mourned.

Louis Hébert was brought to Quebec by Champlain in 1617 to be the doctor to the new colony. Previously, in 1606, he had made a trip to Acadia as a member of Poutrincourt's expedition, and that is how he met Champlain.

Bear River, N.S., near Champlain's habitation, is named after Hébert, whose name in French is pronounced "'Ay-bear." Port Hébert, on the southwest shore of Nova Scotia, is another landmark honoring the memory of this great Canadian. Across the nearby inlet is Louis Head.

Louis Hébert's father had been a physician to the Royal Court in Paris. He had attended Catherine of Medici when she was dying after instigating the Massacre of St. Bartholemew's. It was said that she was haunted by ghosts. In any case, young Louis Hébert had seen enough of court intrigue and was glad to get as far away as possible. When he was ready to sail he did not look back, even after learning that the directors of the company backing Champlain had reduced his salary sharply.

When they arrived at Quebec, the Héberts decided quickly that they could not live in the rat-infested rubble of Lower Town, and they investigated the land at the top of the cliff. There they built what was probably the first stone home in Canada, and cultivated ten acres of land. They grew enough vegetables to support not only themselves but also many poor families. Louis Hébert may, therefore, deserve to be known as the first farmer in Canada.

His son-in-law is believed to have used the first plough in 1628. It was drawn by an ox, since horses were not used until 1647. The Indians called them "the moose from France." The first wheat is believed to have been sown in 1644.

Monument to Louis Hébert at Quebec City

Other Events on January 25:

1688   Plague took a heavy toll of lives at Fort Niagara.

1791   Quebec was divided into Upper and Lower Canada by Royal proclamation.

1835   Sir Francis Bond Head was made Lieutenant-Governor of Upper Canada.

1870   A convention of Red River rebels considered proposals from the federal government put forward by Donald A. Smith on January 19.

1905   The Liberal government under G. W. Ross was defeated in Ontario.

1909   Premier McBride announced a deal to bring a third transcontinental railway to British Columbia.

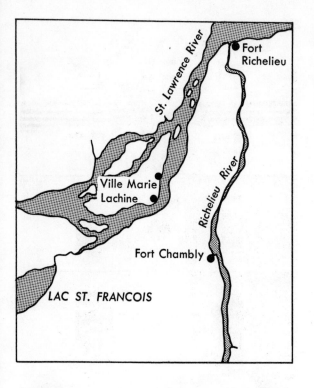

Frontenac Jails Perrot

In early Canada, and probably in many countries, it sometimes paid to be a big criminal, but not to be a petty thief. People might, for example, be hanged for stealing food. As late as 1824, an eighteen-year-old boy was hanged in Saint John, N.B., for stealing twenty-five cents from his employer's till.

In the years 1672 to 1674, one of the biggest racketeers was François Perrot, Governor of Montreal. He established a base on an island between Lake St. Louis and Lake of Two Mountains, above Lachine rapids. Indians bringing their furs to Montreal were induced to stop there and, having been plied with brandy, usually left without part of their valuable cargo.

As in most criminal operations, there was a flaw. The drunken Indians would go on sprees in Montreal and terrify the inhabitants. A delegation of leading citizens, including Charles Le Moyne, called on Perrot and protested to no avail. In fact, the Governor put one of them in prison. Protests were then made to Governor Frontenac in Quebec, who had supreme authority, and he sent an officer to Montreal to investigate. Perrot put him in prison. Fortunately, La Salle saw what happened and brought word to Frontenac by secretly leaving Montreal.

Frontenac then played a trick on Perrot. He wrote to him and Abbé Fénelon, who supported Perrot, inviting them to come to Quebec to clear up their misunderstandings. As it was winter, they had to walk most of the way on snowshoes. When they arrived on January 26, Frontenac immediately had Perrot arrested and put in jail. Abbé Fénelon was allowed to return to Montreal, but he created such an agitation in favor of Perrot that Frontenac brought him back to Quebec. Eventually Perrot and Fénelon were sent to France to face the King. Fénelon was forbidden to return to Canada, and Perrot was put in the Bastille for three months. However, on his release the governorship of Montreal was restored to him, and, in 1684, he even became Governor of Acadia!

Other Events on January 26:

1604   Biencourt sailed for Port Royal with Jesuit missionaries.

1657   The Viscount d'Argenson was made Governor of New France.

1679   The keel of La Salle's ship *Griffon* was laid. It was the first ship built above Niagara Falls.

1911   A Reciprocity Agreement with the United States was made public. It was ratified by the American Senate in July, but in the Canadian general election of September, the Liberals were defeated on the issue and reciprocity was dropped.

1917   The biggest electric steel plant in the world opened in Toronto.

1924   The Canadian Red Ensign was approved as the official flag for government buildings at home and abroad.

1951   General Eisenhower, Supreme Commander of NATO, visited Ottawa.

Ottawa, Canada West, 1855

Ottawa Chosen Capital by Queen Victoria

On January 27, 1858, it was officially announced that Ottawa would be the capital of Canada which then consisted of Ontario and Quebec. The choice was made by Queen Victoria after the Legislative Council had refused to vote money to build a Parliament at Quebec. The matter was referred to her in March 1857 by Prime Minister John A. Macdonald, and she announced her decision on December 31.

There was consternation in Quebec, Montreal, Kingston, and Toronto when her choice became known. They had all been vying for the honor, and little consideration had been given to Ottawa. One critic described Ottawa as "a sub-Arctic lumber village converted by royal mandate into a political cockpit."

There is a story that Queen Victoria had been influenced by a painting that had been sent to her by Lady Head, wife of the Governor-General. Lady Head, who was an amateur painter, captured some of the beauty of the area on canvas when she was taken on a picnic at what is now Major's Hill Park, where the Rideau River flows into the Ottawa River.

However, there is little doubt that Queen Victoria's decision was influenced by military authorities including the Duke of Wellington, who had earlier drawn attention to the strategic advantages of Ottawa. It was far enough from the United States border to be protected; it had good water transportation routes connecting the St. Lawrence and the Great Lakes; and it was on the Ontario-Quebec border.

Even so, after the Queen had chosen Ottawa there was doubt that the capital really would remain there. When the Prince of Wales, later King Edward VII, laid the cornerstone of the original Parliament Building on September 1, 1860, the inscription read "cornerstone of the building *intended* to receive the legislature of Canada."

Other Events on January 27:

1721 A mail stage coach service was established between Quebec and Montreal.

1826 Upper Canada was made a separate diocese by the Pope, with Kingston as its see.

1847 Nova Scotia appointed a committee to study postal operations. Its report resulted in a special conference arranged by Lord Elgin which led to uniformity of postal services in the Maritime provinces and Canada.

1854 The Great Western Railway opened between London and Windsor, Ontario.

1916 Manitoba gave the vote to women.

1961 The city of Montreal authorized the building of a subway.

Caughnawagas Join Attack on Indian Villages

The Caughnawaga Indians, who have a reserve on the St. Lawrence River across from Montreal, are known all over North America for their ability to work on steel girders on high buildings and bridges. Among many famous structures, they worked on the Empire State Building and Waldorf-Astoria Hotel in New York, and on the Golden Gate Bridge in San Francisco. Their sure-footedness and lack of fear are inherited from their forefathers who could run across the rolling logs being boomed down fast-flowing rivers.

In 1693 the Caughnawagas took part in an operation that was nearly too much for them, perhaps because it was on the ground. Count Frontenac organized an attack on important Mohawk villages in New York, and the Caughnawagas were included in the force that set out on January 28. It was led by Nicolas de Manthet and many of Frontenac's best officers.

Caughnawaga Indians

The operation was successful in that 300 Mohawk prisoners were taken after a bloody battle, but then a British force under Peter Schuyler came to the aid of the Mohawks. De Manthet had to withdraw his men quickly and try to get to the border. The situation became desperate because the ice on Lake George had broken, and they had to make their way through the woods around the shore. A supply of food hidden at Lake Champlain had gone bad. De Manthet took what food he had and gave it to the most hardy followers in the hope it would give them enough strength to reach Montreal and get help. The remainder of the force stayed alive by eating nuts, bark, squirrels, and even boiling their own moccasins.

Peter Schuyler's British forces might have caught them if they too had not been starving. During the chase, the Mohawks invited Schuyler's men to share some stew they were cooking in open pots. The offer was gratefully accepted—until a human hand appeared in the stew! With nothing to eat, Schuyler and his men gave up the chase, and help arrived not one day too soon for de Manthet and his force.

Other Events on January 28:

1689   A French force left Trois Rivières to attack New England.

1832   The Commercial Bank was incorporated in Upper Canada.

1870   The *City of Boston* sailed from Halifax and disappeared with 191 passengers.

1916   The Manitoba Legislature passed a Temperance Act.

1952   Viscount Alexander ended his term as governor-general.

Yonge Street Opens

One of the most famous streets in Canada is Yonge Street in Toronto, named in honor of Sir George Yonge, a member of the British cabinet in 1793.

Yonge Street was a military road from Lake Ontario to Lake Simcoe planned by Colonel John Graves Simcoe, Lieutenant-Governor of Upper Canada from 1791-1796. It was opened on January 29, 1796, and provided a route to Penetanguishene, a naval base on Lake Huron.

Another well-known thoroughfare in Toronto is Dundas Street. It was also a military road, which Simcoe hoped to build all the way from Detroit to Kingston, Ontario. In those days Detroit belonged to Britain, which was at war with France. Simcoe was convinced that the United States would help France by attacking Canada, and he built Yonge and Dundas Streets to enable him to move troops quickly to strategic points.

He was so sure the United States would attack that he moved the capital of Upper Canada from Niagara to Toronto which was farther away from the American border. There was no settlement in Toronto then, except the remains of old French Fort Rouillé, built in 1749. Simcoe did not like the Indian name "Toronto" and changed it to York to commemorate the Duke of York's victories in Flanders. It was changed back to Toronto when it became a city in March, 1834.

Simcoe's activities might have brought the United States into the war against Britain in 1794. Acting on instructions from Lord Dorchester, Governor-in-Chief of British North America, Simcoe built Fort Miami near Toledo, Ohio. Its purpose was to prevent the Americans from marching on Detroit. The British Government was horrified because it did not want to be involved in a war with the United States as well as France. Detroit and other posts were returned to the United States on June 1, 1796.

John Graves Simcoe (1752-1806)

Other Events on January 29:

1820   George III died, and George IV came to the throne.

The Bank of New Brunswick was founded.

1829   McGill University was opened.

1847   Lord Elgin, the new Governor-General of Canada, arrived at Montreal.

1856   The Victoria Cross was instituted by Queen Victoria. Alexander R. Dunn was the first Canadian to receive it for gallantry in the Crimean War (1854).

1859   Parliament met at Toronto.

1885   A statue of Sir George Etienne Cartier was unveiled at Ottawa.

1921   Canada and France signed a trade convention.

Lord Elgin (1811-1863)

Lord Elgin Arrives

You may perhaps Americanize, but depend upon it, . . . you will never Anglicize *the French inhabitants of the province. Let them feel, on the other hand, that their religion, their habits, their prepossessions, their prejudices if you will, are more considered and respected here than in other portions of this vast continent, who will venture to say that the last hand which waves the British flag on American ground may not be that of a French Canadian?*

—LORD ELGIN, 1848

Being Governor-General of Canada in the 19th century was no sinecure. The job killed Durham, Sydenham, Bagot, and Metcalfe who served between 1838 and 1845. The Earl of Cathcart followed them for two years, but he was a soldier, and kept away from the troublesome political situation, leaving it to Tory leader William Henry Draper.

Lord Elgin may therefore be considered a brave man for accepting the post. He arrived in Montreal on January 30, 1847, and stayed on the job for seven years. Although he had some of the roughest times of all, the experience did not kill him; in fact, he later went on to become Viceroy of India.

Lord Elgin's greatest test came when he had to sign the Rebellion Losses Bill in April, 1849. During the rebellions of 1837-1838, a great deal of property was destroyed in Upper and Lower Canada, especially in the latter. Damages were readily paid to property owners in Upper Canada, but there was great indignation among the English-speaking minority in Lower Canada when French-speaking property owners demanded reparations.

Lord Elgin opened Parliament in 1849 in both French and English, but the lid blew off when he announced that his government would provide £90,000 to compensate property owners in Lower Canada. English-speaking citizens said that the French were being rewarded for treason. As he left Parliament after signing the bill, he was pelted with eggs and was nearly killed a few days later when he was struck by a heavy stone. The rioters even burned the Parliament Buildings at Montreal.

Many leading Tories and some Liberals were so indignant that they signed a manifesto urging that Canada should join the United States.

Other Events on January 30:

1815   Bishop Strachan of York wrote to ex-President Jefferson of the United States protesting the actions of American forces in the War of 1812.

1869   Joseph Howe joined the Macdonald government as President of the Privy Council.

1923   The Grand Trunk Railway was taken over by the Canadian Government, beginning the organization of the Canadian National Railways.

1934   The constitution of Newfoundland was suspended.

Durham Suggests Unity

Not government merely, but society itself seems to be almost dissolved; the vessel of the State is not in great danger only, as I had been previously led to suppose, but looks like a complete wreck.

—LORD DURHAM, 1838

Lord Durham (1792-1840)

It was on January 31, 1839, that the most celebrated study of Canada, the Durham Report, was issued in London. It came at the most troubled time in Canadian history, following the rebellions in Upper and Lower Canada in 1837-1838.

Britain was involved in great reform movements at the time. More people were being given the right to vote, child labour in factories was being abolished, and slavery was ended in 1838. It was shocking that rebellion and bloodshed should take place in Canada in the name of reform.

Lord Durham, who had helped devise the British Reform Bill of 1832, was sent to Canada as governor-general in April, 1838. Although he was a reformer, Durham, a former ambassador to Russia, loved pomp. He crossed the Atlantic in a warship, with six secretaries, eight aides, plate for elaborate dinners, horses and grooms. Two days after arriving in Quebec he paraded through the city mounted on a white horse.

Nevertheless, Durham did an amazing amount of work. He stayed in Canada only until November 1, when he returned to London because one of his ordinances had been disallowed. During this time he conferred in Quebec with the leaders of all the colonies in British North America, and travelled through a great deal of country to Niagara. Although this seems a short distance now, you must remember that in those days there were no trains and only a few rough roads.

The great problem was that of "two nations warring in the bosom of a single state." French and English-speaking Canadians were not getting along together. Durham recommended uniting Upper and Lower Canada, and giving them one Parliament. He thought that French- and English-speaking children should go to the same schools, and that English should be the only official language because he hoped that gradually the French would be assimilated.

Durham pointed out that Britain was a democracy, and one democracy cannot rule another. Therefore Canada should have its own responsible government.

These, and a number of other sound recommendations, led, according to historian G. M. Wrong in *The Canadians*, to a new and contented British Colonial Empire.

Other Events on January 31:

1690   The Duchess d'Aiguillon gave 18,000 francs for a hospital at Quebec.

1821   The Upper Canada Parliament opened the session that dealt with uniform currency.

1839   New Brunswick and Maine lumbermen fought along the border.

1906   Britain and Japan signed an agreement concerning Japanese trade with Canada.

1955   A 109-day strike ended at Ford plants in Ontario.

Canadian Prime Ministers since Confederation

Sir Mackenzie Bowell

W.L. Mackenzie King

Sir John Thompson

Arthur Meighen

Sir John Abbott

Sir Robert Borden

Alexander Mackenzie

Sir Wilfrid Laurier

Sir John A. Macdonald

Sir Charles Tupper

Mounties Join Forces

If people around the world were asked what they knew about Canada, chances are that the Mounties would get the most mention. It was on February 1, 1920, that the original force, the Royal Northwest Mounted Police, was amalgamated with the Dominion Police, and its name was changed to the Royal Canadian Mounted Police. The official motto is *Maintiens le Droit*, meaning *Uphold the Right*, but most people are more familiar with the saying, "the Mounties always get their man."

Some form of protection was needed for the settlers moving onto the prairies, and for the Indians, who were being victimized by illicit whisky peddlers from the United States. The federal government formed a civil organization under military discipline and planned to call it the Northwest Mounted Rifles. The United States objected to having what appeared to be an armed force along the border, so Sir John A. Macdonald changed the name to Northwest Mounted Police to prevent any misunderstanding. The men were recruited in Eastern Canada and assembled at Collingwood on Lake Huron in July, 1874. They trekked 800 miles west, and set up their headquarters in the heart of the Blackfoot country, with detachments at Forts Walsh, Calgary, McLeod, Saskatchewan, and Carlton, covering what are now Saskatchewan and Alberta.

The Mounties' control of the Indians attracted world wide attention in 1877 when Sitting Bull and his Sioux poured into Saskatchewan after annihilating the U.S. Seventh Cavalry under General Custer at Little Big Horn River, Montana. The Indians set up camp at Wood Mountain near the Cypress Hills, and refused to return to the United States.

Later in the year, a conference was arranged between Sitting Bull and General Terry, a representative of the American Government, who was accompanied by newspaper correspondents from Washington and New York. They were amazed to see how Commissioner

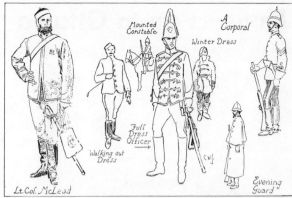

Northwest Mounted Police (1874-1885)

McLeod and 150 Mounties controlled Sitting Bull and his 4,000 highly-excited followers, many of whom were armed with rifles.

Sitting Bull rejected the American proposals and stayed in Canada until 1881, when starvation compelled the Sioux to return to their reservations in the United States.

The Mounties kept control over many other equally dangerous situations, including the Klondike gold rush.

Other Events on February 1:

1796   The capital of Upper Canada was transferred from Niagara to York.

1814   The 8th Regiment began its march from Fredericton to Quebec.

1854   The Parliament Buildings were burned at Quebec.

1858   The Douglas Law concerning miners obtaining licences in order to search for gold in the Fraser Valley came into effect in British Columbia.

1881   C.P.R. bill was approved by the House of Commons.

1890   Canada Atlantic Railway opened a bridge over the St. Lawrence at Coteau.

1904   The Dominion Railway Commission was established.

1955   Prime Minister St. Laurent was presented with the Freedom of the City of London during the Commonwealth Conference.

Pioneers go to Ottawa

*We came to build, and building, a mighty
    structure grew,
And ever as we builded, builded better
    than we knew;
And through the darkening wilderness,
    lo! we were led in might,
Our log-heaps made a smoke by day, a
    pillared flame by night.
Now, when across the continent we've
    seen our task expand,
To our children's children and their chil-
    dren's children we do bequeath this
    land.*

—ROBERT K. KERNIGHAN, 1925

Over the years there have been periods
when more Americans came to live in Canada
than Canadians went to the United States.
The first heavy influx of settlers from the
United States was that of the United Empire
Loyalists, who came to Nova Scotia, New
Brunswick, and Upper Canada after the
American Revolutionary War.

Sir Clifford Sifton organized one of the
most successful population drives in Canadian history when he was Minister of Immigration from 1896-1905. Although he induced
people in many parts of the world to come
to Canada, most of his settlers were from the
United States and Britain.

One of the most picturesque and successful
settlers was Philemon Wright, one of the
founders of Ottawa-Hull. Although he was a
successful farmer in Massachusetts, he was
attracted by offers of free land in Upper and
Lower Canada and spent several years exploring the possibilities. Finally, he decided that
the area near Chaudière Falls on the Ottawa
River offered the best opportunities. Huge
pine trees grew there and by climbing them
Wright could see the country for miles
around. Sometimes he would have to climb
nearly 100 feet before reaching the first
branch.

On February 2, 1800, Wright left Woburn
with twenty-five men to help him. They
brought their wives and fifteen children and
traveled in sleighs drawn by fourteen horses
and eight oxen. The women and children
slept in the sleighs while the men, after clearing away the snow, wrapped themselves in
blankets and lay on the ground.

The most difficult part of the journey along
the frozen rivers was at the Long Sault
rapids where Dollard Des Ormeaux and his
colleagues had made their gallant stand
against the Iroquois years before. A road had
to be cut through the woods to get around the
rapids.

The party arrived at Chaudière Falls on
March 17, and began clearing land right
away. The first summer they reaped 1,000
bushels of potatoes and 40 bushels of wheat.
In 1806 Wright was ready to ship his first
boom of logs down the Ottawa River to the
St. Lawrence. An industry that was to become
the commercial backbone of Ottawa had
started.

Other Events on February 2:

1628   King Charles I gave William Alexander islands in the St. Lawrence.

1807   The Upper Canada Legislature provided schools for every district.

1848   The first Liberal government in Nova
Scotia was elected; J. B. Uniacke was
elected Premier.

1869   Lord Lisgar was made Governor-
General of Canada.

1926   H. H. Stevens, in the House of
Commons, charged that customs officials were accepting bribes and illegal
favors. This led to an investigation
in which a number of cases of graft
were uncovered.

1947   Snag, Yukon, registered 81 below zero,
the lowest temperature on record in
North America.

1963   Premier Stanfield of Nova Scotia
turned the first sod for the Fathers of
Confederation building at Charlottetown, Prince Edward Island.

Fire Ruins Parliament

Canada's original Parliament Buildings were destroyed by fire on the night of February 3, 1916. World War I was at its height, and it is possible that the fire was set by an enemy agent. The Providence, Rhode Island, *Journal* had issued a warning several weeks before that the Parliament Buildings in Ottawa would be set on fire, but the information which came from a source in the German Embassy in Washington was disregarded. The Ottawa *Citizen* named a suspect a few days later, but the man disappeared after being interviewed by a police constable.

The fire broke out in the Centre Block in which the House of Commons, Senate, offices of the members, press gallery, and many other important offices were situated. Fortunately, the Senate was not in session or there would probably have been many more casualties. The fire started in the newspaper reading room and spread through the dry wooden corridors so quickly that members had only a few minutes to escape. Dr. Michael Clark, member for Red Deer, Alberta, and one of the all-time humorists of Parliament, barely managed to crawl out on his hands and knees. He wasn't being humorous on that occasion.

The death toll of seven included Bowman K. Law, member for Yarmouth, N.S., and two ladies who were guests of Mrs. Albert Sévigny, wife of the Speaker. They had gone for their overcoats after the alarm was given and were overcome by smoke. Four other casualties were employees in the building.

There was a dramatic moment exactly at midnight. The big clock on the 160-foot tower at the foot of the building crashed into the flames just as its bell rang out the final note of twelve o'clock. That bell is now on display in the grounds outside the Parliamentary Library, the only part of the building saved. The library had its own fire in 1952, but has been maintained almost in its original form.

The first Parliament Buildings, 1890

After the fire, Parliament met in the Museum for four years. The new building was not completed until the Peace Tower was erected in 1927.

Other Events on February 3:

1767 A group of citizens signed a petition asking that there be no religious discrimination.

1811 Alexander Henry left on his trip to find the source of the Saskatchewan River.

1831 Lord Aylmer was made Governor-General of Canada.

1865 The Canadian Government returned Confederate saboteur Bennett Burley to the United States.
The Canadian Legislature resolved in an address to the Queen to ask for union of the provinces of British North America.

1916 Seventeen Ottawa schools closed owing to a strike of teachers over bilingualism.

1956 British Prime Minister Sir Anthony Eden addressed a joint session of the Senate and House of Commons at Ottawa.

1960 Canada contributed $35,000,000 to the building of a transpacific cable.

1961 Government approved the merger of the Imperial Bank of Canada and the Canadian Bank of Commerce.

John A. McDougall (1842-1917)

Town Fights for Bridge

Edmonton, Alberta, made a deal with the government at Ottawa on February 4, 1897, to build a bridge over the North Saskatchewan River. This was not the most important event that happened in Canada on February 4 over the years, but it is a good example of the pioneering spirit that built the West.

Edmonton's growth was impeded for years by lack of a railway. When Canadian Pacific Railway engineers decided to put the transcontinental through Calgary, 200 miles to the south, some people predicted the end of Edmonton. However, its early settlers had faith, and hung on. In 1891, the C.P.R. built a branch line from Calgary to Strathcona, across the river from Edmonton. This meant that traffic had to be brought across the river in an old-fashioned ferry. It appeared that Strathcona would become the most important centre in northern Alberta.

John A. McDougall, who had gone to Edmonton from Ontario as a young man, had been elected mayor by acclamation in 1896. His fascinating story is told in the book *Edmonton Trader* by J. C. MacGregor. McDougall would only agree to act as mayor for one year, but in that time he accomplished a great deal, including persuading the village council and Board of Trade to put all the pressure they could on Ottawa to build a bridge.

On February 4, 1897, a telegram came from the federal government saying that it would build the bridge if Edmonton would put up $25,000 towards its cost. This was a tremendous undertaking for a community of only 1,500 people. It was charged in some quarters that Ottawa was only bluffing, believing that Edmonton could not accept the offer.

If so, the bluff was called by evening, and a telegram was sent to Ottawa agreeing to the deal. At first, the money was subscribed by McDougall and some leading citizens. Later, the ratepayers endorsed the action and assumed liability.

The bridge took five years to complete, during which time Edmonton became the gateway to the Klondike gold fields. Eventually, Strathcona became part of the city, ending years of intense rivalry.

Other Events on February 4:

1623   Louis Hébert received a seigniorial grant at Quebec (see January 25).

1667   The first ball in Canada was held at Quebec to celebrate a victory over the Iroquois.

1783   Fighting stopped between Britain and the United States. The armistice was signed on January 20.

1793   Governor Simcoe began his tour of Upper Canada.

1826   The first issue of *La Minerva*, Montreal, was published.

1876   Manitoba abolished the legislative council.

'Quake Moves "Sinners"

Sometimes people say, "it would take an earthquake to move him" when commenting about someone who is stubborn. It took an earthquake on February 5, 1663, to move people to stop selling liquor to the Indians, and even then the effect didn't last long.

One of the worst problems in early Canada was caused by people who plied the Indians with liquor and then stole their furs. Even in the late 1800's, unscrupulous traders persuaded many Indians and Métis in western Canada to give up their allotments of land in exchange for bottles of whisky.

Laval, the first Bishop of Quebec, waged a continual battle against the liquor trade. When his own appeals did not have any effect, he urged King Louis XIV and his minister, Colbert, to take action. There was considerable discussion but no effective action was taken. Finally, Bishop Laval decreed that people selling liquor to the Indians would be excommunicated from the church. Even this was unsuccessful, and Laval persuaded Governor d'Avaugour to impose the death penalty on people who were guilty.

People were hanged until the day a woman was caught. She was a widow with a family to support, and Father Lalemant appealed to Governor d'Avaugour for clemency. The Governor, who had not wanted to impose the death penalty in the first place, took this opportunity to end it. He said, "Since this is not a crime for this woman, it shall not be a crime for anybody."

On the night of February 5, 1663 came the earthquake. It was so severe that great fissures were opened in the snow; streams were diverted from their courses; new waterfalls appeared; houses rocked, and church bells rang wildly.

People were terrified. They flocked into the churches, believing that the world was coming to an end. Many of those guilty of selling liquor to the Indians felt that they were being punished for their sins and resolved to "go straight."

Bishop François de Laval (1623-1708)

Other Events on February 5:

1692   The Abenaki Indians from Nova Scotia massacred the British at York, Maine.

1759   Prime Minister Pitt gave Wolfe secret orders for the Quebec campaign.

1790   Chief Justice W. T. Smith wrote to Lord Dorchester suggesting Confederation.

1841   A proclamation was issued declaring the union of Lower and Upper Canada.

1857   The British House of Commons appointed a committee to investigate the affairs and governing powers of the Hudson's Bay Company.

1920   King's College, Windsor, Nova Scotia, was destroyed by fire.

1946   A Royal Commission was appointed to investigate Russian spy charges as a result of the defection of Igor Gouzenko.

1963   John Diefenbaker's Conservative government was beaten in the House of Commons. It was only the second time since Confederation that the government had been beaten in the Commons.

Louis Riel (1844-1885)

Riel Refuses to Leave

Louis Riel would have been a hero in Canada had he not killed Thomas Scott, a federal employee who had been sent to Manitoba during the Métis uprising in 1870 (see March 4). The gruesome execution caused religious and political strife, as Scott was an Orangeman and Rièl was a Roman Catholic. Edward Blake, then Premier of Ontario, offered a reward of $5,000 for Riel's capture.

Prime Minister Sir John A. Macdonald was caught in the crossfire of the controversy. Riel was a hero among French-speaking Canadians, but he was regarded with hatred by English-speaking Canadians. Sir John had to try to appease both sides. Through Bishop Taché at Fort Garry, he privately sent Riel $1,000 and asked him to leave the country. Riel took the $1,000 but demanded more. On February 6, 1872, Governor Archibald of Manitoba got Donald A. Smith to put up $3,000 so that Riel and his comrade Lépine would leave the country. Once again Riel took the money, but failed to leave.

In August of 1872, Riel was nominated as the candidate for Provencher in a federal election. Sir George Etienne Cartier was beaten in Montreal in that election, so Sir John A. Macdonald asked Governor Archibald to find a safe seat for him in Winnipeg. Elections in those days did not take place on the same day all over the country, but were spread over several weeks. Riel and his opponent in Provencher were asked to withdraw, which they did, and Cartier was elected in their place.

Cartier's death soon afterwards necessitated a by-election in Provencher. Although he was a fugitive from justice, Riel was elected by acclamation. He thought that the government would grant him an amnesty because he had withdrawn in favour of Cartier. This did not happen, so he was unable to take his seat in Ottawa. Following the C.P.R. scandal, there was another general election in 1874, and Riel was elected again. He went to Ottawa and signed the register of members, but four days later he was expelled from the House before he had taken his seat. A bill banishing Riel was enforced, and as a result, he lived in Montana until 1884. Then he was persuaded to return to Canada and lead the second serious rebellion on the prairies, which led to his capture and hanging.

Other Events on February 6:

1682   La Salle and Tonty reached the Mississippi River.

1813   Americans from Ogdensburg, New York, raided Brockville, Ontario, and took back fifty-two people as hostages (see February 22).

1865   The Canadian Parliament began its debate on Confederation.

1894   Ontario held a plebiscite on prohibition.

1952   King George VI died at Sandringham; Elizabeth II was proclaimed Queen.

1956   British Prime Minister Anthony Eden addressed a joint session of Parliament at Ottawa.

1963   The Twenty-Fifth Parliament was dissolved after the Conservative government under Prime Minister Diefenbaker was defeated on a vote of confidence.

1965   The Conservative Party National Executive rejected demands to hold a leadership convention.

Citizens Protest in B.C.

To the native of the prairies Alberta is the far West; British Columbia the near East.
—EDWARD A. McCOURT

Alberta, Prince Edward Island, and Newfoundland appear to be the only Canadian provinces that haven't had rebellions. There was a rebellion in Nova Scotia (which included New Brunswick) in 1776 during the American Revolutionary War. Upper and Lower Canada, now Ontario and Quebec, had serious rebellions in 1837-1838. In 1870 Louis Riel led a rebellion in Manitoba that was more of an "uprising." The same Riel led a far more serious affair in Saskatchewan in 1885. British Columbia experienced a "rebellion" on February 7, 1874, but it was more comical than serious.

British Columbia came into Confederation in 1871 on the understanding that a railway to the Pacific coast would be completed within ten years, and that work on it would start in two years. When nothing had happened by 1874, British Columbians were angry, and there was considerable talk about joining the United States.

At this time Amor de Cosmos had become Premier of British Columbia. He was a colorful figure, born plain William Smith in Nova Scotia, who had made his way to Victoria by way of the California gold fields. He then changed his name to Amor de Cosmos, meaning "lover of the world." As the editor of a newspaper, he was one of the men who got British Columbia into Confederation.

People were not only angry with the federal government for delaying the railway, but also with De Cosmos, who had proposed changing the Act of Union so that a dry-dock could be built at Esquimalt. On February 7, 800 citizens held a protest meeting in the Parliament buildings, which they angrily called "bird cages." They marched into the debating chamber, denounced the members, and drove

Amor De Cosmos (1825-1897)

out the Speaker. They marched out chanting: *We'll hang De Cosmos on a sour apple tree, We'll hang De Cosmos on a sour apple tree, As we go marching on.*

Two days later, the legislature passed a resolution that no change could be made in the railway clause of the Act of Union, and De Cosmos resigned as Premier.

Other Events on February 7:

1758 The Governor and Council of Nova Scotia passed resolutions organizing a legislature, the first in Canada.

1867 The Earl of Carnarvon introduced the British North America Act in the House of Lords.

1918 The War Purchasing Board was created.

1926 The gold rush at Red Bank, Ontario, began.

Come all you jolly lumbermen,
Whose better years have fled,
And I will sing of halcyon days
Before we had Confed;
When title to respect was writ
Upon each horny hand,
And the man who swung a broadaxe
Was a power in the land.

—HEADLEY PARKER, 1899

The whole territory we were wrangling
about was worth nothing.

—LORD ASHBURTON, 1843

Breaking a jam, 1908

Loggers Dispute New Brunswick-Maine Border

Canada and the United States have not fought a war against each other officially since 1814, but in 1839 there was a "war" fought mostly with fists and axe handles. It was along the New Brunswick-Maine border and the warriors were lumbermen. Hence, it is known in history as "the war of pork and beans," or the Aroostook Controversy.

The root of the problem was that the border had never been clearly defined. The King of the Netherlands was asked to arbitrate, but his recommendations were rejected by the United States immediately, and later by Britain.

Logging along both sides of the border was controlled by powerful lumber "barons" who were not always careful about the areas into which they sent their gangs. One of the barons was "General" Sam Veazie, who owned a railroad and fifty sawmills.

Most of the trouble was in the richly pine-clad Aroostook Valley, now one of the finest potato-growing districts on the continent. The worst battle broke out on February 8, 1839. Under normal circumstances, the fighting among loggers might not have caused much alarm, but the situation was dangerous because of the dispute about the location of the border. Furthermore, the rebellions in

Upper and Lower Canada in 1837-1838 had led many Americans to believe that Canadians wanted to join the United States.

Maine and New Brunswick called out their militia. Nova Scotia passed an appropriation for defense, and British troops were rushed from Halifax to guard the border along the St. Croix River. The United States Congress voted $10,000,000 to raise a force of 50,000 men if required.

Fortunately, London and Washington, realized the seriousness of the situation. President Van Buren persuaded the Governors of Maine and New Brunswick to arrange a truce. Britain and the United States then took steps to agree on a border, and the Ashburton-Webster Treaty provided a settlement in 1842.

Other Events on February 8:

1850 Prime Minister Lord Russell of Britain predicted Canada's independence.

1855 A railway opened from Halifax to Truro and Windsor, Nova Scotia.

1905 Sir James Pliny Whitney formed the first Conservative government of Ontario since 1872.

French Raid Schenectady

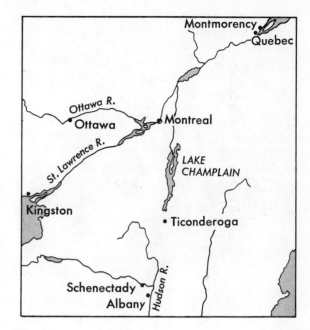

When Frontenac returned to Canada in 1689, he had instructions to attack the British wherever possible, and even to capture New York in the hope of restoring French prestige and hence, respect from the Indians.

One of the first campaigns he organized was against Albany. The force of 160 French and 140 supposedly Christian Indians was led by Nicolas de Manthet. His second-in-command was Ste. Hélène Le Moyne, a member of what must be the most famous fighting family in Canadian history. His brother Pierre was also with the force.

The Indians could not believe that the French had become bold enough to attack Albany, but stayed with the force under terrible conditions, travelling for days in slush and bitter cold. By the time the force reached the Hudson River, it had been reduced to 250. Manthet and Ste. Hélène decided that they were not strong enough to attack Albany, but believed they would have a better chance against Schenectady, sixteen miles northwest.

Albany had been warned of the French plans and had notified Schenectady although there was great jealousy between the two communities. Nevertheless, Schenectady was entirely unprepared for the early-morning attack on February 9, 1690. There had been a party the evening before and even the soldiers were asleep. Two gates were wide open and sentries made of snow were posted on either side, facing Albany in derision! What force of Frenchmen would ever be able to make its way to Schenectady in such weather!

The slaughter was awful. Even women and children were hurled into the flames of their blazing homes, or dashed to pieces against the doors and window frames. Yet, modern historians ask, was it any more cruel than the effect of an atom bomb today?

Sixty old men, women and little children were allowed to remain in Schenectady or escape. Manthet and Ste. Hélène went back to Montreal with ninety prisoners, including a number of young boys. Fifty horses, the most valuable booty, were used to draw sleighs loaded with captured supplies.

Other Events on February 9:

1686　The Intendant made a second issue of card money; it was recalled in October.

1846　The United States Congress ended joint occupancy of Oregon.

1853　Work began on a railway between Peterborough and Cobourg, Ontario.

1879　The North Shore Railway was completed between Montreal and Quebec.

1883　The first public library in Ontario opened at Guelph.

1931　The Earl of Bessborough was made Governor-General of Canada.

George III (1738-1820)

Treaty of Paris Signed

The Treaty of Paris, signed on February 10, 1763, ended the war between Britain and France, so that Britain obtained Canada.

The Peace of Paris in 1783 ended the war between Britain and the United States.

George III had a hand in both of them. He was only a young man when he insisted in 1763 that the "bloody and expensive" war with France must end. Twelve years later he blundered into the war that cost Britain the United States.

France did not appear to care much about losing its possessions in North America after more than 150 years of colonization. Voltaire said that France had simply got rid of "acres of snow." On another occasion he said, "the King must amuse himself, and this ruinous colony is one of his playthings." Before signing the Treaty of Paris, France gave Louisiana to Spain so that Britain would not acquire it, and thereby gave up all her possessions in North America except the islands of St. Pierre-Miquelon, off Newfoundland. They were retained as bases for French fishermen which they still are today.

Wolfe took Quebec in 1759, and Montreal fell to Amherst in 1760. The war for North America was really over then although General Lévis staged an amazing campaign until the end. He wanted to establish a base on St. Helen's Island off Montreal, the site of Expo '67, and go on fighting.

However, the Marquis de Vaudreuil signed the surrender of Canada in 1760. French citizens were allowed to retain their property and their slaves; Roman Catholics were given full religious liberty which they did not have in Britain. Later, the British Parliament arranged for Canada to have French civil law. The Treaty of Paris did not guarantee that French would be an official language in Canada, but this was assumed and eventually became official.

Other Events on February 10:

1604　De Monts made an agreement with merchants of St. Malo and Rouen to colonize Canada.

1794　Lord Dorchester told the Indians that British patience was exhausted with the United States and predicted war.

1802　Alexander Mackenzie was knighted for being the first man to cross the North American continent by land.

1829　King's College, Fredericton (now the University of New Brunswick), was granted a Royal Charter.

1838　The Imperial Government suspended the constitution of Lower Canada; a special council was created.

1841　Upper and Lower Canada were united as the Province of Canada, with Kingston as capital.

1961　Mrs. Gladys Porter seconded the Speech from the Throne in the Nova Scotia legislature; she was the first woman to do so.

1962　Paul Enock of Toronto set a world's record in speed skating in Norway.

British Force Destroyed

*This is the forest primeval; but where are
the hearts that beneath it
Leaped like the roe, when he hears in the
woodland the voice of the huntsman?
Where is the thatch-roofed village, the
home of Acadian farmers,—
Men whose lives glided on like rivers that
water the woodlands,
Darkened by shadows of earth, but reflecting an image of heaven?*

—H. W. LONGFELLOW, *Evangeline*, 1847

Embarkation of the Acadians, 1755

The American poet, Longfellow, wrote the poem *Evangeline* about the expulsion of the Acadians from Nova Scotia in 1755. It aroused great sympathy for them for many years, but modern historians, adding up the score, contend that they deserved their fate.

France controlled Cape Breton because Britain had traded the fortress of Louisburg to France for Madras, India, in an amazing deal in 1748. The French were also installed in the Isthmus of Chignecto where Amherst and Sackville now stand, for troops had been sent from Quebec.

Between Cape Breton and what is now the boundary of New Brunswick, the British were trying to establish a colony that included more than 6,000 Acadians, descendants of the days when Champlain established Port Royal.

It was a highly dangerous situation because if France attempted to regain Nova Scotia, it was likely that the Acadians would side with the invading forces and bring the Indians with them. Many efforts were made to have the Acadians take an oath of allegiance to Britain, but they failed.

One of the incidents that led to the expulsion of the Acadians from Nova Scotia took place on February 11, 1747. A British force of 470 men from New England had set up a base at Grand Pré, meaning "great meadow," where Prime Minister Sir Robert Borden was born in 1854. A French force under M. de Ramezay was based at Chignecto, having marched from Quebec. It comprised about 1,600 men including the Indians who had joined along the way.

Acadians told de Ramezay about the weakness of the British position at Grand Pré, and urged him to attack. The march was made on snowshoes, with the Acadians acting as guides, and the assault on Grand Pré took place in a blinding snowstorm. The British force was wiped out. From then on it was felt that the Acadians could not be trusted and their expulsion took place eight years later.

Other Events on February 11:

1813   104th Regiment of New Brunswick, 1,000 strong, began a march to Quebec and did not lose a man.

1839   Lord Durham's report was submitted to Parliament.

1869   James Patrick Whelan was hanged in Ottawa for the murder of D'Arcy McGee; it was the last public execution in Canada.

1887   C.P.R. arranged the Pacific Ocean freight and passenger service to the Orient.

1907   The Supreme Court of Alberta was established.

1922   The discovery of insulin was announced in Toronto.

1940   Governor-General Lord Tweedsmuir died in Montreal.

David Lloyd George (1863-1945)

Canada on War Cabinet

For Canada as a nation, February 12 is a landmark. It was on February 12, 1867, that the British North America Act was given its first reading in the House of Lords. On the same date in 1917 Prime Minister Sir Robert Borden arrived in London to sit as a member of the British War Cabinet. It was an unprecedented step which led to the nations of the British Commonwealth achieving complete control of their own affairs.

Canada had been pouring troops overseas in the first World War, the battle of Vimy Ridge alone costing more than 10,000 casualties. Battle losses were exceeding enlistments by two to one. Canadian forces were under the British High Command, but the Canadian government was not being informed about plans for how they were to be employed. Prime Minister Borden complained officially that his government knew only what was being published in the daily newspapers, and that it should have a share in making important decisions.

David Lloyd George had succeeded Herbert Asquith as Prime Minister of Britain, and invited the leaders of the Dominions to come to London for consultations. During the session of the War Cabinet, Borden and Prime Minister Smuts of South Africa put forward a resolution urging that the Dominions should have full recognition as self-governing nations and that they should be consulted in all matters of common Imperial concern.

The resolution was adopted by the British Government and led eventually to the Statute of Westminster in 1931 which gave the Dominions complete independence within the framework of the British Commonwealth.

Other Events on February 12:

1793 Spain agreed to pay compensation for seizure of British ships at Nootka, British Columbia.

1800 New Brunswick College was founded at Fredericton.

1816 St. John's, Newfoundland, was nearly destroyed by fire.

1863 Parliament met at Quebec; the big issue was representation by population.

1894 Nova Scotia Legislature voted to hold a plebiscite on prohibition.

1902 The Territorial Grain Growers Association was founded in Saskatchewan.

1953 The first Canadian "Silver Star" jet was delivered to the Department of National Defence.

1963 Prince Albert of Belgium visited Canada on an economic mission.

Troops Keep Order in British Columbia

A Scotsman who was born in British Guiana and came to Canada to work for the Hudson's Bay Company when he was fifteen years old was largely responsible for British Columbia's being part of Canada today. The first governor sent out by Britain to Vancouver Island when it was made a Crown Colony in 1850 was a failure, and James Douglas, Chief Factor of the western division of the Hudson's Bay Company, was asked to take over.

It was a fortunate choice. While working with the company Douglas had seen how the United States took over what is now the State of Washington. Had there been more foresight it might now be part of Canada. When gold was discovered in the Queen Charlotte Islands in 1851, Douglas sensed the danger of an influx of prospectors from the States which could have led to the loss of British Columbia.

The Queen Charlotte gold strike was a minor affair compared with the 1855 strike which led to a gold rush along the Fraser and Thompson rivers that reached a climax in 1858.

Douglas had acted in time, urging the British government to send troops. A detachment of Royal Engineers arrived late in 1858, and a force of marines from Hong Kong arrived at Esquimalt naval base on February 13, 1859. They were just in time to help Douglas preserve order. It was a big job because at the height of the gold rush there was an influx of 30,000 gold seekers, most of them Americans.

The United States was aware of the opportunity to take over British Columbia if there was trouble and sent a special agent, John Nugent, to Victoria. He issued a proclamation to Americans working in British Columbia promising them protection against injustice.

Sir James Douglas (1803-1877)

The American miners themselves were singing:

> *Soon our banner will be streaming,*
> *Soon the eagle will be screaming*
> *And the lion—see it cowers,*
> *Hurrah—boys, the river's ours.*

Douglas did keep order in a most remarkable way and British Columbia was saved for Britain, and later Canada.

Other Events on February 13:

1644 Montreal was granted to the Society of Notre Dame.

1764 The Earl of Egremont devised a feudal scheme for the Island of St. John (Prince Edward Island).

1833 Hamilton, Ontario, was incorporated as a city.

1841 Kingston, Ontario, was made the capital of Canada.

1947 The discovery of oil at Leduc started an oil boom in Alberta.

1963 Brock University, Niagara Falls, received a charter to open in 1964.

Sir Sam Hughes (1853-1921)

Canadians Land in France

On February 14, 1915, the 1st Canadian Division commanded by General Alderson landed in France to fight in World War I. It had been preceded by a hospital unit that had established a base at Le Touquet, and by the famous Princess Pat's regiment.

The story of Canada's great record in World War I will be told at a later date. This is an opportunity to portray briefly Canada's Minister of Militia and National Defense at that time, Colonel Sam Hughes. Ralph Allen, in *Ordeal by Fire,* describes him as "one of the most bizarre and unlikely figures in all of Canadian history."

Sam Hughes, publisher of a newspaper in Lindsay, Ontario, had offered to muster a battalion to fight for Britain in the Boer War. On refusal of his offer, he obtained a commission as a transport officer. When the war ended, he felt that he was entitled to the Victoria Cross and wrote to the King about it.

Nevertheless, Sir Robert Borden made him his Minister of Militia and National Defense in 1911. Sam Hughes threw himself into the job. One of his plans was to have all Canadian boys trained for military service by the time they were twelve. He said, "Give me 1,000,000 men who can hit a target at 500 yards and we would not have a foe who could invade our country."

When war broke out he established a military camp at Valcartier, near Quebec city, and occasionally rode through it on horseback wearing his colonel's uniform, but with a feathered hat. If he liked the appearance of a unit he would promote a captain to the rank of major immediately. He also advanced his own promotion to lieutenant-general and received a knighthood.

Hughes, wasting no time, had Canada's first contingent off to Britain two months after war had been declared.

Exactly two years before the war ended on November 11, 1918, Sir Robert Borden requested Hughes' resignation and dismissed him from the cabinet over a munitions scandal.

Other Events on February 14:

1826   Colonel John By arrived to build the Rideau Canal from the Ottawa River to Lake Ontario.

1836   George Jehoshaphat Mountain was made Anglican Bishop of Montreal.

1858   Governor Douglas fixed the price of land in British Columbia at $2.50 per acre.

1868   Joseph Howe sailed for Britain to try to get Nova Scotia out of Confederation.

1920   The University of Montreal was incorporated.

1956   A strike against General Motors ended after 148 days; it was the costliest strike in Canadian history

P.E.I. – Tax or Unite?

Prince Edward Island will have to come in, for if she does not we will have to tow her into the St. Lawrence.
— THOMAS D'ARCY MCGEE, 1865

Confederation Room, P.E.I., as it appeared in 1864

Prince Edward Island is known as "the cradle of Confederation" but it did not join Canada until July 1, 1873. "The Garden of the Gulf" is the "cradle" because delegates from Canada and the Atlantic provinces met there in 1864 and took the first steps that led to Confederation. The 95,000 islanders, however, mostly Scots, wanted to retain their independence, and felt that they would be swallowed up if they joined Canada.

At the time of Confederation, Canada was embroiled in a railway building boom, and Prince Edward Island was caught in it. By 1873 the cost of laying tracks had mounted so alarmingly that the island was on the brink of bankruptcy. The Legislative Council advised the Assembly that Prince Edward Island had two alternatives: either to submit to a sharp increase in taxes to pay off the railway debts, or to become a province of Canada. On February 15, 1873, a delegation led by Premier Haythorne went to Ottawa and made a deal with Sir John A. Macdonald. When they returned, the government decided to let the people decide, and called an election.

During the campaign Conservative leader J. C. Pope contended that he could make a better deal with Ottawa, and won the election. He took another delegation to Canada, and came back with an offer that would pay off the railway debt, grant the island 50 cents per citizen, establish a ferry service to the mainland, and pay off British landholders who had obtained their property in Prince Edward Island in a lottery in 1767.

The motion to join Canada was introduced in the Assembly by Premier Pope, and seconded by David Laird, leader of the Opposition. It was passed almost unanimously.

When Governor-General Lord Dufferin visited Prince Edward Island soon after it joined Confederation on July 1, 1873, he wrote: "I found it under a high state of jubilation and quite under the impression that it is the Dominion that has been annexed to Prince Edward."

Other Events on February 15:

1625   Champlain was made representative of the viceroy to Canada and was asked to find a route to China.

1839   Six political prisoners were hanged for their part in the rebellion of 1837-1838.

1872   Parliament opened the session that dealt with banking and a uniform system of currency.

1889   Militia from Manitoba suppressed a riot in North Dakota.

1910   Canada made a trade agreement with Germany.

1965   Canada's new maple leaf flag was raised at a special ceremony in Ottawa.

Baroness Macdonald of Earnscliffe

John A. Weds in London

When John A. Macdonald went to London in 1866 he could not have imagined the adventures that lay ahead. The purpose of the trip, with George Etienne Cartier and Alexander Galt, was to prepare the British North America Act, and see it through the British Parliament. Premiers Tupper of Nova Scotia and Tilley of New Brunswick had arrived in London in July and were annoyed when the delegates from Canada did not sail until November 14.

Altogether there were sixteen delegates from Canada, Nova Scotia and New Brunswick. They met with British representatives at the Westminster Palace Hotel. Joseph Howe remained opposed to federation, until as late as 1869, when he surprisingly joined the federal cabinet.

The conference began on December 4, and the work was completed by December 19. Now the delegates from North America could only wait for the bill to be approved by Parliament.

On the night of December 12, John A. Macdonald went to bed early to read some Canadian newspapers. He fell asleep while reading and wakened to find the room on fire because a curtain had blown into the flame of the candle by his bed. Shouting for Cartier and Galt to help him, he tried to beat out the flames with a pillow. They rushed in with pitchers of water and finally put out the fire. Macdonald was quite badly burned and had to stay in bed until after Christmas.

A happier development then came. While walking along Bond Street, Macdonald met Miss Susan Agnes Bernard, sister of his secretary, Colonel Hewitt Bernard. They began a whirl of theatres and restaurants and were married on February 16 in St. George's Church, Hanover Square, with the Bishop of Montreal conducting the service.

Macdonald had been a widower for nine years. Lady Macdonald, as she became when her husband was knighted on Confederation Day 1867, proved to be a great source of strength to him during the difficult years ahead.

Other Events on February 16:

1693   Canadians battled against the English and Indians near Albany, New York.

1838   An Act of Parliament suspended the constitution of Lower Canada.

1870   A plebiscite on Confederation was proposed at the opening of the Legislative Council of British Columbia.

1872   The first legislature of British Columbia opened after Confederation.

1881   The Canadian Pacific Railway Company was incorporated by an Act of Parliament.

1934   Newfoundland was taken over by a Commission Government.

1958   A conference on education opened at Ottawa.

Wolfe Sails to Canada

Major-General James Wolfe sailed from Britain on February 17, 1759, on his last great adventure, the capture of Quebec. He and Admiral Charles Saunders stood on the bridge of the flagship *Neptune* and watched England fade into the mist.

After he and General Amherst captured Louisburg in 1758, Wolfe wanted to go on and attack Quebec right away. He was so angry when Amherst refused that he wanted to resign from the army. Probably to give him some action, Amherst sent Wolfe to attack small French settlements along the Gulf of St. Lawrence. Wolfe didn't like that job either, and reported later: "I have done a great deal of mischief and spread the terror of His Majesty's arms through the Gulf, but have added nothing to the reputation of them." There was little military value in destroying the homes and food supplies of innocent people facing the approach of winter.

Wolfe's return to Britain annoyed Prime Minister Pitt. He told Pitt that he needed to take the cure of the mineral springs at Bath. Actually, he had met Katherine Lowther there the year before and was greatly interested; this time they became engaged.

Pitt had endured a number of bad experiences with incompetent British generals serving in North America. Benjamin Franklin described one of them as being, "about as effective as a painted soldier on a tavern sign." After the capture of Louisburg in 1758, Pitt knew that in Amherst and Wolfe he had the leaders for whom he had been searching. On February 5, 1759, he asked Wolfe to come to see him. He gave him secret instructions for the campaign against Quebec. The armada that set sail on February 17 was the greatest fleet that had ever sailed from Britain up to that time.

James Wolfe (1727-1759)

Other Events on February 17:

1869 The Society for the Prevention of Cruelty to Animals was organized.

1891 Sir John A. Macdonald, at a mass meeting in Toronto, charged the Liberals with conspiring to have Canada join the United States.

1919 The death of Sir Wilfrid Laurier was announced.

1958 Former Prime Minister St. Laurent (1948-1957) announced his retirement from politics.

1960 Prime Minister Diefenbaker opened the new National Gallery of Canada at Ottawa.

1965 The government announced a plan, to take effect gradually over five years, whereby old age pensions would be made available at age sixty-five instead of seventy.

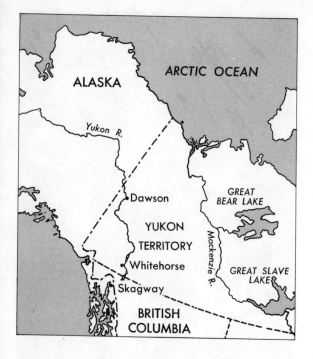

Klondike Railway Expands

Of all the gold rushes in history, the Klondike in 1898 caused the greatest hardships. The worst problem was to get to the gold fields. Some prospectors traveled 3,000 miles by ship to the mouth of the Yukon River in the Bering Sea, and then another 1,700 miles up the river to Dawson. Others went to Edmonton, "the gateway to the north," and trekked into the Yukon from there. The most popular route was by ship to Skagway, Alaska, and then overland through the mountain passes. In one year, only 2,000 out of 10,000 men who set out from Skagway completed the trip. Many died along the way, while others turned back.

At first, the horse-drawn Red Line Transportation Company carried supplies for the miners at $1 per pound. Everyone using it had to sign a pass reading "this pass is not transferable and must be signed in ink or blood by the person who, thereby accepting and using it, assumes all risk of damage to person and baggage. The holder must be prepared to mush behind. Passengers falling into the mud must first find themselves and remove the soil from their garments."

In May, 1898, a group of promoters began to build a narrow-gauge railway called "The White Pass and Yukon." It reached the summit of White Pass on February 18, 1899, and eventually completed the 110 miles to Whitehorse. Its construction was not only a battle against the elements but also against the owners of the Red Line Transportation Company. One of them was a character called "Soapy" Smith, who operated so many rackets in the Skagway area that Al Capone would be like a choir boy in comparison. Yet "Soapy" was regarded as a "Robin Hood" by many because he used some of the revenue from his crooked gambling to build churches and help the poor. His slogan was, "the way of the transgressor is hard—to quit."

"Soapy," trying to prevent the building of the railway, got involved in a gun duel with Frank Reid, Skagway engineer, and both were killed. Smith's body was put in a cart and exhibited throughout the area as a warning.

Other Events on February 18:

1686   A convent was established at Lachine, Quebec.

1886   Archbishop Taché baptized Poundmaker and twenty-eight braves at the Stoney Mountain penitentiary, following the Riel rebellion of 1885.

1941   Sir Frederick Banting, co-discoverer of insulin, died in an airplane crash.

1949   Royal Assent was given to the Terms of Union with Newfoundland.

1963   Justice Minister Fleming resigned after twenty-five years in public life. The Canada Council was given an anonymous gift of $4,250,000.

1966   A bill was passed approving the Ontario Medicare Plan.

Patrick Laurie Honored

Some of Canada's best newspapers were founded on shoestrings by men like Patrick Laurie who began his career by publishing the Owen Sound *Times* in the 1850's at the age of twenty.

Laurie's next venture was the Essex *Recorder,* but his ambition was to publish a newspaper in the prairies and he moved to Fort Garry in 1869, just as Canada bought the territory that had been controlled by the Hudson's Bay Company.

During the Red River uprising Laurie was such a thorn in Riel's side that Riel took over his paper, the *Nor-wester,* and offered $2,000 for his arrest. Laurie had to escape across the border and go to Windsor, Ontario.

Laurie's heart was still in the West, and in 1878, he loaded four Red River carts with equipment and set out for Battleford. He began publishing the Saskatchewan *Herald* in 1878. Although the railway had not reached Battleford, it was on the telegraph line connecting Winnipeg and Edmonton so Laurie was able to send news to other parts of Canada. The Saskatchewan *Herald* kept people informed about the events that were leading up to the Northwest Rebellion of 1885. Battleford itself was besieged by Poundmaker's Indians for nearly a month (see April 24), and Laurie took his place in the Home Guard.

After the rebellion, the people in the Battleford area paid Laurie a magnificent tribute, collecting a purse of $220 for him. This does not seem much today, but it was "the widow's mite." The entire budget of the government of the Northwest Territories in 1879 was only $237.37!

On February 19, 1887, the Edmonton *Bulletin* said: "If any editor ever deserved such recognition, the editor of the *Herald* is that man. He has been engaged in publishing a two-horse paper in a one-horse town for so many years, that it is about time the latter tried to even up a little."

Other Events on February 19:

1631 The first Lutheran baptism in Canada took place at Quebec.

1732 Religious houses were forbidden to shelter fugitives from justice.

1860 The ship *Hungarian* was lost off Cape Sable, Nova Scotia, with 205 lives.

1864 Parliament met at Quebec.

1873 C.P.R. received its charter. (It was later replaced by a new company as the result of a campaign funds scandal.)

1889 Gabriel Dumont was pardoned for his part in the Northwest Rebellion.

1897 The Women's Institute was organized by Mrs. Adelaide Hunter Hoodless at Stoney Creek, Ontario. Later it spread through Canada and Britain.

1911 Japan renounced a trade treaty with Canada.

1920 Shareholders of the Grand Trunk Railway ratified its sale to the government.

Laurie's office at Battleford, 1878

Stefansson's expedition, 1916-17

Arctic Charms Explorer

This is an opportunity to outline the story of Vilhjamur Stefansson, one of the greatest Arctic explorers, who was born at Arnes, Manitoba, in 1879. His parents were among the Icelanders who settled in Canada so successfully, although the Stefanssons moved to the United States after Vilhjamur was born. He was educated there and spent three years at Harvard.

It was on February 20, 1915, that Stefansson set out on an expedition that took him along the coast of Banks Land to Alfred Point, and then to Prince Patrick Island. He and his assistants found land that had never been seen before and claimed it for Canada. This expedition was only one of a number of achievements Stefansson recorded between 1913 and 1918 when he was employed by the Canadian government to explore the Arctic. The five-year expedition above the Arctic Circle was the longest on record and Stefansson and his men lived like Eskimos, depending on hunting for their food.

During his ten winters and thirteen summers in the Arctic, he claimed many islands for Canada, including Borden, Brock, Meighen, and Lougheed.

Stefansson's great claim to fame, however, was his insistence that the Arctic was habitable by white men, and even hospitable. He wrote a book called *The Friendly Arctic* which was heartily criticized by other explorers including Amundsen, the first man to reach the South Pole.

He not only exploded many myths about the Arctic, but claimed that it was capable of commercial development. He forecast the use of air transport and submarines for getting over and under icy wastes. His argument that there was mineral wealth in the Arctic was confirmed not long ago by the discovery of the world's richest deposit of iron ore on Baffin Island.

Other Events on February 20:

1667   La Salle settled in Montreal.

1808   Joseph Willcocks was arrested for contempt of the Assembly.

1836   Governor Sir Francis Bond Head invited Reformers to join the Upper Canada Council.

1865   The Legislative Council of Canada voted 45-15 for Confederation.

1894   The Supreme Court of Canada refused the appeal of Manitoba Roman Catholics concerning the abolition of separate schools.

1915   Field Marshal Sir John French inspected the 1st Canadian Division on the western front.

1950   The Princess Patricia Canadian Light Infantry was in action in Korea.

1961   Prime Minister Diefenbaker conferred with President Kennedy at Washington.

1966   The Lieutenant-Governor of Quebec, Paul Comtois, died in a spectacular fire which destroyed the historic residence of Bois de Coulonge.

Buchan Appointed Governor-General

In 1935 R. B. Bennett was Prime Minister and W. L. Mackenzie King was Leader of the Opposition. A successor was needed for Governor-General Lord Bessborough and, since a general election had to be held, the British government felt that Mackenzie King should be consulted. Prime Minister Bennett agreed and conferred with the Opposition Leader. They came up with one of the best governors-general Canada has ever had. John Buchan, author of exciting adventure stories, was appointed on February 21, and created Baron Tweedsmuir.

During his term of office, Lord Tweedsmuir saw as much of Canada as he could, even making a trip down the Mackenzie River. As Bennett and King probably hoped, he also managed to write about Canada, including *The Long Traverse*, and *Sick Heart River*, books about Indian life.

One of the most delightful stories about his travels in Canada concerns his visit to Val Marie, Saskatchewan, in the summer of 1938. He wanted to see an irrigation project at Val Marie, and news of his visit caused a commotion. Nothing as exciting had happened in twenty years. Fronts of buildings were painted (there wasn't time to do the sides and backs), cows and chickens were cleared off the streets, and school children dramatized a John Buchan story.

The welcoming committee felt it was important that the Scottish lord should be "piped" into town. By making appeals on the radio and in newspapers, a piper was found, and gradually a proper highland uniform was put together.

When the great day arrived, Lord Tweedsmuir was piped into Val Marie to *Cock o' the North*, and he was delighted. He called over the piper and asked, "What tartan do you claim?" The piper, who did not know one tartan from another, replied, "My name is Olson and I come from Minnesota."

Lord Tweedsmuir (1875-1940)

Other Events on February 21:

1642   Charnisay was commissioned to arrest La Tour as a traitor.

1812   The Lower Canada Parliament voted money for war.

1824   An eighteen-year-old boy was hanged in Saint John, New Brunswick for stealing 25 cents.

1834   The Ninety-two Resolutions on public grievances were passed by the Assembly of Lower Canada.

1949   Newfoundland's Commission Government announced approval of the Terms of Union with Canada.

1952   Canada and the United States signed an agreement to use radio as a safety measure on the Great Lakes.

1961   The Ontario Royal Commission recommended fluoridation of water supplies.

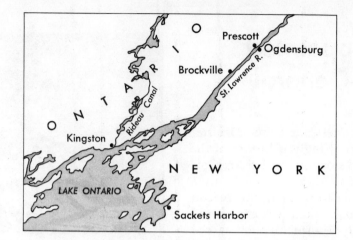

Canadians Defeat Americans at Ogdensburg

One of the world's great examples of international co-operation is the St. Lawrence Seaway, built and maintained jointly by Canada and the United States. Near its western end is a new bridge linking Prescott, Ontario, and Ogdensburg, New York. Strangely, it could equally be a memorial to some bitter fighting which occurred there during the War of 1812, or to the raid by American members of the Hunters' organization in 1838. They were hoping to "liberate" Canada from Britain.

It was on February 22, 1813 that British-Canadian troops won a hard battle against the Americans at Ogdensburg. Earlier in the month the Americans under Major Forsyth had come over the ice from Ogdensburg and raided nearby Brockville. They took fifty-two Canadians back to Ogdensburg as hostages, as well as all the horses, cattle, pigs and chickens they could round up.

Major Macdonnell of the Glengarries, stationed at Prescott, wanted to hit back, but Governor Sir George Prevost would not allow him to attack. Perhaps he felt the hostages might be killed. However, Macdonnell persuaded Prevost to allow him to put on a "demonstration" on the river.

Macdonnell took 480 men and three pieces of artillery out on the ice. The river is more than one mile wide there. The "demonstration" was suddenly turned into a real attack.

The Canadian troops had no shelter, but they advanced through the American gunfire. There was a bloody battle as they fought their way into Ogdensburg and the Americans fled into the woods.

Macdonnell returned to Prescott with seventy-four prisoners, twelve guns, three hundred tents and a large quantity of food and ammunition. There were no more raids on the Prescott-Brockville area during the rest of the war. Later in the year, American General Wilkinson left Sackets Harbor, New York, with 8,000 men and sailed past Prescott with the intention of attacking Montreal. They landed below Prescott and suffered disastrous losses at Crysler's Farm.

Other Events on February 22:

1724   Edmé Nicholas Robert was appointed Intendant.

1785   British Law was established in Cape Breton, Nova Scotia.

1851   The Bytown *Packet* became the *Ottawa Citizen*.

1887   The Conservatives under Sir John A. Macdonald won the general election with a majority of thirty seats. The hanging of Riel in 1885 was an important factor in the election campaign. Wilfrid Laurier and Edward Blake were the Liberal leaders.

Burns Wins Boxing Crown

Canada once produced a world heavyweight boxing champion who became an ordained minister in Vancouver. He was Tommy Burns, born Noah Brusso in Hanover, Ontario.

Although Tommy Burns won the world heavyweight title on February 23, 1906 by defeating Marvin Hart in a 20-round fight in Los Angeles, he wasn't a real heavyweight at all. Burns was only five feet seven inches tall, and usually weighed about 170 pounds in the ring. Most of his fights were against men who were from 30 to 60 pounds heavier. However, he had an extraordinary reach of 74½ inches. Perhaps more important, he was highly intelligent, self-sufficient (he never had a manager) and knew how to get into the best condition. His training methods were copied not only by boxers but other athletes, and he wrote a book about scientific boxing.

When Burns beat Hart in 1906, his claim to the world's championship was disputed by other fighters, and so he took on all the challengers. He defended his title successfully ten times before he lost to huge Jack Johnson in Australia in 1908. The fight was no contest. Johnson was far too big, and Burns could not land a blow. Finally the police stopped the fight during round 14 to save Burns from further punishment. Still, he made $30,000, the biggest purse ever won by a fighter at that time. Altogether, Burns won about $200,000 from the fight game and lifted it into the big-money class.

After Burns lost the championship, he fought in Calgary, Saskatoon, and Prince Rupert, winning every time. He was over forty when he was finally defeated by Joe Beckett in England. Then he retired to Vancouver where he became a church minister. Later, Tommy became an honored member of the Canadian Sports Hall of Fame.

Tommy Burns (1881-1955)

Other Events on February 23:

1770 Samuel Hearne began his second search for the Coppermine River, lasting until November 25.

1879 The first issue of *La Patrie* was published in Montreal.

1909 J. A. D. McCurdy made the first airplane flight in the British Commonwealth at Baddeck, Nova Scotia (see September 30).

1914 A rock slide into the Fraser River nearly destroyed the salmon fishing industry there.

Company of 100 Associates Loses Charter

One of the biggest development companies was formed by Cardinal Richelieu in 1627. It was called The Company of One Hundred Associates and its shareholders were some of the leading citizens of France. The company had exclusive control of the fur trade from Florida to the far north and from the Atlantic to the western end of the St. Lawrence River. In return, the company was supposed to settle 4,000 people in Canada within 15 years.

Almost from the start the Company was unlucky. Its first act was to send out a fleet of twenty ships carrying men, women, and children to Canada. There were 150 guns to protect the new settlements. The convoy was guarded by four warships under Admiral de Roquemont.

Cardinal Richelieu (1585-1642)

Unfortunately, the Kirke brothers who worked for the rival English organization, the Merchant Adventurers, were in the vicinity. They caught Admiral Roquemont's fleet in Gaspé Bay, sheltering from a storm and unprepared for action. The French fleet was destroyed and surrendered quietly. The Kirkes took the transports to Newfoundland, and the prominent prisoners to England. Champlain was left without supplies for the winter.

By 1659 the affairs of the Company were in such bad shape that a French lawyer, Dumesnil was sent to Quebec to see what was going on. He soon learned that there were swindlers operating there. They tried to scare Dumesnil from continuing his investigations by murdering his son and raiding his office. They gagged him while they went through his papers, and carried off the evidence he had collected.

Eventually Dumesnil got back to France, where Louis XIV was now king with Colbert as his minister. They cancelled the charter of the One Hundred Associates on February 24, 1663, and the Crown took over the development of Canada.

Other Events on February 24:

1653   Charles La Tour married Madame Charnisay (see April 13).

1662   Bishop Laval excommunicated people selling liquor to the Indians.

1865   A telegraph line to Russia was begun at New Westminster, British Columbia, but never was completed.

1887   Vancouver lost its city charter over rioting against Chinese labor.

1915   Canadian troops went into action at Armentières.

1925   Canada signed an agreement with the United States, setting up control of the Lake-of-the-Woods waterways.

Montmorency New Viceroy

In the early days of Canada the kings of France appointed viceroys to represent them, but they did not have to come here. They were really contact men between the court and the companies doing business in Canada.

Champlain was fortunate to have a backer like de Monts who spent most of his fortune organizing the early trips. Strangely enough, de Monts should not have been in the company at all because he was a Huguenot (Protestant) and Huguenots were not even allowed to leave France, let alone develop colonies. De Monts was able to play the part he did because Henry IV was a Huguenot before he became King, and had to change his faith in order to ascend to the throne.

When Henry was assassinated, Champlain and de Monts knew they had to get someone close to the court to be head of their company. After an unsuccessful experiment, they chose the Prince de Condé, a member of one of the most famous families in France. They gave him shares in the company and a salary of 1,000 crowns a year to be their contact man along with young King Louis XIII and his mother, Marie de Medici, who was the power behind the throne.

Condé was appointed viceroy in 1613, but was later sent to the Bastille when found to be involved in a conspiracy against the King. His wife was so beautiful that he had kept her hidden from amorous Henry IV. She was so annoyed that she was about to divorce him when he was put in prison. She changed her mind and joined him in the Bastille, bringing with her several servants, a cook, barber and a confessor! They lived there for three years and had a son who became the most famous Condé of all. Fortunately for the development of Canada, the Prince de Condé sold his position in the company to the Duke of Montmorency, Admiral of France, for 11,000 crowns. Montmorency was appointed viceroy on February 25, 1620, and he quickly

Duke of Montmorency, Viceroy, 1619-24

reorganized the company. He bought out some shareholders who had been hindering progress, and proved to be a solid supporter of Champlain. Montmorency River, with its beautiful waterfall, near Quebec City, is named after him.

Other Events on February 25:

1651   Charles La Tour was made governor of Acadia.

1813   The Parliament of Upper Canada opened the session that prohibited the sale of liquor to Indians, and the export of grain, owing to food shortage.

1832   The Champlain and St. Lawrence Railway was incorporated; this was the first railway legislation passed in Canada.

1858   Parliament met at Toronto; the session included the first legislation on protective tariffs.

1880   The legislature of New Brunswick was destroyed by fire (Fredericton).

1918   McGill University received $1,000,000 from the Carnegie Foundation.

1963   Prime Minister Diefenbaker was made a Freeman of the City of London, England.

Sir Samuel Leonard Tilley (1818-1896)

Lords Pass B.N.A. Act

On February 26, 1867, the House of Lords passed the British North America Act establishing the Dominion of Canada. The bill still had to go to the House of Commons, but there was no doubt that it would be passed.

The name "Dominion" of Canada came about in an interesting way. John A. Macdonald had wanted "Kingdom" of Canada, but Prime Minister, the Earl of Derby, objected to a colony having a title that would make it equal to Britain. His son, Lord Stanley, who was Secretary for Foreign Affairs, also objected because the United States might not like having a kingdom on its border! Premier Tilley of New Brunswick finally solved the problem. He read the Bible every morning, and Psalm 72 seemed to leap from its pages: "He shall have dominion also from sea to sea, and from the river unto the ends of the earth." What more appropriate description could there be of Canada? His suggestion that the name of the new nation should be "Dominion of Canada" was approved by Queen Victoria and all the delegates.

When Colonial Secretary Lord Carnarvon presented the British North America Act for its second reading, he said: "We are laying the cornerstone of a great state, perhaps one which at a future day may even overshadow this country. But, come what may, we shall rejoice that we showed neither indifference to their wishes nor jealousy of their aspirations."

The day after the Act passed the Lords, Macdonald, Cartier, Galt, Tilley and Tupper, the senior members of the delegation, went to Buckingham Palace for an audience with Queen Victoria. They wore blue court uniforms which would have caused some commotion in their own home towns. After all, they were only two colonial lawyers, two businessmen, and one country doctor. They reported later that the Queen looked sad. She was wearing black, still mourning for her husband, Prince Albert, who had died five years before. She approved the Act in a few words, and then John A. Macdonald said: "We have desired in this measure to declare in the most solemn and emphatic manner our resolve to be under the sovereignty of Your Majesty and your family forever." Then the delegates backed out of the room.

Other Events on February 26:

1790   Prime Minister Pitt demanded that Spain make restitution for British ships captured at Nootka, British Columbia.

1798   David Thompson explored the headwaters of the Mississippi.

1857   Parliament met at Toronto and asked Queen Victoria to choose a site for the capital.

1919   The session of Parliament began that passed the Soldiers' Settlement Act, established an air board, and abolished further titles for Canadians.

1954   Dag Hammarskjold, Secretary-General of the United Nations, visited Ottawa.

1960   Anne Heggtveit of Ottawa became the first Canadian to win an Olympic gold medal for skiing.

Canada's Demands Ignored

Sir John A. Macdonald was such a powerful figure in Canadian affairs that it is difficult to imagine his taking a back seat. Yet it happened on February 27, 1871, when he went to Washington as a member of a British delegation to try to settle problems that had arisen among Britain, Canada and the United States.

The United States was demanding reparation for the damage done by the British-built Confederate steamer *Alabama* during the Civil War. The States also wanted a discussion on coastal fishing rights. Canada wanted reparation for damage caused by the Fenians. The question of ownership of San Juan Island just south of Vancouver Island was also causing bad feelings.

Britain was fearful of what was happening in Europe and the Middle East, and had no time for trouble with the United States. The British delegates were not too concerned about Canada's problems; they wanted to make the best deal they could to repay the damage done by the *Alabama*. The delegation was led by the Earl de Grey and Ripon whom W. D. Hardy describes in *From Sea Unto Sea* as being "a handsome man with a scorn for colonials and a beard that would have graced any bull bison."

Since the agenda made no mention of the Fenian raids, the Americans refused to discuss them. Macdonald had hoped to make a deal giving the United States better fishing rights off Canadian coasts in exchange for an easier entry of Canadian products into the American market. He was shunted into the background by his four British colleagues and the upshot was that Britain paid the United States $15,500,000 for the damage done by the *Alabama*. The United States acquired San Juan Island, fishing rights and free navigation of the St. Lawrence River "in perpetuity" for which Canada was eventually paid $5,500,000. Britain lent Canada £2,500,000 for forgetting to put the Fenian raids on the agenda.

Macdonald and British delegates, 1871

Sir John A. Macdonald had to sign the agreement knowing that his political opponents would describe him as being "Judas Iscariot and Benedict Arnold rolled into one."

Other Events on February 27:

1629   Louis Hébert was made a seignior with the authority to grant land.

1742   France issued additional card money worth 120,000 livres.

1839   The Upper Canada Parliament advocated the union of Upper and Lower Canada.

1867   Queen Victoria approved the British North America Act.

1896   The Manitoba Legislature protested federal interference in its Separate Schools Act.

1900   The government of British Columbia was dismissed by Lieutenant-Governor McInnes; all but one member left the legislature when the governor arrived to prorogue.

1951   Canada posted an Army officer with the Supreme Allied Commander's staff: the first step in providing Canadian ground troops for Europe.

Twenty-one crude stills at Petrolia refinery, 1893

Oil Deposits Found at Enniskillen (Petrolia)

In recent years oil development in Alberta and Saskatchewan has stolen the limelight from Canada's original "oil capital," Petrolia, Ontario. The first oil well brought into production on the whole North American continent was at Oil Springs, a few miles south of Petrolia, in 1857. The United States disputes this, and claims that the first oil well was drilled at Titusville, Pennslyvania, in 1859. Both claims are correct. The oil well at Oil Springs, two years before the Pennsylvania discovery, was "dug." The oil well at Titusville was "drilled."

The pioneer of oil in Canada was Charles N. Tripp of Woodstock, Ontario. He contrived a method of making asphalt from what he called "gum beds" in the Oil Springs area. He sold his holdings to James Miller Williams of Hamilton, Ontario, who although only thirty-nine years of age, had already made a fortune building carriages and railway cars.

Tripp used to boil the "gum" from which he made asphalt. Williams found that by digging he could obtain oil in liquid form and began operations in 1857 on the banks of the Thames River at Bothwell, Kent County. When he got down to 27 feet, he found oil mixed with water. Operations were then shifted to Enniskillen where better oil was found at 65 feet. The first wells produced from five to one hundred barrels a day.

This began the oil boom of the late 1850's. Hugh Nixon Shaw found the gusher at Enniskillen on February 28, 1860. The name of the community was changed to Petrolia, which it is still called today. By 1895 production reached 800,000 barrels a year. There were fifteen refineries operating and the oil was taken to markets in carts drawn by teams of oxen.

In the 1880's, Imperial Oil was organized, and it built the largest refinery in Canada. Canadian Oil Companies then followed and built a pipeline to Froomfield on the St. Clair River where the oil flowed directly into ships.

Other Events on February 28:

1820   Mississauga Indians surrendered 2,000 acres, now part of Peel County, Ontario, to the Government.

1825   A treaty between Britain and Russia defined the Alaska boundary.

1952   Vincent Massey became Governor-General of Canada; he was the first native-born Canadian to hold the position.

French Attack Deerfield

This story may be read only once every four years, but historian J. L. Rutledge in *Century of Conflict* says that it led eventually to France's losing Canada. There might have been peaceful co-existence between French Canada and what is now the United States if Governor Vaudreuil had not persisted in the policy of attacking settlements in New England.

On February 29, 1704, Deerfield, near the northwest frontier of Massachusetts, was the target for destruction. It was a peaceful village with no military significance. The attack was led by Hertel de Rouville, whose force included four of his brothers, fifty soldiers and two hundred Abenaki and Caughnawaga Indians. Dragging their supplies on sleighs, they marched 300 miles on snowshoes in bitter winter weather from Montreal to Deerfield. When they arrived on the night of February 28, they were starving and cold, but they could not light fires without causing an alarm.

Deerfield's forty-one homes were quickly destroyed when Rouville's men made their vicious attack at dawn. Forty-eight citizens were killed, including women and children. Reverend John Williams, who was spared, saw two of his children killed, and then he and Mrs. Williams were included in a group of 100 prisoners who were forced to march to Montreal with the troops. Mrs. Williams had given birth to a child only one week before, and was unable to wade across the swift and unfrozen Green River. As she stumbled in the stream, an Indian killed her with a blow of his hatchet.

The march to Montreal was comparable in cruelty to that inflicted by the Japanese on British and American prisoners during World War II. Reverend Williams survived the ordeal and wrote a book about it called *The Redeemed Captive Returning to Zion*. Eventually, fifty-seven of the prisoners were returned to Boston in exchange for French prisoners taken in New England. One of the

Marquis de Vaudreuil (1698-1778)

Deerfield residents who did not return was the Williams' seven-year-old daughter, Eunice. One of the Indians had taken pity on her during the march, and carried her practically all the way. She was taken to the mission at Caughnawaga and educated. A few years later, she married the Indian who had saved her.

Other Events on February 29:

1680 Father Hennepin left to explore the Mississippi.

1712 Montcalm was born at Candiac, France.

1892 The Treaty of Washington between Britain and the United States allowed both sides to submit the Bering Sea fishing dispute to arbitration.

1960 President Segni of Italy visited Canada until March 2.

Canada was honored to have Vincent Massey as its first native-born Governor-General. Mr. Massey served with distinction from 1952 to 1959 as the Queen's representative in Canada. Before becoming Governor-General, Mr. Massey held many important government positions. He was Canada's first minister to the United States, 1926-30; President, National Liberal Federation, 1932-35; high commissioner for Canada to London, 1935-46.

Mr. Massey, as trustee or chairman of many cultural institutions, has contributed much to the development of the arts and education in Canada.

Georges Philias Vanier, soldier and diplomat, succeeded Vincent Massey as Governor-General until his death on March 5, 1967. The late Governor-General selflessly devoted his energies to strengthening the bonds of Confederation. In his New Year's Message in January, 1967, he said that the settlement of Canada dated back three and a half centuries "during most of which the two founding peoples, first the French and then the British, then both together, with peoples of other origins, have co-existed and co-operated . . . but to emphasize now our quarrels and shortcomings leads only to bitterness best forgotten . . ."

Labrador Granted to Newfoundland

When Jacques Cartier sailed along the coast of Labrador on his first voyage to Canada in 1534, he described it as "the land God gave to Cain." He felt there was a more promising future for the New World a few days later when he discovered Prince Edward Island.

Today, Labrador would be too rich a gift for the most deserving man in the world. Billions of dollars are being poured in to develop its mineral resources, especially iron ore. Newfoundland, which took over Labrador on March 1, 1927, by a decision of the Privy Council in Britain, earns $10 million a year in royalties from the iron ore alone. Electric power from the Churchill River in Labrador (see April 15) is to supply industries in eastern Canada and the United States and may even help to light New York. There is a waterfall on the Churchill 245 feet high, and the plan is to converge the river so that there will be a drop of 1,040 feet. It will provide 4,700,000 horsepower of electricity, twice as much as the output of Grand Coulee, the biggest producer in the United States.

The story of Labrador's belonging to Newfoundland rather than to Quebec is long and complicated. Newfoundland fishermen used the Labrador coast from the earliest days, and when France handed Canada over to Britain by the Treaty of Paris in 1763, Newfoundland's claims to Labrador were recognized. The boundary was supposed to be determined by watersheds of rivers running to the ocean. It was the same ambiguous kind of definition that caused difficulties between New Brunswick and Maine for many years.

After periods of recurring disputes, the problem was handed to the Privy Council in Britain in 1921. No decision had been made by 1925, and Newfoundland offered to sell Labrador to Quebec for $30 million. Since the United States had bought Louisiana from Napoleon for $27 million, perhaps it wasn't surprising that Premier Taschereau turned down the offer. Two years later the Privy Council made its decision. The boundary between Newfoundland and Quebec is still the same today, although Quebec disputes it.

Other Events on March 1:

1632 Champlain was appointed the first governor of Canada.

1815 The troops of Lower Canada were disbanded.

1838 Six hundred Lower Canada rebels under Dr. Nelson surrendered to United States authority in Vermont.

1868 Canada issued a three-cent stamp.

1888 A parcel post was established between Canada and the United States.

1898 The first Intercolonial Railway train arrived at Montreal.

1939 Trans Canada Airlines (now Air Canada) inaugurated the transcontinental airmail service.

1953 The United States removed an embargo on Canadian livestock imports.

1963 The British Columbia government converted Victoria College to the University of Victoria and established the Simon Fraser University at Burnaby.

Sieur D'Iberville (1661-1706)

River Mouth Sighted

On his first voyage to Canada, in 1534, Jacques Cartier sailed in a 20-ton caravel and made the trip across the Atlantic in twenty-one days. He was an expert navigator, and as he sailed up the Strait of Belle Isle, between Newfoundland and Labrador, he could tell from the movement of the water that there was a great river ahead and so he discovered the St. Lawrence.

One of the greatest military leaders in the history of Canada, Pierre Le Moyne d'Iberville used his knowledge of the sea in somewhat the same way to find the mouth of the Mississippi River. Pierre Le Moyne, usually called Iberville, was one of ten brothers born and raised in Montreal. The Le Moynes must have been one of the greatest fighting families in the history of the world. Their exploits

ranged all the way from Hudson Bay to the Gulf of Mexico. It has been said of Iberville that if his campaigns had taken place in Europe instead of in the wilds of North America, he would have been acknowledged as a military leader ranking with Napoleon.

French explorers from Canada, notably La Salle, had worked their way down the Mississippi River but had never reached its mouth. In January, 1685, La Salle tried to find it from the sea but sailed by without recognizing it.

King Louis XIV decided to entrust Iberville with the task. On March 2, 1699, Iberville was sailing along the coast of the Gulf of Mexico and saw the blue water turning gray. He knew there must be a muddy river not far away and later in the day sailed between high rocks into the mouth of the Mississippi. Some of the mud flowing into the Gulf had come all the way from the prairies.

Iberville was a military adventurer, not a colonizer. He left that job to his younger brother Bienville, who had accompanied him; and so, the famous city of New Orleans, still proud of its French traditions, was founded by the Le Moyne brothers of Montreal.

Other Events on March 2:

1804   Four mutineers and three deserters were executed in Quebec city in what was described as a "revolting public spectacle."

1831   The Upper Canada Parliament passed an act legalizing marriages by Methodist ministers.

1916   Ontario passed a Temperance Act.

1932   The Senate killed a bill legalizing sweepstakes.

1943   Income tax was put on a pay-as-you-earn basis.

1951   The first Canadian casualty list from Korea was issued: six soldiers had been killed.

1965   Lucien Rivard escaped from Bordeaux prison, Montreal.

Simpson Circles World

Philanthropy is not the object of our visits to these Northern Indians.
—GEORGE SIMPSON, *1821*

One of the most colorful characters in Canadian history was Sir George Simpson, Governor of the Hudson's Bay Company. On March 3, 1841, he began a trip around the world that took twenty months.

Scottish-born, he was only thirty-three when the Hudson's Bay Company sent him in 1821 to govern what is now western Canada. The Hudson's Bay Company had just taken over its bitter rival, the Northwest Company, and a strong, wise leader was needed to blend the two together. Simpson virtually ruled western Canada for forty years.

Simpson was a fur-trader, not a farmer, but he tried to help the settlers in the Red River area by buying their surplus products. He even organized an experimental farm on the Assiniboine River and imported the best thoroughbred cattle and horses from Britain. Even so, late in his career, he told a special committee of the House of Commons in London that the soil in western Canada was useless for farming. He wanted to protect the area for fur trading.

Simpson made his trips across Canada by canoe. Traveling would begin every day at 3 a.m., after Simpson had had a swim, and continue almost without pause until dark. Colin Fraser, Simpson's piper, was always a member of his party. On approaching a settlement, Fraser would stand in the stern and play his bagpipes, while Simpson, wearing top hat, cloak, and gaiters, would stand erect in the bow.

On one trip in 1828, Simpson traveled from Hudson Bay to the mouth of the Fraser River in ninety days. This included paddling down the Fraser River itself, which Simon Fraser had done only twenty years before. It was one of the most dangerous journeys ever undertaken by man.

Sir George Simpson (1792-1860)

Simpson was not a Pacific coast fan. He thought that living in what is now British Columbia was unhealthy and would only allow his traders to stay there for two years, after which they had to go to Fort Garry (Winnipeg) to "recuperate."

Other Events on March 3:

1722   France divided Canada into "parishes."

1838   Five hundred American sympathizers of the Canadian "rebellion" were repelled at Point Pelee, Lake Erie.

1870   Thomas Scott was condemned to death after his trial at Fort Garry.

1887   The United States passed the Fisheries Retaliation Act against Canada.

1945   Canadian and American troops linked in Germany as Nazis retreated along the Rhine.

1962   The death of Cairine Wilson, the first woman senator in Canada, was announced.

The Scott Tragedy

Thomas Scott Executed

It cannot be said that Riel was hanged on account of his opinions. It is equally true that he was not executed for anything connected with the late rebellion. He was hanged for Scott's murder; that is the simple truth of it.

—WILFRID LAURIER, 1885

An event on March 4, 1870, in Fort Garry, now Winnipeg, is still causing political repercussions in Canada. Louis Riel had Ontario Orangeman, Thomas Scott, executed in the prison yard at Fort Garry. The outcry in Ontario was so great that Riel was hanged in Regina in 1885, after leading a rebellion on the prairies. In Quebec, Riel was regarded as a martyr, and the Conservatives were blamed for his death.

Scott's trial had been held on March 3, 1870, and was called "a council of war." It was presided over by Ambroise Lépine, who was one of Riel's chief aides. Riel was the prosecutor and one of the three witnesses who were called. Scott was not allowed to call any witnesses in his own defense.

The charge against Scott was that he had taken up arms against Riel's provisional government. It was "phoney" because dozens of others had done the same thing and had been released. Later, Riel told federal mediator Donald A. Smith (Lord Strathcona) the real reason. It was that Scott had been rough and abusive to the guards and insulting to Riel himself.

When the time came for the execution on March 4, Scott stood before a wall of the prison and was allowed to pray with Methodist minister Young. He then knelt in the snow, a coffin beside him. There were six Métis in the firing party, and they had all been drinking. Three of their rifles contained blank charges so it would not be known who actually fired the bullets that killed Scott. After the guns blasted the kneeling Scott, another Métis had to dash up with a revolver and put a bullet through his head because he was only wounded.

The body was buried secretly and its resting place has never been found. It is believed that the coffin was dropped into the river through a hole in the ice.

Other Events on March 4:

1791 The Constitutional Act divided Quebec into Upper and Lower Canada. It was introduced to the British House of Commons by William Pitt, the younger.

1814 British and American troops fought the Battle of Longwoods between London and Thamesville, Ontario.

1865 Confederation was defeated in the New Brunswick Legislature.

1871 Sandford Fleming was appointed to survey the C.P.R. route from Fort William, Ontario to the Pacific coast.

1925 Quebec rejected Newfoundland's offer to sell Labrador for $30 million.

1971 Prime Minister Trudeau, 51, married Margaret Sinclair, 22, of Vancouver, thus becoming the first Prime Minister since the confederation to wed during his term of office.

Brown Publishes *Globe*

On March 5, 1844, the first issue of the *Globe*, edited and published by George Brown, appeared in Toronto. Brown was a Scot who had emigrated to the States and then moved to Toronto where he became interested in the Reform movement.

As time went by, George Brown and the *Globe* became John Macdonald's sharpest opponents. Clashes between Macdonald and Brown, who gradually became the leader of the Clear Grit wing of the Reform (Liberal) Party, were often the highlight of parliamentary sessions. All the same, it was Brown who manoeuvred Macdonald into supporting Confederation (see June 22).

Although Brown was dead, it was, strangely enough, on the anniversary of the first issue of the *Globe*, March 5, 1891, that Macdonald turned the tables on it. His government was facing a general election, and things were going badly for the Conservatives when Macdonald got the break for which he had been waiting.

Edward Farrer, editor of the *Globe*, had been persuaded by some Americans to write a private treatise suggesting steps the United States might take to annex Canada. It was a purely theoretical argument of the type used by debating societies. Somehow, Macdonald got a copy of it and reread excerpts at a huge election meeting in Toronto, claiming that here was proof of a conspiracy by the Liberals to force Canada into union with the United States. It was then that he uttered his famous campaign slogan: "a British subject I was born, a British subject I will die."

Conservative speakers across the country took his cue, waved the Union Jack and shouted, "the old man, the old policy." When the votes were counted, an expected Liberal victory had been turned into defeat. The Macdonald government had won a majority of thirty-one but its jubilation soon diminished because Sir John died a few weeks later.

George Brown, (1818-1880)

Other Events on March 5:

1496   King Henry VII authorized John Cabot and his sons to claim lands they discovered.

1648   The Constitution of Canada was revised, with a council at Quebec to be the governing body—the Council of New France.

1764   Governor Murray ordered citizens to declare holdings of French-Canadian money.

1838   The town of Kingston, Ontario, was incorporated.

1844   The seat of government moved from Kingston to Montreal.

1870   Britain and Canada agreed to send a military expedition to Red River.

1874   The first session of the Prince Edward Island Legislature after Confederation was held.

1957   Guy Mollet, Premier of France, addressed a joint session of Parliament at Ottawa.

Toronto, circa, 1840

York Officially Becomes Toronto

Toronto was originally named "Toronto" by the Indians, who used its sheltered bay as a harbor. Later, French fur traders used the bay, and built Fort Rouillé there in 1749. There was, however, little habitation until 1793, when Governor Simcoe chose the site to be the capital of Upper Canada. He called it "York" to commemorate victories won by the Duke of York in the war with France.

As the community grew, the inhabitants tried several times to get the name changed to Toronto because so many other places were called York. The Assembly passed a bill to this effect in 1822, but the Governor and his Council ignored it.

Quebec and Montreal were incorporated as cities in 1832, and using this as a precedent, the people of York finally got their way. An Act of Incorporation was passed on March 6, 1834, and the city was named Toronto.

By this time there were 10,000 people in Toronto, and the first municipal election was held on March 27. Every male citizen could vote whether he was an owner or a tenant. The city was divided into five wards, each having two councillors and two aldermen. They appointed the mayor from their own ranks and the man they chose was William Lyon Mackenzie. This was intended to be an affront to the Governor and his Council, known as the Family Compact. Mackenzie was a militant reformer and had already been expelled from the legislature. This happened a number of times but he was always re-elected.

Mackenzie's first act as mayor of Toronto was to order wooden sidewalks to be built and drains to be dug. When it became known that this work would increase taxes by three-pence per pound, there was a riot in which six people were killed and others were injured. Toronto "the good" got away to a turbulent start.

Other Events on March 6:

1837 Lord Russell put ten resolutions about Canada before the British Parliament.

1884 A free public library was established in Toronto.

1889 Toronto Customs officers destroyed novels by Zola for being "obscene."

1957 The Supreme Court of Canada nullified the Quebec "padlock law."

Cook's ships Resolution *and* Discovery *in Nootka Sound, 1778*

Captain Cook Sights Oregon, Rests at Nootka

It is amazing to realize that nearly thirty years before Champlain was active in Canada, Sir Francis Drake tried to find the Northwest Passage by sailing around the Horn and exploring the Pacific coast. He made that voyage in the *Golden Hind*, in 1579, and claimed what is now California, Oregon, Washington and British Columbia for England.

Drake blamed the "stinking fogges" (fogs) for his failure to discover the Northwest Passage, although he sailed as far north as Alaska. His voyage was a success, however, because when he returned to England, the ballast in his ships was gold and silver taken from the Spaniards.

Other romantic buccaneers followed Drake. The most successful was Captain Cook, who was also sent to try to find the Northwest Passage from the Pacific. Cook had done a wonderful job as navigating officer for General Wolfe in 1759, guiding the armada of British ships safely up the St. Lawrence. When the Admiralty sent him to the Pacific to look for the Northwest Passage, Cook's navigating officer was the cruel Captain Bligh, who had been made famous by the book, *Mutiny on the Bounty*. Another of Cook's officers was young George Vancouver.

On March 7, 1778, Oregon was sighted by Cook's ships, *Resolution* and *Discovery*. Sailing north, they unluckily missed the mouth of the Columbia River. A storm drove them out to sea when they reached Cape Flattery and they missed the Strait of Juan de Fuca leading to the water between Vancouver Island and the British Columbia mainland.

However, Cook did find the beautiful harbor of Nootka Sound where he rested the crew for a month. Scurvy was cured by making a brew of spruce bark. (Cartier learned a similar recipe when wintering at Quebec in 1535.)

From Nootka, Cook sailed north until turned back by ice in the Bering Sea. From there he sailed south and was murdered by natives in Hawaii. Drake and Cook had paved the way for Vancouver and the others who mapped and colonized British Columbia.

Other Events on March 7:

1610   Champlain sailed on his fourth voyage.

1657   King Louis XIV prohibited the sale of liquor to Indians.

1842   Queen's University opened at Kingston, Ontario.

1867   The New Brunswick Legislature rejected Confederation.

1878   The University of Montreal, and the University of Western Ontario (London), were incorporated.

1965   Roman Catholic churches in Canada celebrated mass in English for the first time.

Canadian delegates in London, December, 1866

Commons Pass B.N.A. Act

On March 8, 1867, the British North America Act was passed by the House of Commons in Britain, less than a month after it had been introduced in the House of Lords. It was a speedy job of legislation, so much so, that the Canadian delegates were a little "miffed" because it had not caused more debate. John A. Macdonald grumbled: "The English behave as though the British North America Act was a private bill uniting two or three parishes."

Some British M.P.'s were suspicious that the bill was being rushed through, but the only man who offered any opposition was John Bright, free-trader and reformer. In this case, he was on the side of the underdog, Joseph Howe, who had been in London since July trying to keep Nova Scotia out of Confederation.

Howe even went to Lord Carnarvon and claimed that fifty-two of the seventy-two resolutions leading to the British North America Act had been drawn up by Macdonald who had probably been drunk at the time. Carnarvon, greatly upset, wrote to Governor-General Lord Monck in Canada asking him to investigate. Evidently he was reassured because the bill went through without delay.

John Bright tried to have the bill set aside by criticizing the colonial system generally. He said that if the provinces of British North America were going to keep asking Britain for money for defense and railways, then it would be better if they were given their independence and paid their own way.

M.P.'s were so little concerned that many of them were not in their seats when the British North America Act got its final reading on March 8. They came rushing in immediately after, because the next item of business was a bill to place a tax on dogs, and most of them owned dogs!

The British North America Act was officially proclaimed on March 29, and Queen Victoria set July 1 as the date for Confederation.

Other Events on March 8:

1765   The House of Lords passed the Stamp Act, one of the aggravations that led to the American Revolutionary War.

1799   David Thompson was exploring along the North Saskatchewan River.

1836   The New Brunswick and Canada Railway received a charter to operate between St. Andrews, New Brunswick, and Quebec City.

1837   The Bank of British North America opened in Montreal.

1855   The Niagara Suspension Bridge was opened.

1873   The Northwest Territories Council prohibited the sale of liquor.

1907   The Supreme Court of Saskatchewan was established.

1922   The first session of the Fourteenth Parliament opened with W. L. Mackenzie King as Prime Minister. Legislation included the establishment of the Department of National Defence.

Cartier's Plans Crushed

Jacques Cartier was more than a good navigator. He was a showman. After spending the winter of 1535 at Quebec and losing twenty-five of his men through illness, he knew that it was important to put on a good show when he returned to France, if he were ever going to get back to Canada.

Before sailing from Quebec, he invited Chief Donnacona and some of his braves to a feast. When they entered the stockade, they were taken prisoner and put on board a ship. Cartier didn't exactly force them to accompany him to France, but told Donnacona that he would be treated like a king and that he and his braves would be given many presents.

Donnacona agreed, but there was great weeping and wailing on shore. Donnacona explained the situation to the Indians from the deck and gave them gifts of two brass frying pans and eight steel hatchets.

All went well. Donnacona was taught enough French to talk to the king. The Indians have great imaginations and spin good yarns. Donnacona was no exception and did such a good sales job that King Francis decided to send a large expedition to Canada.

Then Cartier's plans went sour. King Francis appointed a nobleman, Sieur de Roberval, to be in charge of the expedition because he felt that it was not good enough to have a mere sea captain represent him. More blows fell. Life in France was not good for Donnacona and his men and they soon died.

Cartier had great plans to bring some of the best French artisans to Canada to build homes and found a colony. Roberval would not allow Cartier to recruit the type of men he wanted. Instead, on March 9, 1541, he obtained authorization to take criminals to Canada. Greatly disappointed, Cartier broke away from Roberval and went to Canada on his own.

. . . They are by no means a laborious people and work the soil with short bits of wood about half a sword in length. With these they hoe their corn which they call ozisy, in size as large as a pea. Corn of a similar kind grows in considerable quantities in Brazil. They have also a considerable quantity of melons, cucumbers, pumpkins, pease and beans of various colours and unlike our own. Furthermore they have a plant, of which a large supply is collected in summer for the winter's consumption.

They hold it in high esteem, though the men alone make use of it in the following manner. After drying it in the sun, they carry it about their necks in a small skin pouch in lieu of a bag, together with a hollow bit of stone or wood. Then at frequent intervals they crumble this plant into powder, which they place in one of the openings of the hollow instrument, and laying a live coal on top, suck at the other end to such an extent, that they fill their bodies so full of smoke, that it streams out of their mouths and nostrils as from a chimney. They say it keeps them warm and in good health, and never go about without these things. We made a trial of this smoke. When it is in one's mouth, one would think one had taken powdered pepper, it is so hot. The women of this country work beyond comparison more than the men, both at fishing, which is much followed, as well as at tilling the ground and other tasks. Both the men, women and children are more indifferent to the cold than beasts; for in the coldest weather we experienced, and it was extraordinary severe, they would come to our ships every day across the ice and snow, the majority of them almost stark naked, which seems incredible unless one has seen them. While the ice and snow last, they catch a great number of wild animals such as fawns, stags and bears, hares, martens, foxes, otters and others.

Taken from Cartier's writings, a description of Indians.

Other Events on March 9:

1812   The letters of British spy John Henry were read to Congress; these triggered the War of 1812.

1815   The Treaty of Ghent (December 24, 1814) was proclaimed at Quebec.

1855   The first locomotive crossed the Suspension Bridge at Niagara Falls.

1870   The British Columbia Legislature passed a resolution to send a delegation to Ottawa to negotiate for Confederation.

1907   A news dealer at Hamilton, Ontario, was fined $30 for selling American newspapers on Sunday.

Huault de Montmagny (1622-1654)

New Governor Appointed

When Champlain died at Quebec on Christmas Day, 1635, the man who was given the unenviable task of taking his place was Charles Huault de Montmagny. He was appointed Governor of Canada on March 10, 1636, and arrived at Quebec in June.

Montmagny was a soldier and a knight of the Maltese Order, as was his aide, Bréhaut l'Isle. It was an inspiring sight when they stepped on shore wearing their black robes with white eight-pointed crosses on their breasts. They were followed by soldiers in scarlet uniforms and flashing breastplates. The party numbered forty-five in all, including six daughters of two of its members. Their arrival nearly doubled the population of Quebec!

Canada needed trained military men. Montmagny and his aide, Bréhaut l'Isle, had fought the Turks on land and sea, and were believed to be the leaders who could handle the Iroquois. The Five Nations had declared war on the French to revenge the defeats inflicted on them by Champlain and had taken strategic positions along the rivers. It was not safe for small parties of white men to go into the woods, and small communities were always in danger.

The Iroquois were armed with guns, most of which had been supplied by the Dutch who had a base at what is now Albany, New York. They were remarkable warriors and planned their campaigns on lines that would be considered modern today. They established positions along the St. Lawrence and Ottawa Rivers, from Three Rivers to Chaudière Falls. This separated the French from the Hurons and Algonquins who were their allies.

The Iroquois "army" was divided into ten sections with most of the strength around Montreal Island, which was the crossroads of the trade routes. One of the sections was a large mobile force that could be moved quickly to any sector. The Iroquois did not commit large numbers of warriors to single actions, but used small bands to kill the French in what is now called "guerilla warfare." If the French could be weakened sufficiently, that would be the time for a united attack.

Montmagny made the first plans for countering the Iroquois but it took another thirty-six years to make much headway. Count Frontenac had arrived by that time to take charge.

Other Events on March 10:

1816   Jean-Baptiste Lajimonière, father of the first white child born in western Canada, traveled 1,800 miles in winter from Red River to Montreal to bring Lord Selkirk news of the colony.

1865   The Parliament of Canada asked Britain to unite the North American colonies.

1871   The first Legislative Council of Manitoba opened.

1910   Prince Rupert, British Columbia, was incorporated.

1915   Canadian troops were in action in the battle of Neuve Chapelle.

Presentation of commission to Blanshard at Fort Victoria, 1850

Blanshard Arrives to Govern Vancouver Island

Blanshard is the name of an important street in Victoria. It commemorates Richard Blanshard, the first Governor of Vancouver Island which was made a British colony in 1849. Previously it had been governed by the Hudson's Bay Company.

Richard Blanshard must have been one of the most disappointed men who ever came to Canada. He was a London merchant who had spent some time in the West Indies and India, and became ambitious to make a name for himself in the British diplomatic service. When Vancouver Island became a colony, he applied for the job of governor, even though it meant serving without pay. There was some talk in London, though, that he would be given a beautiful mansion and an estate of 1,000 acres with beautiful lawns and gardens.

His chagrin can be imagined when he stepped on shore from H.M.S. *Driver* on March 11, 1850, and read the proclamation establishing the new colony with himself as governor. It was a dreary day, mixed with rain and snow. The only estate available for Blanshard was 1,000 acres of uncleared land which he was expected to develop at his own expense. There wasn't a place for him to live on shore, let alone a mansion and he had to go back to the ship.

In one of his first letters to the Colonial Office he complained that there were only three other settlers on the island. One of them, Captain Colquhon Grant, had arrived the previous year with coaches and carriages, only to learn that there were no roads. He also brought equipment for playing cricket, which requires a smoother surface than a baseball diamond!

Blanshard only lasted until November when he resigned. James Douglas, Chief Factor of the Hudson's Bay Company, was appointed governor in his place. It was a good thing, because Douglas had seen the United States take over Oregon and knew the steps that had to be taken to preserve British Columbia from annexation.

Other Events on March 11:

1848   The second Baldwin-Lafontaine ministry took office.

1855   Joseph Howe was in Georgetown, Virginia, on a "cloak and dagger" mission to recruit Americans for the British army in the Crimean War.

1885   Inspector Crozier of the Northwest Mounted Police gave warning that rebellion was imminent in what is now Saskatchewan.

Chartier de Lotbinière (1748-1822)

Jesuits Lose Estates

The Constitutional Act in 1791 divided Quebec into two provinces, Upper and Lower Canada, each with its own Parliament. For several years, this helped to bring about better understanding between English and French-speaking Canadians. When the new legislature of Lower Canada opened in 1792, one French member said that as they lived under the best of kings it was only courteous that English be the language used in the debates. This wasn't practicable because few of the French members understood English. Probably, few of the English understood French. In the end both languages were adopted.

On the question of English being the "loyal" language, Chartier de Lotbinière said: "Remember the year 1775! Those Canadians who spoke nothing but French showed their attachment to the sovereign. . . . They helped to defend this province. You saw them join with faithful subjects of His Majesty and repel attacks on this city by people who spoke very good English. It is not, you see, uniformity of language that makes people more faithful or more united."

The trend toward better understanding was reversed after March 12, 1800, when estates formerly owned by the Jesuits were taken over by the government of Lower Canada. The income from the land was to be used for educational purposes. The English-speaking minorities in Quebec and Montreal were still powerful. The Anglican Bishop Mountain insisted that schools with English Protestant teachers should be established in every parish so that the French-speaking children would gradually become Protestants.

When the bill was presented to the legislature, French-speaking members added paragraphs safeguarding church schools and making it necessary for the majority of people in any parish to vote in favor of having one of Bishop Mountain's schools before it could be established. The purpose of the bill was killed, but resentments which had been dying away were renewed.

Other Events on March 12:

1613   Colonists were sent from France by the Marchioness de Guercheville.

1672   Father Dollier de Casson laid out Montreal's main street, Notre Dame.

1857   Gold miners were reported to be flocking to British Columbia.

1868   The first session of the Second Parliament opened; measures included the organization of the Civil Service.

1883   *Duke of Abercorn* landed the first steel at Port Moody, British Columbia, for the building of the Pacific section of the C.P.R.

1903   The third session of the ninth Parliament opened; measures included authority for the Grand Trunk Railway to build a transcontinental line and a $500-a-head tax was put on the Chinese.

1926   Coal miners accepted wage contracts recommended by a Royal Commission —a reduction of 10 per cent.

1930   Colonel W. G. Barker was killed in a crash at Ottawa. During World War I he had brought down fifty-two German planes.

Dog Signals Indian Raid

Maisonneuve fighting the Indians, 1644

There is disagreement among historians as to whether the following incident took place on March 13 or March 30, 1644. Maisonneuve's settlers who had founded Montreal in 1642 were spending their second winter there. Their activities were restricted because the Iroquois often waited in the woods outside the stockade ready to kill anyone who ventured out.

Maisonneuve's men usually knew when the Iroquois were there because in the garrison was a dog called "Pilot," who would howl the moment she scented the Indians. She had six puppies who learned the same trick.

On March 13 or 30, as the case may be, Pilot and her puppies began to howl. Maisonneuve's men clamored to be allowed to go out and attack the Indians. Maisonneuve realized the danger but agreed to lead the assault.

It was a mistake. No sooner had they entered the woods, than they realized that there were a great many Indians there. Furthermore, they had guns as well as bows and arrows. The Iroquois, greatly outnumbering the French, spread out in an encircling movement. Maisonneuve knew then that he was trapped. The only hope for survival was to retreat along a path in the snow that had been made by hauling logs into the stockade. The Indians came racing out of the woods, leaping over snowbanks and firing their guns and arrows at the retreating French. It was only by the narrowest of margins that the survivors got back into the stockade and closed the gate. Maisonneuve was the last to enter. Three of his men had been killed, and others were wounded.

Pilot has been commemorated as one of a group of figures in a statue in Montreal. Perhaps Walt Disney's organization will produce a film about her as it did for "Greyfriar's Bobbie," of whom there is a statue in Scotland.

Other Events on March 13:

1521   The King of Portugal granted islands in the St. Lawrence to Joam Alvarez Fagundez.

1812   David Thompson left on his last journey from Saleesh House to Fort William and Montreal, where he arrived on August 24.

1859   John Brown, made famous in song, brought fugitive slaves to Windsor, Ontario, by "underground railway."

1885   The British Columbia government refused to allow Chinese to land.

1900   J. W. Tyrrell began a 1,729-mile survey from Great Slave Lake to Chesterfield Inlet.

1909   Lord Strathcona established a fund to provide military training in schools.

1916   Manitoba was the first province to vote for prohibition.

1928   Eileen Vollick, of Hamilton, Ontario was the first Canadian woman to obtain a pilot's license. She was the first woman flyer to take off and land a plane on skis.

1961   Major-General Jean Victor Allard became the first Canadian to command a British Army Division.

The founding of Victoria, B.C.

Fort Victoria Founded

James Douglas, Chief Factor of the Hudson's Bay Company, founded Fort Victoria, on Vancouver Island on March 14, 1843, when he landed at Clover Point with fifteen men to build a base for the Hudson's Bay Company. Until this time the huge fur trading company had controlled the Pacific coast area, including what are now the states of Idaho, Montana, Utah, Washington, and Oregon. American settlers were rushing in and it was becoming increasingly clear that the United States was taking over. In fact, the Democratic Party won an election in 1844 with a slogan, "fifty-four forty or fight", which meant that the United States claimed the Pacific coast all the way to Alaska (see June 15).

When Blanshard was appointed Governor of Vancouver Island in 1850, Douglas had seen the withdrawal of the Hudson's Bay Company from what is now the United States. Even though the boundary had been estab-lished along the 49th parallel, he knew that the United States might still make an effort to acquire the Pacific coast all the way to Alaska. It was ridiculous that a man without any experience should be placed over him. Fortunately, it worked out that Douglas took over the job.

Douglas had actually chosen the site of Victoria in 1842 to be a new post of the Hudson's Bay Company. After he landed with his fifteen men on March 14, 1843, they went to work with determination, and although they had only the most primitive tools, they had built a stockade by October. It included two dwellings, a storage house, a three-story bastion armed with blunderbusses and muskets, and was surrounded by a cedar fence 18 feet high. The protection was against the Indians, not the Americans.

Sir George Simpson, governor of the company, who always considered the climate of British Columbia to be unhealthy, had to admit that the climate helped Douglas that summer. There was hardly a drop of rain from June to November, which made it possible for the building of Fort Victoria to progress so quickly.

Other Events on March 14:

1682   La Salle claimed north Arkansas for France.

1783   Sir John Johnson became Super-intendent-General of Indian Affairs in British North America.

1864   Sir Etienne Taché and John A. Macdonald formed a government.

1879   National Policy came into effect with "Tilley's tariff."

1907   Technical schools were established at Montreal and Quebec.

1916   Women were granted the right to vote in Saskatchewan.

1925   The first transatlantic radio broadcast was made.

1961   Massey College for graduate students was established at Toronto.

Parliament Buildings ("bird cages") at Victoria, B.C.

Legislatures First Open in Rink, House, "cages"

When the provinces of Canada were formed, the openings of some of their legislatures were mildly amusing. The first legislative assembly in Manitoba opened on March 15, 1871, in the home of A. C. B. Bannatyne because there was no building suitable for the purpose. Outside the Bannatyne residence there was a ceremonial guard provided by the Ontario Rifles.

The first session of the Alberta Legislature also took place on March 15, but the year was 1906. It was held in the Thistle skating rink and sessions continued there until a suitable building became available.

British Columbia had the first legislature west of the Great Lakes. It opened in August, 1856. After using temporary headquarters until 1860, the legislative members moved into buildings which became known as the "bird cages." They were made of brick, painted various shades of red and had roofs like pagodas. An 800-foot bridge had to be built across James Bay to connect them with Government Street in Victoria.

There is an amusing story about the opening of the legislature at Regina in 1905 when Saskatchewan became a province. Originally, the capital of the Northwest Territories had been at Battleford, but was moved to Pile O'Bones (Regina) when the C.P.R. went through there instead of Battleford.

Among the furniture that had to be shifted was an oak table that had been sent to the capital of the Northwest Territories by the Fathers of Confederation. It was supposed to have been the table on which the Confederation pact had been signed at Charlottetown.

There was more than a little consternation later when it was learned that Charlottetown still had the original Confederation table. It was then explained that there had been two tables, one used for the preliminary discussions and the other for the actual signing. Just which table had been sent to Saskatchewan may be open to argument. In any case, it became necessary to shorten the table by six feet in order to provide wood for repairs to it!

Other Events on March 15:

1603 Champlain sailed on his first voyage to Canada.

1650 The Iroquois defeated the powerful Neutral Indians.

1691 Abenakis from Nova Scotia attacked Haverhill, Massachusetts.

1746 The Marquis de la Jonquière was made Governor of Acadia and Louisiana.

1827 King's College, Toronto, was given a Royal Charter.
Shades Mills, Ontario, became Galt.

1894 Nova Scotia voted for prohibition.

1928 Canada signed a trade treaty with Czechoslovakia.

Martyrdom of Brébeuf and Lalemant, 1649

Indians Murder Priests

In Canada, not a cape was turned, nor a mission founded, nor a river entered, nor a settlement begun, but a Jesuit led the way.

—GEORGE BANCROFT, 1834

In 1930, the Roman Catholic Church canonized a number of Jesuit missionaries who had been massacred in Canada. Among them were Fathers Brébeuf and Lalemant who were murdered at the mission of St. Louis on March 16, 1649.

The Iroquois had resolved to wipe out the Hurons. They left northern New York during the winter on a hunting expedition. Gradually they worked their way into Huronia, destroyed the village of St. Ignace and rushed to the mission at St. Louis. They stripped the priests and made them march between a double row of warriors who clubbed their naked bodies. Then, a leisurely torture began.

Father Brébeuf's turn came at one in the afternoon. For three hours he stood silently in prayer, except when he tried to encourage the other prisoners. He endured the worst tortures the Iroquois could inflict, until he died from a blow on the head.

Father Lalemant was a much younger man, and frail. He was forced to watch Brébeuf suffering and his own torture began at six o'clock. The torture of the frail priest lasted most of the night, during which the Indians tore out his hair, then his eyes, cut off a hand and put hot axes around his neck.

When the Iroquois left the area, they took some prisoners with them but tied women and children to posts in their homes and set them on fire. The settlement went up in flames to the accompaniment of the shrieks of those who were burning to death.

The Hurons were finished. After attempting to develop a new settlement on St. Joseph's Island, many of them were encouraged to go to Quebec for safety. Others went west and formed a new tribe, the Wyandots, who played a part in the conspiracy of Pontiac, which will be described in May and June.

Other Events on March 16:

1605 Champlain, after a hard winter on Dochet Island, St. Croix River, set out to look for a better location for his settlement.

1846 The Earl of Cathcart was appointed Governor-General of Canada.

1856 A railway was incorporated to operate between Saint John and Shediac, New Brunswick.

1861 Parliament met at Quebec.

1900 The Strathcona Horse sailed for the South African War. The regiment was raised and equipped by Lord Strathcona.

Fenians Plan Attack

*We are a Fenian brotherhood, skilled in
the arts of war.
And we're going to fight for Ireland, the
land that we adore;
Many battles have we won, along with the
boys in blue,
And we'll go to capture Canada, for we've
nothing else to do!*

—FENIAN BATTLE SONG, 1866

Canadian volunteer bivouac, 1870

Canada had an invasion scare on March 17, 1866, that helped to speed up Confederation. The enemy was the Fenian Brotherhood, an organization of Irish revolutionaries dedicated to damaging Britain in any part of the world. One of their objectives was to capture Canada.

In 1863 they held a convention in Chicago, at which they drew up a new constitution for Canada as a republic and appointed a cabinet to govern it. Their scheme called for a fund of $15 million and battle forces of 30,000 men. The money was available. Appeals to "help the dear auld sod" drew generous support from many Americans. The troops were also available, battle-hardened Irishmen who had fought in the American Civil War. Many of them assembled at Portland, Maine, early in March and rumors circulated that an attack would be made on New Brunswick on St. Patrick's Day. New Brunswick had been "on again, off again" about Confederation, but the invasion rumor became so alarming that sentiment swung sharply in favor of joining Canada.

In Canada itself, Sir John A. Macdonald called out 10,000 militia.

There was no attack on New Brunswick but the Fenians began their raids in June on Fort Erie, Niagara Peninsula. They were waving green flags, emblazoned with a harp and crown of gold. The raids were not successful, partly because they were badly led. There were too many "generals" and "colonels" and it seemed that few of the Fenians were willing to be ordinary foot-slogging soldiers.

An interesting point about the Fenian plan to capture Canada was that Canada's name would be changed to "New Ireland." New Brunswick was actually called "New Ireland" for a short time when it was made a separate province from Nova Scotia in 1784.

Other Events on March 17:

1765   St. Patrick's Day was celebrated for the first time in Canada at Quebec City.

1776   British forces left Boston for Halifax after General Washington seized Dorchester Heights in a night attack.

1800   Philemon Wright arrived at the site of Hull, Quebec, across the river from Ottawa (see February 2).

1810   The first issue of the Kingston, Ontario, *News* was published.

1866   The United States terminated a reciprocal trade agreement with Canada. This had a bearing on swinging opinion in New Brunswick and Nova Scotia in favor of Confederation.

1885   The Métis formed a provisional government with Riel as President, as they had done at Red River in 1870.

1907   A Royal Commission was appointed to investigate the Civil Service.

1955   The suspension of Maurice Richard from hockey caused a riot in Montreal.

1959   The death of Dr. Sidney Smith, Minister of External Affairs, was announced.

Battle at Duck Lake, 1885

Riel Arrests Hostages

Had I been born on the banks of the Saskatchewan, I would myself have shouldered a musket to fight against the neglect of governments and the shameless greed of speculators.

—Sir Wilfrid Laurier, 1885

By March 18, 1885, there was no hope of turning back the forces of rebellion in the Northwest. At Mass, the previous Sunday, Father Fourmand had announced that anyone taking part in a revolt would be deprived of the sacraments. Riel, in one of his Hitler-like rages, told his armed Métis that the spirit of God had left the church of Rome and the Pope. He said that he had appointed Bishop Bourget as Pope, and he (Riel) would be their priest.

This caused a division among the Métis, many of whom were devoted to the church and on March 18, Riel and Dumont arrested a number of men as hostages. To regain support, Riel shouted that Inspector Crozier was leading a force of the Northwest Mounted Police from Fort Carlton to attack them.

The first bloodshed came when Crozier sent his interpreter, Thomas McKay, to Duck Lake to bring back rifles and ammunition from Mitchell's trading establishment. McKay and his police escort were suddenly surrounded by a force of Métis led by Riel and Dumont who demanded surrender. They refused and returned to Fort Carlton.

Crozier then took action. Instead of waiting for reinforcements, he and fifty-seven police and forty-one members of the militia set out for Duck Lake.

Dumont set up an ambush for Crozier's approaching force. When it was stopped, Dumont's brother Isadore, and an Indian approached Crozier waving a white blanket. Crozier went forward with McKay to meet him. The Indian tried to snatch McKay's rifle and a struggle began.

Meanwhile, Dumont had his men begin a flanking movement to encircle Crozier's men. Dumont said later that he only intended to force the police to surrender and hold them as hostages. This would make it necessary for the government at Ottawa to negotiate.

Crozier dashed back to his men and both sides opened fire. Isadore Dumont and the Indian were killed. The police had twelve men killed and eleven wounded before Crozier ordered them to retreat to Fort Carlton. The Northwest Rebellion had begun in earnest.

Other Events on March 18:

1836 The Hudson's Bay Company steamer *Beaver,* the first on the Pacific coast, arrived at Fort Vancouver, near present Portland, Oregon.

1886 The first stone of the Lachine Bridge over the St. Lawrence was laid by the C.P.R.

1907 Canadian Pacific and Grand Trunk Railways were ordered to reduce fares to three cents a mile.

1957 Canada took part in a Disarmament Conference in London with Britain, the United States, Russia and France.

Feast Saves Jesuits

There is a history which, if it were only recorded or capable of being recorded, would be interesting indeed, and would furnish us with a religion of gratitude. It is the history of the pioneer in all his lines. The monument of that history is the fair land in which we live.

—Goldwin Smith, 1883

Sometimes when people describe a boring party they say, "After dinner we escaped." The phrase was grimly true on March 19, 1658, but the escape was from murder, not boredom.

Despite the horrible massacre of Fathers Brébeuf and Lalemant (see March 16), the Jesuits agreed to establish a mission in Iroquois country where the city of Syracuse, New York, now stands. The Iroquois pretended they wanted a mission but in reality they were hostile to the French and planned to drive them from Canada so that they could control all the territory from the Atlantic.

During the winter, the Jesuits began to realize the true intentions of the Iroquois and knew they had to escape. It was necessary to wait until the ice broke in the rivers; in the meantime, they secretly built two flat-bottomed boats in the attic of their fort.

Young Pierre Radisson was working for the Jesuits. He had been brought up by Mohawks and knew their legends. One of them was that impending disaster could be warded off by having a feast, at which every morsel of food must be eaten. He told the Indians that he had dreamed of a disaster and that the Jesuits were going to help by putting on an "eat-all" feast.

The banquet was held just outside the gate of the fort. The festivities began with songs, dancing and games. The food was served: venison, bear meat, wild duck, fish and everything that had been collected for the occasion. It has even been suggested that the food was spiked with drugs.

Radisson meets the Indians

In any case, the Iroquois were made to keep on eating until every one of them fell on the ground exhausted and asleep. The Jesuits and members of their party then dragged the boats they had made down to the river, which took them to Lake Ontario. Five weeks later, after battling the spring storms and floods and always aware that the Iroquois might be following, they arrived at Quebec.

Other Events on March 19:

1649   The Iroquois left Huron country after the Brébeuf-Lalemant massacre.

1687   La Salle was murdered by one of his own men while trying to reach the Mississippi River from the Gulf of Mexico.

1825   The Hudson's Bay Company established Fort Vancouver on the Columbia River, near the present Portland, Oregon.

1867   The British Columbia Legislative Council approved an act enabling the province to enter Confederation.

1922   Stefansson claimed Wrangel Island for Britain.

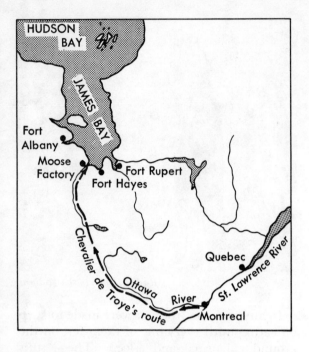

French Attack Hudson's Bay Company Posts

Charles II of England established the company of "Merchant Adventurers of England trading into Hudson's Bay" in 1670. It is still known as the Hudson's Bay Company. Within a few years its presence was felt by French fur traders in Montreal who decided that the English must be driven from the area.

There was a minor difficulty in that England and France did not happen to be at war at that time. Governor Denonville contrived a plan whereby the Compagnie du Nord, the private fur trading company, would take action on its own behalf. Leadership of the campaign was entrusted to the Chevalier de Troyes of Montreal. Three of his lieutenants were Le Moyne brothers; Pierre known as Iberville, Paul, and Ste. Hélène.

It was decided not to attack Hudson Bay by sea because the expedition would have been sighted by English ships. On March 20, 1686, de Troyes and the Le Moynes left Montreal with about one hundred men and went

overland, up the Ottawa River to Lakes Temiskaming and Abitibi, and then north on the Abitibi River.

First, they attacked Fort Hayes on the shore of James Bay and took it without bloodshed. Then they raced along the shore to Fort Rupert. While de Troyes attacked it, Iberville took another group in small boats to a ship anchored off the shore. Some lives were lost in the fighting, but the captives included Governor Bridgar of the Hudson's Bay Company and some valuable guns. Fort Albany was next. It tried to put up a fight, but was soon set on fire by the guns Iberville had taken from the ship. Hudson Bay was now under control of the French.

England had a Catholic king, as Louis XIV had wished, and they were supposed to be friends. When the news of the attack reached London and Paris, King James II and King Louis XIV were positively embarrassed. Louis sent a special envoy to London where France and England signed a "neutrality pact." Both monarchs had their tongues in their cheeks, and it wasn't long before England and France were at war officially.

Other Events on March 20:

1831 The King of Netherlands' boundary award for New Brunswick-Maine was rejected by the United States.

1846 Parliament met at Montreal.

1862 Parliament met at Quebec.

1910 Finance Minister Fielding met President Taft secretly at Albany, New York, and drew up plans for the reciprocity treaty that became the issue of the general election in 1911.

1917 Prime Minister Sir Robert Borden attended a British War Conference until May 2.

1930 The federal government transferred natural resources to Saskatchewan.

1944 General H. D. G. Crerar was appointed Commander-in-Chief of the first Canadian Army.

First Census Taken

One of the best moves France made in the development of Canada was to appoint Intendants to help the governors. They were really business managers and some of them were excellent. The best was Jean Talon; the worst was François Bigot. Their stories will be told later.

The first Intendant was appointed on March 21, 1663. He was Louis Robert, but he did not come to Canada at all! Talon's first term as Intendant began in 1665. He took the first census of Canada, also on March 21 the following year. The tabulation showed 3,000 people! English colonies to the south were growing far more quickly. The English (as they were until the Act of Union with Scotland made them *British*) brought their wives and children to Virginia and New England. Most of the French who came to Canada never had any intention of staying, and did not bring their families; they were great explorers and fur traders, but they wanted to return to their own homeland.

The English colonists who went to what is now the United States did so to escape restrictions at home. They set up their own governments and controlled their own affairs. When London tried to interfere they often disregarded its instructions.

On the other hand, Canada was ruled by the King of France. He appointed the governors and high officials and told them what to do. He even drew on his own funds to pay for the development of Canada. When the king lost interest, or money was tight owing to war, the development of Canada suffered. Eventually, when France lost Canada to Britain, Voltaire shrugged it off by saying: "The King must amuse himself and Canada was one of his playthings."

Even so, the 3,000 French who were in Canada in 1666 began to have good times. There were hardships and great danger from the Indians, but they evolved a way of life that made them better off than their counterparts in France.

Jean Talon (1625-1694)

Other Events on March 21:

1629   Champlain was appointed Richelieu's lieutenant in Canada.

1663   An ordinance was issued stating that all lands not cleared in three months must be returned to the Crown.

1821   A medical school was incorporated at Montreal. The school later became part of McGill University.

1864   The Sandfield Macdonald-Sicotte government was replaced by the Taché-John A. Macdonald government.

1896   A commission was appointed to try to settle the Manitoba separate schools problem.

1911   The Duke of Connaught was made Governor-General of Canada.

1918   Germany began an offensive that came near to victory in World War I.

1955   Fire destroyed fifty-five buildings at Nicolet, Quebec.

Canadian Rumrunner Sunk

There was an incident on March 22, 1929, that put the name *I'm Alone* into the headlines of newspapers all over the continent. *I'm Alone* wasn't a song on the hit parade. It was the name of a Canadian rumrunner sunk by an American coast guard vessel in the Gulf of Mexico. There were hot words between Ottawa and Washington, but Canada did not have a legal leg to stand on.

It was regarded as very unsporting of the Americans. Prohibition was in force in the United States and the smuggling of liquor across the border was treated like a game. As the manufacture of liquor was legal in Canada, the government took the position that it could not forbid its export. If the Americans did not want the liquor to enter, it was their job to stop it. The problem from the States' point of view was that many of their Customs officers did not want to stop the smuggling. Some had been bribed to close their eyes. Canadian authorities would phone their counterparts across the border and warn them that shipments were on the way, but would often be told to stop bothering them with such trivialities, or to write letters instead of phoning!

Some of the Atlantic rumrunners, as they were called, used clever tactics. Perhaps twenty of them would approach the coast together. When a patrol boat began to chase them, they would scatter, so only one could be caught. When the patrol boat did bring a vessel to a halt, there would be no liquor on board. It had been dumped overboard in a net, weighted with bags of salt. The net would have a buoy attached to it which would float under the surface of the water. The salt would dissolve in a few days, and then the rumrunner would be able to see the buoy and regain the sunken liquor.

It was all part of the frenzy of the "Roaring Twenties" before the stock market crash of 1929.

Other Events on March 22:

1700   Bienville Le Moyne explored the Red River.

1723   The Reverend George Henry, a Presbyterian, began preaching in Quebec in a room provided by the Jesuit College.

1764   The first book was printed in Canada; it was a catechism.

1765   The Stamp Act received Royal Assent.

1849   Baldwin, Mackenzie and Blake were burned in effigy in Toronto.

1885   Troops were mobilized all over Canada because of the Northwest rebellion.

1894   The first Stanley Cup game was played.

1914   Stefansson embarked on an expedition to Cape Kellet.

Britain Regains Nootka

If Washington Irving, author of *Rip Van Winkle*, had not been asleep at the switch, the United States might own half of Vancouver Island!

In 1790 Britain and Spain nearly went to war over an incident at Nootka Sound on the west coast of Vancouver Island (see January 4). Spain backed down, paid reparations and agreed to share Vancouver Island equally with Britain. Britain regained possession of Nootka officially on March 23, 1795.

In 1819 the United States bought Florida from Spain. The deal included all Spanish territory west of the Mississippi and north of latitude 42. Washington Irving was American ambassador to Spain at the time. He was supposed to have made a thorough search of documents in Madrid to find out exactly what territory was involved. Somehow, he missed the agreement giving Spain equal rights to Vancouver Island.

Fortunately for Britain and Canada, the Americans did not find out about this until years after the Oregon Boundary Treaty had been signed in 1846. It established the present boundary between Canada and the United States, dipping to give Canada all of Vancouver Island.

Another strange feature about the story was that Washington Irving was greatly interested in the romance of fur trading in Canada. He had visited the famous "Beaver Club" in Montreal, where the great fur traders gathered. He also wrote a story about Fort Astoria on the Pacific coast, when it was involved in the rivalry among the Hudson's Bay Company, the Northwest Company and John Jacob Astor.

If it seems far-fetched that the States might own half of Vancouver Island, look at a map of the southern tip of the mainland of British Columbia. The strict boundary of the 29th parallel leaves Point Roberts as part of the States although for all practical purposes it is Canadian.

It is always a joke for residents of Greater Vancouver to go to the United States by entering the few square miles that comprise Point Roberts.

Other Events on March 23:

1633   Champlain left France for the last time.

1665   Jean Talon was commissioned as Intendant of New France.

1670   Fathers Dollier de Casson and Galinée claimed Lake Erie for France.

1752   The Halifax *Gazette*, the first newspaper in Canada, was published.

1764   Captain Holland was commissioned to survey the Island of St. John (Prince Edward Island).

1832   A political riot broke out at York (Toronto).

1865   The Imperial Parliament voted £50,-000 (pounds) for the defense of Canada owing to tension over the *Alabama* incident.

1893   The Bering Sea tribunal met at Paris.

1949   Royal assent was given to the North America Bill passed by the British Parliament for the union of Canada and Newfoundland.

Louisburg British Goal

Although one incident may be the spark that sets off the explosion of war, usually a number of provocations have preceded it, some of them trivial. Such was the case in 1739 when Britain went to war with Spain. One of these seems almost unbelievable today. A British sea-captain was said to have cut off the nose of a Spanish pirate of noble birth and made him eat it. So, a Spanish sea-captain boarded a British ship, cut off one of Captain Jenkins' ears and threw it at him, with an insulting message to the king.

The story probably wasn't true at all—it was reported later that Jenkins had both ears when he died. In any case, there was so much resentment in Britain that Prime Minister Walpole declared war on Spain, and France became involved five years later.

As soon as France became entangled, a message was rushed to her fortress at Louisburg, Cape Breton. Governor Du Quesnel acted quickly, sending a force to capture the nearest British settlement at Canso. The garrison, which had not been notified of the war, was taken by surprise, and surrendered on the understanding that the troops would be taken to Port Royal or Boston, after they had been held as prisoners at Louisburg for one year.

When they arrived at Louisburg, Governor Du Quesnel realized that he did not have enough food for the prisoners so he sent them to Boston as soon as possible. However, the British had spent enough time in Louisburg to acquire some important information, namely that the famous fortress was not nearly as strong as it was supposed to be. Food and ammunition were in short supply. Many of the soldiers were Swiss mercenaries who had not been paid for a long time. They were unhappy and there was bad feeling between them and the French.

When this information became known in Boston, an expedition was organized to attack Louisburg. It sailed on March 24, 1745 (see June 17).

Other Events on March 24:

1670   Silver and copper coins were minted for use in Canada.

1694   Jean Talon, former Intendant, died in France.

1761   The first Lutheran Church in Canada was established at Halifax.

1786   An Imperial order prohibited imports from the United States.

1803   Egerton Ryerson, the famous educator in Upper Canada, was born.

1865   Macdonald, Cartier, Brown and Galt went to Britain to discuss the possibility of Confederation.

1878   Letellier de St. Just, Lieutenant-Governor of Quebec, dismissed the cabinet.

Boundary Established

An exchange of notes between Britain and the United States on March 25, 1905, established the Alaska Boundary the way it is today. Canada was helpless to do anything about it, although it was one of the worst deals ever foisted on the nation.

The Alaska boundary had been a problem for years. Finally, Britain, who controlled Canada's international affairs, and the United States agreed to have the boundary decided by an "impartial commission." Britain appointed Sir Louis Jetté and A. B. Aylesworth of Canada to serve with Lord Chief Justice Alverstone. The United States appointed Elihu Root, Secretary of War, Senator Henry Cabot Lodge, and Senator George Turner of the State of Washington. Root and Lodge had already opposed Canada's claims, saying they were "baseless and trumped up." Turner represented the City of Seattle which competed with Victoria and Vancouver for trade in the Yukon. This was important because of the Klondike gold rush. Thus, the American members of the tribunal were far from impartial.

The commission began its work early in 1903, but nothing had been settled by the end of August. Roosevelt, the American President, believed in the policy of the "big stick," and sent a message to the British government stating that the boundary must be fixed the way the United States wanted, or troops would be sent to enforce it. Britain had no desire to become involved in a war with the States and Lord Alverstone was instructed to side with the Americans. The boundary decision which was announced on October 20, 1903, was supposed to be a compromise, but Canada was blocked from any seaport in northern British Columbia or the Yukon.

One result of the decision was that the Laurier government decided that Canada must handle her own foreign affairs, and the Department of External Affairs was created in 1909.

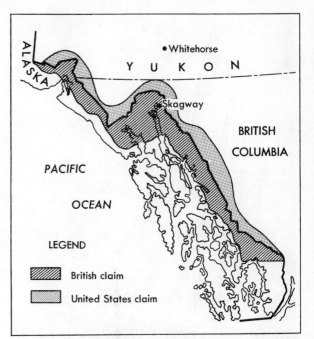

Other Events on March 25:

1820   The Bank of New Brunswick was incorporated. It was the first bank in the colony.

1839   The Aroostook agreement ended the "war of pork and beans."

1880   George Brown was shot in the *Globe* office, and died on May 10. George Bennett was hanged for murder.

1886   The first Workmen's Compensation Act was passed by the Ontario Legislature.

1893   Magistrate Baxter of Toronto fined a cab driver $2 or ten days in jail for driving a lady on Sunday.

1897   The Manitoba Legislature passed a compromise act on the separate schools question.

1957   Prime Minister St. Laurent held a conference with British Prime Minister Macmillan in Bermuda.

1958   The maiden flight of the Canadian-built CF—105 took place. It was supposed to be the most advanced fighter aircraft of its time.

Schooner Bluenose I

Bluenose I Launched

If a poll were taken of the greatest achievements by Canadians in the world of sports, there would be many nominations. The greatest all-around athlete would have to be Lionel Conacher who could play everything well. There would be the greatest runners like Tom Longboat and Percy Williams; boxers like Tommy Burns and Jimmy McLarnin; skaters and skiers like Charles Gorman, Barbara Ann Scott, and Anne Heggtveit.

How about the Nova Scotian fishing schooner *Bluenose*, now commemorated on Canadian 10-cent pieces? She was launched at Lunenburg on March 26, 1921, built entirely of Canadian materials except for her masts of Oregon pine. In order to challenge for the International Schooner Racing Trophy, *Bluenose* had to be a bona fide fishing vessel. Her first job was to go to the Grand Banks and catch fish. She returned as highliner of the Lunenburg fleet, having caught more than the others.

Now *Bluenose* was qualified to race against the champion of the Gloucester, Mass., fleet. The first contest was held in October, 1921, and *Bluenose* was fifteen minutes ahead at the finish line. From that time until her last race in 1938, *Bluenose* defeated all other challengers.

In 1935, *Bluenose* crossed the Atlantic to attend the Silver Jubilee of King George V and was received with royal honors by the yachtsmen of Britain. She even raced the fastest schooner yachts in Britain and came third. Her opponents were designed for racing, not fishing.

W. J. Roue of Halifax, who designed *Bluenose*, built other vessels to try to beat her, but was unsuccessful. It is believed there was something freakish about her hull, an accident of building, that could not be detected and copied.

During World War II, *Bluenose* was sold to the West Indies Trading Company and carried general cargo between Cuba, Haiti, Guatemala and Honduras. On the night of January 28, 1946, she hit a reef off Haiti and sank the next day. Not a sliver of her got back to Canada, although a replica now operates in Halifax as a cruise ship.

Other Events on March 26:

1616   Bylot and Baffin sailed on their Arctic expedition.

1789   Pictou Academy was established by Nova Scotia statute.

1821   The Hudson's Bay Company and the Northwest Company amalgamated.

1831   The *Royal William* was built at Quebec and launched April 27. It was claimed to be the first steamer to cross the Atlantic entirely under steam power.

1885   The Métis, led by Riel and Dumont, clashed with Northwest Mounted Police at Duck Lake. Twelve police were killed.

1961   A snowstorm created a state of emergency in Prince Edward Island.

New Capital for N.W.T.

When the federal government bought the Hudson's Bay Company territory in 1869, Manitoba was made a province almost immediately. What are now the provinces of Saskatchewan and Alberta were called the Northwest Territories, with Battleford as the capital. In 1882 the C.P.R. engineers decided that the transcontinental line should be built two hundred miles south of Battleford and the capital was shifted to Pile O' Bones on March 27, 1883.

Before 1882 there was virtually nothing at Pile O' Bones. It had been a camping place for buffalo hunters and got its name from the buffalo carcasses left there. The fact that the new capital was going to be there brought droves of settlers. Of course a more dignified name had to be found.

The popular choice was Victoria but that had already been chosen for the capital of British Columbia. After a great deal of discussion the problem was referred to the Governor-General, the Marquis of Lorne. His wife, Princess Louise, daughter of Queen Victoria, came up with the happy answer. If the people of the Northwest Territories wanted the capital to be called after the Queen, why not use the Latin word for "queen"—Regina?

In 1905, the provinces of Saskatchewan and Alberta were separated from the Northwest Territories. Regina remained the capital of Saskatchewan, while Edmonton was chosen as the capital of Alberta.

The entire area had to overcome the effects of bad publicity. Even as late as 1865, Sir John A. Macdonald believed that it was of "no present value to Canada." The British government then sent out a special expedition under Captain John Palliser. After studying conditions as far west as the Rockies for two years, the Palliser expedition marked out a triangular area as unfit for settlers. It included a great deal of what is now southern Saskatchewan and Alberta.

Princess Louise

Fortunately there were some who disagreed with these findings, amongst them Dominion Botanist Dr. John Macoun, and settlers flocked into the country by rail.

Other Events on March 27:

1647 The first political constitution was drawn up for Canada.

1834 York became the City of Toronto.

1848 Fredericton, New Brunswick, was incorporated as the "celestial city."

1950 The federal government transferred water rights on the Niagara River to Ontario.

1951 Canada and the United States ratified an agreement for civil defense along the border.

1953 Canada presented the United Nations with main doors for its new building.

1955 His Excellency Mario Scelba, Prime Minister of Italy, visited Ottawa.

Province Building, Charlottetown

Nova Scotia to Send Delegates to Charlottetown

On March 28, 1864, Nova Scotia became the first maritime colony to authorize a delegation to go to Charlottetown in September to discuss maritime union with representatives of the other Atlantic colonies. New Brunswick and Prince Edward Island decided to send delegations soon after. To unite politically would allow the maritime colonies to achieve what they all urgently needed, a railway to Canada.

In the 1860's, Canada was in the middle of a railway-building boom. Tracks were being laid everywhere; sometimes they started in a community and ended in the woods! Government subsidies made it profitable for promoters to build railways. Some promoters made fortunes as a result.

One of the problems of building a railway between Canada and the Atlantic colonies was to decide the route it should take. The most profitable route would have been from Montreal to Portland, Maine, and then along the coast to Saint John and Halifax. British military authorities objected to this proposal because such a rail line would be useless in the event of war with the United States. They preferred the line followed by the present C.N.R. tracks; that is, along the St. Lawrence River and south to Halifax.

As early as 1862, delegates from Canada and the Atlantic colonies had met at Quebec to discuss the building of a railway connecting Canada and the Maritimes. An agreement had been reached, but it was necessary to obtain the approval of the British Government. This was not forthcoming.

By 1864, the Atlantic colonies were quickly reaching the conclusion that if they were to have a railway, they would have to form a union among themselves. On March 28, 1864, Nova Scotia officially committed itself to discussing maritime union.

It was this meeting of Atlantic colonies that Canada asked permission to attend. It became the famous Charlottetown Conference that eventually led to Confederation.

Other Events on March 28:

1684   Tonty repulsed the Indians after a siege of six days at Fort St. Louis, Illinois.

1851   New Brunswick passed legislation to co-operate in the building of the European and North American Railroad.

1918   Conscription riots broke out in Quebec.

1960   The Ontario Legislature announced a plan to build a bilingual university at Sudbury; it is now Laurentian University.

New Governor-General Appointed

Sir Charles Metcalfe (1785-1846)

In the days when Canada was becoming a nation, it took courage to be a governor-general. Durham, Sydenham, and Bagot were the governors between 1838 and 1843, and the work led to their deaths. On March 29, 1843, Sir Charles Metcalfe took over the unenviable task.

Metcalfe had been born in India and was the governor of the huge district of Delhi by the time he was twenty-six years old. Among his achievements were the abolition of the slave trade and of the custom of burning wives on their husbands' funeral pyres.

Metcalfe was sent to Jamaica where there was danger of a rebellion, and then on to Canada where there had been rebellions in 1837-1838. When he arrived, Kingston was the capital of recently united Upper and Lower Canada. The government soon moved to Montreal which was able to provide more accommodation. Montreal then had 40,000 people!

Although Metcalfe was a reformer in India, he was not in favor of the reform movement in Canada that was trying to win responsible government. He complained that his ministers, instead of doing what he wished, were trying to force him to do what they wanted.

Baldwin and Lafontaine, leaders of the Liberal or Reform government, resigned, and Metcalfe was forced to govern almost alone. In September, 1844, he called a general election and campaigned himself. He branded the Reformers as "disloyal" to Britain, and won the election by a small majority.

Ironically, one of the new members was a young lawyer from Kingston, Ontario, John A. Macdonald. Although he was elected as one of Metcalfe's supporters, he was destined to take the lead in bringing about nationhood for Canada.

Metcalfe was the fourth successive governor to lose his life through disease. He returned to Britain in 1845 and died soon after.

Other Events on March 29:

1632   France recovered Canada from England through the Treaty of St. Germain-en-Laye.

1778   Captain Cook landed at Nootka Sound, British Columbia.

1848   The Niagara River went dry owing to an ice jam at Lake Erie.

1867   The Confederation bill received Royal Assent.

1906   A riot of street railway employees broke out at Winnipeg.

1912   A trade conference with representatives of the West Indies was held at Ottawa.

1927   Government control replaced prohibition in Ontario.

Front and back of La Vérendrye's tablets

La Vérendrye Leaves Tablet

Sieur de La Vérendrye began his adventures when he was only nineteen, taking part in a raid on Deerfield. After campaigning in Newfoundland he went to France to fight for Louis XIV. He was left for dead on the battlefield of Malplaquet with three bullets and six sabre wounds in his body.

La Vérendrye did not die, but returned to Canada where he became a fur trader. From 1731 to 1743 he set up chains of forts from what is now Fort William to Portage La Prairie. He was convinced that he could find the route to the western sea because he had heard so many promising stories from the Indians, although he did not accept them at face value. He said: "These people are great liars, but now and then they tell the truth."

In the spring of 1742, La Vérendrye's two remaining sons and two Indians set out for Fort La Reine (Portage La Prairie) to track down a rumor that the Mandan Indians farther west could lead them to the western sea. They did not get back until July the following year, during which time they had gone south, crossed the Missouri River and made their way to a place where they could see high mountains. It is believed they were the Big Horn range of the Rockies. They were probably the first white men to see the Rockies.

They did not find the river that led to the western sea, but while conferring with the Little Cherry Indians, Chevalier de La Vérendrye left a metal plate as a souvenir.

It was uncovered in 1913 by some young people who were walking near (appropriately enough) Pierre, the capital city of South Dakota. The inscription read: "Placed by the Chevalier de la Vérendrye—the 30th of March 1743."

Other Events on March 30:

1809   The Labrador Act gave Labrador to Newfoundland. This was later disputed by Quebec and a final decision was not made until 1927.

1814   The American General Wilkinson was forced to retreat at La Colle, Quebec. It was the last attempt by Americans to invade Canada during the War of 1812.

1832   The Bank of Nova Scotia was incorporated. It was the first in the province.

1838   Lord Durham was made Governor of British North America, except Newfoundland.

1874   Louis Riel arrived at Ottawa as a member of Parliament but was not allowed to take his seat.

1901   In the Delpit marriage case, it was ruled that marriages of Roman Catholics by Protestant clergy were valid.

1954   The Toronto subway train system opened; it was the first in Canada.

Welcome, Nfld.!

On July 1, 1873, Governor-General Lord Dufferin went to Charlottetown to preside over the ceremonies as Prince Edward Island joined Confederation. He passed under an archway with a sign that read: "Long Courted, Won at Last."

It took six years to get Prince Edward Island into Confederation, but Newfoundland held out for eighty-two years! The oldest Dominion in the British Commonwealth became part of Canada officially on March 31, 1949.

Newfoundland delegates attended the Quebec Conference in 1864 and reported favorably, but in 1869 the Confederation party was badly beaten in a general election and the plan was dropped.

In 1894, Newfoundland was in a period of depression, largely owing to a bank failure, and the proposal to join Canada was revived. This time, Canada was the unwilling suitor and would not accept the marriage contract.

The world-wide depression in the 1930's hit Newfoundland hard and Dominion status was lost. A commission government took over, appointed by Britain. After the war, the commission government called a national convention, to which the people of Newfoundland sent delegates to decide how the country should be governed. There was little interest and only thirty per cent of the people voted.

Two referendums had to be held after that. In the first, nearly ninety per cent of the people voted and the proposal to resume commission government was defeated. The second referendum on July 22, 1948, resulted in a very close vote: Confederation with Canada 78,323; Newfoundland with its own responsible government 71,334. The city of St. John's wanted Newfoundland to govern itself, but the "outports" swung the balance in favor of joining Canada.

Agreement with the government of Canada was reached on December 11, 1948, and New-

Premier Joseph Smallwood

foundland became Canada's tenth province on March 31, 1949. Joseph R. Smallwood, who had led the drive for joining Canada, was the first Premier.

Other Events on March 31:

1713 The Treaty of Utrecht returned Nova Scotia to Britain. France retained Cape Breton and the Island of St. John, now Prince Edward Island.

1821 McGill University received a Royal Charter.

1831 Quebec and Montreal were incorporated as cities.

1854 A railway from Truro to Pictou, Nova Scotia, was opened.

1872 The first issue of the Toronto *Mail* was published.

1885 The federal government disallowed the British Columbia Chinese Immigration Act.

1890 The Manitoba Legislature passed an act suppressing separate schools.

Dr. Wilder Penfield has gained the respect and admiration of doctors everywhere for his work in neurosurgery. In 1934, Dr. Penfield organized the building of the world-famous Montreal Neurological Institute, of which he was director for more than twenty years of distinguished service. Neurological associations here and abroad have awarded Dr. Penfield many honors for his research in epilepsy. In 1953, Queen Elizabeth awarded him the Order of Merit. In 1958, the French Academy of Surgery honored Dr. Penfield with its highest award, the Médaille Lannelongue.

This photo of Frederick Banting and Charles Best was taken in 1921. It shows them with one of the first diabetic dogs to have its life saved by insulin. After years of research, Banting and Best discovered life-saving insulin during the summer of 1921. Since then, insulin has saved the lives of countless thousands of people all over the world.

Diefenbaker Wins Biggest Victory

In the early morning hours of April 1, 1958, Canadians were rubbing their eyes in amazement as they watched the completion of election returns. Could it be an April Fool's joke? The Conservatives, led by Right Honorable John G. Diefenbaker, had won 208 seats, the Liberals 49, C.C.F. (now N.D.P.) only 8, and the Social Credit party had been completely wiped out.

It was by far the biggest election victory in Canadian history. Even the people of Quebec, who had been solidly Liberal since the hanging of Louis Riel in 1885 (see November 16), had given Diefenbaker's Conservatives 61 percent of their votes.

Diefenbaker might be described as the Abraham Lincoln of Canadian politics. Like Lincoln, he survived a number of defeats that would have crushed most men before becoming leader of the nation.

Diefenbaker grew up in Prince Albert, a sparsely-populated area in northern Saskatchewan. This constituency has the remarkable distinction of being represented by three Prime Ministers: Wilfrid Laurier in 1896, W. L. Mackenzie King in 1927, and Diefenbaker.

As a newsboy in 1909, the young Diefenbaker sold Laurier a paper, and somehow he became convinced that he was also going to be Prime Minister. He never lost sight of that ambition. Although he became a successful criminal lawyer, his great love was politics. First, he tried to be elected mayor of Prince Albert, but he was defeated. Then voters rejected him four times when he was a candidate in provincial and federal elections. Eventually, in 1940, Prince Albert Conservatives needed a candidate and chose Diefenbaker. This time he was successful, and he began his career in the House of Commons.

The next step was to become leader of the Conservative party. He was rejected twice by party members, who preferred John Bracken and then George Drew. These men made no headway against the Liberals in federal elections, and finally Diefenbaker was given his opportunity in December 1956.

From then on, his progress was meteoric. There was a general election in June, 1957, which resulted in the return of 112 Conservatives, 105 Liberals, 25 C.C.F. members, and 19 Social Crediters.

So Diefenbaker finally ended the long rule of the Liberals, who had been in power since 1936, after only six months as leader of the Conservative party. However, as his government was in a minority position, he seized an opportunity to call a general election in 1958. That election resulted in the most spectacular victory in Canadian history.

One of Diefenbaker's first achievements after becoming Prime Minister was to have Parliament pass a Bill of Rights for Canadians.

Other Events on April 1:

1734 The first lighthouse in Canada was opened at Louisburg, Cape Breton.

1776 American General Wooster succeeded General Benedict Arnold at the siege of Quebec.

1885 Indians began their siege of Battleford, Northwest Territories, and the siege continued until April 25.

1892 The North American Canal Company was incorporated to deepen the St. Lawrence River and to build canals from Lake Erie to Lake Ontario and from Lake Francis to Lake Champlain and the Hudson River.

1901 The population of Canada was 5,371,315: 3,063,000 English-speaking, 1,649,000 French-speaking.

1924 The Royal Canadian Air Force was organized.

1927 The United States put an immigration quota on Canadians seeking employment.

1949 Sir Albert J. Walsh was appointed the first lieutenant-governor of the Province of Newfoundland.

1951 The Department of Defense Production was organized.

Victoria Voted Capital

One of the most incredible stories from the early days of the provinces tells how Victoria was chosen to be the capital of British Columbia on April 2, 1868.

Vancouver Island and the mainland, which had been separate British colonies, were united as the single colony of British Columbia in November, 1866. Governor Kennedy, who had been unpopular, was recalled to London and Frederick Seymour appointed in his place. There is an interesting sidelight on Governor Kennedy's departure. Dr. Margaret Ormsby, in her book *British Columbia: A History*, recounts that an official wrote: "The Governor's family departed in a shower of tears. 'Twas most affecting—entre nous, only an Irish family could have got up such a scene. One would have thought they had been beloved and revered all the time."

On April 2, 1868, the legislative council of British Columbia had to vote on whether Victoria or New Westminster should be the new capital. Captain Franklin, the magistrate of Nanaimo, was supposed to make a strong speech in favour of New Westminster because there was great jealousy between Nanaimo and Victoria. Before the Council opened its

meeting, Franklin spent some time in a bar and wasn't thinking clearly when the time came for his speech. Gold Commissioner Cox, who was in favour of Victoria, reshuffled the pages of Franklin's speech so that he read the introduction three times. When Franklin laid his spectacles on the table, Cox pressed the glass from their frames and Franklin was not able to read at all.

The chairman called a recess for half an hour, but when Franklin rose to resume his speech there was an objection. It was that he had already made his speech and could not be heard again. The objection was put to a vote and upheld. Victoria was then chosen to be the new capital.

Gold Commissioner Cox and Magistrate Franklin were both dismissed by Governor Seymour shortly after.

Other Events on April 2:

1663　King Louis XIV issued an edict stating that Canada would be governed by the laws of France.

1667　Louis XIV issued a civil code for Canada and established courts.

1778　Quebec merchants petitioned for the repeal of the Quebec Act.

1838　A special council of twenty-two members was appointed to govern Lower Canada.

1871　The first Dominion census was taken. The population of 3,689,257 consisted of 2,110,000 English-speaking and 1,082,000 French-speaking Canadians.

1873　A charge was made in the House of Commons that Sir John A. Macdonald and cabinet ministers had accepted campaign funds from the promoters of C.P.R. This led to the downfall of Macdonald's government in November.

1885　Indians massacred whites at Frog Lake, Saskatchewan.

1887　Canadian sealing vessels were seized by the Americans in the North Pacific.

Prairie War Spreading

*In the little Crimson Manual it's written
    plain and clear
Those who wear the scarlet coat shall say
    good-bye to fear.*
                —ROBERT W. SERVICE, 1909

On April 3, 1885, the Prairies were aflame with revolution and the Indians were beating their tom-toms as far west as Edmonton. News of the defeat of the Northwest Mounted Police at Duck Lake on March 26 was spreading like a prairie fire. The Indians' hunting grounds were disappearing and they were starving. Many of the Métis had sold their land holdings for bottles of whisky. This looked like the opportunity to seize supplies and force the federal government to give them better deals.

The Northwest Mounted Police had to abandon Fort Carlton and leave it in flames while they galloped through the night to Prince Albert where many families were in danger. Settlers in the Battleford area left their homes and sought refuge in the fort. Wearing war paint, the Crees, under Big Bear and Little Pine, burned their homes and charged into Battleford itself. The five hundred people in the fort on top of a hill could see them raiding every building, looting and destroying.

Similar scenes were taking place in other areas, as far west as Battle River Crossing between Calgary and Edmonton. The one bright spot was Qu'Appelle where the newly constructed C.P.R. line brought militia from Winnipeg on April 2. The Blackfoot in Alberta heard about this and did not go on the warpath, although they were restless.

In the thick of the trouble was Inspector Francis Dickens, son of the famous author Charles Dickens. When the Crees raided Fort Pitt, they found the watch that had been given to him by his father. It was recovered later, still containing a picture of his mother and a lock of her hair.

Louis Riel, who went into battle holding a crucifix, did not like bloodshed, but he was

The Mounties attack Big Bear, 1885

in favor of the Indians' going on the warpath. After Duck Lake, he wrote to Poundmaker saying: "Praise God for the success he granted us. Arise. Face the enemy. If you can take Fort Battle, destroy it."

Other Events on April 3:

1834   W. L. Mackenzie was chosen mayor of Toronto.

1875   Construction of the C.P.R. transcontinental began at Thunder Bay, Lake Superior.

1907   The University of Saskatchewan at Saskatoon was granted a provincial charter.

1940   The Earl of Athlone was appointed Governor-General of Canada.

1962   General A. G. L. McNaughton resigned as chairman of the Canadian section of the International Joint Commission.

1965   Parliament prorogued after its longest session, 248 days.

A mule team at Yale, B.C.

Gold Strike Brings Thousands to British Columbia

Californians were singing "British Columbia here I come" on April 4, 1858. A Pacific mail steamer had arrived at San Francisco the day before, bringing the news that people in the Seattle area were rushing for the Thompson River where gold had been found. Mills were closing down and soldiers and sailors were deserting.

Thousands who had taken part in the California gold rush packed their bags and headed north. Some sailed for ports in Puget Sound and tried to get to British Columbia by trekking through the State of Washington. This was dangerous because the Indians in the interior were on the warpath.

Most of the Californians took ships to Victoria. The first to arrive was a wooden paddlewheeler. Victorians wondered what was going to happen as the *Commodore* unloaded hordes of men, wearing red flannel shirts and carrying spades and firearms. Instead of being the "dregs of society," as expected, they turned out to be well-behaved, with money to spend.

Although most of the newcomers crossed to the mainland, many others stayed in Victoria to establish businesses. Six weeks after their arrival, Victoria had 225 new buildings, of which 200 were stores. Building sites along the harbor front rose in value from $50 to as much as $3,000.

By the first of June, 10,000 miners had gone up the Fraser River, the total reaching 25,000 by the end of the year. The first gold was found on a sandbar near Hope; the river was productive from that point to Yale. The best return was about $50 a day.

The great problem was to preserve order. If the miners began fighting among themselves, or if the Indians attacked them, Governor Douglas knew that the States would send in troops "to protect our nationals," and would almost certainly absorb British Columbia. Douglas did preserve order and was helped by a remarkable man, Judge Begbie (see November 19).

Other Events on April 4:

1629   William Alexander and the Kirke brothers formed a company to monopolize the fur trade in Canada.

1853   King's College, Windsor, Nova Scotia, was incorporated.

1881   The second Dominion Census showed Canada's population as 4,324,810: English 2,548,000, French 1,299,000.

1887   Sir Alexander Campbell and Sandford Fleming represented Canada at the First Imperial Conference in London.

1917   Women were granted the right to vote in British Columbia.

1949   Canada signed the North Atlantic Treaty at Washington, D.C.

Louis XIV Introduces Baby Bonuses

There were many jokes in Canada when the system of "baby bonuses" was introduced in 1944. Nevertheless, it wasn't the first time it had happened in Canada. Louis XIV inaugurated baby bonuses on April 5, 1669! A family with ten children received a pension of 300 livres a year, while twelve children were worth 400 livres.

There weren't many French people who were willing to settle in Canada. Most of those who came hoped to make some money and then return to their homeland. Louis XIV, his First Minister Colbert, and the great Intendant Talon realized that the population of Canada must be increased.

One of the first steps was to send out "King's Girls" to marry the bachelors in Canada. They were carefully chosen, mostly from the provinces of Normandy, Brittany and Picardy. City girls were apt to be lazy. Thomas B. Costain in *The White and the Gold* says: "The sturdy young inhabitants had no desire for wives of that type (city girls), even though they might be prettier and trimmer than the broad-beamed candidates from the farms."

The King's Girls arrived in shiploads of one hundred or more, carefully chaperoned. They were displayed in halls while the bachelors looked them over. The girls could also question the men who were interested in them and find out about their homes, habits, and possessions. The bachelors in Three Rivers and Montreal complained a good deal because the Quebec boys got the first choice and they were left with the culls!

As soon as a boy and girl agreed to be married, the wedding ceremony took place. They were given an ox, cow, two pigs, a pair of chickens, two barrels of salted meat and a purse of eleven crowns.

There was no escape for the bachelors. Parents were fined if their sons were not married by the time they were twenty and their daughters when they were sixteen. They were hauled into court every six months until their children were married!

Other Events on April 5:

1745 A New England force, led by William Pepperell, arrived at Canso on its way to attack Louisburg.

1832 Brockville, Ontario, was incorporated as a town.

1842 The Gesner Museum, the first public museum in Canada, opened in Saint John, N.B.

1871 Prince Edward Island authorized the building of a railway.

1891 The third Dominion Census showed the population as 4,833,239, an increase of 500,000 in ten years.

1908 Edmonton installed one of the first dial telephone systems in North America.

1958 Ripple Rock in Seymour Narrows, British Columbia was removed by the world's biggest non-atomic explosion.

Jean Colbert (1619-1683)

Trudeau Elected Prime Minister

On the night of April 6, 1968, after seven hours of voting, Canadians suddenly realized that their next Prime Minister would be Pierre Elliott Trudeau, a perfectly bilingual bachelor playboy who had flashed from obscurity to the most powerful position in the nation in one year. In fact, he had only been a member of Parliament since 1965 and did not enter the cabinet until April 4, 1967, when he became Minister of Justice.

Trudeau's victory was the result of a spectacular leadership convention conducted in American hullabaloo style. The nation watched on television as he defeated seven other strong contenders in the most fantastic political spectacle in Canadian history. One of them was Paul Martin who had been a member of Parliament for thirty-five years and who had often served as acting Prime Minister. The others were Robert Winters, Joseph Greene, Paul Hellyer, Allan MacEachern, Eric Kierans, and John Turner.

Trudeau's election as leader of the Liberal Party meant that he would become Canada's fifteenth Prime Minister on April 20. Yet some of the most experienced political observers in Ottawa knew little about his background. Few Canadians know much about it today.

He was born in Montreal in 1919, son of wealthy lawyer Charles-Emile Trudeau and Grace Elliott. He studied law at the University of Montreal and political economy at Harvard, with further studies in Paris and London. Then he spent years travelling through most of the world.

Gradually Trudeau became active in Quebec politics and supported the socialist New Democratic Party in the general election of 1963. He attacked Liberal leader Lester Pearson for reversing his stand on nuclear arms for Canada, saying, "Power offered itself to Mr. Pearson; he had nothing to lose except his honour. He lost it, and his entire party lost it with him."

Yet Trudeau became Liberal M.P. for a Montreal constituency in 1965. The Liberal party accepted him reluctantly, but they had to admit him in order to get the powerful Quebec Labor leader, Jean Marchand, to be a candidate.

The new Prime Minister's flamboyant life style and eccentric manner in conducting government affairs soon attracted attention the world over. Many people for the first time sat up and took notice of Canada because of this man who took it upon himself to ignore the conventions of statesmanship. In 1971, at the age of 51, Trudeau became the first prime minister to wed while in office when he married 22-year-old Margaret Sinclair. On Christmas day of the same year a son was born to them. Justin Pierre Trudeau was the second child born to a prime minister during his term of office (see Dec. 25).

Other Events on April 6:

1609 Henry Hudson, an Englishman in the service of Holland, began the voyage that took him along the coast of Newfoundland.

1851 Britain transferred control of post offices to Canada. A uniform rate of postage was introduced.

1860 The Allan Steamship Line won the contract for a weekly postal service to Liverpool.

1885 General Middleton set out from Qu'Appelle to attack Riel's force at Batoche.

1886 Vancouver was incorporated.

1908 Robert F. Peary sailed from his base at Sydney, Cape Breton, on the first leg of his successful voyage to the North Pole.

McGee Murdered

It was 1:30 in the morning, April 7, 1868. The first Parliament to meet since Canada had become a nation had adjourned for the Easter recess. The House of Commons sat late in order to finish its business so that its members could get away for the holidays. One of the members who spoke that night was D'Arcy McGee, the former Irish revolutionary who had done so much to bring about Confederation.

McGee left the House of Commons with a friend and they walked together to the corner of Sparks and Metcalfe Streets. McGee then strolled along Sparks Street to Mrs. Trotter's boarding house, where he stayed when Parliament was in session. Tomorrow he would return to his home in Montreal, and next week he would celebrate his forty-third birthday with his wife and daughters.

As he was searching in his pocket for his key, a man stepped from the shadows and shot him. McGee fell back on the wooden sidewalk, mortally wounded. He was found a few minutes later by young Will Trotter, a page boy in the House of Commons. At first, young Trotter did not know what to do, but then dashed into the office of the nearby Ottawa *Times* and shouted: "Mr. McGee is lying dead in the street."

A doctor was called, but the boy was right. D'Arcy McGee was dead. After the police had looked over the scene of the crime, a message was sent to Sir John A. Macdonald who came right over. There was no trace of the murderer except footprints in the snow.

Parliament held a special session later in the day and voted an annuity for McGee's family. A reward of $20,000 was offered for the arrest of his murderer. Many suspects were questioned and finally a charge was laid against James Patrick Whalen, a Fenian. The motive for the murder was supposed to be revenge, because McGee had warned that the Fenians planned to invade Canada. Whalen protested his innocence but was hanged in public execution, the last in Canada, on February 11, 1869.

Thomas D'Arcy McGee (1825-1868)

Other Events on April 7:

1623   George Calvert (Lord Baltimore) was granted the province of Avalon, Newfoundland.

1672   Count Frontenac was appointed Governor of New France for the first time.

1849   Fire destroyed a large part of Toronto.

1869   A public execution was held in Prince Edward Island.

1885   Troops left Toronto for action against Riel's rebellion.

1890   Ontario municipalities were granted a local option in the matter of the sale of liquor.

1914   The Grand Trunk Pacific Railway was completed at Nechako, British Columbia. The first train arrived at Prince Rupert on April 9.

1917   A Royal commission was appointed to study the high cost of living.

1965   Leon Balcer left the Conservative party.

Mowat Rides for Help

We muster but three hundred
In all this great lone land,
Which stretches o'er the continent
To where the Rockies stand;
But not one heart doth falter,
No coward voice complains,
That few, too few, in numbers are
The Riders of the Plains.

Our mission is to plant the rule
Of Britain's freedom here,
Restrain the lawless savage, and
Protect the pioneer;
And 'tis a proud and daring trust
To hold these vast domains,
With but three hundred men,
The Riders of the Plains.

—ANONYMOUS

Nearly everybody knows the story of Paul Revere's famous ride when the American Revolutionary War began. Who knows the story of James Mowat and his desperate ride from Edmonton to Calgary to get help during the Northwest rebellion? Mowat is one of the unsung heroes of Canadian history.

Riel and Dumont had stirred the Indians into going on the warpath late in March, 1885. The war drums, keeping up a continual beat day and night, were heard as far west as Edmonton. The situation in Edmonton was critical because its only defenders were thirty volunteers armed with muzzle-loading muskets used in the Indian mutiny of 1857. There was no ammunition, so they had to make their own lead balls and gunpowder.

It was essential to get word to Calgary and ask for help, but the telegraph line had been cut. James Mowat volunteered to ride to Calgary on horseback, and left early on the morning of April 8. Sneaking out of Edmonton was dangerous. The Indians were camping all around and Mowat had to make his way so quietly that even the dogs would not bark. Somehow he managed to get through and ride the two hundred miles to Calgary **in** thirty-six hours, with no sleep and little food.

Fortunately, General Strange was at Calgary with six hundred men and their march to Edmonton began on April 20. Meanwhile, Mowat had made his way back to Edmonton with copies of the Calgary *Herald,* containing news to April 13.

When the Indians heard that General Strange was coming with a large body of troops, they stopped beating their drums. The Edmonton *Bulletin* reported: "Since the Indians heard that troops are on the way, their desire to get on with their farming is marvellous." Nevertheless, it had been a close call for Edmonton.

On another sector, General Middleton was leading a strong force from Qu'Appelle to attack Riel's centre at Batoche. It wasn't easy going. The temperature at Qu'Appelle on April 8 was twenty-three below zero! James Mowat's ride from Edmonton to Calgary that day and night, must have been through similar, bitterly cold weather.

Other Events on April 8:

1669   Louis XIV approved the building of a hospital at Montreal.

1671   Marquette founded a mission at Sault Ste. Marie, Michigan.

1785   An ordinance prohibited imports from the United States by sea.

1873   A select committee was appointed to examine charges that Sir John A. Macdonald and members of his cabinet had accepted large sums of money from promoters of the C.P.R.

1880   The first passenger train of the Grand Trunk Railway went from Port Huron to Chicago.

1963   General election: Liberals 129, Conservatives 95, Social Credit 24, New Democratic Party 17.

Vimy Under Attack

One of the most striking war memorials is at Vimy Ridge, near Arras, France. It commemorates the part played by Canadian troops in an important battle of World War I on April 9, 1917. The commander of the Canadian forces in the attack was General Sir Julian Byng, who later became Lord Byng of Vimy and Governor-General of Canada.

Early in 1917, it was decided to try to dislodge the Germans from their position in Vimy, and the assault was entrusted to the Canadian Corps, and a British brigade; a force of 170,000 men. The battle was carefully planned, even rehearsed. This could be done because there was a network of underground tunnels running from Arras toward Vimy Ridge. Twenty-five thousand men could be hidden underground and moved to the jumping off places for the assault.

April 9 was Easter Monday and by dawn most of the Canadian force had moved to within 100 yards of the enemy, guided through the darkness of the tunnels by white tapes laid along the floors. The attack was preceded by a heavy artillery barrage that had been going on for two weeks, but intensified during the first hours of the morning. Nevertheless, the 100 yards up the slope to the enemy trenches were 100 yards of hell. A combination of snow and rain before the attack made the ridge muddy and slippery.

Just as the assault began, the weather suddenly cleared. The Canadian divisions climbed the open slope firing Lewis guns and throwing grenades. When they reached the trenches, bayonet fighting began. Overhead the planes of the Royal Flying Corps, manned by many Canadians, were acting as spotters and tangling with German aircraft trying to stop them.

More than 3,000 Germans surrendered in the first assault, and after heavy fighting, Vimy Ridge was taken. Unfortunately, the battle was not decisive. After three years of similarly terrible casualties, the French soldiers to the south were on the verge of revolt. Marshal

Canadian War Memorial at Vimy, France

Pétain took over after 20,000 desertions, herded 200 mutinous men into an artillery range and blew them up. He exiled another 100 men and shot 20 more after courtsmartial. These were harsh measures, but the morale of the French army was restored in time to withstand a final German assault that nearly broke through to Paris.

Other Events on April 9:

1682   La Salle reached the mouth of the Mississippi and claimed Louisiana for France.

Louis XIV recalled Governor Frontenac.

1914   The first train arrived at Prince Rupert, British Columbia, from Winnipeg.

1961   British Prime Minister Macmillan arrived at Ottawa for discussions with the Canadian government.

Lloydminster in 1904

British Settlers Arrive in Saint John

A wise man once said: "The history of Ireland is something for Englishmen to remember and Irishmen to forget." A parallel might be drawn with Canadians and Englishmen. Canadians who have gone to live in England have usually been welcomed. Too many Englishmen, after coming to live in Canada, have been treated with resentment and disdain.

Yet, many settlers from England proved to rank with the best citizens of Canada, although enduring terrible hardships. The journey made by the founders of Lloydminster on the Saskatchewan-Alberta border exemplifies their courage.

In 1903, Canada was enjoying a great immigration boom, thanks to an almost worldwide drive for new settlers. One of the immigration agents was the Reverend I. M. Barr, a silver-tongued orator in England. Anxious to earn the $5 paid for every head of family and the $2 for every individual sent to Canada, he persuaded a large group of people that life in western Canada was much better than in England. Their ship, an old tub called the *Manitoba*, arrived in Saint John on April 10, 1903, after a dreadful crossing. Men, women and children slept in the cargo holds. There was no privacy, the most primitive of toilet facilities, and the food and water were unfit to eat or drink.

When they arrived in Saint John, they were loaded into "colonist cars." The train was so slow it was said that the people in the front coaches could shoot a rabbit from a window,

jump out, pick it up and get back on one of the coaches to the rear.

When they arrived at Saskatoon, they lived in tents for two weeks before journeying on. The wagons they traveled in were overloaded; baggage dropped into mudholes and coal oil spilled into the food. The temperature was often below zero as blizzards gusted across the prairies.

Many of those people were ordinary cityfolk. Yet, they stuck it out, encouraged by one of their members, Reverend G. E. Lloyd. They were the founders of present day Lloydminster, which they named after their fellow member who did so much to keep them going.

Other Events on April 10:

1606   James I gave large grants in North America to the Plymouth and London Companies.

1684   An ordinance prohibited emigration from French Canada to English colonies in the south.

1812   The United States called out the militia in preparation for the war against Canada that began on June 18.

1841   Halifax obtained its city charter.

1865   Premier Tupper of Nova Scotia moved for Maritime Union rather than Confederation.

1959   A nuclear research reactor began operating at McMaster University in Hamilton.

Britain and France Sign Treaty of Utrecht

The Treaty of Utrecht signed by Britain and France on April 11, 1713, ended the war that made the Duke of Marlborough famous. Before becoming a duke, he was John Churchill, the most distinguished member of his family until Sir Winston Churchill gave leadership to the free world in 1940-1945.

It took Britain and France fifteen months to work out the details of the Treaty of Utrecht. Both sides made concessions. France gave up Hudson Bay and Newfoundland, although Iberville had captured them, and also Acadia to the British. She retained Canada (New France), Cape Breton and Prince Edward Island (called the Island of St. John) to protect the entrance to Canada via the St. Lawrence River. France also kept her possessions in what are now the United States and West Indies.

Nominally, there was a long period of peace between Britain and France after the Treaty of Utrecht, but preparations were made for war. France began building the mighty fortress at Louisburg and tried to persuade the Acadians to move there. The land at Louisburg was not suitable for farming, so the Acadians stayed where they were, even though it meant living under British rule. They made it clear, however, that they would never take up arms against France if there was a war. This led to their expulsion.

Eventually, Britain had to develop an army and naval base at Halifax to counteract the French fortress at Louisburg.

One troublesome feature of the Treaty of Utrecht was its failure to establish a border between Nova Scotia and Massachusetts (New Brunswick and Maine did not exist). Sometimes, the border was said to be the St. Croix River, as it is today, but there were other occasions when France claimed the territory as far south as Boston. This resulted in a number of raids by the British and French on each other's settlements. The French joined the Abenaki Indians in a number of fierce sorties into Massachusetts and massacred entire communities.

In the long run, the Treaty of Utrecht resulted in France's losing her North American possessions, including Canada.

Other Events on April 11:

1617   Champlain brought Louis Hébert to Canada as the first permanent settler.

1768   Montreal was badly damaged by fire.

1872   The fifth session of the First Parliament began; legislation included legalizing the trade unions.

1884   The Amateur Athletic Union of Canada was formed.

1904   Sydney, Nova Scotia, was incorporated as a city.

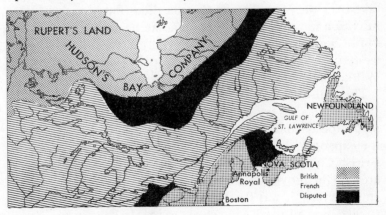

Upper Fort Garry, 1857-58

American Plans for Canada Upset by Civil War

It has to be speculation now, but it could be argued that Canada would not be an independent nation today if the American Civil War had not taken place. The fight began at Fort Sumter on April 12, 1861.

In 1861, the Americans had a big foothold in western Canada and were looking for more. The most important trade route was via the railway that had been built to St. Paul, Minnesota. Six thousand Red River carts were employed in transporting Hudson's Bay Company goods between Fort Garry (Winnipeg) and St. Paul. They were supplying 152 shops, 3,000 traders and 100,000 Indian trappers.

Fort Garry was growing rapidly and dividing into political factions, "The American Party" and the "Canadian Party." Each side had newspapers to express its views, and hotels for headquarters. With Confederation looming as a possibility in the East, the States had agents working in Fort Garry to try to take over the West before Canada did. The intention was to establish the Canadian north-south boundary along longitude 90, at the western end of Lake Superior, just past Fort William and Port Arthur.

The United States was interested for several reasons. Its own good lands were being occupied rapidly, and the prairies provided room for expansion. Gold had been discovered in British Columbia, and it was thought that the area might provide a route to the goldfields. In any event, it was the United States' policy to take over all the Pacific coast up to Alaska.

The Americans might have pursued this policy if they had not become involved in a war with Mexico. Rather than fight Britain too, they settled for a boundary along the forty-ninth parallel. The Americans might also have absorbed the Prairie Provinces, if they had not become involved in their own civil war in 1861. Four years later, Sir John A. Macdonald said about the Prairies: "The country is of no present value to Canada." Sir John's views changed when Confederation became a reality in 1867. He and his colleagues then saw the need for quick action to prevent the West from falling into American hands. The action was so quick that it caused the Riel uprising in 1870.

Other Events on April 12:

1776 Thomas Frobisher was sent to build a fort on the Churchill River.

1819 The Earl of Dalhousie was made Governor of Canada.

1838 Samuel Lount and Peter Mathews were hanged in Toronto for taking part in the Upper Canada rebellion.

1853 Five small railways amalgamated into the Grand Trunk Railway.

1867 The British Government authorized a loan of £3,000,000 for Halifax and the St. Lawrence Railway.

1876 The Canada Shipping Company was established by Montreal merchants.

1917 Women were granted the right to vote in Ontario.

Mme. La Tour valiantly defends the garrison

Charnisay Attacks Rival Fort La Tour

Someone should write an opera about the rivalry in Acadia between Charles La Tour and D'Aulnay de Charnisay. It would have a dramatic and surprising finale.

Charles La Tour was one of the first Europeans to settle in Acadia. He was such a diplomat or villain (It depended on who was describing him!), that he was given a monopoly of the fur trade along the Saint John River by the King of France, and was made a Baronet of Nova Scotia by the King of England. Nobody could be sure which side he was on.

D'Aulnay de Charnisay, a close relative of Cardinal Richelieu, was given Port Royal, while also controlling a good deal of Nova Scotia. He used his influence at court to try to have La Tour put out of business, but was unsuccessful.

On April 13, 1645, while La Tour was away, Charnisay attacked Fort La Tour. Mme. La Tour was in charge of the fort and organized a heroic defense. She was described as being "an Amazon of a woman" but very beautiful. Although there were only fifty men to defend the fort, they held back the much larger Charnisay force until a traitor let Charnisay's men into the enclosure.

There was a fierce battle but Mme. La Tour finally surrendered on a promise by Charnisay that the lives of the garrison would be spared. Instead, he spared only one, a man who volunteered to act as the executioner of his comrades. Mme. La Tour was forced to stand with a halter around her neck and watch the execution of her men, one by one. She died of a broken heart soon after.

Charnisay then had his date with destiny. He was drowned when his canoe overturned. There is a story (unconfirmed), that one of the Indians made sure he drowned by holding his head under water!

Then followed the amazing finale. Charles La Tour sailed across the bay to Port Royal and married Charnisay's widow. Of course, it was a good business arrangement. It ended the dispute over property rights, and, in the words of the marriage contract "served to restore the peace and tranquility of the country, and concord and unity between the two families."

Other Events on April 13:

1608   Champlain sailed to Canada for the third time.

1713   The Iroquois were joined by the Tuscaroras to become Six Nations.

1859   The University of New Brunswick was incorporated.

1870   Donald A. Smith reported to the federal government at Ottawa on the negotiations with Louis Riel at Fort Garry.

1961   His Excellency, Constantine Caramanalis of Greece visited Ottawa.

St. Lawrence River Swells, Floods Montreal

This is the time of year when many parts of Canada are menaced by spring floods. Under normal conditions the floods are kept under control, but occasionally there will be a combination of unusual weather conditions and then the high spring waters run wild.

Even in recent years there have been desperate conditions in the Fraser Valley of British Columbia (1948) and the Red River, Manitoba (1950). Both situations were saved by thousands of citizens turning out to make restraining walls with sandbags. Even so, the Red River flood extended over 700 square miles and caused $27 million damage.

Until 1901, when a stone wall was built along the river banks, Montreal had often been damaged by spring floods. One of the first floods destroyed a cemetery established by Maisonneuve who founded Montreal in 1642.

The worst Montreal flood happened on the evening of Sunday, April 14, 1861. Almost without warning, the St. Lawrence River rose so suddenly that the water poured into the lower part of the city, stranding many people who were attending evening services in the churches. St. Stephen's Church on Dalhousie Street, and the Methodist Church on Ottawa Street were completely surrounded by water in a few minutes. The people had to stand on the pews as it poured in at the doors. Even then, with the water 6 feet deep, they could only keep their heads above it. Some people had to stay there all night in the freezing cold and darkness because the lights were extinguished. Others were rescued by small boats which were rowed into the churches.

By morning, there was an icy blizzard and one-quarter of Montreal was under water. Small boats served as taxis from St. James Street to Beaver Hall Hill, at a fare of five cents per passenger. The Grand Trunk Railway was unable to operate as its lines were flooded as far as Lachine. Victoria Bridge, an important link in the Grand Trunk which spanned the St. Lawrence River, was also temporarily closed. Then considered one of the engineering wonders of the world, it had just been opened the previous year by Edward, Prince of Wales, representing his mother, Queen Victoria.

Other Events on April 14:

1849   Mount Allison University, Sackville, New Brunswick received its charter.

1851   Britain disallowed the currency regulations introduced by Sir Francis Hincks.

1871   An act was passed, establishing the use of uniform currency throughout Canada.

1892   Windsor, Ontario, received a city charter.

1896   The House of Commons deadlocked on the Manitoba separate schools remedial bill.

1918   General Foch was named Commander-in-Chief of the Allied Forces in France. In practice, the national commanders (Haig, King Albert, and Pershing) retained extensive control.

1919   President Wilson rejected the Italian claim to Fiume and the coast south of it, whereupon the Italians withdrew from the Paris Peace Conference.

1928   The famous Russell House Hotel, Ottawa, was destroyed by fire.

First Steamboat Appears on the Red River

One of the most colorful stories in Canadian history tells of the days when steamboats began operating on the Red River, carrying freight and passengers between Fort Garry (Winnipeg) and St. Paul, Minnesota.

As explained on April 12, the building of a railway to St. Paul created tremendous traffic to Fort Garry. The next step of encroaching civilization was taken on April 15, 1859, when Captain Anson Northrup brought his ship *North Star* to the Red River. St. Paul merchants figured that if steamboats could operate on the Mississippi, they could also navigate the Red River to Fort Garry. Captain Northrup had the *North Star* on Crow Wing River, but offered to transfer it to the Red for $2,000. In order to do this, he had to dismantle *North Star* and have its parts freighted across country in winter in sleighs drawn by oxen. All the parts were there on April 15 and a few weeks later the ship was ready for its first run to Fort Garry. Its name had been changed to *Anson Northrup*.

There was a certain amount of fear as the old paddle-wheeler thrashed her way down the river, deck barely above water, funnel pouring out smoke and sparks, and boiler leaking clouds of steam. Amongst the cargo were 100 kegs of gunpowder, with sparks falling all around!

The first trip took eight days. The Indians along the banks of the Red River were terrified when the *Anson Northrup* came into view and especially when she blew her whistle. On the other hand, the new settlers came rushing from their homes cheering, weeping, praying and even firing guns! The ship would stop at frequent intervals so that the crew could go ashore and cut wood for fuel.

The *Anson Northrup* arrived at Fort Garry in June, the first steamer of any size to do so. It was a great event for the rapidly growing community. Cannons were fired in salute and church bells rang.

Other steamers followed the *Anson Northrup* and there was great rivalry among them until 1877, when one of the ships brought a railway locomotive to Winnipeg. That was the end of the steamers on the Red River (see December 2).

Other Events on April 15:

1672   A royal edict prohibited fur traders from going to Indian villages. The Indians had to bring their furs to the settlements.

1720   Three ships left France with three hundred settlers for the Island of St. John (Prince Edward Island).

1814   The warships *Prince Regent* and *Princess Charlotte* were launched at Kingston, Ontario.

1861   Joseph Howe introduced a resolution proposing union of the North American provinces.

1907   Coal miners went on strike until May 6 in Alberta and eastern British Columbia.

1928   A Canadian airplane discovered the German airship *Bremen* that had been forced down on Greenly Island, Strait of Belle Isle.

1958   The Queen Elizabeth Hotel opened in Montreal.

The Anson Northrup, *1859*

Roberval's Shield

Roberval Sent to Canada

On January 15, the story was told of how King Francis I downgraded Jacques Cartier and made the Marquis de Roberval viceroy of New France. Roberval did not leave for Canada until April 16, 1542. He had three ships, and several hundred colonists, some of whom were useful, but most were hardened convicts who were taken on board in chains.

It was a terrible winter in Quebec. There was a scarcity of food and the convicts were difficult to control. There were fights and thefts, and Roberval had to hang one of the men, keep others in chains and even flog some of the women. Many of the party died of scurvy. Roberval went back to France soon after the ice broke in the river and he and Cartier had to appear before a court of enquiry. Eventually, the king forgave them for their quarrel.

There is a legend about Roberval's voyage to Canada that may be true. His niece, Marguerite, was in one of the ships and fell in love with one of the men. There was so much talk about their behaviour that Roberval put Marguerite ashore on an island off Newfoundland, called the Isle of Demons. It was avoided by ships because it was supposed to have been inhabited by evil spirits.

Roberval left Marguerite and her old nurse Bastienne on the island, with four muskets and a supply of gunpowder. Marguerite's lover jumped off the ship and swam ashore to join them. Eventually they had a baby, but all of them died except Marguerite who lived alone for two years. It is said that she shot three polar bears and was never afraid of the demons who screamed at her through the strong winds.

One day, a fishing vessel was brave enough to sail close to the island and its crew was amazed to see a woman waving to them. She was dressed in skins. They took her off the island and sailed back to France where she told her fantastic story.

Other Events on April 16:

1739 La Vérendrye sent his sons to explore the rivers flowing into Lake Winnipeg.

1833 English-speaking residents of Quebec protested the proceedings in the Assembly.

1853 Toronto Locomotive Works completed the *Toronto*, the first locomotive built in Canada.

1856 Governor Douglas announced that gold had been discovered in British Columbia.

1874 Louis Riel was expelled from the House of Commons by a vote of 123 to 68.
The Guelph Agricultural College and Experimental Farm was opened.

1903 Canada raised the tariff on imports from Germany in retaliation for a similar move by Germany.

Marco Polo Launched

The *Marco Polo* was launched at Saint John, New Brunswick, on April 17, 1851. In those days the harbors of the Maritimes were ringing with the hammers of men making wooden ships to sail the Seven Seas.

Marco Polo was the fastest ship in the world in her day, and her speed was said to be due to an accident that occurred when she was launched. She went down the launching ramp too quickly, shot across Marsh Creek where she was built and settled in the mud. Fortunately, the heavy spring tide was enough to get *Marco Polo* righted and there did not seem to be any great damage. Later, when the ship showed such speed, it was said that the accident had twisted her frame in such a way that she sailed faster than had ever been intended.

The *Marco Polo* was an ugly duckling that became a luxurious passenger liner. She was built as a "drogher" for carrying lumber to Britain. Even then, she showed such speed that she was bought by the Black Ball line which needed ships for the Australian trade. *Marco Polo* was transformed into the most luxurious passenger liner afloat, with a copper-sheathed hull, maple-panelled cabins, mirrored pillars ornamented with coins, deep pile carpets, and red velvet upholstery, all set off by mahogany with gilt and silver fittings.

Marco Polo's first captain was "Bully" Forbes, who predicted that his ship would astound the world. She spread her great white sails for the first voyage to Melbourne with 930 passengers, and was back in Liverpool in six months. It was a record, and *Marco Polo* had a sign strung between her masts that read "Fastest Ship in the World." In 1867, the year of Confederation, *Marco Polo* made a trip from Australia to Britain in seventy-six days, beating the new-fangled steamer *Great Britain* by more than a week!

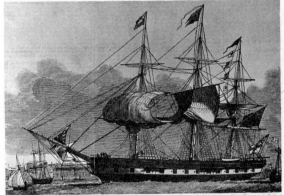

The Marco Polo, *1851*

Unfortunately, steamers with iron hulls replaced the "wooden ships with iron men", and the *Marco Polo* was transformed into her original ugly-duckling form, as a lumber carrier. A wreck, she went home to die on Cape Cavendish, Prince Edward Island.

Other Events on April 17:

1610   Henry Hudson sailed from London to discover Hudson Strait.

1760   Brigadier de Lévis left Montreal to try to recapture Quebec.

1790   The export of wheat, oats, flour and meal was prohibited to try to reduce high prices.

1840   Benjamin Lett blew up Brock's Monument at Niagara Falls.

1855   Charlottetown was incorporated as a city.

1862   The legislative council of Prince Edward Island was made an elective assembly.

1866   The Nova Scotia Legislature voted for union of the maritime colonies.

1903   Barr colonists arrived at Saskatoon (see April 10).

1916   A New York grand jury indicted Baron Von Papen for conspiracy to blow up the Welland Canal.

Card Money, 1714, Public Archives of Canada

Cards Become Money

Perhaps the most successful money-reformer in Canada was the first Intendant, Jacques de Meulles.

The intendants acted as business managers for the governors of French Canada. One of their problems was to keep enough currency in circulation. Coins were sent to Quebec to pay the members of the garrison, but they were returned to France to pay for the purchases. Most trade among the inhabitants had to be carried on by barter. Merchants were legally bound to accept wheat and moose skins as payment for goods, while other pelts, like beaver and wildcat were equally acceptable. One blanket could be bought for eight wildcat skins.

In 1670, France minted special silver and copper coins for use in Canada, but they dis-

appeared quickly and none arrived at all in the spring of 1685. A large number of soldiers who were billeted with private families were De Meulles' responsibility. They were not hunters capable of trapping their own pelts, but they still needed coins to pay for their board and lodging. De Meulles, in desperation, hit on the idea of issuing paper money that would be redeemed when the coins arrived.

There was a good deal of card playing in Quebec, especially among the soldiers. The most popular game was called "maw" and the lucky cards to turn up were, *Tiddy, Gleek, Tup-tup* and *Towser*! There was probably a good deal of grousing when De Meulles gathered up the playing cards and cut them into four pieces. He marked them as being worth various amounts of money and stamped them with the word "bon", meaning "good". Each piece of paper money also carried his signature and seal.

The system worked so well that it was used again many times. On April 18, 1749, the King authorized an issue of card money to be increased from 720,000 to one million livres! It was the forerunner of the Canadian paper money in use today.

The Château de Ramezay Museum in Montreal has a collection of the coins used in those days and even some of the card money, although it is only exhibited by special request.

Other Events on April 18:

1793　The Upper Canada *Gazette* was published at Niagara. It was the first newspaper in Upper Canada.

1846　A special commission was appointed to study rebellion losses in Lower Canada.

1960　President de Gaulle of France arrived in Ottawa for a four-day state visit. Canada and Russia signed a three-year agreement. Russia undertook to spend $2 in Canada for every dollar Canada spent in Russia.

Panama Treaty Signed

It was on April 19, 1850, that Britain and the United States signed the Clayton-Bulwer Treaty to build the Panama Canal as a joint venture. Later the States decided to go it alone. Great Britain withdrew, accepting the promise that the canal would be open to the ships of all nations, at equal rates.

It might be asked what the building of the Panama Canal had to do with Canada, but there are some interesting sidelights.

In the first place, Panama might easily have been called Nova Scotia. After Scotland and England united in 1707 (after this date it is correct to use the term Britain rather than England), the people of Scotland had better opportunities to migrate. One group decided to go to Panama and develop a colony called New Scotland (Nova Scotia). It was a failure for the same reasons that caused Napoleon to abandon his plan to recapture Canada for France years later. The natives and the mosquitoes were too fierce, even for Scotsmen! Samuel Vetch, a Scotsman who went to live in Boston, interested the British government in a plan to capture Acadia from France. Eventually he became Governor of Nova Scotia as we know it, with its capital at Annapolis Royal, formerly Port Royal.

Britain's agreeing to withdraw from ownership of the Panama Canal also had a bearing on the unfortunate agreement made in 1905, establishing the Alaska boundary. The British government thought that as it had given way to the United States on the Panama Canal question, the Americans would be willing to compromise on the boundary between Canada and Alaska, then in dispute. This was not the case (see March 25).

In fairness, it must be said that the building of the Panama Canal was a great help to the development of British Columbia. Ships sailing to and from British Columbian ports carrying the trade of western Canada have never been prevented from using the Panama Canal, thus saving themselves the long journey around South America.

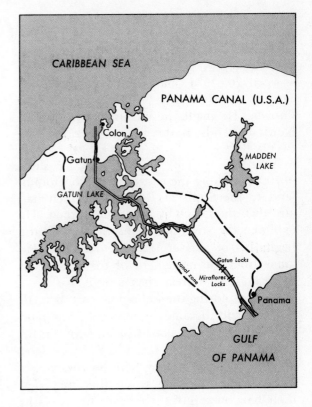

Other Events on April 19:

1627   Cardinal Richelieu signed the charter of the Company of One Hundred Associates which was supposed to develop Canada.

1750   Representatives of the Acadians asked the Governor of Nova Scotia for permission to leave the country. Permission was denied.

1775   A skirmish at Lexington led to the outbreak of the American Revolutionary War and the withdrawal of British troops from Boston to Halifax.

1883   The Parliament buildings were burned at Quebec.

1904   A fire at Toronto caused $12 million damage.

1927   New Brunswick put liquor under government control.

Cartier Makes His First Voyage to Canada

April 20, 1534, marked the beginning of Jacques Cartier's first historic voyage to Canada. He made the crossing to Bonavista, Newfoundland, in the incredible time of twenty days.

After an overhaul, Cartier took his ships northward along the east coast of Newfoundland to the Strait of Belle Isle, which had already been named by French fishermen. He explored the strait which he hoped was the beginning of a river leading to China. He knew from the movement of the water that there must be a great river ahead.

After exploring the Labrador coast in small boats, Cartier became discouraged. The land was so desolate and poor that he wrote in his diary: "I believe that this was the land God allotted to Cain." Along here he saw natives for the first time and wrote that they tied their hair on top of their heads like wreaths of hay!

Cartier made his way along the west coast of Newfoundland which he saw only occasionally through the fog. Gradually, the country improved, especially along the north shore which is now Prince Edward Island. He was still hoping to find the route to Cathay (China) and was fired with hope when he sailed into a deep inlet in the Gaspé. The inlet opened out into a bay which he named "Chaleur", the French word for "heat". The weather was so hot that Cartier expected to find figs growing there.

When Cartier landed he was greeted by the natives who sang, danced and waded out into the water. The French raised a huge wooden cross on the shore, and nailed a shield on it, with a crest bearing the *fleurs-de-lis* and the words, "Vive le Roy de France." A monument was erected there 400 years later.

Although it was only July, Cartier felt that he should hurry back to France before winter came. He persuaded an Indian chief to let him take two of his sons, promising to bring them back the next year. Cartier, in return, gave the natives all the presents he could, especially shirts, red caps and other clothing.

One of the most valuable features of the exploit was the careful diary Cartier kept, in his own writing. It is one of the world's truly historic documents.

Other Events on April 20:

1769 Chief Pontiac was murdered at the present site of St. Louis, Missouri.

1808 Explorer David Thompson tried to discover the route of the Columbia River from British Columbia into the State of Washington.

1864 Frederick Seymour arrived to be Governor of British Columbia (mainland).

1907 Port Arthur and Fort William were incorporated as cities.

1918 Men from eighteen to twenty-two years of age were called to military service.

1941 Prime Minister Mackenzie King and President Roosevelt signed the Hyde Park declaration of joint defense and economic co-operation.

Jacques Cartier at Gaspé, 1534

King Sets Record

On April 21, 1948, William Lyon Mackenzie King established a record as having been prime minister longer than any other man in the history of the British Commonwealth. He had served for 7,825 days, during which time he won six general elections.

Grandson of the rebel William Lyon Mackenzie (see January 2), he became the most controversial leader in Canadian political history. Many books have been written about him, and the title used by Bruce Hutchison illustrated the common impression of him: *The Incredible Canadian*. People who were closely associated with Mackenzie King are still not sure that they really knew or understood him. Although some authors and commentators maintain that Mackenzie King was a spiritualist, others declare that his interest in the occult has been greatly exaggerated.

Over the years Mackenzie King became a labor expert and was made Deputy Minister, then Minister of the Department of Labour when he joined the Laurier government. He was defeated in the reciprocity election in 1911 and spent the next three years in financial straits, with his father going blind, his beloved mother seriously ill and a brother suffering from tuberculosis.

It was then that the tide turned. A rich English lady, Violet Markham, gave him an annuity of $1,500 a year. This was followed by an invitation to work for the Rockefeller Foundation of New York, where he earned $20,000 a year while Canada was involved in World War I. He was bitterly attacked for this by political opponents in later years.

Nevertheless, in 1919, the Liberal party needed a leader to replace the great Sir Wilfrid Laurier and Mackenzie King was chosen in a contest with four other candidates. In 1921 he led the Liberals to their first election victory since the defeat of 1911.

Mackenzie King was not Prime Minister continuously from 1921 until 1948, when he resigned in favor of Louis St. Laurent. He

William Lyon Mackenzie King (1874-1950)

was out of office a few days in 1926 during one of Canada's most exciting political struggles. In 1930 he was defeated in a general election by the Conservatives under R. B. Bennett, and was Leader of the Opposition until 1935. He was at the helm during the "ordeal by fire" of the Second World War.

Mackenzie King was at his best when the political storms were at their worst. His biography makes fascinating reading.

Other Events on April 21:

1668   Father Marquette left Montreal for Sault Ste. Marie.

1785   Trial by jury was established by an ordinance.

1821   The Bank of Upper Canada was incorporated.

1918   Canadian fighter pilot, Roy Brown, shot down the German ace, Baron von Richthofen.

1952   Queen Juliana of the Netherlands visited Ottawa. She and her children had lived there during World War II. One of her children was born in the Civic Hospital in Ottawa, and to satisfy the Dutch Law on constitutional succession, the hospital room was declared a part of Holland!

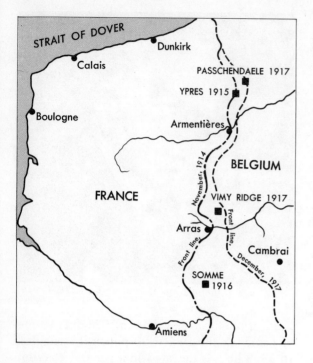

STRAIT OF DOVER

Dunkirk
Calais
PASSCHENDAELE 1917
YPRES 1915
Boulogne
Armentières
BELGIUM
FRANCE
November, 1914
VIMY RIDGE 1917
Front line
Arras
Front line
Cambrai
Front line
December, 1917
SOMME
1916
Amiens

Germans Use Deadly Gas

No troops ever received a more severe baptism of fire in World War I than the Canadians who moved into the front line in mid-April, 1915. They were assigned to hold Ypres in Belgium, gateway to the channel ports of Dunkirk, Calais and Boulogne. The Germans had nearly broken through in 1914, as they did in 1940.

Nothing exciting happened until the afternoon of April 22, when a little breeze blew up. Suddenly the Canadians saw gas drifting like fog across the fields toward them. Algerian conscripts on the left flank broke and ran, throwing away their rifles. As the gas was moving at 6 miles an hour, many were overtaken by it and fell into canals and ditches clutching their throats.

Soon, two French divisions to the left of the Canadians were over-run and the Germans came pouring through the gap, bayonets high. The flank of the Canadian division was turned and virtually trapped.

Ralph Allen in *Ordeal by Fire* says: "Three things stopped the Germans: their lack of any master plan, . . . the terror and discomfort the advancing soldiers met as they stumbled over their writhing enemies into the gas cloud they had created; and perhaps above all else the valor of the Canadian division."

The battle raged back and forth until May 4, under the most terrible conditions. There were no gas masks but the Canadians learned they could get some protection by holding urine-soaked rags over their noses and mouths. The gas destroyed the will to live. Victims usually cried, "Go away and let me die."

On the first day of the battle, one battalion was down to 193 of its 800 men. Another had 250 left. By May 4, the Canadians had lost 6,000 men; either killed, wounded, or missing, one man out of every five who had been rushed into battle.

In all, the Allies lost 60,000 men in the defense of Ypres, a tragedy made deeper by the aftermath. Military historians still cannot decide whether it was worthwhile. At this great cost Canadians proved that they ranked with the best of fighting men.

Other Events on April 22:

1635 William Alexander (Earl of Stirling) was given further grants in Canada and Long Island.

1737 The first smelter in Canada was established at Three Rivers, Quebec.

1745 A British naval force under Admiral Warren joined Pepperell at Canso for the attack on Louisburg.

1786 Lord Dorchester was again appointed Governor of Canada.

1844 The *Bytown Packet*, later the Ottawa *Citizen* was founded.

1897 Finance Minister Fielding introduced new tariffs.

1960 Field Marshal Montgomery arrived at Ottawa for a four-day visit.

1963 Lester B. Pearson became Prime Minister of Canada.

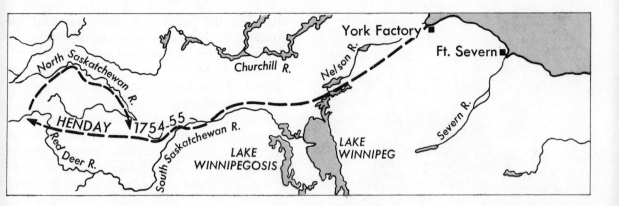

Henday Celebrates St. George's Day by Feasting

Perhaps the most successful St. George's Day dinner ever given was by Anthony Henday on April 23, 1755. At that time the Hudson's Bay Company had its trading posts around the bay itself. Business was getting worse because the French were establishing posts farther and farther west and the Indians could deal with them.

In June 1754, the governor of York Factory decided to send a trouble-shooter west to see what could be done. Anthony Henday, a former smuggler from the Isle of Wight, volunteered for the job, and set off with a band of Indians.

Henday was told to live like an Indian, which he did with much enjoyment, keeping a diary which was both informative and amusing. The hunting was marvelous and there were many feasts along the way. Commenting that, "You can never fill an Indian," Henday wrote: "I am not behind, thank God, a good stomach, and as I am looked upon as a Leader, I have Ladies of different ranks to attend me; please to observe the men do nothing but hunt, and we Leaders hath a Lady to hold the thogin with water to our heads when we drink."

By October, Henday's party had reached what is known as the Red Deer River today, and Henday could see the Rocky Mountains. He met the Blackfoot Indians who lived in a village of 200 teepees in parallel rows. He sat on a sacred white buffalo robe while he conferred with the chief, whom he tried to persuade to send braves with furs to Hudson Bay. The chief pointed out that his tribe did not know how to paddle canoes but traveled on horses. They lived on meat, not fish, and would starve.

Henday then traveled north and spent the winter at what may have been the Thickwood Hills. On April 23, 1755, he gave a great St. George's Day feast at which he displayed the flag and spoke about the patron saint. He knew that the Indians could not have cared less about St. George, but they loved a feast! There was drumming, dancing and especially eating! When he was ready to go back to Hudson Bay, he had sixty canoes laden with furs.

Other Events on April 23:

1827   The first steam engine began operation in Nova Scotia.
Shubenacadie Canal was begun to connect Halifax with the Bay of Fundy.

1842   The cornerstone of King's College, Toronto, was laid by Sir Charles Bagot.

1851   The first Canadian postage stamps were issued.

1879   Guelph, Ontario, was incorporated as a city.

General Middleton (1825-1898)

Battleford Relieved

April 24, 1885, marked the turn of the tide in the Northwest Rebellion. Ottawa had been moved to act by the news of Duck Lake (see March 18) and rushed a force of 3,000 men from the east under British General Middleton. Middleton also had 2,000 men from the west and 500 Northwest Mounted Police.

One of his first decisions was to order Colonel Herchmer to take fifty Mounted Police to Battleford and try to rescue the besieged inhabitants. Herchmer acted contrary to the spirit of Tennyson's *Charge of the Light Brigade,* "Theirs not to reason why. Theirs but to do and die." He did something unheard of in the annals of the famous force, and refused to go! The order meant a march of 200 miles from Regina to Battleford, when only half his men had horses. They would have to ford the South Saskatchewan River in spring flood and would be easy targets for Poundmaker's Indians.

Middleton then revised his plan and divided the force that was destined for Edmonton. Half of it was ordered to take the train to Swift Current and go to Battleford. Colonel Otter was in command and was joined by the fifty police Herchmer had refused to squander.

When they reached the South Saskatchewan River, they waited for the paddle-wheeler *Northcote* to bring supplies from Medicine Hat, a trip that took a week. Since in some places, the water was only 20 inches deep and the *Northcote* drew 26 inches, the ship had to become amphibious to get over the shoals. General Middleton later wrote: "The long expected steamer arrived after a tedious voyage most of which seems to have been made on land. All the steamers are stern-wheelers and have four strong spars fastened, two on each side of the bow, by a sort of hinge. These spars are lowered when the vessel runs on a shoal or sandbar, and the vessel is forced over; made to walk, as it were."

On April 24, Middleton's own force was almost ambushed by Dumont and 130 Métis at Fish Creek. A more important development on April 24 was that Otter and Herchmer reached Battleford. It was like the relief of Lucknow to the people who had been besieged there for nearly a month. It must have been a thrilling event to hear the music of a military band approaching from the distance.

Other Events on April 24:

1626 Champlain sailed from Dieppe on his eleventh voyage to Canada.

1851 Prince Edward Island obtained responsible government with George Coles as Premier.

1896 Lord Strathcona (formerly Donald A. Smith) was appointed Canadian High Commissioner to Britain.

1951 Princess Patricia Canadian Light Infantry was sent into action in Korea.

1952 The first shipment of oil from Alberta by pipeline and freighter arrived at Sarnia, Ontario.

The smouldering ruins of the Quebec Parliament

Rebellion Losses Bill Signed, Rioting Ensues

On April 25, 1849, Lord Elgin signed the Rebellion Losses Bill. Thomas Raddall wrote in *The Path of Destiny*: "It was a memorable date in Canadian history, for he signed the bill and in that one firm signature made clear that from now on Canada (and British governors-general) were to be ruled by Canadians though the heavens fell."

The Rebellion Losses Bill provided payment for people who had suffered property damage during the rebellions of 1837-1838. The English-speaking people in Quebec went wild with anger. How could the Queen's own representative in Canada sign a bill rewarding treason? The answer was that the bill had been passed by Parliament and therefore, under the principle of responsible government, the Queen's representative had to sign it, whether he agreed with it or not.

Lord Elgin was booed in Parliament and pelted with rotten eggs when he left. The *Gazette* called him "the last governor of Canada" and urged Tory sympathizers to attend a mass meeting in the Place d'Armes. Rioting then got completely out of control. People stormed from the meeting and rushed into Parliament which was in session. Someone yelled that the "French Parliament" was dissolved and stole the mace. In a few minutes the interior of the building was a shambles, with furniture, doors and windows smashed and pictures torn from the wall.

The end of the Parliament building came when the gas jets were torn from the wall and caught fire. The mob would not allow the fire department to try to stop the flames and the building was burned to ashes.

Rioting went on for days. Lord Elgin was nearly killed when his carriage was wrecked by heavy stones. He could have called out troops to quell the rioting, but they were under British control. This would have meant that the Imperial Government was interfering in a Canadian civil matter.

Eventually, more responsible elements of the English-speaking population established order by enlisting a force of special constables. Even so, riots broke out periodically for a year. There was even a movement on the part of leading Tories to have Canada join the United States (see July 26).

Other Events on April 25:

1720 A governor and council of Nova Scotia were appointed.

1858 The first gold miners heading for Fraser River arrived at Victoria, British Columbia.

1862 John A. Macdonald's motion for a more efficient militia led to the defeat of the government on May 20.

A Red River expedition, 1871

Speculators Grab Lands

Danny Kaye has a story about four kittens named Un, Deux, Trois and Quatre who went sailing on a block of ice. The story has a sad ending because Un, Deux, Trois and Quatre cinq! There's a happier ending to a true story about eight men who sailed down the Red River on a raft and arrived at Fort Garry on April 26, 1871. They were land speculators from Ontario, and their arrival heralded a flood of people who rushed to grab up land being made available to the Indians, Métis, and new settlers. Even so, the story had an unhappy ending for many of them: they were "conned" into giving up their holdings.

When the federal government took over the Northwest Territories from the Hudson's Bay Company, the land was surveyed so that it could be divided among the original settlers. First, treaties were made with the Indians to encourage them to live on reservations. Generally speaking, each family of five received 640 acres. Every Indian was given a present of $12, and an annuity of $5, plus an extra $15 to every head man. They were given new suits of clothes every three years, and provided with farm implements, cattle and grain.

Similar arrangements were made with the Métis although they did not live on reservations.

The first treaty was made in 1871 in Manitoba, and then others covered New Ontario (now Saskatchewan) and southern Alberta. Commissioner Laird made the treaties with the Blackfoot Indians and the Piegans in 1877. They required very careful negotiating as the Indians were waging war south of the border. Commissioner Laird was helped a great deal by Blackfoot Chief Crowfoot, who he said was the shrewdest Indian he ever met. It was remarkable that the treaties were negotiated without a drop of blood being shed, although there were many anxious moments.

Unfortunately, unscrupulous speculators obtained a great deal of land from the Métis. Until the area was surveyed and the Métis were allocated their holdings, they were given a scrip proving their claim to ownership. The land speculators often bought this scrip for $15, or even for a few bottles of whisky.

Other Events on April 26:

1610 Champlain arrived at Tadoussac on his fourth voyage to Canada.

1625 Jesuit Fathers, Brébeuf and others, sailed from Dieppe.

1792 Captain Vancouver sailed into the Strait of Juan de Fuca.

Survivors of the War of 1812, photo take in 1859

Americans Attack York, Destroy New Legislature

In the early morning hours of April 27, 1813, the people of York, the capital of Upper Canada, were startled to hear gunfire. American troops had landed on what is now Sunnyside Beach, and were fighting their way along the shore.

The Americans had sailed from Sackets Harbor, New York, two days before, but the only opposition on Lake Ontario had been rough weather. General Dearborn, who was so stout that he had to be carried in a special carriage, became seasick and his second in command, General Pike, directed the landing of 1,700 men.

The garrison at York was commanded by General Sheaffe who had not expected an attack and so had spent the winter at Niagara. Consequently, arrangements for defense were very poor. The only new artillery guns were lying in the mud near the shore, where they had been unloaded from a ship the previous autumn. Two companies of red-coated "regulars" happened to be staying at the fort on a march from Kingston to Niagara. They brought the strength of the garrison to 510 regulars, 250 militia and 40 Indians. Sheaffe ordered them to try to stop the Americans who were working their way through the woods towards the west battery, where Toronto Argos now play their football games. British bayonets were ineffective against American guns and the fight was over in half an hour.

General Dearborn then led a victory parade through the muddy streets of York in his special carriage. Some of the Americans were undisciplined volunteers and spent four days looting the town. They even let the prisoners out of York jail and urged them to help themselves. Finally, they decided to burn down the new Parliament Buildings of Upper Canada.

While they were looting the legislature, they found the Speaker's wig which they sent to Washington as, "an example of British barbarity." They thought it was a human scalp!

After storing as much loot as possible in their ships, including York's only fire engine, the Americans sailed away to attack the British at Niagara.

The British retaliated for the attack on York by raiding Washington the following year and burning the Capitol and other government buildings.

Other Events on April 27:

1628 Sieur Couillard, son-in-law of Louis Hébert, was the first man in Canada to use a plough drawn by oxen.

1644 Wheat was first sown in Canada.

1831 The steamer *Royal William* was launched at Quebec.

1896 Sir Mackenzie Bowell resigned as Prime Minister and was succeeded by Sir Charles Tupper.

1961 Canada gave Sierra Leone a $5,000 book credit to mark its independence.

Chevalier de Lévis (1720-1787)

Lévis Defeats General Murray

When the hockey experts pick their "three stars", they usually choose two players from the winners and one from the losers. For much the same reason, history has not accorded Montcalm and Lévis the recognition they deserve as great soldiers.

François Gaston, Chevalier de Lévis, was one of Montcalm's most valuable officers. He refused to give up the battle for Canada after the fall of Quebec and spent the winter of 1759-1760 in Montreal, building up a new army. The British had not been able to capture Montreal in the autumn of 1759 because the news of Wolfe's victory at Quebec reached General Amherst too late in the year.

By April, 1760, General Lévis had recruited 7,000 men and was ready to try to recapture Quebec. One of his biggest problems was to transport this large force down the St. Lawrence River without being detected. He managed this, somehow or other, and landed at Cap Rouge (where the Quebec Bridge is), on a wild, rainy night.

Unfortunately for Lévis, at this moment one of his men fell overboard, but saved himself by grabbing a large piece of floating ice. A British sloop, patrolling off Quebec, heard the man's cries and picked him up. He was brought before General Murray, commander of the garrison at Quebec, at three in the morning. He told the general everything. Murray had just enough time to blow up an ammunition dump at Ste. Foy, so that it would not fall into Lévis' hands, and to establish a line of defense outside the city walls.

The battle of Ste. Foy was fought on April 28, 1760, and was one of the bloodiest in Canadian history. Murray was beaten and had to return to Quebec. Each side lost 1,000 men. Now it was a question of time. Murray hoped he could hold on until British reinforcements could get up the St. Lawrence. Lévis knew he had to bombard the city into submission before that happened. Murray was the victor eventually, because British ships began to arrive on May 10, before Lévis was able to break through. The French had to return to Montreal to get ready to fight again.

Other Events on April 28:

1726 Charles Le Moyne was made the first governor of the French fort at Niagara.

1817 The Rush-Bagot Treaty was signed. Britain and the States agreed not to have guns or ships of war on the frontier waters of the Great Lakes.

The steamer *Ontario*, the first on the Great Lakes, made the round trip between Lewiston and Ogdensburg in ten days.

1967 Expo '67 opened.

"Personal Approach" Fails

Benjamin Franklin (1706-1790)

When the American Revolutionary War began in 1775, George Washington and the newly-formed Congress of the United States made two mistakes. The first was a military one. Instead of capturing Nova Scotia (which was largely sympathetic to the American cause) and preventing British reinforcements from getting up the St. Lawrence to Montreal and Quebec, the Americans decided to make simultaneous attacks on the two cities. Montreal fell relatively easily, but Arnold failed to capture Quebec.

The other mistake the Americans made was one of politics, or perhaps "public relations." Although they invited Canada and Nova Scotia to join the union, they did not send emissaries soon enough to try personal sales appeals. It was April, 1776, before Benjamin Franklin led a carefully chosen delegation to Montreal, which had already been captured. It arrived on April 29, and included Charles Carroll and his cousin John, two eminent Catholics who were supposed to persuade Roman Catholic leaders in Quebec that their church would have as much freedom in an American State as it had under British rule. Canadian church leaders were not impressed. In fact, they disciplined a Montreal priest who allowed John Carroll to celebrate mass.

There were a number of American businessmen living in Montreal who had gone there from New York when Britain took Canada from France. They were heartily disliked by Governor Murray, the first British military governor of Quebec. He called them "licentious fanatics trading here." They, and some of the Canadian businessmen in Montreal, gave the Franklin commission a warm welcome, but generally speaking, the reception from most people was cold.

The Americans brought a good supply of "Continental dollars" to pay their bills, but even the cab drivers refused to accept them.

The expression "not worth a continental damn", heard even today, originated from the Continental dollars.

The Franklin delegation was too late. One week after it arrived in Montreal, British warships began arriving at Quebec. When the Americans fled from there, Franklin led his party back to Philadelphia for the signing of the Declaration of Independence. It was then that Franklin made his famous quip. One of the signers said: "We must all hang together." Franklin quickly added: "Or we shall all hang singly."

Other Events on April 29:

1627　The Company of the One Hundred Associates was established to develop Canada.

1742　Pierre de la Vérendrye sent two of his sons to try to find the route to the Pacific.

1891　The first Canadian Pacific Steamship *Empress of India* arrived at Vancouver from Yokohama. Mail arrived in New York three and a half days later. This finally established the short route to "Cathay" for which explorers had been searching since the days of John Cabot.

Louisiana Sold to U.S.

One story that isn't well known is that Napoleon planned to recapture Canada for France. He made himself dictator of France in 1799, on the pretext of "saving the Revolution," but then went on to conquer most of Europe.

Napoleon's plan to recapture Canada was inspired by Sir Alexander Mackenzie, who in 1793 became the first man to cross the continent from the Atlantic to the Pacific. Mackenzie wrote a book about his trip which Napoleon had translated into French to help him plan his campaign.

His first step was to regain Louisiana. France had owned the Mississippi Valley all the way to the Gulf of Mexico but had handed over this territory to Spain before signing the Treaty of Paris in 1763 so that Britain would not acquire it.

In 1800, Napoleon regained Louisiana from Spain as part of the secret treaty of San Ildefonso. He planned to move his troops up the Mississippi from the Gulf of Mexico. In order to do this, he sent a large navy and army to recapture the former French colony of Haiti, which had been lost in a rebellion led by a mighty black warrior, Toussaint L'Ouverture. This was to be the base for the attack up the Mississippi, led by Napoleon's favourite general, Count Bernadotte. His campaign was defeated by the same elements that beat the Scotsmen who wanted to establish a colony in Panama and make it New Scotland. The natives and the mosquitoes were too fierce. They killed 60,000 French troops in two years!

In the meantime, the British fleet had moved powerful units to the West Indies, and Napoleon knew that it would be too risky to try to move an army to the mouth of the Mississippi. He abandoned the plan to recapture Canada, and sold Louisiana on April 30, 1803, to the United States for $27 million. The actual area included all the territory between the Mississippi and the Rocky Mountains. Spain still retained claims on the Pacific coast as far north as Oregon, which had an important bearing on the future development of British Columbia.

Other Events on April 30:

1630 Charles La Tour and his son received 4,500 square miles of Nova Scotia from William Alexander.

1658 The Ville Marie school, the first in Montreal, opened in a stable.

1745 A force from New England under Sir William Pepperell began the siege of Louisburg.

1835 Sir Francis Bond Head was appointed Lieutenant-Governor of Upper Canada.

1852 A delegation from Canada and the Maritimes met with the Earl of Derby, Prime Minister of Britain, to discuss the possibility of building railways.

1864 Chilcotin Indians massacred road builders in British Columbia.
      Prince Edward Island's Legislature authorized a delegation to discuss the proposed maritime union.

1890 Lethbridge *News* reported a battle between Crees and Blackfoot Indians.

1960 The centennial of the Queen's Own Rifles of Canada was celebrated.

Charles Hatfield "Makes" Rain – and $5,000

There has been a good deal of controversy in recent years about making rain artificially. An inch of rain on the prairies, when it is needed, is worth a million dollars. It can make all the difference between a good or bad wheat crop, and also in providing better feed for beef cattle.

A most colorful and exciting experiment was conducted in Alberta in 1921. The Medicine Hat United Agricultural Association decided that a "rain-maker" would be good crop insurance, and signed up Charles M. Hatfield of California, who was said to be "a rain-making wizard." The contract ran from May 1 to August 1, and gave Hatfield the credit for half the rain that fell during the period, at a rate of $4,000 per inch. The maximum he could be paid was $8,000.

Hatfield did not claim to be able to make rain, but said he could offer nature certain aids. Eight thousand farmers each subscribed one dollar to see him do it. The area was within a 100-mile radius of Chappice Lake, which is about 20 miles northeast of Medicine Hat. Gauges for measuring the rainfall were distributed at intervals of 50 miles.

What excitement there was when Hatfield built a 20-foot tower by the lake! It had an open vat on top, into which he poured secret chemicals, like a witch's brew. People watched anxiously, or placed bets to see if distant clouds would be drawn into the area. Nothing happened for three days, and then came nearly half an inch of beautiful rain! Two days later even more rain fell, and again on May 11th. Now the farmers were becoming apprehensive! Let's not overdo this thing! Too much would be almost as bad as too little. Some of them asked Hatfield to quit for a while.

The story was different in June. Hatfield said that chinook winds were blowing the clouds away. People began to watch him with field glasses to make sure that he was on the job. Prayer meetings were held for rain, and

a whole inch fell towards the end of the month. Even the rain-maker seemed greatly relieved!

The story was the same in July when the temperature was often 90 degrees in the shade. Then, near the end of the month, came one of those million-dollar rains, all the way from Winnipeg to the Rockies. The people of Medicine Hat were paying for it, but they didn't mind. In fact, they tried to get Hatfield to come back the next year but he had had enough. He was so relieved when the rain came in July that he would not accept more than $5,000 for his services. Swift Current offered him $10,000 to operate there the next year, but he rejected it.

In Ontario, where rain falls more easily, the chief of the Dominion Meteorological Bureau described the experiment as "the most absurd thing ever perpetrated in the West."

The average rainfall for May, June and July in the Medicine Hat area had been 6.22 inches for 37 years! Still, who can be sure what would have happened in the summer of 1921 if Hatfield had not been there?

Other Events on May 1:

1822   A general hospital opened at Montreal to accommodate eighty patients.

1885   Ottawa was the second city in Canada to have electric lights.

1888   Lord Stanley (donor of the Stanley Cup) was made governor-general.

1896   Sir Charles Tupper became prime minister.

1909   Prohibition came into effect in Ontario.

1919   The Winnipeg general strike began.

1963   The Quebec government took over eleven private power companies.

1965   The United States consulate was bombed in Montreal.

His Majesty receives traditional gifts, 1939

Hudson's Bay Company Granted Charter

On May 2, 1670, King Charles II granted a charter to the "Merchant Adventurers of England trading into Hudson's Bay," which came to be known as the Hudson's Bay Company. It was a momentous charter in the history of Canada.

The head of the company was the king's cousin, Prince Rupert, who rated in warfare as Bobby Hull and Gordie Howe do in hockey. He would go into battle clad in scarlet, adorned with silver lace, and mounted on a black Arabian charger. He was also a good mathematician, understood chemistry and made gunpowder. The trading area granted to the Hudson's Bay Company was known as Rupert's Land, which extended from Labrador to the Rocky Mountains (although the Rockies had not then been seen by white men).

The company was given absolute power to control the fur trade, rule the inhabitants, make laws and even go to war. Its duties included finding the Northwest Passage to China, gold, silver and anything precious. It was not required to bring in settlers, or try to convert Indians to Christianity, as was the Company of New France. In fact, 100 years passed before a clergyman went to the trading posts.

There was a condition that if the king visited the area he must be given two black elks and two black beaver skins. These were given to King George VI and Queen Elizabeth when they visited Winnipeg in 1939.

The company nearly always made a good profit, sometimes as high as 200 percent in a single year, but it had its lean years as well, especially when it was in competition with the Northwest Company, a rivalry that came close to civil war.

The activities of the company were also challenged by France. In October, only a few months after it had been formed, Intendant Talon sent a mission to Hudson Bay where the Le Moyne brothers of Montreal captured the Hudson's Bay Company posts. The most famous Le Moyne of them all, Iberville, won the biggest naval victory in French history in Hudson Bay.

Despite the opposition, the Hudson's Bay Company was a major force in the development of Canada.

Other Events on May 2:

1864 The Merchants' Bank of Halifax opened (now absorbed in Royal Bank of Canada).

1881 C.P.R. syndicate broke ground for the transcontinental railway at Fort William, Ontario.

1882 The House of Commons passed a Civil Service Bill.

1945 Fighting ended in Italy in World War II.

1961 His Excellency Habib Bourguiba, President of Tunisia, visited Ottawa.

1962 The Canadian dollar was pegged at 92.5 cents.

Poundmaker Wins Battle

Otter versus Poundmaker sounds like a fight between two Indians. Poundmaker was an Indian, Chief of the Crees, but Otter was a colonel in the British army, serving with General Middleton in the Northwest Rebellion of 1885. Pleased with himself because he had relieved Battleford while his general was being pushed around by Gabriel Dumont and his Métis, Otter thought it would be a good move to attack Poundmaker, Riel's ally. He would try to defeat Poundmaker before he could join forces with Big Bear, and go on to help Louis Riel at Batoche. Riel was pleading with both to get there in a hurry.

Instead of having his plan approved by General Middleton, Otter wired Governor Dewdney and was given his permission. He began his march from Battleford on the afternoon of May 1, with 325 men, including 75 members of the Northwest Mounted Police.

On the moonlit night of May 3, 1885, the force was spotted by an Indian scout. There was a race for the top of Cut Knife Hill and the Mounties got there first. If Otter had attacked then, while the Indians were disorganized, he might have won his objective

Colonel Otter

easily. Instead, he decided to station his infantry on the hill first, and this gave Poundmaker time to conceal his men in fissures on the slope, behind trees and shrubs. Otter's force was surrounded. The Gatling gun and the seven-pounders which the American army had provided fired aimlessly into the night. The hidden Indians would hold up bonnets or rags on sticks and then shoot the soldiers who exposed themselves to fire.

Although the Indians were outnumbered three-to-two, the fighting went on for seven hours. Otter's men were exhausted. The gun-carriages had broken down. Reluctantly, Otter retreated to Battleford.

Father Cochin, who had been a prisoner in Poundmaker's camp, said later that if Poundmaker had not restrained his Indians, Otter's force would have been slaughtered. It is believed that the great Indian leader knew the rebellion would be crushed soon, and thought there was no point in being charged with the slaughter of government troops at Cut Knife Hill.

Other Events on May 3:

1631 Captain Thomas James of Bristol began his voyage to Hudson Bay.

1776 Americans tried to set fire to ships at Quebec.

Chief Poundmaker

Landing of the Loyalists, 1783

Loyalists Seek New Home

There are many Canadians today who are proud to be descendants of the United Empire Loyalists. They were the people who lived in the United States until the American Revolutionary War led to the break with Britain. Remaining loyal to Britain, they decided to move to Canada, many of them giving up beautiful homes.

Some of them went back to Britain but found it difficult to fit in there. An exception was the famous Boston painter Copley, whose son became Lord Chancellor as Baron Lyndhurst. Another was Benjamin Thompson, who went to live in Germany where he became Minister of War. He created the English Garden in Munich and was eventually made a member of the Institute of France, a fellow member with Napoleon.

George M. Wrong in his excellent history, *The Canadians*, makes an interesting point. When the American Revolutionary War broke out, there were people in Britain and Canada who favored the American cause, and spoke out for it. They were not punished.

In the United States, however, those who were against the war were given rough treatment. When the British evacuated Charleston, twenty-four Loyalists were executed. Many more suffered the same fate.

Although Sir Guy Carleton did not finish evacuating New York until November, 1783, the Loyalists began crossing to Canada in 1782. Gradually the trickle built up into a flood. On May 4, 1783, 471 families from New York landed at Shelburne, Nova Scotia. Eventually, 35,000 Loyalists settled in the Maritime Provinces. Many others went to Upper Canada and turned the scale against Canada's being a predominantly French country.

By 1785, Shelburne had received so many Loyalists that it became a bigger city than Halifax. The British government supplied food and other needs, but when this aid stopped, Shelburne's growth collapsed.

By May 18, 1783, more than 7,000 Loyalists had landed at Saint John. They resolved to make it a greater seaport than New York. It didn't work out that way, but the Saint John River, 400 miles long, provided forest and farmland for settlement. Saint John is known as the "Loyalist City" today.

Another 20,000 Loyalists sailed all the way up the St. Lawrence to Quebec or Montreal, and then made their way to Upper Canada. Others escaped from New York and crossed into the Niagara area.

The Americans never honored the agreement to repay the Loyalists for their losses. Britain offered partial reparation but payments did not begin until 1790. Until then, the Loyalists in Canada went through some very hard times. Nova Scotia, in particular, was called "Nova Scarcity."

Other Events on May 4:

1639 Madame de La Peltrie and others sailed from Dieppe to Quebec:

1804 Selkirk brought colonists from Isle of Mull, Scotland, to settle at Baldoon, near Chatham, Ontario.

1859 Parliament prorogued. Offices were moved from Toronto to Quebec.

Siege of Quebec Begins

Wolfe choosing his battleground, 1759

Although Quebec did not surrender to Wolfe's forces until September 18, 1759, after the battle on the Plains of Abraham on September 13, the campaign began on May 5. When Wolfe sailed from England in February, with twenty-two warships, as well as frigates and sloops of war, he went to Halifax and stayed there because Louisburg harbor was closed by ice. Work began on the assembling of an army. Most of the units had been engaged in the attack on Louisburg the previous year. When the troops were assembled and counted, there were only 9,000 men. The battle plan called for 12,000. Wolfe refused to be discouraged and wrote to Prime Minister Pitt: "If valour can make amends for lack of numbers, we shall probably succeed."

It was an optimistic point of view, because Montcalm had 15,000 regulars and 1,000 militia. Quebec was supposed to be an impregnable fortress, and under those conditions the attacking force should be far greater than the defenders.

Then came another blow. On May 5, Captain Durell sailed from Halifax with a number of warships to block the St. Lawrence. The plan was to prevent reinforcements arriving from France. Durell was too late. Twenty-three French transports under Admiral Bougainville had already made their way up the river to Quebec.

Durell took his ships up the river after them until they arrived at Isle-aux-Coudres, 60 miles below Quebec. Montcalm had wanted to fortify the island, but had been over-ruled by Governor Vaudreuil, who, with Intendant Bigot, was his biggest handicap. The opportunity to establish a base there was seized by Colonel Guy Carleton, later to play a greater part in the development of Canada as Lord Dorchester. He was in charge of the troops in the Durell expedition.

There were many notable players in the drama of Quebec. Cook, who became an explorer of the Pacific coast, was a "Master" or navigating officer of Wolfe's armada, and guided it safely through the almost uncharted waters of the St. Lawrence during May and June. Sometimes the armada stretched for miles as it made its way up the river. It was one of the greatest feats of navigation of all time, as not a ship was wrecked. The French were dumbfounded when they saw the British ships sail through "the traverse" where they would seldom risk a ship of their own.

Other Events on May 5:

1660 Bishop Laval announced that he would excommunicate people caught selling liquor to the Indians.

1665 Twelve horses were brought to Quebec. The Indians called them "the moose from France."

1789 Captain Martinez claimed Nootka Sound, British Columbia, for Spain.

1813 Sir James Yeo arrived at Quebec with 450 seamen. He was made Commodore of the Royal Navy on Lake Ontario.

1814 Yeo attacked Oswego, New York, with 1,100 men.

1859 New Westminster was made capital of British Columbia. (Vancouver Island was a separate colony.)

1929 C.N.R. radio operators established two-way telephone links from trains.

Sitting Bull

Sioux Enter Canada

Every American knows the story of "Custer's last stand" when he and 264 men of the United States Seventh Cavalry were wiped out by Chief Sitting Bull and his Sioux warriors. How many Canadians know its sequel? It was a tense situation in western Canada when Sitting Bull crossed the border on May 6, 1877, with 500 of his braves, 1,000 squaws and 3,500 horses. Gradually others joined them until they numbered 4,000, armed with the latest-type rifles captured from the defeated Americans. They settled at Wood Mountain, now the Cypress Hills Provincial Park, on the Saskatchewan-Alberta border.

When Major Walsh of the Northwest Mounted Police made his first visit to Sitting Bull's camp, he had 150 scarlet-coated mounties with him. As the two leaders talked, the Sioux rode around the camp carrying their rifles. They had defeated a far larger force of United States Cavalry. Why

not attack 150 men of the Mounted Police? If they had done so, they might have been joined by the Blackfoot and the Cree Indians in an Indian war to massacre every white man in western Canada.

There was another danger. These two tribes might resent the Sioux' having come into their hunting grounds, and go to war against them.

Major Walsh tried to persuade Sitting Bull to return to the United States. The Americans had promised to forgive the attack on General Custer and provide them with a reservation. Sitting Bull would not go. He said that the Sioux had been British subjects in the past and had been promised safety in the "Great Mother's land."

The American government even sent General Terry to negotiate with Sitting Bull, who refused to talk to him at a colorful conference attended by a group of nervous American newspapermen. Who wouldn't be nervous watching a handful of Mounties guard 4,000 armed Indians?

The explosive situation continued for four years. On one occasion Sitting Bull pulled a knife on Major Walsh, who grabbed him by the shoulders and the seat of his pants and threw him out of the tent. The Sioux warriors only watched.

Starvation finally drove the Sioux back to the States in 1881. W. G. Hardy in *From Sea Unto Sea* says: "A brave and free people had been forced into surrender, not by battle or by persuasion, but by the shabbiest of all tricks, denial of food for men, women and children."

Other Events on May 6:

1708 Bishop Laval died.

1720 The first meeting of the Council of Nova Scotia was held.

1776 Sir Guy Carleton drove the American forces from Quebec.

1777 General Burgoyne arrived at Quebec to succeed Carleton.

1910 King Edward VII died. He was succeeded by George V.

Pontiac Plans Massacre

Sitting Bull was dangerous, as recounted in yesterday's story, but an Indian Chief who did far more actual damage was Pontiac in 1763. Before his uprising was brought under control, more than 2,000 British, including women and children, had been killed.

Many Indians in what is now western Ontario did not like Britain's taking Canada from France. When the red-coated soldiers occupied the French forts at Detroit and Michilimackinac, between Lakes Huron and Michigan, they were led to believe that the King of France would soon drive them out again.

Pontiac was chief of the Ottawas who lived near Detroit. At a secret meeting he vowed to drive the British "off the face of the earth." Fortunately, Major Gladwyn, who was in charge of the fort at Detroit, was told of Pontiac's boast.

Pontiac, professing undying friendship for the British, asked for a peace conference. He and 300 followers arrived at Detroit on May 7, 1763, and were received in the fort. Pontiac's followers included a number of squaws who concealed weapons under their blankets.

The custom was that in a conference of this kind, the Indian chief would offer the white leader a belt of wampum. Pontiac had arranged that when he stood up to offer the belt, the Indians would grab their concealed weapons and begin the massacre.

However, Gladwyn was prepared for the masquerade. He pretended to go along with the peace conference, but took obvious precautions to deal with any trouble that might occur. When Pontiac looked around he saw that an uprising would have had no chance to succeed. He gave no signal.

The conference proceeded as though it were genuine, and the Indians left with promises of goodwill and other friendly meetings in the future. Soon after they were out of the fort they surrounded it and kept it

Pontiac meets Gladwyn, 1763

under siege for more than a year until British reinforcements arrived. This was only one of a number of manoeuvers organized by the wily Pontiac.

Other Events on May 7:

1586   John Davis began his second voyage to Baffin Land.

1792   Lower Canada was divided into twenty-seven electoral districts with fifty members.

1865   The Canadian Land and Immigration Company of London bought ten townships in Upper Canada, settling Haliburton and Minden.

1866   St. Francis Xavier University at Antigonish, Nova Scotia, received its charter.

1873   Joseph Howe was appointed Lieutenant-Governor of Nova Scotia.

1907   The Vancouver Stock Exchange was incorporated.

1945   Germany surrendered unconditionally in World War II.

1953   Prime Minister St. Laurent paid an official visit to the United States.

American Plan Includes Acquisition of Canada

There have been a number of occasions when the United States nearly took possession of Canada. One of them was in 1782 when negotiations were taking place to end the American Revolutionary War.

Britain had been fighting France and Spain in Europe, as well as the Americans overseas, and was greatly tempted to end the war as quickly as possible. The United States had obtained a secret document, prepared by the French ambassador in Washington, stating that France would oppose American claims to fishing rights in Canadian waters. It was also clear that Spain, which owned Florida and the lands west of the Mississippi, would oppose American expansion to the south and west. The Americans thus had every reason to suspect the future intentions of their allies, and were willing to conclude a separate peace with Britain.

Benjamin Franklin, American ambassador in Paris, was told to try to make a deal with Britain as quickly as possible. Lord Shelburne, then Colonial Secretary, sent Richard Oswald to Paris to negotiate with Franklin. Oswald did not even know the geography of North America, and was no match for a wily trader like Franklin, who persuaded him that the surrender of Canada was a logical part of the peace plan. Oswald sent the proposal to Shelburne, who is believed to have shown it to the King, but kept it from the members of the cabinet.

Fortunately, Charles Fox who was Secretary for Foreign Affairs, sent his own agent to Paris on May 8 to see what was going on. He learned about the proposal to give up Canada and rushed the information back to Fox. There was a row in the cabinet during which Prime Minister Rockingham died, and Shelburne became Prime Minister. He immediately got rid of Fox and it looked as though the Canada deal would go through.

Just then, Britain received some favorable news from Admiral Rodney in the West Indies: he had beaten the French fleet there. He wrote: "In two years I have taken two Spanish, one French, and one Dutch admiral." This, and the obvious conflict between the United States, France and Spain, strengthened Britain's hand at the conference table. When the Treaty of Paris was finally signed in September 1783, Canada remained a British possession.

Other Events on May 8:

1604   Champlain arrived at the mouth of the Lahave River, Nova Scotia.

1620   Champlain sailed for Canada, bringing his young wife with him (see November 3).

1642   Maisonneuve and colonists left Quebec to found Montreal.

1756   Indians attacked Mahone Bay, Nova Scotia, as a reprisal for the expulsion of the Acadians (see December 9).

1818   Samuel Leonard Tilley was born at Gagetown, New Brunswick.

1849   Joseph Howe wrote his famous letter to the British North America League concerning Confederation.

1858   John Brown, American abolitionist, held a convention at Chatham, Ontario.

1871   New Brunswick adopted a school system similar to Ontario's; this led to rioting.

1882   Northwest Territories were divided into four districts: Alberta, Saskatchewan, Assiniboia, and Athabaska.

1906   The University of Alberta at Edmonton received its charter.

1915   The War Purchasing Board was appointed.

1945   The Armistice, ending the Second World War with Germany, was signed.

Quebec Saved by Ships

Britain owes her position as a world power to the Royal Navy. What would have happened if it had not been for the decisive victories of Drake, Rodney, Howe and Nelson at crucial periods in world history?

Canadian independence is due in large measure to actions fought by the Royal Navy, or its arriving in the nick of time to remedy a desperate situation. Yesterday's story told how Rodney's victory was a factor in Britain's decision not to give Canada to the United States in 1783. Spain might have taken possession of British Columbia in 1790, if it had not been for Admiral Howe. Many other famous British seamen, including Cook and Vancouver, played their parts.

One of the most dramatic scenes took place on May 9, 1760. Quebec had fallen to Wolfe in September, 1759, but now General Lévis (see April 28) had struck back. General Murray, defeated in the Battle of Ste. Foy, had withdrawn his troops into the fortress and was hanging on for dear life. It was simply a matter of time. Both Murray and Lévis were hoping for help from the sea. The ice was melting in the St. Lawrence. Would Britain or France get ships up the river first?

At noon, on May 9, the tall sails of a frigate could be seen rounding the Island of Orleans. Both sides waited, fingers crossed. A broad red pennant fluttered to the masthead, and a salute was fired. It was the British ship *Lowestoft*.

General Lévis, who had been hoping for reinforcements from France, decided to launch his final assault. The arrival of the *Lowestoft* was not serious in itself. One ship would not make any difference between victory and defeat, but others were probably following. He gave orders to his artillery to fire all the ammunition they had. The walls of Quebec began to crumble after three days of the bombardment, and the time had come for an assault by the troops.

At that moment three more British ships rounded the Island of Orleans. General Lévis

Hon. James Murray (1721-1794)

knew that more were following. The battle was over and he ordered his men to retreat to Montreal, but to be ready to fight again. Many of them were *habitants* who were anxious only to return to their farms. Hence, many deserted Lévis.

Much the same thing happened on May 6, 1776. While the Americans were besieging Quebec, three British warships appeared. Following that, the invaders were singing the old song: "I'll be here just three more seconds, and after that I'll be gone."

Other Events on May 9:

1783 Sir Guy Carleton arrived at New York to evacuate British forces and Loyalists.

1853 The British Parliament approved of Canada's right to dispose of clergy reserves.

1916 General Byng succeeded General Alderson as commander of Canadian forces.

1926 Admiral Byrd and Floyd Bennett flew over the North Pole.

Allen's Green Mountain Boys Attack Ticonderoga

If the name "Ethan Allen and His Green Mountain Boys" appeared in the newspapers today, it would look like an advertisement for a group of folk-singers. Ethan Allen performed in the American Revolutionary War in the same way as General George Patton did in World War II. He was the militia commander in Vermont who, loving to take his soldiers on daring sweeps into enemy territory, could not be restrained by superior officers.

As soon as possible after war began in the spring of 1775, Ethan Allen led his leatherstockings to the Lake Champlain area where the British had garrisons at Ticonderoga and Crown Point. These garrisons were supposed to block the route from New York to Montreal, but their defenses had been neglected. The British in Canada had not expected to go to war with their fellow-countrymen south of the border.

When Ethan Allen led his force of 200 men (including Benedict Arnold) to Ticonderoga on May 10, everyone in the fort was asleep. Allen called on it to surrender and finally aroused the commanding officer, who asked him by what authority he was making such a demand. Allen is quoted in history books as having replied: "In the name of the great Jehovah and the Continental Congress." There is a more realistic school of thought which believes his actual words were, "You damned old rat, come down from there."

Crown Point and then Fort St. John fell as easily. The Americans took three British forts in a space of 125 miles without firing a shot. The easy victories encouraged the Americans to believe that Montreal and Quebec could be taken with little opposition. General Arnold persuaded George Washington to adopt that strategy, rather than try to capture Nova Scotia and close off the St. Lawrence to British reinforcements. This was an unfortunate decision for the Americans, because British sea power did relieve Quebec and force the invaders to retreat.

Other Events on May 10:

1534 Jacques Cartier arrived at Cape Bonavista, Newfoundland, on his first voyage to Canada.

1632 Isaac de Razilly was made Lieutenant-Governor of Acadia with instructions to drive out the British.

1746 Admiral La Jonquière sailed from La Rochelle to capture Acadia.

1783 A large group of United Empire Loyalists arrived at Saint John, New Brunswick (see May 18).

1796 Edward, Duke of Kent (father of Queen Victoria), was made commander of the garrison at Halifax.

1844 The capital of Canada was moved from Kingston to Montreal.

1853 The steamer *Genova* arrived at Quebec, beginning a regular fourteen day service between Montreal and Liverpool.

1870 British Columbia delegates left for Ottawa to discuss terms for entering Confederation.

1886 W. S. Fielding introduced a resolution in the Nova Scotia Legislature asking for an end to Confederation.

1921 Canada made a preferential tariff agreement with the West Indies.

1963 Prime Minister Pearson conferred with President Kennedy at Hyannis Port. It was announced that the former home of F. D. Roosevelt on Campobello Island, New Brunswick, would be shared by Canada and the United States for public purposes.

More Sail to Port Royal

The first permanent settlement in Canada by white men was at Annapolis Royal, Nova Scotia. It was discovered by Champlain in 1604, when he made his first voyage to Canada with de Monts and Pontgravé. They called it Port Royal, and so it remained for many turbulent years, sometimes in the possession of the French, sometimes occupied by Britain.

One of the most delightful stories about Port Royal is that of the creation of the "Order of the Good Time," in the winter of 1606-1607. De Monts had returned to France in 1605, and with the help of Sieur de Poutrincourt, fitted out a second expedition which sailed from La Rochelle on May 11, 1606.

Champlain organized the "Order of the Good Time," the first social club in North America. Each of the fifteen members of the colony took his turn at being the Grand Master of the day and wore the insignia of office. At dinner he led the way to the table, at the head of the procession of members.

It became a point of honor with each member to try to outdo the others in providing the finest possible dinners. The party made friends with the Indians and went hunting and fishing. The dinner table groaned with the luxuries of the forest and streams. There were roasts of moose, caribou, beaver, otter, bears, porcupine and rabbits. For poultry, they had wild ducks, geese and ruffled grouse. Seafood was usually represented by salmon, trout, bass and cod, caught through the ice.

The Indian chiefs were invited to the feasts while warriors, squaws and children crouched in the corners of the dining hall where they would be given biscuits and bread which were novel treats for them.

One of the members of the group was Marc Lescarbot, who might be called Canada's first historian. He wrote: "Whatever our gourmands at home may think, we found as good

The Order preparing for a "meeting"

cheer at Port Royal as they at their Rue Aux Ours in Paris, and that, too, at a cheaper rate."

Other Events on May 11:

1615   Captain Richard Whitbourne was appointed commissioner to establish order in Newfoundland.

1676   Begging without the permission of a priest was prohibited in Montreal.

1690   Port Royal surrendered to Sir William Phips.

1717   Commercial exchange began in Montreal when merchants were given permission to hold meetings.

1760   Lévis attacked Quebec with a heavy artillery barrage.

1839   The College of Physicians and Surgeons was established in Upper Canada.

1870   Canada paid Hudson's Bay Company $1,500,000 for its territory.

1880   Sir Alexander Galt was appointed first Canadian High Commissioner to Britain.

1938   Lord Tweedsmuir visited Val Marie, Saskatchewan (see February 21).

Government Passes Manitoba Act

Manitoba owes its name to two controversial characters, Thomas Spence and Louis Riel. If it had not been for them, Manitoba would have been called "Assiniboia" and included in the Northwest Territories.

When the federal government, in 1869, took over the territory that had been governed by the Hudson's Bay Company, Louis Riel occupied Fort Garry and established a provisional government. Sir John A. Macdonald sent Donald A. Smith to negotiate with Riel (see January 19) who stipulated that part of the area should be made a province and called Manitoba, not Assiniboia. He got the name Manitoba from Thomas Spence who had created a somewhat comic "Republic of Manitoba" in 1868 (see May 31).

Delegates from the provisional government were sent to Ottawa, but two of them, Richot and Alfred Scott, were arrested when they arrived. Ottawa was seething over the execution of Thomas Scott. Later, Richot and Scott were released and "received but not recognized" by Prime Minister Macdonald, Joseph Howe, and George Etienne Cartier.

Their discussions led to the Manitoba Act being prepared and passed by Parliament on May 12, 1870. It came into effect on July 15. Manitoba was to be a new province with a legislative council and assembly, a constitution similar to the other provinces, and representation in the federal parliament.

Although Ottawa retained control over "public lands" to be used for railway building and settlement, a land grant of 1,400 million acres was kept in reserve for the children of half-breed families. This helped to solve the problem that had started the Riel uprising.

The Manitoba Act also included official use of the French language, and a guarantee of the continuation of educational rights of the various denominations at the time of union. Twenty years later this led to one of the hottest issues in Canadian political history: the Manitoba separate schools question.

When Manitoba became a province, a census was taken which showed its population to be 11,963 of whom 558 were Indians, 5,757 Métis, 4,083 English half-breeds, and 1,565 whites. Catholics numbered 6,247 and Protestants 5,716.

Manitoba wasn't nearly as big then as it is now. In relation to surrounding territory, it looked like a postage stamp until 1884 when the boundary was extended north to Hudson Bay.

Other Events on May 12:

1501 Gaspar Corte Real sailed from Lisbon to Conception Bay, Newfoundland.

1628 Charles La Tour was made a baronet of Nova Scotia (see October 18).

1678 The King of France authorized La Salle to build forts down the Mississippi to the Gulf of Mexico.

1781 The Chippewas ceded the Island of Michilimackinac to George III for £5,000 (pounds).

1846 An address to Queen Victoria asked for better trade arrangements with the United States.

1870 Manitoba, Rupert's Land, and Northwest Territories were established by a Dominion statute (proclaimed July 15).

1874 Prince Edward Island Railway opened.

1915 The Roblin government in Manitoba resigned following corruption charges.

1922 The Royal Canadian Navy was reduced to only three small ships on each coast.

1937 The coronation of King George VI took place.

1943 Fighting ended in North Africa when the Germans surrendered Tunisia.

J. Ward Launches Steamer

Tibbets' Reindeer, *c. 1848*

There were some weird and wonderful ships operating in the East, especially on the mighty Saint John River.

The United Empire Loyalists who settled along its shores were enterprising people. John Ward, a member of the large group of Loyalists who landed at Saint John in 1783, put the first steamer on the river on May 13, 1816. He obtained an exclusive charter for ten years, and operated between Saint John and Fredericton. The first ship he built was the *General Smyth*. It could carry sixty passengers at a speed of six knots and was described as a "floating palace."

As John Ward had an exclusive steamship contract, William Peters, a farmer up the river, invented a way to compete without using steam. He thought steam was unsafe anyway, as boilers could blow up! He built a paddle-wheeler 100 feet long with a large circular platform on the deck. In the centre of the platform was a capstan from which twelve bars projected. Peters hitched a strong horse to each of the bars and shouted, "giddy-up." The horses trotted around the platform, turning the capstan, which was connected with the paddle-wheel, and away they went!

This was a real 12-horsepower vessel! As it moved away from shore, some prankster shouted, "whoa!" The horses stopped. Every time Peters got the horses started, someone would yell "whoa", and progress was mighty slow. Peters tried stuffing the horses' ears with rags but they wouldn't stay there. Finally he gave up. He took the horse-boat to Grand Lake, beached it, and used it as a hotel for lumberjacks! One of the most remarkable craft on the Saint John River was the *Reindeer*, built by Benjamin Franklin Tibbets. He had a scientific turn of mind and was apprenticed to a watchmaker. His favorite hobby was to sit by the river and watch the steamers moving along. He noticed how steam escaped from the engines and decided that it should be recaptured and used again.

In order to gain some engineering training, he left his job with the watchmaker and went to the United States to work for engineering companies. While he was there, he read all the technical books he could and returned to Fredericton to build the world's first compound steam engine, which he put into the *Reindeer*. There were many skeptics and Tibbets had to prove his point. *Reindeer* was matched in a race to Woodstock against the fastest ship on the river, *Forest Queen*. It left *Forest Queen* far behind. Furthermore, *Reindeer* burned only four cords of wood to *Forest Queen's* nine! Tibbett's compound steam engine revolutionized steam navigation everywhere.

Other Events on May 13:

1604   De Monts named Port Mouton, Nova Scotia, because a sheep jumped overboard there. Now it is locally known as Port "Mootoon."

1707   Colonels March and Wainright sailed from Boston to attack Port Royal.

1724   A Royal edict ordered a stone wall to be built for the defense of Montreal.

1919   The Winnipeg general strike began.

1950   The Red River flood was at its height at Winnipeg; it covered 700 square miles and caused $27 million damage.

1954   President Eisenhower signed a bill approving the St. Lawrence Seaway agreement with Canada.

Henry IV Assassinated — Champlain Loses Friend

In this book so far, several stories have described the terrible tortures and massacres inflicted by the Indians. An impression might be given that Indian torture and cruelty was unique, but this was far from being the case. So-called civilized people could be just as barbarous.

On May 14, 1610, King Henry IV of France was assassinated by François Ravaillac, a religious fanatic. Ravaillac was put in prison, tortured by red-hot pincers, and had his legs crushed. While thousands of people, including princes and leaders of France, lined the streets or watched from windows, Ravaillac was drawn from the prison in a scavenger's cart and taken to the Place de Grève. Boiling lead was poured into his wounds, and then his body was torn apart by four white horses pulling in opposite directions. The people in the crowd scrambled to pick up pieces of his flesh. The house where he was born was burned to the ground, and his mother and father were exiled from France.

Champlain was in Paris at the time and was glad that the Indians had not seen what had happened. He had often told them that the French killed, but did not torture their enemies.

Henry IV's death was a serious loss to Champlain. He had made Champlain a royal geographer, and granted trading monopolies to Chauvin, Chaste, and de Monts. Just before he was assassinated, Champlain had given him a belt of porcupine quills, the head of a garfish, and two little birds, scarlet tanagers. The king was greatly pleased, and listened to Champlain's stories about Canada. Now no one of authority in France took any interest in Canada and the fur trade got out of control. Unauthorized traders rushed to Canada and obtained furs by plying the Indians with brandy. The situation became so bad that some of the Indian chiefs prohibited their braves from taking their furs to the French.

Champlain had to find someone to take control in France, and finally persuaded Charles de Bourbon, a prince who ranked next to the king. He was already governor of Normandy and Dauphiné from which he drew substantial revenue, but he agreed to become lieutenant-general for the king in Canada, provided that he was paid a salary, plus a share of the profits from the fur trade. It was a hard bargain, but Champlain was pleased because the prince made him a lieutenant of France. This position gave him authority to control the traders on the St. Lawrence River. Champlain was told to make Quebec his capital.

Other Events on May 14:

1501   Gaspar Corte Real left Portugal on his second voyage to Newfoundland but was not heard of again.

1747   A French fleet under La Jonquière was captured by the British.

1789   Martinez seized British ships at Nootka, British Columbia, which were flying Portuguese flags.

1793   General Ogilvie took the islands of St. Pierre-Miquelon and deported the inhabitants.

1825   Four hundred families from Ireland settled in Peterborough County, Ontario.

1850   The third session of the Third Parliament opened; it passed legislation to control bank notes, protect Indians, and establish schools.

1866   A railway was chartered to serve Windsor-Annapolis in Nova Scotia.

1880   Construction of the C.P.R. began in British Columbia.

1965   The Anglican and United Churches of Canada announced an agreement in principle on union.

Riel Surrenders

Although Poundmaker and Big Bear were still at large, Louis Riel surrendered to General Middleton on May 15, 1885, and the Northwest Rebellion was over. The decisive battle had been fought at Batoche two days before. Gabriel Dumont escaped across the border into the United States, but Riel wrote a note on an envelope and had two Métis take it to Middleton. It said: "I don't like war."

Middleton would not receive Riel until May 15, and then sent him to Medicine Hat on board the *Northcote* under close guard. From there he was taken to Regina by train and put in prison. Middleton later described his meeting with Riel in an official report: "I found him a mild-spoken and mild-looking man, with a short beard and an uneasy frightened look about his eyes, which gradually disappeared as I talked to him." He decided that Riel was sane enough to stand trial.

The *Northcote* played an important part in the battle. As it arrived with supplies at Middleton's jumping-off place for the assault on Batoche, it was supposed to blow its whistle as the signal for the attack to begin. The Métis had strung a cable across the river, and it ripped off the *Northcote's* funnels. The whistle came down with them and was not able to blow!

The Métis were hidden in pits, with breastworks of earth and logs. They were placed in such a way that Middleton's troops had to attack across the skyline and could be easily seen. Middleton moved cautiously for two days, though some of his officers were impatient for a more daring type of attack.

On the third day, Middleton decided to attack the rifle pits. He took the Gatling gun and a small force of men to one sector, and arranged for the main body of troops to attack from the south when they heard his guns firing. However, there was a strong wind and his gunfire could not be heard. Middleton galloped to the main position on his white

Lt. A. Howard behind a Gatling gun

horse to scold the Midlanders and Grenadiers for not having gone into action. This was exactly what Colonel Williams and Colonel Grassett wanted. When they saw Middleton galloping towards them, they ordered their troops to rush the rifle pits in a daring charge. The battle was over in a few minutes, as the Métis had run out of ammunition and were only firing small stones and nails.

Other Events on May 15:

1650   The Iroquois defeated the powerful Neutral Indians.

1760   Admiral Swanton and the British fleet arrived at Quebec, causing General Lévis to retreat to Montreal.

1789   The final report on payments to United Empire Loyalists for losses was made.

1814   United States troops burned Port Dover, Ontario.

U.S. Fishing Rights Extended—Canada Prospers

There have always been three important factors in relations between Canada and the United States: fisheries, transportation, and markets. Canada has usually held the trump cards in fisheries and transportation, while the United States bargaining power has come through its markets. The question of water-power and resources is rapidly becoming an important fourth factor.

In the past, Canada has been able to use fishing rights as a bargaining lever to gain better deals with the United States. One of the most profitable came into effect on May 16, 1855. It had been negotiated in Washington the previous year by Lord Elgin, in one of his last acts as Governor of British North America, and William L. Marcy, United States Secretary of State. The story of the negotiations, including bribery in New Brunswick and Nova Scotia, is vividly described by W. G. Hardy in *From Sea Unto Sea*.

Since 1818, American fishermen had not been allowed to fish within the three-mile limit. Their ships were seized if they were caught. In 1851, 300 American fishermen were drowned in a storm off Prince Edward Island when they would not risk going into Charlottetown for shelter.

Feelings were inflamed because Britain had sent thirteen ships to help patrol the Maritime fishing waters. One of them was a 74-gun frigate. There were a number of incidents that might have been fanned into war.

On the other hand there was depression in Canada. Britain had adopted free trade and removed the preferences on the import of Canadian wheat, flour and timber. In three years the value of property in Canadian towns had fallen 50 per cent, and three-quarters of the businessmen were said to be bankrupt. It was of the utmost importance for Canada to find markets in the United States for these other products.

Usually in these stories it has been the Americans like Benjamin Franklin who have been the expert negotiators. On this occasion, Lord Elgin took the lead. For tcn days he wined and dined members of the American Senate, telling them spicy stories until two in the morning. Finally at midnight, June 5-6, he and Marcy signed an agreement that was to last ten years, when either side might cancel it. Americans were given the right to fish within the three-mile limit, land anywhere to dry and cure their fish, and have free navigation in the St. Lawrence River. The States agreed to admit a wide range of Canadian products duty free.

Depression in Canada gave way to prosperity while the treaty lasted.

Other Events on May 16:

1613 Saussaye and Courtier arrived at Lahave, Nova Scotia, with settlers.

1619 Jens Munck of Denmark discovered Churchill River, Hudson Bay. He returned with only two members of his crew of sixty-five.

1677 Quebec Council fixed fur prices.

1760 Admiral Swanton destroyed a French fleet in the St. Lawrence.

1762 Settlers from New England arrived at Maugerville (pronounced Majorville), New Brunswick. It was the first British settlement in what is now New Brunswick.

1853 The Northern Railway opened from Toronto to Aurora, Ontario; it reached Barrie on October 11.

1865 Macdonald, Cartier, Brown, and Galt were presented to Queen Victoria.

1871 An Imperial Order-in-Council authorized British Columbia to join Canada.

1961 President Kennedy and his wife paid a state visit to Ottawa until May 18.

Edward To Head Forces

A number of members of the British Royal Family have been closely connected with Canada. Edward, Duke of Kent, was commander of the garrisons at Quebec and Halifax. King William IV was noted for his escapades in Halifax and other Canadian ports when he was a member of the Royal Navy. King Edward VII, as Prince of Wales, toured Canada in 1860 and laid the cornerstone for the first Parliament Buildings. Edward, Prince of Wales, later the Duke of Windsor, served with Canadian forces in World War I; he laid the cornerstone of the present Parliament Buildings and owned a ranch in Alberta. King George VI and Queen Elizabeth paid a memorable visit to Canada beginning on this day in 1939. Since then, the present Queen and Prince Philip have made several visits to Canada.

On May 17, 1799, Edward, Duke of Kent, was made Commander-in-Chief of British forces in North America, with headquarters in Halifax. He tried to make the old port into a fortress as powerful as Gibraltar. He also tried to establish a signal system from mountain top to mountain top all the way to Quebec, a route now used by microwave telephone. The visual signal system was never completed, because fog often obliterated the signals between Nova Scotia and New Brunswick!

The most romantic part of Edward's stay in Canada was when he was commander of the garrison at Quebec in 1791. He fell in love with Alphonsine Thérèse Julie de Montgenet de St. Laurent Baronne de Fortisson whom he called "Julie" for short. As he was a king's son and could not marry a commoner, they lived as man and wife for a number of years. Through "Julie," Edward made lasting friendships with many leading French-Canadian families. He quelled a racial riot in Quebec by shouting in his military voice: "Let me hear no more of these odious dis-

Prince Edward, Duke of Kent, at Halifax

tinctions of French and English. You are all His Britannic Majesty's beloved Canadian subjects."

When the time came for him to give up "Julie" so that he could marry someone of Royal blood and provide an heir to the throne, "Julie" retired into a convent in Belgium. The heir Edward produced was Queen Victoria.

Other Events on May 17:

1657 Jesuits set out to establish a mission in Iroquois country (see March 19).

1673 Joliet and Marquette began their exploration of the Mississippi.

1774 The Quebec Act was introduced to the House of Lords.

1849 The Hudson's Bay Company monopoly was broken.

1882 Queen's achieved university status.

1939 King George VI and Queen Elizabeth began their visit to Canada.

1949 The Canadian Government granted full recognition to Israel.

1963 The Quebec Government offered $50,000 reward for information leading to the arrest of terrorists.

1971 Prime Minister Trudeau began an eleven-day tour of Russia.

Sieur de Maisonneuve (1612-1676)

Montreal Is Founded

Surely no city had a more romantic beginning than Montreal. In 1635, Jerome de la Dauversière, a tax collector in Anjou, had a vision of an island called Montreal. He felt inspired to found an order of nuns who would establish a hospital there. Dauversière had never heard of Montreal, so he went to Paris to learn something about it. On the way he met a priest, Jacques Olier, and together they founded the Sulpician order, which secured a grant of the island. A distinguished crusader and warrior, the Sieur de Maisonneuve, agreed to go as governor.

The party arrived at Quebec in August, 1641, but Governor Montmagny was opposed to their going farther up the river, knowing the danger from the Iroquois. He tried to get them to establish a mission on the Island of Orleans, below Quebec.

Maisonneuve said: "Were all the trees on the island of Montreal to be changed into so many Iroquois, it is a point of duty and honor for me to go there and establish a colony." The winter was spent building boats and they began their journey on May 8, Montmagny going with them.

The morning of May 18 was clear, with sunshine touching the top of Mount Royal and lighting up the forests. Maisonneuve went on shore first and dropped to his knees in prayer. The twenty other members of the party followed. The actual place was where a small stream they named St. Pierre flowed into the St. Lawrence. Now it is an area of tall buildings.

An altar was built, and Father Vimont conducted the first Mass while soldiers with muskets stood guard. At the Mass, Father Vimont uttered some prophetic words: "That which you see is only a grain of mustard seed. But it is cast by hands so pious and so animated by faith and religion that it must be that God has great designs for it. He makes use of such instruments for His work. I doubt not that this little grain may produce a great tree, that it will make wonderful progress some day, that it will multiply itself and stretch out on every side."

Other Events on May 18:

1675   Marquette died in the Lake Michigan area.
The Feast of the Assumption Mass was first celebrated at the church of Notre Dame de Bon-Secours, the first stone church in Montreal.

1783   Seven thousand United Empire Loyalists landed at Parrtown (Saint John).

1785   Parrtown was incorporated and its name changed to Saint John; it is the oldest incorporated city in Canada.
Reverend Dr. Stuart opened the first school in Upper Canada at Kingston, Ontario.

1824   William Lyon Mackenzie founded the *Colonial Advocate*.

1837   Lower Canada banks suspended payments until June, 1838.

1846   Kingston received a city charter.

1861   The College of Bytown became Ottawa College.

Iberville Ordered to Hudson Bay

On May 19, 1697, Pierre Le Moyne d'Iberville was resting at Placentia Harbor, Newfoundland. Iberville and his men had marched across the Avalon Peninsula the preceding November, through swamps and icy waters to rendezvous with another French force under Governor Brouillon, who was jealous of Iberville. In fact, after they met at Ferryland, Brouillon and Iberville drew swords because the French Governor went back on an agreement he had made about division of the spoils. The fight was prevented but Iberville lost the argument and had to give Brouillon a bigger share.

They besieged St. John's on November 26 but it was bravely defended by Governor Miners who tried to hang on because he knew reinforcements were coming from Britain. Iberville knew it too and devised a trick (or what would be called a propaganda move today) to make Miners give in. He captured a settler, William Drew, and had the Indians cut all around his scalp and then strip the skin from the forehead to the crown. He then sent Drew into St. John's with a message to Miners saying that unless St. John's was surrendered immediately, all its inhabitants would get the same treatment. Miners gave in.

There was a good deal more fighting and devastation elsewhere, but by May 19 Iberville had returned to Placentia. Now he planned to rest his troops, capture the remainder of Newfoundland and then organize a campaign to drive the English from the New England states. He was going to capture Boston and perhaps even New York!

Iberville's hopes and plans were dashed on May 19, when five ships of war sailed into Placentia Harbor. His brother Joseph de Sérigny was on board one of them, bringing a message from King Louis XIV. Iberville was to give up the Newfoundland campaign and once again drive the English from Hudson Bay (see September 3). The tragedy from his point of view was that the Newfoundland campaign had been a waste and the plan to capture Boston would never be carried out.

Other Events on May 19:

1535 Cartier sailed on his second voyage to Canada.

1587 John Davis began his third voyage to the Arctic.

1745 British and French fleets fought a battle off Louisburg.

1780 This was known as the "dark day" in Canada and New England States because darkness fell at 2 p.m. The cause has never been made known.

1790 Various Indian tribes surrendered 2 million acres in Ontario.

1859 The first steamboat on the Red River arrived at Fort Garry.

1876 The British Columbia Legislature passed a Schools Act supporting public schools, and taxing male residents $3 a year for education.

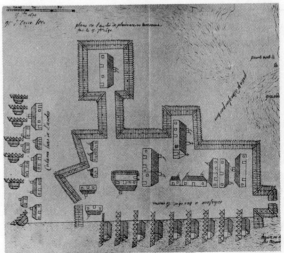

French fort at Placentia, 1690

British troops march to Quebec

Militia Bill Defeated

Someone should write a drama called "The Trent Affair" starring James Mason, because there was a "Trent Affair" and James Mason was a real character in it. Canada became involved to such an extent that the Macdonald-Cartier government was defeated on May 20, 1862.

During the American Civil War a British ship, the *Trent*, sailed from the United States. James Mason and John Slidell, southerners on their way to take up ambassadorial posts for the Confederates in Europe, were on board. A Northern warship stopped the *Trent* on the high seas and took them off. Britain was so angry there might have been war if the Prince Consort had not toned down a note sent to Washington by Prime Minister Palmerston.

In the event of war, Canada would have been attacked immediately by the Northern armies. Fortunately, President Lincoln felt that they had all they could do to defeat the South, and Mason and Slidell were freed.

Meanwhile Britain had rushed 14,000 troops to British North America. They landed in winter, and marched to Quebec on snowshoes. It must have been a comical sight—British soldiers trying to wade through Canadian drifts on snowshoes!

In the midst of the excitement, a bugaboo of many years raised its ugly head: conscription! The Macdonald-Cartier government called out the militia of 40,000 men. Many of them were farmers from Canada West (Ontario) and turned out with shotguns and pitchforks, confident that any Canadian could lick seven Americans!

The government proposed a militia bill providing for compulsory military service to raise an additional 30,000 men. Feelings ran high in French Canada. Why should they fight Britain's wars? In any case the danger was over.

When the militia bill came up for the vote on May 20, 1862, a bloc of French-Canadian members of the Macdonald-Cartier party voted against it. A new government was formed under John Sandfield Macdonald and Louis Victor Sicotte. It lasted for only one year, then Macdonald-Cartier were returned. Strangely enough, Cartier died in London, England, on May 20, exactly ten years after the defeat of the militia bill.

Other Events on May 20:

1656   The Iroquois descended on the Island of Orleans and took eighty Hurons prisoners. The garrison at Quebec did not dare try to rescue them.

1690   Fort Loyal (now Portland, Maine) was captured by the French and Indians from Nova Scotia.

1776   The Americans were defeated at Quinze Chênes on the Ottawa River.

1798   David Thompson arrived at Sault Ste. Marie after a long trip.

1803   Chief Justice Osgoode in Montreal declared that slavery was inconsistent with the laws of Canada.

1859   George Barston was elected mayor of Nanaimo, British Columbia. Only one vote was cast!

1879   The Department of Railways and Canals was organized; Sir Charles Tupper was Minister.

1959   Prime Minister Menzies of Australia visited Ottawa.

"Overlanders" Begin Quest

One of the most amazing stories in Canadian history came from the gold rush to the Cariboo in 1862. It began with an advertisement in London, England, newspapers: "The British Columbia Transit Company will punctually despatch on May 21 at 12 noon from Glasgow, a party of first and second class passengers for Quebec, Canada, and over the Grand Trunk Railway to Chicago and St. Paul and via the Red River settlements, in covered wagons to British Columbia. This is the speediest, safest and most economical route to the gold diggings. The land transit is through a lovely country unequalled for its beauty and salubrity of climate."

The adventures of the "Overlanders" as they came to be known, began when they arrived at Fort Garry, after coming down the Red River on a steamboat. They were greeted by the cannons of the Hudson Bay fort, and treated to dinners and dancing. All that remained for them now was to buy Red River carts and journey to the Cariboo.

One of the largest groups started with 150 people, including Mrs. August Schubert, who had three children with her and was expecting her fourth. There was a great deal of rain that summer, carts bogged down to their wheel hubs while the oxen sank to their bellies in "muskeg." Members of the party who had never handled axes had to build bridges across the swollen rivers. By July 21, they had finally reached Edmonton. Now they only had to cross the Rockies!

The Hudson's Bay men at Edmonton persuaded them to exchange their Red River carts for pack horses. They pressed on, and by August 2 had reached Cowdung Lake, the Great Divide, where the water began to flow to the west. By this time, they had eaten practically all their food and were living on skunks and porcupines, and even horses.

Prospectors going in; gold coming out

Occasionally they got salmon from the Indians. The fish had come 700 miles from the Pacific and were half-rotten.

It was October 13 before one party reached Fort Kamloops. Many had died through drowning or other accidents. Among the survivors were Mrs. Schubert and her three children. The new baby was born the following day, the first white girl born in the interior of British Columbia.

Few, if any, of the "Overlanders" found gold.

Other Events on May 21:

1690   Sir William Phips captured Port Royal, Nova Scotia.

1765   The first agricultural fair in Canada was held at Windsor, Nova Scotia.

1784   A large party of Loyalists left Sorel, Quebec, to settle at Kingston, Ontario.

1901   Captain John C. Voss sailed from Victoria, British Columbia, to Britain, in an Indian canoe *Tilikum*. He went via Australia and arrived September 2, 1904 (see July 6).

1914   Gurdit Singh and 396 Hindus were forbidden to land at Vancouver.

1939   King George VI unveiled the National War Memorial at Ottawa.

Coal Creek, near Fernie, B.C.

Tremor Causes Disaster

Frances Shelley Wees, in a wonderful prose-poem called *A Geography Lesson*, described the Rockies: "They are like giants sleeping under a ragged green blanket piled with snow. Some day, you think, watching them crowd up against the sky, some day they will wake, or turn in their dreaming, and shatter the world."

Occasionally the Rockies have turned in their dreaming, or perhaps just shuddered a little, and results have been devastating. On May 22, 1902, the little mining town of Coal Creek, near Fernie, experienced disaster when a tremor caused the cave-in of a coal mine and 128 men were killed.

After the Coal Creek disaster, a policeman in town said openly that he wished a few hundred more men had been killed. The miners who were left held a court-martial and were ready to hang him. Calmer heads prevailed. They stripped him of his uniform and hustled him through all the mining towns of Alberta, showing him off. The policeman never came back.

Life was exciting in the foothills of the Rockies in those days. There was danger from nature, Indians, wild animals and rustlers from the north and south. During the Klondike gold rush, the Northwest Mounted Police chased out as many of the gamblers, swindlers and suspected murderers as they could. Many of them went to the mining towns like Fernie. The gamblers would wait for the paydays of the miners and railway construction workers, and take their money from them. There were thirteen hotels in the Crowsnest Pass, running wide open, and the gamblers would get most of the workers' money between Saturday and Monday.

The only doctor in the area, Saul Bonnell, worked for the C.P.R. He spent most of his time patching broken heads and stitching up wounds from knife fights. During 1898, when the Crowsnest Pass was under construction, there was a typhoid epidemic. Dr. Bonnell would have as many as sixty patients lying on the straw. Whenever a blanket was shaken, lice would jump out everywhere.

Other Events on May 22:

1808   Simon Fraser left Fort St. James, British Columbia, for a trip down the river that now bears his name.

1815   Fort Niagara was restored to the United States.

1820   Lord Dalhousie laid the cornerstone of Dalhousie University.

1867   Queen Victoria proclaimed at Windsor Castle that the British North America Act would go into effect July 1, and named seventy-two senators—thirty-six Conservatives, and thirty-six Reformers.

1872   The Earl of Dufferin was made Governor-General of Canada.

1893   The Earl of Aberdeen was made Governor-General of Canada.

1906   British forces were withdrawn from Esquimalt, British Columbia; they were the last British forces in Canada.

1919   The House of Commons passed a bill prohibiting titles for Canadians.

1945   The government announced that Japanese incendiary balloons had been found in Western Canada.

"374" arrives in Vancouver

Citizens Welcome First Train to Vancouver

The short route to China, which explorers from Cabot onwards had hoped to find, really came into being on May 23, 1887 when the first C.P.R. transcontinental passenger train arrived at the new west coastal terminal, the city of Vancouver. It was drawn by engine 374, now displayed in Kitsilano Park, Vancouver, and clambered through every day by children.

Vancouver had only been incorporated as a city the previous April, and was completely destroyed by fire in June. Yet, when 374 puffed in on May 23, it had been rebuilt and was a vivid sight with fir arches, garlands and slogans. There were many rounds of "three cheers and a tiger" for the C.P.R.

Port Moody, farther up Burrard Inlet, was supposed to be the Canadian Pacific terminal and still is officially, but William Van Horne moved the end of the line to Vancouver, to allow deeper berthing water for a shipping service. The C.P.R. had already made its plans for steamship routes across the Pacific. The *Abyssinia* of 3,000 tons had sailed from Yokohama and arrived at Vancouver on June 14, with first class passengers and a cargo of tea. She had crossed the Pacific in thirteen days. Her passengers reached Montreal twenty-seven days after leaving Japan. Things were speeding up in the world! The *Abyssinia* also carried the first transpacific mail and the pioneer cargo of silk. For many years, the fast "silk trains" were something to behold, as they roared across the continent with their precious cargo, some to Prescott, Ontario, from whence they were ferried to Ogdensburg, N.Y.

Vancouver grew quickly with the arrival of the railway. By the end of the year its population was 5,000 with new settlers arriving every day. Two years later it had grown to 8,000, and eventually it became the third largest city in Canada.

Other Events on May 23:

1633   Champlain was made the first governor of New France.

1873   Parliament passed an act establishing the Northwest Mounted Police.

A proud chief surrenders, 1885

Poundmaker Surrenders

The law is a hard, queer thing. I do not understand it.

POUNDMAKER, *at his trial, 1885*

Louis Riel surrendered to General Middleton on May 15, 1885, and the Northwest Rebellion was over, although the Indian Chiefs Poundmaker and Big Bear were still at large. Poundmaker was in the bag first, but Big Bear did not give up until July 2. He scattered his braves, eluded dozens of military scouts, and reached Fort Carlton, where he surrendered personally to Sergeant Smart of the Northwest Mounted Police.

Poundmaker had captured a supply train and twenty-two prisoners on May 14, but realized the game was up when he heard the news of Riel's capture. He released Indian agent Jefferson, who had been one of his prisoners, and sent him with a message to Middleton on May 24. He asked for surrender terms in writing so there would be no misunderstandings.

Middleton adopted a stern attitude. He sent a message back to Poundmaker saying that he had completely defeated the half-breeds and Indians at Batoche. No terms had been made with them, and he would make no terms with Poundmaker. He must surrender unconditionally. The date was set for May 26.

When Poundmaker arrived, General Middleton was sitting on a chair, with his officers in a semi-circle behind him. The proud chief came forward all prepared to shake hands. The general brushed him off. Some observers said later that Poundmaker impressed them as the greater man. He had risked his own position more than once to prevent his braves from massacring white people. He was fighting for the right to get food for his hungry people, and to assure them of their share of the lands they had lost.

Middleton told Poundmaker that he was charged with high treason, but Poundmaker did not understand the expression. The interpreter finally got the message across by saying, "You are accused of throwing sticks at the Queen and trying to knock her bonnet off." Poundmaker was arrested with four of his braves, taken to Regina and charged with treason and murder.

Big Bear was also put in prison after he surrendered. Public opinion caused the sentences of both chiefs to be shortened. The confinement was too much for both men and they died soon after being released.

Other Events on May 24:

1833　The first university degree in medicine was given to W. Logie of Montreal.

1856　The Taché-Macdonald government was formed. It remained in office until November 1857.

1881　The steamer *Victoria* sank in the Thames River, near London, Ontario, on Victoria Day, with the loss of 200 lives.

1932　Parliament passed a bill establishing a nationally-owned broadcasting system.

1955　The C.N.R. and the C.P.R. reduced the running time between Montreal and Vancouver by sixteen hours.

1965　A separatist demonstration began in Montreal.

Conscription Opposed

One of Canada's most serious political crises was brewing on May 25, 1917. Prime Minister Sir Robert Borden had just returned from a tour of Canadian forces fighting in World War I. Although he had hoped to avoid it, Sir Robert felt that compulsory military service was necessary to fill the ranks, even though it would split the nation.

Quebec Nationalist ministers and members of Parliament opposed conscription. There was opposition from farm and labor organizations and others. The only possibility was to form a coalition with members of the Liberal Party, who had been the official Opposition since the reciprocity election of 1911.

Borden met the Leader of the Opposition, Sir Wilfrid Laurier, on the morning of May 25, and urged him to unite in a government. The cabinet would be composed equally of Conservatives and Liberals. Sir Wilfrid replied that a referendum on conscription, or a general election, should be held first. After some discussion, Sir Wilfrid asked for a few days to think things over.

The talks between the leaders continued well into June. Sir Wilfrid refused to join the coalition, believing that he was being asked to accept a decision already made, not one on which he had been consulted. On June 24, Parliament passed the Military Service Bill by 102 votes to 44. Laurier saw his friends in the Liberal Party slipping away, one by one. When Frank Carvell of New Brunswick, one of his oldest friends, voted for conscription after a moving speech, Laurier sent him a note via a House of Commons messenger: "Frank, that was a noble speech."

The battle went on until December 17 when an election was held. In the meantime, Sir Robert had formed a Union Government without a single French-Canadian member! It was sustained in the election: Union Government 153, Laurier 82, 62 of which came from Quebec. Laurier had won 42 per cent

Sir Robert Borden reviewing troops in France

of the popular vote. Mackenzie King was defeated in North York, but the 42 per cent was what he had to build on when he became leader of the Liberal Party in 1919.

Conscription enlisted 83,000 men, of whom 47,500 went overseas. In all, 35,000 French-speaking Canadians served in the armed forces—and with distinction.

Other Events on May 25:

1660　The Company of the One Hundred Associates sent lawyer Dumesnil to Quebec to enquire into company affairs.

1849　An act of Parliament stated that postage stamps should be engraved to prevent forgery.

1870　Fenians raided eastern townships.

1883　The Grand Trunk and Great Western Railways were amalgamated.

1905　Peterborough, Ontario, was incorporated.

1907　The University of Saskatchewan was founded at Saskatoon by Dominion charter.

Dollard Des Ormeaux

Dollard Saves Montreal

In 1660 Adam Dollard defended Montreal against the Iroquois. There is some dispute about the date, various authorities giving it as May 10, 21 and 26.

Dollard had come to Canada as a young man under the cloud of an unfortunate event in France. He wanted to do something big and brave to blot out its memory. His opportunity came when it became known that the Iroquois were embarking on a campaign to wipe out Montreal.

Dollard Des Ormeaux, as he is usually called, received Maisonneuve's permission to lead a small party of soldiers to the Long Sault rapids on the Ottawa River. He would try to stop the Iroquois in that area from uniting with their brothers on the Richelieu.

The Long Sault is a stretch of rapids, ideal for catching a foe in ambush. The French established a position behind a barricade of logs that had already been built, and were joined by two Huron chiefs with forty braves.

The first Iroquois party coming down the river was ambushed. The second attack was made by 200 Iroquois, who were driven back with heavy losses. The Iroquois then sent a party to parley with the French, who made a mistake and fired on them, killing several.

Wave after wave of Iroquois then tried to storm Dollard's fortification and set it on fire. The French turned them back every time. Gradually most of the Hurons deserted, and the arrival of 500 Iroquois from the Richelieu made Dollard's position impossible. The end came when Dollard tried to throw a hand grenade over the burning fort walls. It struck the top, fell back inside and exploded. The Iroquois poured in, tomahawks and scalping knives in their hands. Dollard was the first to be killed.

After the battle, the Iroquois gave up their plan to attack Montreal, at least for the time being. If such a small group could do so much damage, what chance would they have against the larger fortification?

In the interests of historical accuracy, it should be added that Dollard Des Ormeaux's motives have been questioned by some authorities, who believe that Dollard went to Long Sault to hijack the Indians and take their furs, not to defend Montreal.

Other Events on May 26:

1577 Martin Frobisher explored Baffin Land on his second voyage.

1611 Champlain visited the site of Montreal and cleared land there.

1828 An Imperial act allowed naturalized citizens from the United States to vote in Canada and become members of Parliament.

1868 The Great Seal of Canada was prescribed by Royal Warrant.

1874 The Dominion Elections Act instituted voting by secret ballot, and abolished property qualifications for members of the House of Commons.

1887 The Imperial Government empowered Canada to negotiate commercial treaties with foreign countries.

1896 The Imperial Privy Council gave the federal government rights over the fisheries.

Champlain Seeks China

In 1867 an historic find was made near Renfrew, Ontario. It was an astrolabe belonging to Champlain who lost it in 1613 while making a portage from the Ottawa River to Muskrat Lake.

Champlain always hoped to find the great river that would lead to the Pacific. During one of his visits to France, he met a young man named Vignau, who had been in Canada. He told Champlain about a trip he had made up the Ottawa River until he reached an ocean. A wrecked English ship was seen on the shore. This looked as though it might lead to the route to China, so Champlain brought Vignau back to Canada to act as guide.

On May 27, 1613, Champlain and Vignau left St. Helen's Island near Montreal, and paddled up the Ottawa River. Champlain knew an Algonquin chief who lived at Muskrat Lake. He walked there carrying four paddles, other supplies and his astrolabe, an instrument used for reading the stars to determine latitude and longitude.

Every fisherman who has portaged through the woods in June, carrying equipment while fighting off mosquitoes and blackflies, will appreciate what happened to Champlain. He dropped the astrolabe along the way, and it was lost for 254 years. That was the first bad break.

The Algonquin chief, after hearing Vignau's story, laughed, and the young Frenchman confessed that he had made up the story. Champlain decided to return to Quebec and was accompanied by the Indians as far as Chaudière Falls. They carried the canoes to the foot of the falls, and performed a ceremony to ensure protection against all enemies. A plate was passed, into which every member of the party dropped a piece of tobacco. The plate was then placed on the ground, while the Indians moved around it, singing and dancing. One of the braves made

Champlain's astrolabe

a long speech, always part of Indian ceremonies, and the plate was hurled into the midst of the cauldron. Loud shouts rang out as Champlain departed.

The astrolabe was found in 1867 by a farmer who was ploughing land near Renfrew. It was in a remarkable state of preservation; the date of its manufacture, 1603, could clearly be seen.

Other Events on May 27:

1732 La Vérendrye sent his eldest son to build a fort on the Winnipeg River. He was probably the first white man to see Lake Winnipeg.

1813 General Dearborn and Commodore Chauncey took Fort George, Niagara.

1818 Halifax and Saint John were declared free ports.

1949 Newfoundland held its first election as a province of Canada; Joseph Smallwood became premier.

The Ross rifle

Government Advised to Abandon Faulty Rifle

One of the greatest controversies in Canada was brought about by national pride, and may have cost thousands of lives. It was over the Ross rifle, used until August 1916 by Canadian troops in World War I.

The problem began several years before the war. The government tried to order British Lee-Enfield rifles for the Canadian forces, but Britain had priority on them, and would not release the quantity required. In 1901 tests were begun on a rifle designed by Sir Charles Ross and continued until after the beginning of war in 1914. It became a matter of pride that Canadians would have rifles so good that Britain would come begging for them. The Ross rifle compared well with the Lee-Enfield in target shooting but jammed when it became hot. It was redesigned and special Canadian ammunition was made for it but it still jammed. Sir Sam Hughes, the Minister of Militia, was a keen amateur marksman, and the lightweight Ross rifle appealed to him. He did not seem to see its faults, and Ross rifles were issued to Canadian soldiers fighting in World War I. They cost up to $28 each, at least 25 per cent more than Lee-Enfields, and by this time had been altered so much that they were seven inches longer and a pound heavier than the British rifle.

The Canadian soldiers themselves got rid of the Ross rifle. During the battle of Ypres, nearly 1,500 threw them away and picked up Lee-Enfields lying beside dead British troops. Their own rifles had jammed in battle as tests had always shown they would.

British General Alderson made repeated representations to Sir Sam Hughes about the loss of confidence in the Ross rifle. Sir Sam did nothing. Finally, in desperation, General Alderson wrote to the Governor-General, H.R.H. the Duke of Connaught.

The Ottawa *Citizen* received permission to print this letter which appeared on the front page of the *Citizen,* May 16, 1916. It produced the desired reaction: Sir Robert Borden cabled Field Marshal Sir Douglas Haig, asking him to have a decisive test made.

On May 28, 1916, Haig advised the Canadian Government to abandon the Ross rifle "without delay," and his recommendation was accepted.

Other Events on May 28:

1664   The West India Company secured a Royal grant of all French colonies in North America.

1754   Major George Washington was defeated by the French at Great Meadows (near Pittsburgh, Pennsylvania).

1845   Fire destroyed two-thirds of Quebec and the suburb of St. Roch.

1881   Britain awarded the United States £15,000 (pounds) reparation for the attack on American fishermen in Fortune Bay, Newfoundland.

1927   The House of Commons approved Old Age Pensions.

1934   The Dionne quintuplets were born near North Bay, Ontario.

1958   President Heuss of the Federal Republic of Germany paid a state visit to Canada. He was the first German head of state ever to have done so.

Cariboo Road Planned

A mule train at Barkerville, B.C.

It was a dangerous, hard journey on May 29, 1861 when Governor Douglas began a tour to see how roads could be built into the interior. Gold had been discovered in the arid Cariboo country. How could he build a road 500 miles long, through difficult country, with only 20,000 people in British Columbia to pay for it?

Douglas managed to get the miners to help build the road voluntarily, and Royal Engineers sent out from Britain built roads, parts of which can be seen today. They deserved the slogan used by United States Marines: "The impossible we do at once. The miraculous takes a little longer."

Mule trains comprised of sixteen mules, each carrying 250 pounds of freight, were used to carry the supplies along the narrow trails, covering about 10 miles a day. Teamster Frank Laumeister had the amazing idea that camels would be better. They could carry more freight and last longer without water. This was important in the hot, dry Cariboo country. Somehow, Laumeister managed to buy twenty-one camels and began using them on the trail. It looked as though he would make a fortune. Each camel carried 1,000 pounds and made about 30 miles a day. He overlooked one problem; camels smell awful! When they passed a mule train, the mules would be terrified, dash into the woods, or fall down the canyon and be killed. Jackass Mountain is supposed to be named after a mule train that had dashed down the canyon to death. Laumeister was involved in so many lawsuits that he had to abandon the plan.

There is an amusing story about the arrival of the camels in Victoria on their way to the Fraser. A small boy came running home and told his father breathlessly that he had seen two wild beasts with humps on their backs coming along the road. Although he could hardly believe the boy, his father took a heavy stick and went to see for himself. A Victoria paper reported the incident: "As soon as his eyes fastened upon the monsters, his own courage departed, and with blanched cheek and trembling steps he hastily regained the shelter of his own home."

Other Events on May 29:

1733   Intendant Hocquart upheld the right of Canadians to have Indians as slaves and to sell them.

1775   The Continental Congress issued an address to Canadians inviting them to join the Union.

1794   Bishop Mountain was given a seat in the legislature of Lower Canada and the title of Lord Bishop of Quebec.

1815   An Order-in-Council declared Canada opened to citizens of the United States for commerce.

1838   Members of Hunters' Lodges burned the ship, *Sir Robert Peel*.
The Bank of Montreal issued pennies: they are now rare coins.

1914   The C.P.R. liner *Empress of Ireland* sank after a collision in the St. Lawrence River: over 900 lives were lost.

1950   The Royal Canadian Mounted Police supply ship, *St. Roch,* arrived at Halifax. It was the first ship to sail around North America, via the Northwest Passage and Panama Canal.

1963   The Hall of Canadian Eskimos opened in the National Museum, Ottawa.

Bourassa, leader of Quebec Nationalists

Senate Kills Navy Bill

The importance of this story is its anti-climax, which occurred on May 30.

For three years, the Commons had been discussing the question of naval help for Britain. When the Liberals were in power, Sir Wilfrid Laurier had proposed that Canada should build a navy. This was opposed by the Conservatives under Sir Robert Borden, who said that this was disloyal to Britain. Instead, Canada should give Britain money to build battleships. Winston Churchill was then First Lord of the Admiralty. He made a deal with Sir Robert Borden to send him two messages: one confidential, outlining the military facts, the other for public consumption.

The Quebec Nationalists under Henri Bourassa supported the Conservatives, not because they wanted to help Britain, but because they opposed the building of a Canadian navy.

The Conservatives won the election in 1911 with the slogan: "One Flag, One Fleet, One Throne," and now Sir Wilfrid Laurier, as leader of the Opposition, asked them what

they were going to do about the navy, or naval aid for Britain.

Sir Robert Borden introduced a measure to give Britain $35 million to build British battleships. He quoted Churchill as saying that it would be foolhardy and presumptuous for Canada to go ahead and build a navy for which it did not have trained men.

The Liberals, trying to force another election on the issue, launched the biggest fili-buster in the history of the Canadian House of Commons. They kept the House in session twenty-four hours a day for two weeks, with the exception of one Sunday when there was an armistice. Both parties divided their members into eight-hour shifts. Liberals who hadn't spoken for years took their turns, quoting the Bible, reading the British North America Act, or *Janes Fighting Ships* (the bible of shipping), or anything even remotely relevant.

Eventually, Sir Robert ended the debate by invoking the "closure" for the first time in Canada. Closure might be described as a political measure to make prolonged debate impossible, and is used only as a last resort. Sir Robert managed to push his navy bill through the House of Commons and avoid an election.

The anti-climax? On May 30, 1913, the Senate killed the bill!

Other Events on May 30:

1675 Jacques Duchesneau was appointed Intendant; he was the first since Talon.

1811 The Hudson's Bay Company agreed to Lord Selkirk's plan to buy land at the Red River.

1832 The Rideau Canal was opened.

1849 Britain repealed Navigations Laws, and deprived Canada of preferential tariffs.
      A canal was authorized from Lake Champlain to the St. Lawrence to compete with the Erie Canal.

1859 The British Government took over British Columbia from the Hudson's Bay Company.

Manitoba to be "Republic"?

One of the "characters" of Canadian history was Thomas Spence, who proclaimed himself "President of the Republic of Manitoba" in 1868. He really meant "President of the Prairies"; Spence had big ideas!

He was first in the limelight at Fort Garry in 1866, when the community was divided into camps supporting union with Canada or the United States. Spence did some "grand-standing" by posing as a leader for Confederation. He wrote a letter on birchbark to the Prince of Wales, inviting him to come to the Red River and hunt bear and buffalo with the Indians. The Prince rejected the invitation "with profound regret."

Spence then opened a store in Portage la Prairie. On May 31, 1868, he proclaimed the "Republic of Manitoba." Its boundaries were vague, but seemed to extend south to the United States' Border, west to the Rockies and east to Fort Garry, or as far as it was safe to go. Spence was, of course, President, and said his purpose was to hold the country for Canada. He intended to levy taxes to build a Government House and jail!

Spence seemed to be getting along quite well until the time came to collect taxes. Charges were heard that he and his "cabinet ministers" were spending most of the money on whisky! One of the most vocal objectors was shoemaker MacPherson. Spence sent two of his cabinet ministers, who doubled as police constables, to arrest MacPherson, and after a struggle, MacPherson was bundled on a sleigh to be taken to Portage la Prairie for trial. When they were passing farmer John McLean, MacPherson shouted for help. Mc-Lean advised MacPherson to go peacefully, but said he would attend the trial that night.

The trial was held in Spence's store, with President Spence acting as judge and accuser. McLean entered with three friends and pro-tested against the unfair trial. One of the

Thomas Spence (right)

policemen tried to throw him out, and a fight started. The policeman was hurled across the room and in the course of his flight upset the lamp, table, and president! The melee con-tinued in the darkness until someone fired a shot into the ceiling. The defenders of the Republic scurried out the door and when the lamp was lighted President Spence was found cowering behind the upset table, pleading for mercy because his wife and family needed him.

The Republic of Manitoba came to a sud-den end. Spence left for Lake Manitoba and entered the salt-making business.

Other Events on May 31:

1578   Martin Frobisher left on his third voyage to the Arctic; he discovered Hudson Strait.

1862   The Bank of British Columbia re-ceived a royal charter.

1962   Plans were announced for the estab-lishment of Trent University at Peter-borough, Ontario.

"*The measure of our unity has been the measure of our success . . .*

If we imagine that we can now go our separate ways within our country; if we think that selfish interests can now take precedence over the national good; if we exaggerate our differences or revel in contention; if we do any of these things, we will promote our own destruction."

"*Canada owes it to the world to remain united . . . no lesson is more badly needed than the one our unity can supply, the lesson that diversity need not be the cause for conflict, but, on the contrary, may lead to richer and nobler living.*"

—GOVERNOR-GENERAL VANIER, 1967.

Fenians Raid Niagara

On June 1, 1866, Canada was attacked by a military force which traveled in two rented tugs and some canal boats! The invaders were Fenians (see March 17) who sailed across the Niagara River to Fort Erie, Ontario! As nobody was awake, they had to knock on doors to get people up. They wanted Canadians to join them and be liberated from the "tyranny of Britain." The good folk of Fort Erie couldn't see things that way, but they wanted to be nice to the strangely dressed men carrying green flags with harps and gold crowns on them. They fed them cooked ham, tea and coffee.

The Fenians had intended to spread out through the Niagara Peninsula after landing at Fort Erie, but they had been up all night. The weather was warm, and so they lay down under the trees and slept for a while. The rest of the day was spent in handing out proclamations from "General" Sweezy and "General" O'Neill, saying that their only quarrel was with the oppressors of Ireland, and that they offered Canadians "the olive branch of peace and the honest grasp of friendship."

Meanwhile, official opinion in Canada West (Ontario) wasn't friendly at all. The Queen's Own Rifles of Toronto, the 13th Battalion from Hamilton, and a force of regulars from St. Catharines were rushed to the area. The Caledonian and York Rifles Companies also arrived. The Canadian troops had only thirty-five bullets each and no food or water. Some of their commanding officers had no experience in warfare and little military training.

The Fenians suddenly realized that the invasion was no picnic; there were already casualties. General O'Neill was hoping for reinforcements from Buffalo where 10,000 Fenians had assembled. They were having a good time listening to speeches and drinking whisky, and did not want to leave. The United States Government then decided that

Raid at Ridgeway, near Fort Erie, Ont., 1866

it had better do something, and sent an armed revenue cutter to patrol the Niagara River.

Some of the Fenians who had landed in Canada tried to swim back to the United States and were drowned. General O'Neill then shaved off his whiskers and fled in disguise. The tugs and canal boats came back and took off the rest of the force, towed by the American patrol boat. The skirmishing lasted until Sunday, June 3.

Other Events on June 1:

1797   The Legislature of Upper Canada met at York for the first time.

1813   H.M.S. *Shannon* captured the U.S.S. *Chesapeake* and took it to Halifax (see December 30).

1831   Sir James Ross discovered the position of the North Magnetic Pole.

1873   Joseph Howe, Lieutenant-Governor of Nova Scotia, died (see January 1).

1876   Royal Military College opened at Kingston, Ontario.

1882   Gas lighting was introduced in Winnipeg.

1909   Governor-General Lord Grey donated the Grey Cup to Canadian football.

1916   Manitoba adopted prohibition.

1927   William Phillips, the first United States Minister to Canada, arrived at Ottawa.

The siege of Louisburg

Louisburg Under Attack

Before Wolfe could attack Quebec it was necessary to eliminate the powerful French fortress at Louisburg, Cape Breton. There were 200 cannons, 17 heavy mortars mounted along the fortifications, 3,000 regular troops in the garrison, plus 1,000 militia and about 500 Indians. Powerful units of the French fleet were in the harbor.

Britain was well prepared for the campaign. The land forces, numbering 12,000, were commanded by General Jeffery Amherst. His brigadiers included Whitmore, Lawrence and Wolfe. Admiral Edward Boscawen commanded the fleet of 39 ships and 12,000 sailors. He and Amherst were friends and worked well together.

Louisburg was commanded by the Chevalier de Drucour, a resolute soldier. His wife was a fighter too, and insisted on being with the guns. When the invasion fleet appeared on June 1-2, Drucour placed 2,000 troops along four miles of the coast where landings would have to be made.

The actual invasion was delayed until June 8, 1758 because of rough weather. Brigadier Wolfe was in command of the landing force. At two in the morning, they set out for the shore in small boats. It was bitterly cold, but the defenders provided a hot reception, waiting until the landing craft were close to the shore before opening fire. It was so intense that Wolfe had to order his boats to get out of range. He then saw that one group had made a landing east of the beach and its men were getting some protection behind the rocks. He ordered the boats to head in that direction. As soon as the water was shallow enough, he jumped into the surf and led his men to the land, waving them on with his stick.

The siege and the battle on shore lasted until July 27. While some of Boscawen's ships were sunk trying to enter the harbor, French ships within the harbor were sunk by gunfire. The battle raged continuously until the British troops broke through and forced Drucour to surrender.

Although Amherst was in command of the attacking force, he always gave Wolfe the credit for the victory. It was his dash and determination that saw it through.

Other Events on June 2:

1622   William Alexander, founder of the Baronets of Nova Scotia, sent colonists from Scotland to Acadia.

1755   A New England force attacked Fort Beauséjour near the present boundary between New Brunswick and Nova Scotia.

1800   The Legislature of Upper Canada opened the session that introduced the British Criminal Law.

1847   John A. Macdonald was made a cabinet minister.

1889   The C.P.R. opened a railway through Maine, between Montreal and Saint John.

1915   The government appointed a committee to enquire into war purchases.

1953   Queen Elizabeth II was crowned.

1954   Dr. C. J. Mackenzie of the Atomic Energy Control Board was awarded the Kelvin medal for outstanding service. He was the second Canadian to be so honored.

Mackenzie Journeys West

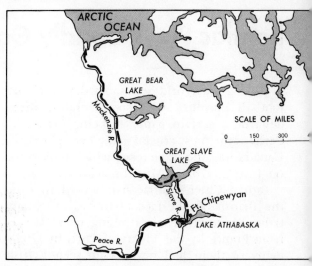

Alexander Mackenzie began his exploration of the Mackenzie River on June 3, 1789, four years before becoming the first man to cross the North American continent.

Mackenzie came to Canada from Scotland when he was fifteen to become a clerk for the Northwest Company in Montreal. He became a minor partner and was sent to take charge of a trading post at Detroit. However, the Nor'westers needed young, rugged men in the north, and Mackenzie was sent to build a post on Lake Athabaska in 1785. He named it Fort Chipewyan.

Mackenzie soon became familiar with the surrounding territory, even Great Slave Lake, larger than Lake Ontario. There was a giant river running north from Great Slave Lake and Mackenzie wanted to know where it went: to the Pacific, or to the Arctic?

He set out in a canoe with a German, four French-Canadian voyageurs and two of their wives. The women's skills were essential on a long trip such as Mackenzie planned. The expedition paddled the 230 miles to Great Slave Lake, where they had to wait for two weeks because it was still frozen. By July 1, they were able to continue down the river which was, at times, six miles wide. After they had gone 500 miles, they met some Indians who tried to stop them from going farther. The Indians told such tales about the horrors of the river, and the evil spirits, that the German and the voyageurs were ready to turn back, but not Mackenzie.

By July 12 they had reached the river mouth. It was dreary and disappointing. The great river divided into narrow channels and flowed through marshy land into the Arctic Sea. Mackenzie spent three days there under the midnight sun, and then turned back. Two months later he reached Fort Chipewyan.

It seems incredible that Mackenzie and his companions could have covered such a dis-

tance by canoe in such a short time, especially as they had to paddle back against the current. From Great Slave Lake, the Mackenzie River is 1,200 miles long. The distance to and from Lake Athabaska, where Fort Chipewyan is located, must also be added.

Other Events on June 3:

1668 Groseilliers sailed from England in *Nonsuch,* on a voyage that led to the forming of the Hudson's Bay Company.

1672 Governor Frontenac left on a trip similar to Courcelles' and built Fort Frontenac at Cataraqui (now Kingston, Ontario).

1778 First issue of the Montreal *Gazette* (Gazette Littéraire) was published.

1799 The Island of St. John was proclaimed as Prince Edward Island.

1870 A delegation from British Columbia arrived at Ottawa to discuss a proposal to enter Confederation.

1889 The first C.P.R. train arrived at Halifax.

1909 W. L. Mackenzie King became Canada's first Minister of Labour.

1918 An airmail service was inaugurated between Montreal, Boston, and New York.

Pontiac Plays Deadly Game of Lacrosse

During the World Series, Stanley Cup, and football playoffs, sport commentators often describe a certain game as being "crucial." Perhaps the most crucial game ever played in Canada was one of lacrosse, which took place on June 4, 1763 at Michilimackinac.

Indian Chief Pontiac had vowed to wipe the British off the face of the earth. Many tribes resented Britain's taking over Canada from France by the Treaty of Paris in 1763—many of them had never even seen British redcoats until after the fall of Montreal, when General Amherst sent troops to take over Detroit and Michilimackinac. (Michilimackinac was an important fort at the junction of Lakes Huron and Michigan. It has been preserved as a historic site near one of the longest bridges in the world.)

June 4 was the birthday of King George III, and the Indians arranged to play a game of lacrosse outside the fort. A great many squaws who were there as spectators were hiding tomahawks and knives under their blankets.

The gate of the fort was open and nearly all the members of the garrison were watching the game. The Indians worked the play closer and closer to the gate, and suddenly took their weapons from the squaws and began the massacre. The troops were taken completely by surprise, probably not having heard about Pontiac's treachery at Detroit on May 7. While some of the Indians killed the soldiers outside the gate, others dashed inside and massacred the people there. Few escaped.

It was part of what the distinguished historian, Francis Parkman called, "the conspiracy of Pontiac." Before it was brought under control, 2,000 British, including women and children, were killed along the frontier.

Britain decided to send an army to North America to protect the colonies. The catch was that King George and his ministers demanded that the colonists should bear the cost! This led to the imposition of the Stamp Act, the duty on tea and other forms of taxation. The American Revolutionary War was the result. Britain put down the Indians for the time being, but lost the United States!

The game of lacrosse at Michilimackinac was certainly more "crucial" than any game in the Stanley Cup or World Series!

Other Events on June 4:

1613   Champlain reached the site of the present city of Ottawa during his expedition to find a route to the Pacific (see May 27).

1760   Twenty-two ships with New England planters aboard arrived in Nova Scotia to replace the Acadians.

1843   Victoria, British Columbia, was founded.

1866   Fenians raided Quebec from St. Albans, Vermont; they retreated after causing considerable damage.

1917   Prime Minister Borden told Sir Wilfrid Laurier he could choose the members of the cabinet if he joined a Union government (see May 25).

Pontiac in council

Cadillac Founds Detroit

Detroit, Cadillac, and Pontiac are so identified with automobiles that few people realize their connection with Canadian history. Detroit was founded by La Mothe Cadillac, one of Frontenac's officers. The name is French, meaning "on the strait." Pontiac, of course, was the great Ottawa chief.

When Frontenac was asked to return to Canada in 1689 (see January 11), one of his problems was to try to control the Iroquois. They used two main routes into Canada from their territory in New York. They could cross Lake Ontario and go down the St. Lawrence River, or they could reach the Ottawa River via Lake Huron and French River. Frontenac had blocked the St. Lawrence route by building a fort at Cataraqui. The fort at Michilimackinac was supposed to guard the other route.

Cadillac had been in charge of Michilimackinac for six years, and felt that its location was awkward and out of date. He had snowshoed all the way to Montreal several times for supplies, or to attend to some business connected with the fur trade. How he would enjoy the same trip in a Cadillac today! Cadillac persuaded Frontenac that a better location would be along the strait connecting Lakes Erie and Huron.

Frontenac was impressed, but sent Cadillac to France to get the approval of Louis XIV. It wasn't easy, because Michilimackinac was an important Jesuit mission and they did not want it weakened. Cadillac insisted that his plan would be profitable for France and block Britain from the fur trade. Finally he got his way.

On June 5, 1701, Cadillac left Quebec to found Detroit. He took a party of soldiers and workmen in twenty-five canoes, and traveled the long route via the Ottawa River, Lake Nipissing, Georgian Bay, and Lake Huron, with a stop at Michilimackinac.

There was a marked resemblance between Cadillac and D'Artagnan of the "Three

Cadillac landing at Detroit

Musketeers." Both were Gascons, fast tempered and expert swordsmen. There was nearly a mutiny on the way, with someone knocking Cadillac's hat over his long nose. His sword was out in a flash and he turned on the 100 men, challenging them to fight!

Nobody wanted any part of it, and the journey continued. They reached Detroit on July 23, and began building the fort that has since expanded into one of the automobile centres of the world.

Other Events on June 5:

1673 A Royal decree regulated the activities of the couriers de bois.

1792 Galiano and Valdez of Spain explored the coast of British Columbia and met Captain Vancouver.

1817 The steamship *Frontenac*, the first on the Great Lakes, made the trip from Kingston to York.

1832 Montreal and Quebec were incorporated as cities.

1854 The Elgin-Marcy Agreement established reciprocity between Canada and the United States (see May 16).

1876 Manitoba abolished its legislative council.
      The first session of the Supreme Court of Canada was held.

1940 Nazi, Fascist and Communist groups were declared illegal in Canada.

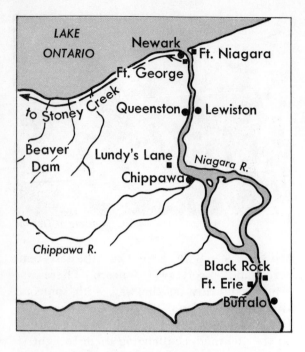

Americans Prepare Raid

There were few bright spots for British forces defending Canada from the Americans in 1813. York, the new capital of Upper Canada, had been captured and looted (see April 27) and Newark soon suffered a similar fate. Fat General Dearborn was well pleased with himself. He now had a solid line of communication from Buffalo to the head of Lake Ontario.

General Vincent, who had defended Fort George at Newark, led his surviving troops to Burlington (near Hamilton) and expected help, if necessary, from Colonel Procter's force in the Detroit area. In the meantime Dearborn missed an opportunity to finish him off. Instead of following up the success at Fort George, Dearborn waited for five days, perhaps because it was raining hard. Then he heard rumors that Procter was sending reinforcements to Vincent and decided that he had better take action before they arrived. Generals Winder and Chandler set out for Burlington with 2,000 infantry, cavalry and artillery, whereas Vincent now had about 1,600 men.

The American force camped at Stoney Creek for the night of June 6, about 6 miles from Burlington, but their movements had been followed and reported by Canadian volunteers. General Vincent sent out a scouting patrol which brought him word that the American tents were strung out in a long line, and that their artillery was badly placed. Vincent immediately ordered an attack. His troops made their way through the woods in the darkness and stormed the camp at two o'clock in the morning. There was a sharp fight in which the British lost 214 men, but both Generals Winder and Chandler were taken prisoner with 123 others.

The Americans still had enough strength to retaliate, but lost heart when Admiral Yeo's ships were seen approaching. Yeo bombarded the American position at Forty Mile Creek, and they decided to retreat to Fort George.

Vincent received help from an unexpected quarter when the 104th New Brunswick Regiment arrived. It had left Fredericton in winter, marched 400 miles on snowshoes to Quebec and was then transported to Kingston by ship. After fighting at Sackets Harbor, New York, it traveled another 500 miles to join Vincent's army. The march of the 104th (New Brunswick) Regiment was one of the notable achievements of the war.

Other Events on June 6:

1821   The cornerstone of the Montreal General Hospital was laid.

1834   Lord Selkirk's heirs returned his territory to the Hudson's Bay Company for shares worth £15,000 (pounds).

1891   Sir John A. Macdonald died.

1929   The Liberals were defeated in Saskatchewan for the first time in the history of the province.

1944   Allied forces invaded France on D-Day.

Laurier Heads Liberals

Sir Wilfrid Laurier was elected leader of the Liberal party on June 7, 1887. The Liberals were then in opposition, but in 1896 Laurier won a general election by opposing the Roman Catholic church, of which he was a devout member, over its Manitoba separate schools question.

Sir Wilfrid remained prime minister until 1911. Although he never again became Prime Minister, he was always a power until his death in 1919. Years after that, there were said to be French-speaking Canadians in the backwoods who believed that Sir Wilfrid was still at the helm!

Laurier's ancestors came to Canada with Maisonneuve. He was born in humble circumstances (the family home at St. Lin, near Montreal, is a museum), but his father helped him obtain an astonishing education. He sent him to school in the village of New Glasgow, a nearby Scottish settlement, where he studied with English-speaking pupils and lived with a Presbyterian family. After a classical education at the College of L'Assomption he joined a law firm in Montreal, and at the same time took night courses at McGill University.

During this time, young Laurier was making a name for himself as a debater. On one occasion he argued that Huguenots (French Protestants) should have been admitted to early Canada, which led the priests to close the debating society!

He was only thirty years old when he was elected a member of the Quebec Legislature, and three years later he entered the House of Commons in Ottawa.

One of the first important functions Wilfrid Laurier attended after becoming prime minister in 1896 was Queen Victoria's Diamond Jubilee and the Colonial Conference in London. His charming manner and beautiful flow of language, in both French and English, won the hearts of everyone. There is a de-

Sir Wilfrid Laurier (1841-1919)

lightful story of how Queen Victoria is said to have tricked him into receiving a knighthood, and he returned to Canada as "Sir Wilfrid."

Other Events on June 7:

1576   Martin Frobisher began his first voyage to Baffin Land.

1585   John Davis made his first voyage to Davis Strait.

1677   La Durantaye claimed the Lake Huron-Lake Erie area for France.

1819   The fourth session of the Seventh Parliament opened. Legislation included a validity act for married women.

1870   The first General Assembly of the Presbyterian Church of Canada was held.

1886   Archbishop Taschereau was made the first Canadian Cardinal.

1904   Lord Dundonald was dismissed as commander-in-chief of forces in Canada for criticizing the Minister of Militia. This ended the practice of having Imperial officers command forces in Canada.

Sir Charles Tupper (1821-1915)

Last Session Begins

On June 8, 1866, Parliament began its last session as the Province of Canada. The next Parliament would be that of the new Dominion, but this was by no means certain on June 8, 1866.

In Nova Scotia, Premier Tupper carried a motion through the legislature authorizing his government to continue negotiations for a federal union. In New Brunswick, the anti-Confederation Smith government had resigned, and an election was in the offing. Actually, Smith was weakening in his opposition to Confederation, angry because the United States had refused to continue the reciprocity agreement made in 1854.

Clear Grit (Liberal) leader George Brown had left the coalition government he had formed with Taché-Macdonald, the deal that had won Macdonald's support for Confederation. Brown was something like Joseph Howe in Nova Scotia. Neither one could play "follow the leader." Howe had been one of the earliest supporters of Confederation, but was one of its strongest opponents when Tupper became premier. Tupper had campaigned effectively against Howe when the latter was in the States, trying to recruit Americans to fight for Britain in the Crimean

War. A friend asked Howe why he had turned against Confederation and he replied, "If you had a circus and had got together a good show, how would you like it if that fellow Tupper came and stood by the door and collected the shillings?"

Once Brown felt that Macdonald was fully committed to Confederation, he left the coalition as quickly as possible. From that time on he never spoke a civil word to the Conservative leader. Macdonald was puzzled and perhaps hurt. He said that during their brief association, which included a trip to Britain, they had dined and gone to public places together. They had even played euchre a good deal while crossing the Atlantic.

Brown did not weaken his support for Confederation. He contributed $500 to a $50,000 campaign fund contribution which Canada sent to the Confederation party fighting the election in New Brunswick. It won and Premier Tilley of New Brunswick and Tupper of Nova Scotia were able to go to London later in the year, to join Macdonald, Cartier and Galt in negotiations with the British Government.

Other Events on June 8:

1731 La Vérendrye and party left Montreal to explore the west.

1789 Spaniards seized Meares' vessel *North West America* at Nootka, Vancouver Island.

1790 King's College opened at Windsor, Nova Scotia.

1824 Noah Cushing of Quebec obtained a patent for a washing machine.

1832 The ship *Carrick* from Dublin arrived at Quebec with half its passengers dead from cholera.

1859 Governor Douglas established the Supreme Court of British Columbia.

1963 Prime Minister Pearson and American Ambassador Butterworth attended the 150th anniversary of the Battle of Stoney Creek (see June 6).

Railways Begin to Boom

There have been a number of exciting booms in Canada: gold, real estate, miniature golf and hula-hoops. In the middle of the nineteenth century, it was railways.

In an effort to stimulate railway building, the government guaranteed interest of not over six per cent on any issue of bonds for half the cost of any railway of 75 miles or more. The effect was magical. Railways sprang up everywhere, starting at one spot and ending nowhere—perhaps in a bush! One of them was the Cobourg-Rice Lake, Plank Road and Ferry Company, which was incorporated on June 9, 1846.

The way to make money was to form a company to build a railway and then borrow from the government. The directors would retain enough shares for control of the company and sell the remainder to the public. Contracts for the building of the railway would then be awarded to companies in which the railway directors held shares.

It was easy to sell shares to the public because most people believed the railways would make great profits. Instead, most of them went bankrupt and had to be bailed out by various governments.

Even so, the boom continued well into World War I. Two of the most spectacular railway barons were William Mackenzie and Donald Mann, both of whom received knighthoods. Mackenzie was a small town teacher who also kept a store. Mann was supposed to enter the ministry, but instead became a lumber camp foreman and construction boss. He could beat most lumberjacks with one hand tied behind his back.

In 1896, Mackenzie and Mann had a railway about 130 miles long, running between Gladstone, Manitoba, and Lake Winnipegosis. They built the Canadian Northern Railway from Quebec to the Pacific coast. By 1914, they owned 10,000 miles of track, hotels, tele-

A lone Mountie stands guard as the CPR moves west, 1881-1887

graph companies, a transatlantic steamship service, iron and coal mines, sawmills and fisheries. They did this without investing a cent of their own money, except for their original 130-mile railway costs!

The Canadian Northern eventually went bankrupt and was merged with the Grand Trunk, to form the present Canadian National Railways, the largest in the world. Mackenzie and Mann did not go bankrupt. They made fortunes.

Other Events on June 9:

1775   Governor Carleton declared martial law due to the American Revolutionary War.

1790   David Thompson began a survey of the Saskatchewan River to Hudson Bay.

1829   The first public temperance meeting in Canada was held at Montreal.

1841   The legislative council held its first meeting at Kingston.

1846   A bad fire at St. John's, Newfoundland, destroyed 2,000 homes.

1946   William Lyon Mackenzie King established a record for the longest service as Prime Minister of Canada.

United Church Conducts First Service

In 1925, Maple Leaf Gardens did not exist and the Toronto team in the National Hockey League played its games in the Arena. The team was called the "St. Pats" and it had some great players.

No group of hockey players ever worked harder than the 800 people who gathered in the Arena on June 10, 1925. They were representatives of the newly-organized United Church of Canada, and some of them had been working for this occasion since 1904.

Methodists, Presbyterians, and Congregationalists in Canada saw no reason why differences in doctrine in Scotland, England and the States should apply to them. Negotiations to unite began in 1904, and years were spent in planning the structure for union.

Sentiment generally favored union but a minority of members of the Presbyterian Church were opposed. The conflict between them was quite sharp and both sides were conducting a propaganda campaign for and against, until 1917, when they agreed to stop until the end of the war.

In 1921 the debate was resumed, but the non-union Presbyterians were more opposed than ever. On the other hand, more than 1,000 congregations had united in one organization on the prairies. If church union had not taken place they would have been forced to return to their isolated groups.

In 1924 the Parliament of Canada passed the United Church of Canada Act and the provincial legislatures passed similar bills. When the first service took place in Toronto on June 10, 1925, all the Methodists, practically all the Congregationalists and two-thirds of the Presbyterians were represented.

The United Church had a difficult time during the depression years from 1930 to 1940. Minimum salaries of some of its ministers fell to $1,200 or lower.

During those tragic years, church members across Canada sent 1,000 carloads of fruit and vegetables, and 25,000 bundles of clothing to destitute families in Saskatchewan, the hardest hit province of all.

Since the union in 1924, the United Church of Canada today counts more than 3 million members.

Other Events on June 10:

1650 Jesuits abandoned the last mission raided by the Iroquois in the Huron country (see March 16).

1810 The Halifax "old town clock" arrived on the H.M.S. *Dart*.

1837 The Upper Canada Academy opened at Cobourg, Ontario.

1857 A bill was passed which put Canada on the dollar system.

1878 Victoria, British Columbia, was fortified because of possible war with Russia.

1884 Louis Riel left a school teaching job in Montana to return to the prairies to lead the rebellion.

1937 Sir Robert Borden died.

1947 President Truman of the United States arrived in Ottawa for a state visit until June 12.

1957 Conservatives won the general election with 112 seats, Liberals 105, Cooperative Commonwealth Federalism (C.C.F.) 25, Social Credit 19.

1963 Three men were identified as leaders of the Quebec Freedom League that had been bombing installations.

Sir John Franklin Dies in Arctic

There are few more dramatic stories in Canadian history than the account of Sir John Franklin's death in the Arctic on June 11, 1847. His expedition to discover the Northwest Passage sailed from Britain in May, 1845. His ships, the *Terror* and *Erebus*, were last seen at the entrance to Lancaster Sound in July. It took fourteen years of searching by many expeditions before it was learned what had happened. A record was found in a cairn at Point Victory giving the history of the expedition until April 25, 1848.

After spending the winter of 1845-1846 at Beechey Island, North Devon, the expedition reached the west side of Cornwallis Island and followed a route that had been especially assigned before Franklin had left Britain. He navigated Peel and Franklin Straits southward, but had been stopped by ice coming down McClintock Channel. The ships were ice-bound on September 12, 1846. Franklin died the following June. By that time, the death toll of the expedition was 9 officers and 15 men of the total of 129 who had sailed from Britain.

The survivors stayed in the *Erebus* and *Terror* until April 22, 1848, when it was decided to trek overland to Back's Fish River. Not a single man survived. Eskimos saw them trying to make their way over the ice, but said they died as they walked.

Sir John Franklin (1786-1847)

At one stage of Franklin's career, he had been Lieutenant-Governor of Van Diemen's Land, Tasmania, where British convicts were sent. When he was lost, the colony gave Lady Franklin £7,000 to finance a search. She not only sent out expeditions but went on one herself. It tried to get to the Arctic by going up the Fraser River from the Pacific, but was stopped at what is now known as "Lady Franklin's Rock."

The record found at Point Victory included the information that Franklin had discovered a channel leading south along the west of North Somerset, discovered by Parry in 1819. Franklin knew he could reach the Bering Sea through it, the long-sought Northwest Passage. Discovery of the Passage, however, was officially credited to Captain McClure who charted it when searching for Franklin in 1850. His was only one of forty expeditions sent during the fourteen-year search.

Other Events on June 11:

1782   William Black, the first Canadian Methodist minister, preached at Halifax.

1815   Duncan Cameron of the Northwest Company attacked the Selkirk colony at Red River.

1863   A legislative council was appointed for British Columbia.

1917   Prime Minister Sir Robert Borden introduced the Conscription Act in Parliament.
     The Canadian Board of Grain Commissioners was established in Saskatchewan.

1945   The Liberals won the general election with 125 seats. The Conservatives had 67 and Co-operative Commonwealth Federation 28. It was Mackenzie King's last election victory.

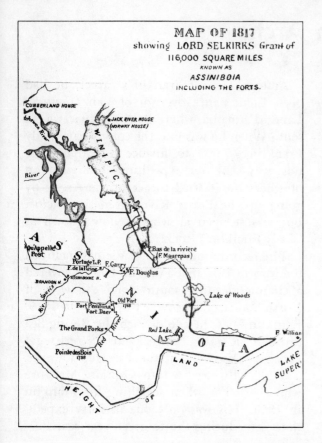

MAP OF 1817
showing LORD SELKIRKS Grant of
116,000 SQUARE MILES
KNOWN AS
ASSINIBOIA
INCLUDING THE FORTS.

Selkirk grant defined by black lines

Selkirk Granted Land

A great Scottish name, Selkirk, is commemorated in many place names in Canada, as it should be. There is the town of Selkirk, Manitoba, and the Selkirk range of mountains in British Columbia, among others. The Earl of Selkirk was the first large-scale colonizer of Canada. His enterprise cost him most of his fortune and eventually his life.

Selkirk was born in 1771, the seventh son of the laird of St. Mary's Isle on the southwest coast of Scotland. One by one his older brothers died until he inherited the title. As he grew up he became the friend of Robert Burns and Sir Walter Scott. He was perhaps a dreamer, as they were, and he wanted to help the needy Scottish people.

The Earl established settlements in Prince Edward Island and Baldoon. Neither worked out well, because the land was said to be poor. This is hard to understand today because Baldoon is an area of thriving corn fields. People weren't eating corn flakes and popcorn in those days!

Like Napoleon, Selkirk had been impressed by Alexander Mackenzie's account of his journey across Canada from the Atlantic to the Pacific. He felt that the Red River area, where Winnipeg now stands, offered the best opportunities because it could be reached from Hudson Bay. This would avoid the costly trip from Quebec. So, Lord Selkirk bought a controlling interest in the Hudson's Bay Company!

It was then that Selkirk made one of the most amazing deals in Canadian, and perhaps any, history. Using his position in the Hudson's Bay Company, on June 12, 1811, he obtained a grant of 116,000 square miles of territory for colonization purposes. It included half of what is now Manitoba, Minnesota and North Dakota! It was an area five times bigger than Scotland, and he received it for a rental of 10 shillings ($2.50) a year on the understanding that he would supply the Hudson's Bay Company with 200 servants a year and develop an agricultural colony.

Other Events on June 12:

1631   King Charles I agreed to return Quebec and Port Royal to France on receiving the remainder of the dowry of his wife, Queen Henrietta Maria.

1690   Henry Kelsey left York Factory, Hudson Bay, to explore the west.

1710   The Hudson's Bay Company gave the widow of Pierre Radisson six English pounds as charity on his death.

1714   The French settlement at Placentia, Newfoundland, surrendered to Colonel Moody.

1958   Prime Minister Macmillan of Britain addressed a joint session of Parliament in Ottawa.

Vancouver, after the fire of 1886

Vancouver Destroyed by Fire

Vancouver is Canada's third largest, and most beautiful, city, although Victoria might like to contend for the beauty title. On June 13, 1886, Vancouver was a mass of smouldering rubble. It was not only costly and inconvenient, but embarrassing, because the first C.P.R. transcontinental train was due to arrive at Port Moody on July 4. Arrangements were being made to extend the railway into Vancouver, and the arrival of the first train must be a gala occasion (see May 23).

The fire began on Sunday afternoon owing to a mistake by a young construction worker, George Keefer. His uncle was one of the contractors building the C.P.R. extension into Vancouver. Young George had been instructed to clear some land along the waterfront, to provide a camping space for a band of Stikine Indians who had been engaged to do construction work. They were due to arrive in canoes. There were big trees to be cleared away and George could think of no quicker way than to burn them. He started a number of fires at strategic places, but suddenly a brisk wind blew up. The flames were carried into the residential district and the entire area was destroyed within an hour. Only Hastings Mill and a few small buildings were saved. Some lives were lost.

As far as it is known, young George was not punished. He lived to see Vancouver become a great seaport, with landing places for ocean liners where he first cleared the space for the Stikine Indian camp.

The rebuilding of the city, which had only been incorporated a few weeks before the fire, was done in record time, even though they did not have today's modern equipment. By three o'clock Monday morning, teams of horses were bringing in new lumber for buildings. The city fathers put up a tent at the foot of what is now Carrall Street, and directed the work from there. By June 15, twenty buildings were underway. The aldermen also obtained Vancouver's first loan, for the purchase of a fire engine!

Strangely enough, the fire took place on the anniversary of the day that Captain George Vancouver explored the area in 1792.

Other Events on June 13:

1611   Champlain met Etienne Brulé with the Hurons. Brulé was the first white man to travel up the Ottawa River.

1673   Cataraqui (Kingston, Ontario) was founded by La Salle.

1799   The name "Prince Edward Island" was first used on an official document.

1818   Richard Talbot sailed for Canada with 200 Irish settlers who founded St. Thomas, Ontario.

1853   The Northern Railroad from Toronto to Bradford was the first in Canada on which a locomotive was used.

1895   The Manitoba Legislature declined to alter the status of schools.

1898   Yukon territory was organized with Dawson as the capital.

1916   The first express train of the Western National left Quebec for Winnipeg.

Lord Sydenham (1799-1841)

Kingston Chosen Capital

When Upper and Lower Canada were united in 1840 there were many difficult problems. Lower Canada had a population of 600,000 and was relatively debt-free. The French-speaking Canadians claimed they were being placed under an English dictator, Governor Sydenham, and that Montreal was being annexed to Upper Canada. Upper Canada had a population of only 400,000 and had piled up a huge debt for those days through the building of roads and canals. English-speaking opponents of Union believed that they would be dominated by the French.

There was also the problem of where the capital should be. Kingston was chosen as a compromise. Quebec was too far to the east, and too French. Toronto was too far to the west, and too English. The new Parliament opened on June 14, 1841, in a hospital. The assembly rooms were airy, members had desks and chairs, and Governor Sydenham claimed they were more comfortable than the members of Parliament in Britain.

French Canada was shocked when Sydenham did not include one of its representatives in his executive council, and only eight French-speaking members in the legislative council of twenty-four. Sydenham claimed that he could not find enough French-Canadians of ability who had not been identified with the rebellion in Lower Canada in 1837-1838.

On the first day of the session, Robert Baldwin, who was leader of the Reform Party in Upper Canada which had a majority, insisted that Sydenham should remove the Tories from the Council and replace them with Reformers, including representatives from Lower Canada. Sydenham refused and so Baldwin resigned from the Council. He and Louis Hippolyte Lafontaine, leader of the Reform Party in Lower Canada, then joined together to lead the Opposition. Lafontaine had been one of the rebels who had fled to the United States. By a strange quirk of fate, he was to become the first joint premier of United Canada.

There was an interesting sidelight to the Baldwin-Lafontaine alliance. Baldwin offered Lafontaine, defeated in Lower Canada, a safe seat in York. Two years later Lafontaine found a safe seat for Baldwin in Rimouski. It was one of the first examples of co-operation between French- and English-speaking Canadians.

Other Events on June 14:

1610   Champlain left Quebec to attack the Iroquois on the Richelieu River.

1776   The retreat of American Generals Arnold and Sullivan marked the end of the invasion of Canada.

1864   John A. Macdonald voted against Confederation (see June 22).

1872   The C.P.R. General Charter was passed, authorizing the construction of a transcontinental line by a private company.

1887   The first C.P.R. steamer arrived at Vancouver from Japan.

1919   Alcock and Brown flew on the first successful flight across the Atlantic from St. John's, Newfoundland.

Oregon Treaty Signed

On June 15, 1846, Britain and the United States signed the Oregon Boundary Treaty. There was a good deal of give and take in the Treaty, which extended the frontier along the 49th parallel, dipping south on the Pacific to give Britain all of Vancouver Island.

Britain had hoped to make the Columbia River "the St. Lawrence of the Pacific." The Hudson's Bay Company had pioneered the area and it had also been claimed by explorers Vancouver, Thompson and Broughton. An amazing mistake by a Royal Naval officer in 1813 may have cost Britain this territory (see October 6).

The Americans hoped not only to acquire the Pacific coast to the 49th parallel, but all the way to Alaska. They were ready to go to war, if necessary. In 1844 the Democratic Party slogan was, "fifty-four forty or fight," and fifty-four forty meant the boundary of Alaska. The Democrats won the election. President Polk said in his inaugural address that Britain had no rights to territory on the Pacific. Britain, however, took a firm stand and American Secretary of State Buchanan (who later became president) warned Polk that there would be war if he pushed the matter too far. War with Mexico was imminent and it would be dangerous for the States to be fighting Britain at the same time.

Under these conditions the Oregon Boundary was signed. The negotiations for Britain were carried out by Lord Aberdeen, the Foreign Secretary. His firmness in the matter was not undermined by the opinions of his brother, Captain Gordon of the Royal Navy, who had been sent to survey the region. Captain Gordon wrote to Lord Aberdeen that he would not give one barren hill of Scotland for what he had seen of the Pacific. The country was worthless because neither salmon nor trout would rise to the fly! Captain Gordon was obviously using the wrong kind of fly!

7th Earl of Aberdeen, Governor-General of Canada (1893-1898), son of Lord Aberdeen

Other Events on June 15:

1616 The first schools for Indians opened at Three Rivers and Tadoussac.

1636 Governor Montmagny arrived at Quebec.

1676 Inhabitants of Quebec were summoned to attend a meeting to fix the price of bread and make suggestions for the welfare of the community.

1815 One hundred and forty Selkirk colonists left the Red River for Upper Canada.

1875 Various Presbyterian churches united as the Presbyterian Church of Canada.

1905 Newfoundland prohibited the sale of bait to foreign vessels.

1915 Canadian troops were in action at Givenchy, France.

1944 The Co-operative Commonwealth Federation Party won in Saskatchewan for the first time.

1962 The first Canadian space vehicle was launched at Wallops Island, Virginia.

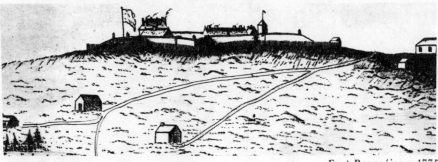

Fort Beauséjour, 1775

Governor Vergor Surrenders Fort Beauséjour

Before the Acadians were expelled from Nova Scotia in 1755, they were caught between the devil and the deep blue sea. There might be some argument about which side was which! Some of the Acadians lived in Cape Breton and what is now New Brunswick, belonging to France, while the others lived in the remainder of Nova Scotia, which was British.

The French governor at Quebec issued a proclamation commanding all Acadians to take an oath of allegiance to the King, and enrol in the French militia. Britain made similar demands on the 9,000 Acadians in her territory, although not requiring them to join the militia.

There was a French fort at Beauséjour (which had been preserved as a historic site), while the British had Fort Lawrence, not far away. Governor Vaudreuil at Quebec sent instructions to Governor Vergor at Beauséjour to devise a plan of attack against Fort Lawrence.

The British had a spy in Beauséjour, who revealed the plan to Governor Lawrence of Nova Scotia and who also got in touch with Governor Shirley in Massachusetts. Shirley, with his usual enthusiasm, raised a force of 2,000 men. When they embarked to sail to Nova Scotia they were instructed: "The men will behave very orderly on the Sabbath Day, and either stay on board their transports, or else go to church, and not stroll up and down the streets."

The force landed at Fort Lawrence on June 4, 1755. Governor Vergor had his men set all the houses on fire between Fort Lawrence and Beauséjour, while a famous Roman Catholic priest, Father Le Loutre, had his Acadians working on the fortifications. In the meantime, Vergor had sent an urgent message to Louisburg for help, but learned on June 14 that none would be coming. The British had been firing their guns at Beauséjour for several days when a shell fell through a roof and killed three officers. That was enough for Vergor and he surrendered the fort on June 16.

As the New England troops could only be kept for one year, and the French were expected to try to recapture Nova Scotia, it was decided to expel the Acadians. Their exodus took place later in the year.

Other Events on June 16:

1659 François-Xavier Laval-Montmorency arrived at Quebec as the Bishop of Petraea in the Holy Land. Canada was not important enough to have a bishop.

1890 Newfoundland ordered a railway from Placentia to Hall's Bay—262 miles.

1891 Sir John Abbott succeeded Sir John A. Macdonald as Prime Minister.

1892 The Edmonton *Bulletin* reported an indication of oil in Alberta.

Louisburg Falls to Pepperell and Warren

Louisburg had always been a threat to the New England colonies. After Governor Shirley of Massachusetts received information that it was not as strong as was supposed (see March 24), he decided to take action.

Shirley managed to raise a force of 3,000 men in New England. They were mere amateurs, farmers who walked to Boston in their working clothes, carrying their own muskets. William Pepperell, a militia colonel from Maine, was placed in command. His only experience had been fighting the French and Indians along the border. Nevertheless, it was an enthusiastic force that sailed from Nantucket on March 24, 1745; destination Canso. Its motto had been supplied by a famous preacher, George Whitefield: "No despair while Christ leads."

At Canso, New Englanders were joined by a British naval squadron from the West Indies under Commodore Warren. This was a stroke of good fortune, because there were powerful French warships at Louisburg and they could have blown Pepperell's small ships out of the water.

A landing was made west of Louisburg on April 30. The troops had to wade through icy water and then drag their cannon into position through a jungle of boulders and marshland. They kept up a bombardment of Louisburg until June 17. During the six weeks of siege there were a number of hard-fought engagements. The knockout punch came on the night of June 16, a combined operation by Pepperell's and Warren's forces. Louisburg surrendered on June 17, 1745.

The British then played another crafty trick. They kept the French flags flying over the fortress for several weeks. During this time they captured twenty French ships that sailed into the harbor unsuspectingly. The value of their cargoes ran into millions of dollars. Under British navy regulations, half of this went to the Crown, while the other half was divided among the officers and men of the fleet. Every sailor received about 25 guineas, which was the equivalent of approximately $125 today! The poor New England soldiers were not entitled to any of this booty. There would have been a mutiny if they had not been promised a raise in pay and land in Cape Breton.

Other Events on June 17:

1616   The Avalon Peninsula, Newfoundland, was sold to Sir William Vaughan who founded a Welsh colony at Trepassey Harbor.

1673   Joliet and Marquette discovered the Mississippi River.

1753   Lunenburg, Nova Scotia, was settled by Germans from Halifax.

1869   Anthony Musgrave, former Governor of Newfoundland, was appointed Governor of British Columbia.

1919   Winnipeg strike leaders were arrested.

1958   The second Narrows Bridge collapsed while being built at Vancouver.

1962   Six buildings were gutted by fire during a riot at the St. Vincent de Paul penitentiary.

Sir William Pepperell at Louisburg, 1745

U.S. Declares War

The annexation of Canada this year as far as the neighbourhood of Quebec, will be a mere matter of marching, and will give us experience for the attack of Halifax the next, and the final expulsion of England from the American continent.

—THOMAS JEFFERSON, 1812

Yesterday's story told how the French flag was kept flying at Louisburg for several weeks after it fell so that French ships would sail in there and be captured. This could not happen today when an important event is known all over the world in a few minutes.

The same kind of thing happened when the United States declared war on Britain on June 18, 1812. The garrison at Halifax received a warning on June 22 from the British ambassador in Washington that there *might* be war. The warning was not confirmed until June 27 when the British frigate *Belvidera*, damaged by gunfire, with two men dead and twenty-three wounded, sailed into the harbor. The *Belvidera*, knowing nothing about the war, had encountered an American squadron of five ships and had been lucky to escape.

There were a number of provocations that led the States to declare war on Britain in 1812, but many Americans wanted the war simply because they thought it was an opportunity to capture Canada while Britain was involved with Napoleon. It looked as though it would be easy. The States had 6 million people and 2 million negro slaves. There were only 500,000 people in what is now Canada, and more than half of them were French. The Americans thought the French would welcome them as "liberators." Dr. Eustis, Secretary for War, said that only officers need be sent, because Canada's "tyrant-ridden people" would fill the ranks! Former president Jefferson predicted that there would be no fighting. After a "joyous march" to Quebec, the Maritimes would fall easily.

It was amazing that they were not right! There were only 90,000 people in Upper Canada. How could they defend a border of 1,000 miles? When the war began, there were only 4,450 British and Canadian regular soldiers to defend the area from Nova Scotia to the head of Lake Huron.

As always in war, there were some imponderables that did not work out as expected. The French-speaking Canadians, the Indians, or any other Canadians did not welcome the American invasion. They fought it. In fact the first attempt at invasion was a complete disaster for the Americans (see July 12).

Other Events on June 18:

1686 Iberville took Moose Factory, Hudson Bay.

1822 A Boundary Commission established the border along the St. Lawrence and through the Great Lakes.

1846 William Henry Draper formed a ministry with Louis Joseph Papineau. Papineau returned to Canada in 1845 after being condemned to death as a rebel in 1838.
The first telegraph system was opened between Toronto-Hamilton-Niagara Falls.

1855 The Sault Ste. Marie Canal was rebuilt. The original canal was built by the Northwest Company in 1797.

1871 The British Columbia Legislature heard Canada's terms for entering Confederation.

1956 Queen Elizabeth II reviewed 300 holders of the Victoria Cross: 30 Canadians were among them.

1959 Queen Elizabeth II and Prince Philip arrived in Newfoundland to begin a forty-five day tour of Canada.

1962 A general election resulted in the return of 116 Conservatives, 99 Liberals, 30 Social Credit, and 19 New Democrats (New Democratic Party).

Selkirk Settlers Killed

In 1811, Lord Selkirk bought a controlling interest in the Hudson's Bay Company so that he could establish a settlement at Red River, now Manitoba. At that time there was great rivalry between the Hudson's Bay Company and the Northwest Company of Montreal. The Nor'Westers, as they were called, were bitterly opposed to agricultural settlers going into the West because it might spoil the hunting and trapping for furs.

The first Selkirk settlers arrived at Fort Douglas, now Winnipeg, in August 1812. The Nor'Westers disputed the legality of the sale of the area to Lord Selkirk and trouble began when they saw the new arrivals ploughing the land and building a storehouse for wheat. When Miles Macdonnell, the leader of the settlers, ordered the Nor'Westers to give up their posts on the Red River, they reacted by destroying the houses and crops of the new settlers and driving many of them out of the country. Others were induced to go to Upper Canada where the Northwest Company offered them land.

There were many skirmishes between the Selkirk settlers and the Nor'Westers. The worst took place on June 19, 1816, after Governor Semple of the Hudson's Bay Company had sent a fearless officer, Colin Robertson, to arrest Nor'Wester Duncan Cameron for having burned a Selkirk village.

On June 19, a force of 70 armed Nor'-Westers and Métis approached Fort Douglas. Governor Semple went out with thirty men and demanded to know what they planned to do. Angry words led to shots being fired, and in a few minutes Semple and most of his followers had been killed. Six managed to get back to Fort Douglas to tell the story. The encounter took place near a group of seven oak trees, and is known in history as "The Battle of Seven Oaks."

Once more the Selkirk settlers were driven from their homes and lands. When Lord Selkirk heard the news he seized the North-west Company's trading post at Fort William, and a number of its most important officers. For this action Lord Selkirk was compelled to go on trial in Upper Canada, and fined £2,000 (pounds)! By this time he was in poor health, and went to the south of France where he died.

Other Events on June 19:

1610   Champlain defeated the Iroquois near the mouth of the Richelieu River.

1687   Champigny seized Indians at Fort Frontenac and sent them to France where they were made galley-slaves. This was one of the reasons for the emnity of the Iroquois towards the French.

1719   Henry Kelsey left Hudson Bay to explore the west for the Hudson's Bay Company and may have been the first white man to see herds of buffalo.

1897   The Allan Steamship Company was formed at Montreal.

1903   Regina was incorporated as a city.

1917   Sir Arthur Currie succeeded Lord Byng as a commander-in-chief of Canadian forces in France.

1924   Postal workers went on strike until June 29.

1964   Canadian Lucien Rivard was arrested in Montreal on a charge of smuggling narcotics into the States from Mexico.

Georges P. Vanier (1888-1967)

Vancouver Is. Bombed

Although Canada fought in both World Wars and suffered heavy casualties, Canadian territory came under shell-fire only once. On June 20, 1942, a Japanese submarine surfaced off Estevan Point, Vancouver Island, and hurled about thirty 5.5″ shells at the wireless station and lighthouse. Little damage was caused, and there were no casualties.

Until the United States came into the war on December 8, 1941, Adolph Hitler would not allow the German navy to operate off Canadian shores. He felt that such attacks would do more harm than good by alienating opinion in the United States. Early in 1942, however, a German submarine fired torpedoes at the entrance to St. John's harbor, Newfoundland. Other German submarines operated in the Gulf of St. Lawrence and sank twenty-two ships. This caused considerable alarm among the local population, who demanded that Army units be sent to guard the coasts. National Defense Headquarters felt that it would be poor policy to allow a few U-boats to tie up a large number of troops, and raised a Reserve Army in the Gaspé Peninsula in September, 1942. It was commanded by Brigadier G. P. Vanier, the late Governor-General of Canada.

The attack on Estevan Point in June 1942 had no significance, but it was followed by a campaign that worried military leaders a great deal more. Between November 1944 and April 1945, the Japanese released about 9,000 unmanned balloons from the island of Honshu. They usually carried one high explosive bomb, and four incendiaries. The idea was that they would float across the Pacific on the prevailing winds, and the bombs would be released by an automatic device. It is believed that only 300 of the 9,000 bombs reached North America, and 90 of them landed in Canada, as far east as Manitoba. The only casualties were a mother and five children who were killed when they tampered with a bomb that had landed in Oregon.

The greatest fear was that the Japanese might use the balloons for chemical or biological warfare. Fortunately, no such efforts were made, and Japan surrendered on September 2, 1945, after being hit by the far more terrible atomic bombs dropped on Hiroshima and Nagasaki.

Other Events on June 20:

1755 Anthony Henday arrived at Fort Nelson after a trip to the Rockies (see April 23).

1838 The Brotherhood of Hunters tried to invade Canada at Short Hills, Upper Canada.

1875 The University of Manitoba was established.

1877 The first commercial telephone service in Canada began at Hamilton, Ontario.
Fire at Saint John, New Brunswick, destroyed 1,600 homes and caused $27 million damage.

1882 The Conservatives under Sir John A. Macdonald won the general election.

Winnipeg Strikers Riot

Citizens turn to violence

Probably the worst strike in Canadian history was the Winnipeg general strike in 1919. The most violent day of the strike was June 21 which became known as "Bloody Saturday."

On May 1, 2,000 workers in the metal trades in Winnipeg walked out. They were asking for a forty-four hour week and a minimum hourly wage of 85 cents. Employers might have met these demands, but resented something new in labor bargaining: negotiation on an industry-wide basis rather than with their own employees. Within a week, fifty-two other unions walked out in sympathy.

Winnipeg was paralyzed. Even essential services like fire, telephone, and food stores were closed down. Policemen were ready to strike but stayed on duty by request of the Strike Committee. Later, all but fifteen of them were fired by the Police Commission because of their sympathy for the strikers.

The population of Winnipeg was 200,000, and 35,000 workers were on strike. Counting their families, it was estimated that the strike was supported by half the population. The other half formed a Citizens Committee which started with 1,000 members but grew to 10,000. They volunteered to work in the public utilities and gradually a number of stores were reopened.

There were many disturbances in which street cars were burned and people killed. The worst was "Bloody Saturday," which took place when the federal Minister of Labor was in Winnipeg trying to settle the strike. A group of returned soldiers held an illegal parade in an effort to get him to make a statement of policy. At 2:30 when the parade was ready to begin, fifty mounted police and some soldiers rode down Main Street swinging baseball bats to get the crowds to disperse. They were booed and stoned. The khaki-clad riders disappeared but the police came back again, revolvers drawn.

They charged into the crowd on William Avenue firing their guns. Two people were killed, thirty wounded. It took the police and soldiers with machine guns six hours to break up the demonstration.

The General Strike Committee ended the strike because many of the strikers' families were on the verge of starvation. Even so, it was an unpopular decision with many of the workers.

Other Events on June 21:

1643 Charles La Tour and his wife escaped from Fort La Tour and went to Boston to get help.

1749 Halifax was founded after the arrival of 2,544 settlers from Britain.

1764 The Quebec *Gazette* of Montreal was founded. It is the second oldest paper in Canada.

1793 Alexander Mackenzie went down the Fraser River as far as Alexandria and turned back.

1946 A national convention was held in Newfoundland to consider the future form of government.

1957 The Liberal government under St. Laurent resigned after its defeat in the June 10 election.
      John Diefenbaker formed the first Conservative government in twenty-two years, with Mrs. Ellen Fairclough as the first woman cabinet minister.

Governor-General Lord Monck (1819-1894)

Brown Unites Government

June 22, 1864, was perhaps the greatest day in the political history of Canada. Parliament was meeting at Quebec, but Canada (Ontario and Quebec) had been without a government for several days because the Conservatives under Sir Etienne Taché and John A. Macdonald had been defeated in the House. Public business was at a standstill.

When the afternoon session began, Macdonald rose to say that the Cabinet had decided to communicate with Governor Monck. This meant another general election. Suddenly, Reform Leader George Brown rose from his seat and announced that he was prepared to take part in a Union government, on the understanding that it would try to form a confederation of the British North American colonies.

There was near pandemonium in the House. It was astounding that Brown, ultra-Protestant champion of reform, would ally with French-Canadian leaders like Taché and Cartier to bring about Confederation. As Brown waited for the uproar to subside, a little French-Canadian member rushed across the floor to embrace him. As Brown was so tall, he had to throw his arms around his neck and hang there!

The story behind this development was that Brown had been chairman of a committee to study Canada's constitutional problems; members included Macdonald, Cartier, Galt and D'Arcy McGee. On the morning of the very day that the Conservative government was defeated, the committee had voted to try for confederation of the British North American colonies. There were only four votes against the proposal, and one of them came from Macdonald!

Brown, who called Macdonald and his party "the Corruptionists," spent the next week negotiating with them. If some form of stable government were not established, the union of Upper and Lower Canada might disintegrate. Brown, who was in favor of Confederation, used this as a political lever to save the government.

Although Macdonald had voted against Confederation, once he agreed to Brown's terms, he went ahead whole-heartedly to become its greatest architect. The coalition government went into effect on June 30. Governor Monck then wrote to the lieutenant-governors of Nova Scotia, New Brunswick and Prince Edward Island, asking if delegates from Canada could attend the Charlottetown Conference on Maritime Union in September. This was the big step towards Confederation.

Other Events on June 22:

1603   Champlain landed in Canada for the first time as both a historian and geographer for the Pontgravé expedition.

1611   Henry Hudson was turned adrift by his mutinous crew.

1774   The Quebec Act was passed.

1825   The Imperial Canadian Trades and Tenures Act abolished feudal and seignioral rights.

1857   The Canadian Rifles Regiment was sent to the Red River.

British Troops Alerted

This day in Canadian history belongs to Laura Secord. The story of the Battle of Stoney Creek was told on June 6. After being reinforced by the arrival of the 104th (New Brunswick) Regiment, General Vincent was ready to counter-attack the Americans on the Niagara Peninsula. He began to move his main force from Burlington, and sent several companies of infantry to Beaver Dam, ready to strike at Queenston.

The American commander, General Dearborn, heard about the move and sent Colonel Boerstler with 570 men and two guns to make a night attack on Beaver Dam. While they were marching there, they stopped to rest at Queenston. Some of the American officers were talking openly about the purpose of their mission.

Laura Secord and her husband, United Empire Loyalists who had left Massachusetts to live at Queenston, overheard the American officers talking about the attack they were going to make on Beaver Dam, and decided that the British must be warned. Laura's husband had been wounded in the fighting at Queenston Heights the previous year and could not make the trip. So, on June 23, 1813, Laura left their home and pretended that she was going to milk the cows. She was barefoot and carried a milking pail.

It was a brave thing to do. Laura Secord had to walk through the woods alone to get to the nearest British position. There were many frightening moments, and she became weary and footsore. On the way she suddenly found herself in the midst of a band of "whooping" Indians. They let her continue on her way when she told them that the "Long Knives" were coming, and that she was going to warn the British. Eventually, she reached a patrol of red coats under Lieutenant Fitzgibbon and related her story.

As it turned out, her journey had been unnecessary. The British had already been warned and the Indians were in place to ambush the Americans. This does not detract

Laura Secord (1775-1868)

from Laura Secord's bravery and self-sacrifice.

Colonel Boerstler and his men walked right into the ambush of 200 Mohawk and Caughnawaga Indians, and after fighting in the woods for two hours, surrendered to Lieutenant Fitzgibbon to escape what they thought would be scalping by the Indians.

Other Events on June 23:

1713   Queen Anne gave the Acadians one year to swear allegiance or leave the country.

1790   Spanish Admiral Quimper claimed Vancouver Island for Spain.

1870   An Imperial Order-in-Council made Manitoba a province and transferred Rupert's Land and the Northwest Territories to Canada.

1896   The Liberals won their first general election since 1874; Laurier defeated Tupper.

1923   Manitoba voted for government control of liquor and repealed the Prohibition Act of 1916 by a narrow margin.

1940   The Royal Canadian Mounted Police patrol vessel *St. Roch* sailed from Vancouver for Halifax via the Northwest Passage. The trip took two years. The *St. Roch* is now on display at the marine museum in Vancouver.

1955   The laying of the first transatlantic telephone cable started from Newfoundland.

First Official Airmail Flight Leaves Montreal

This is the anniversary of Canada's first official airmail flight in 1918. All first class mail now goes by air, except on routes where another method of transportation is more convenient. The first airmail anywhere in the world was flown in India in 1911—five miles!

The inauguration of airmail in Canada was haphazard. Captain Brian Peck was a Royal Air Force officer at a training base at Leaside, Toronto. The Royal Canadian Air Force had not yet been formed. Peck wanted to spend a weekend in Montreal and received permission from his commanding officer to fly there on the understanding that he would do some stunt flying to attract recruits.

Peck arrived in Montreal safely, but it rained all weekend and he wasn't able to put on his flying exhibition. However, the Montreal branch of the Aerial League of the British Empire persuaded postal authorities to sanction the delivery of a sack of mail to Toronto. It was loaded on board Peck's JN IV Curtiss aircraft on June 23. Unfortunately, the flight was delayed because of the heavy rain.

Peck finally got away from the airfield, Bois Franc Polo Grounds, at 10:30 on the morning of June 24. In those days, Montreal was "wet" from more than the weather. The rest of Canada had prohibition as a wartime measure, but not Quebec. There was going to be a wedding at the air base in Toronto, so Peck was carrying a cargo of supplies, as well as the sack of mail. He also had a passenger, Corporal C. W. Mathers.

The plane was so heavily laden that it could hardly take off. Peck had to fly it under telephone and electric wires, and bank clear of a bridge, before he gained altitude! He landed at Kingston for fuel, which was just ordinary automobile gasoline. He then flew on to Toronto where he arrived at 4:55 p.m.

The mail was received by Postmaster W. E. Lemon. Thirty years later, cancelled envelopes from the flight were worth $200 or $250 if they bore Peck's signature. The envelopes are dated June 23 and not June 24, when the flight actually took place, because the flight on June 23 was cancelled after the letters had been sent to the airfield.

Other Events on June 24:

1497 John Cabot sighted the coast of North America. It might have been New-foundland, Labrador, or Cape Breton.

1534 Jacques Cartier discovered Prince Edward Island and landed at St. Peter's Bay.

1604 De Monts named the Saint John River, New Brunswick.

1610 Henry Membertou, Micmac Chief, was baptized at Port Royal, Nova Scotia. It is believed that he was the first Indian to be baptized in Canada. Henry Hudson entered the strait now called after him.

1789 Martinez, at Nootka, claimed the area for Spain. He took four British ships.

1790 Spain agreed to pay reparations for the above incident.

1807 David Thompson arrived at the upper reaches of the Columbia River (see July 15).

1880 The music of *O Canada* was first played at Quebec. A convention invited all French-speaking Canadians to unite; it was directed to the Acadians, but the proposal was rejected.

1890 General Middleton resigned due to criticism that he had looted furs during the Northwest Rebellion.

1917 A conscription bill was passed in the House of Commons.

First Horses Arrive in Canada

There is a dispute about when the first horses arrived in Canada. According to records, the first horse was landed at Quebec on June 25, 1647. It was a present to Governor Montmagny. He was an imposing figure at any time because he was a Knight of the Maltese Order and wore a black cloak with an eight-pointed white cross on the breast. When he mounted his steed and rode like the wind, the Indians thought he was a god.

Other sources state that horses and cattle were landed at Canso and Sable Island, Nova Scotia, perhaps as early as 1518, by Baron de Lery et de St. Just who was supposed to found a colony. The weather was so cold that he left the animals and went back to France, probably intending to return in the spring. He never did return.

Mark Lescarbot says the De Lery expedition was in 1518, but other historians are inclined to give the date as 1538, and even 1552. They say that France was not ready to attempt any colonization work as early as 1518, although hundreds of fishermen were operating off the Nova Scotian and Newfoundland coasts as early as 1504.

The cattle and horses that De Lery landed at Canso all died or were killed by the Indians. The cattle on Sable Island also died, or were removed by pirates and raiders. The horses were the progenitors of the wild horses that roam the desolate island today. During 400 years of exposure, they have become a distinct breed, hardy and undersized. They paw the sand to find fresh water and graze on coarse grass between the sand hills. Sable Island is known as "the graveyard of the Atlantic" because so many ships have been wrecked there.

If the true story of the Norsemen ever becomes known, it may turn out that there were horses in Nova Scotia soon after 1000 A.D. Eric the Red fell from his horse in Greenland when he was planning a trip to Markland and Vinland (Nova Scotia).

Thinking this was an unfavorable omen, he cancelled his trip, but others may have gone and taken horses with them.

Other Events on June 25:

1776 Governor Carleton prohibited the sale of liquor except by license.

1806 Philemon Wright floated the first logs down the Ottawa River and founded a big lumber industry (see February 2).

1855 The Great Western Railway placed the steamers *Canada* and *America* on Lake Ontario and operated a service between Hamilton and Oswego, New York.

1877 Lord Dufferin arrived in Canada to be governor-general.

1927 Prince Edward Island voted to continue prohibition of liquor rather than have government control as adopted by other provinces.

1930 Charles Kingsford-Smith and three companions flew from Ireland to Harbor Grace, Newfoundland, in 31½ hours.

1957 The former Conservative leader George Drew was appointed Canadian High Commissioner to Britain.

1961 J. A. D. McCurdy, Lieutenant-Governor of Nova Scotia, and the first man in the British Commonwealth to fly an aircraft, died (see September 30).

Queen and President Open St. Lawrence Seaway

An outstanding example of co-operation between Canada and the United States is the St. Lawrence Seaway which was officially opened on June 26, 1959, by Queen Elizabeth for Canada, and President Eisenhower for the United States.

The St. Lawrence Seaway is a canal 191 miles long, enabling large ocean freighters to travel from the Atlantic to Lake Ontario and then continue to Lake Superior and Lake Michigan, using other canals that had already been built. The Seaway is also an important source of electric power, generated by the Hydro-Electric Power Commission of Ontario and the Power Authority of the State of New York.

Canada had done a great deal of work on a seaway before the building of the present canal began in 1954. The first canal past the Lachine Rapids above Montreal was built in 1700, and was enlarged in 1821. About that time Canada and the States began talking about building something bigger and better. The Americans were never able to co-operate, and Canada kept enlarging the waterway through Lake Ontario. By 1883 the canal had a depth of 14 feet. Another integral part of the waterway through to Lake Erie was the Welland Canal, by-passing Niagara Falls.

In 1932, it looked at though the dream of attracting ocean-going ships into the Great Lakes was becoming a reality when Canada and the States signed the St. Lawrence Deep Waterway Treaty. However, strong railway, shipping and other interests in the States opposed it, and the Senate would not pass the bill.

Finally, in 1952, Canada decided to "go it alone" and build a deepwater seaway entirely in Canadian territory. This decision led Congress to take swift action and the Seaway was built as a joint venture. As Canada had already spent millions of dollars on the St. Lawrence and Welland Canal, the States spent a larger share on the cost of the St. Lawrence Seaway.

The control dam required by the power project flooded a large area between Cornwall and Iroquois, and necessitated the removal of entire communities. New homes had to be provided for 6,500 people; 40 miles of the C.N.R. had to be rerouted, and Highway 2 relocated. Many improvements were made, including the creation of Upper Canada Village in Crysler's Farm Battlefield Park, now a popular tourist attraction.

Other Events on June 26:

1604   De Monts and Pontgravé established the first settlement in Acadia, with Champlain as a member of the group.

1721   The James Napper expedition to find the Northwest Passage sailed from Fort York, Hudson Bay, and was lost on June 30.

1754   The Hudson's Bay Company sent Anthony Henday west to combat French influence with the Indians. He was the first white man to see the Rockies (see April 23).

1854   Sir Robert Borden was born at Grand Pré, Nova Scotia.

1857   The steamer *Montreal* caught fire and sank 15 miles above Quebec, with the loss of 250 people, mostly Scottish and Norwegian settlers.

1873   An Imperial Order-in-Council authorized Prince Edward Island to join Canada on July 1.

1947   Lord Bennett, formerly Prime Minister R. B. Bennett, died in England where he had gone to live after resigning as leader of the Conservative Party.

1961   Prime Minister Hyato Ikeda of Japan visited Ottawa.
        Upper Canada Village was opened near Morrisburg, Ontario.

British Land at Quebec

Vaudreuil's fire ships, 1759

On June 27, 1759, the British force under General Wolfe and Admiral Saunders completed the voyage up the St. Lawrence to Quebec. They had been guided safely through "the traverse," the most dangerous stretch of the river, by Captain Cook. Actually, Cook tricked some French river pilots into helping him. The first British ships that entered the St. Lawrence flew "fleur-de-lis" flags. The pilots went on board believing them to be French, and were forced to help guide the fleet up the river. They were furious and kept shouting that Quebec would be the tomb of the invaders, and that their scalps would decorate the walls of the city!

The fleet came within sight of Quebec on June 26, and Wolfe's soldiers began disembarking on the Island of Orleans on June 27. Wolfe issued a proclamation to the Canadians, commanding them to remain passive spectators, but many of them flocked to join Montcalm's forces.

Montcalm had arrived at Quebec on May 22. With Brigadier Lévis, he made a tour of the entire area and rearranged artillery batteries. The beach at Beauport gave him the greatest concern, and he installed a floating battery of twelve heavy guns, and six fire ships, loaded with explosives. These ships were bought by the crooked Intendant Bigot, who made a profit for himself even at that hour of danger.

Montcalm had two great handicaps working behind the scene. One was Bigot, and the other was Governor Vaudreuil himself. Montcalm should have sent a strong force to hold the high ground across the river, now Lévis. It is believed that Vaudreuil vetoed this plan. Wolfe quickly took advantage of the opening and installed British guns there. They pounded Quebec until its capture in September.

The fire ships, Vaudreuil's idea, were a complete failure. They were floated down the river towards the British fleet. When the commander of the leading fire ship panicked and deserted, others followed, and finally only one captain remained with his ship and was burned to death. When the fire ships came close, the British sailors simply put grappling hooks on them and towed them to shore. While they burned, the sailors cheered heartily.

This was only the beginning. The battle for Quebec continued until September 13, when it was concluded on the Plains of Abraham.

Other Events on June 27:

1689   The inhabitants of Cocheco (now Dover, New Hampshire) were massacred by the French and Indians.

1772   Matthew Cocking left Hudson Bay for a trip to the Saskatchewan River.

1792   Prince Edward, Duke of Kent, stopped a racial riot at Quebec (see May 17).

1825   John Galt established the Canadian Land Company, buying 1,400,000 acres between Toronto and Lake Huron for settlement.

1922   Jock Palmer attempted the first sanctioned airmail flight from Western Canada. He left Lethbridge but failed to get to Ottawa.

1949   The Liberals under Prime Minister St. Laurent won the general election with 193 seats; the Conservatives won 41.

Red River settlers, contemporary sketch c. 1820

Traders Threaten War

Lord Selkirk's decision to colonize the area near the junction of the Red and Assiniboine Rivers was not received warmly by either the North West Company or the Hudson's Bay Company. Both Companies hunted and traded in the Assiniboia region. They feared that a farming settlement would surely interfere with their business.

Friction between the settlers and fur traders .soon erupted. Miles Macdonnell, appointed Governor of Assiniboia by Selkirk, was angry to see the Nor'Westers transporting bales of pemmican through his territory while many of his own settlers were starving.

Pemmican was made by pounding strips of dried buffalo meat into powder. Wild berries and melted buffalo fat were then mixed with the powder and compressed into bales weighing as much as ninety pounds. Pemmican was the most important food on the Prairies at that time.

In January, 1814, Macdonnell posted his "Pemmican Proclamation," forbidding the export of food supplies from Assiniboia. From the standpoint of the colony, his decision was beneficial, but how were the Métis and the trading companies to survive without their supplies?

Macdonnell was still not satisfied. He sent an armed party to Souris, a North West Com-

pany trading post on the Assiniboine River. There, they confiscated about 600 bales of pemmican. Macdonnell was "pushing his luck." He boasted that he would "crush all the Nor'Westers on the river, should they be so hardy as to resist my authority."

The partners of the North West Company, meeting at Fort William, decided to destroy the Selkirk settlement. A temporary compromise was reached on June 28, 1814, but Miles Macdonnell was nevertheless terribly shaken by the enmity he had aroused. Even the Hudson's Bay Company men turned against him. Macdonnell, a discouraged, beaten man, wrote to Selkirk and asked to be relieved of his command.

Macdonnell spent his later years at his farm in Upper Canada. He died at the home of his brother in Point Fortune, Lower Canada, on June 28, 1828.

Other Events on June 28:

1776 Governor Carleton obtained an oath of allegiance from 300 Iroquois at Montreal.

1829 The Montreal Medical Institute became the Faculty of Medicine, McGill University.

1838 An amnesty was granted to political prisoners from the rebellions of 1837-1838. Some had been banished without trial but this was disallowed by Britain.

1846 A fire at Quebec destroyed 1,300 homes; forty people were killed.

1847 A Boundary Commission made a report on the boundaries of the St. Croix and St. Lawrence Rivers.

1886 The first C.P.R. train left Montreal for Port Moody, British Columbia.

1925 A reception was held at Ottawa for Field Marshal Earl Haig, British Commander-in-Chief during World War I.

1926 The Liberal government under W. L. Mackenzie King resigned to avoid an adverse vote on a customs scandal.

King Resigns—Canada Without Government

Some of the story of William Lyon Mackenzie King was told on April 21. He was Prime Minister of Canada for more than 20 years, a longer record of service than any other man. It was interrupted only twice and one of those occasions happened on June 29, 1926. The episode, one of the most exciting in the history of Canada's Parliament, has come to be known as "the constitutional crisis." Canada had no prime minister or cabinet.

There had been a general election in October 1925, in which the Conservatives under Arthur Meighen won 117 seats to 101 for the Liberals. Mackenzie King had been beaten in his own constituency of North York. Progressives, Independents, and Labor had won another 30 seats among them. Mackenzie King maintained that the so-called "splinter parties" would support him. With their 30 seats plus the Liberals 101, he could carry on the government. Governor-General Lord Byng (who had commanded the Canadian Army at Vimy), agreed that King should be given the opportunity. The Liberal member for Prince Albert, Saskatchewan, resigned to provide a safe seat for Mackenzie King. He won the necessary by-election there and was able to take his place in the House of Commons.

Coalition with the splinter parties might have kept the government in power for a long time. Prime Minister King won their support by promising to bring in old-age pensions and liberalize the Immigration Act, Naturalization Act and Criminal Code. However, there was a scandal in the Customs Department in which a Liberal Minister, Jacques Bureau, was involved. The government faced the possibility of being beaten in the House of Commons. It would have been the first time it had ever happened in Canada.

Prime Minister King paid several calls on Governor-General Byng at Rideau Hall and urged that Parliament be dissolved. He wanted another general election. The first discussions were on an informal basis. On the occasion of his last call, Mr. King arrived in top hat and formal attire. He made it clear that he had come officially as prime minister to advise the Governor-General. Once again he advised Lord Byng to dissolve Parliament to make possible another general election. Lord Byng refused. He felt that Opposition Leader Meighen should be given a chance to form the government. It was a very serious decision for a governor-general to reject the advice of his prime minister.

Thereupon, on June 28, 1926, Mr. King handed his resignation to the Governor-General. So on June 29, technically, Canada had no government.

Lord Byng then asked Mr. Meighen to form a government and he agreed. In those days, when a Member of Parliament was appointed to the cabinet, he had to resign his seat and run in a by-election. Therefore Mr. Meighen, although prime minister, had to give up his seat in the House of Commons. He kept the members of his cabinet there by making them "acting ministers" only. They did not draw pay as cabinet ministers. Neither did they take an oath of office.

The Meighen government lasted until July 2 when it was defeated by one vote, after a very exciting division in the House. It was then necessary to hold another general election. One of the chief issues was whether a governor-general had the right to reject the advice of his prime minister. The Conservatives won only 91 seats and the Liberals had 119. With the support of the Liberal-Progressives and a number of independent members, Mackenzie King formed a government. Once again he was prime minister.

Other Events on June 29:

1871 The British North America Act was amended by Britain, and gave the Canadian Government the right to establish new provinces and alter boundaries.

Regina, Saskatchewan, after the cyclone

Tornado Hits Regina—Hundreds Are Homeless

June 30, 1912, was a Sunday. Regina was decorated to celebrate Dominion Day on the morrow, but the flags hung listlessly in the still air in a temperature of 100 degrees. The sun was a crimson glare in a sullen pink sky.

Regina had made great progress since the days when it was Pile O' Bones, and was enjoying a real estate boom—business lots were selling for $35,000, and houses for $12,000. With prosperity had come lower moral standards, and a large crowd was listening to a sermon on this subject in the Anglican Church of St. Paul's. It was so hot that scores of people fainted. Others tried to escape from the blistering heat by paddling canoes on man-made Wascana Lake near the Legislature. Most people were just sitting at home, sipping lemonade and fanning themselves.

At about 4.30 p.m. two grey clouds were seen racing towards each other, one from the southeast, the other from the southwest. There was a rumble of thunder. The sky began to glow an eerie green, while blue-red flashes of lightning snaked along the ground.

At 4.50 p.m. the two clouds collided with a roar, just over the Legislative Building. They formed a funnel looking like a greasy ice-cream cone, the tip of the cone pointing towards the earth. It swept through the city, writhing and shrieking like 1,000 wailing banshees. Later, someone described it as being like "the black hand of the devil clutching down for us poor mortals." It slashed a path of death six blocks wide, tearing down houses and twisting the steel girders of a building so that they looked like taffy.

A man paddling on Wascana Lake was lifted half a mile in his canoe, and sailed through the third storey window of a building. He was killed. Another paddler flew through the air in his canoe for three-quarters of a mile, and was deposited gently in Victoria Park. He lived to tell the tale.

It was all over in five minutes, but the tornado killed 41 people and injured 300 others. Hundreds of homeless people were sheltered in Albert Public School, or in 250 tents put up by the Royal Northwest Mounted Police. About 500 buildings were ruined with damage rising over $6 million.

Other Events on June 30:

1798   Chippewa Indians traded St. Joseph's Island for goods (see July 8).

1812   A proclamation gave American citizens fourteen days to leave Upper Canada.

1851   Robert Baldwin, Upper Canada Reform leader, retired from public life.

1866   New Brunswick voted for Confederation and the building of the Intercolonial Railway.

1948   William Lyon Mackenzie King made his last speech in the House of Commons as Prime Minister.

BY THE QUEEN!

A PROCLAMATION

For Uniting the Provinces of Canada, Nova Scotia, and New Brunswick, into one Dominion, under the name of CANADA.

VICTORIA R.

WHEREAS by an Act of Parliament, passed on the Twenty-ninth day of March, One Thousand Eight Hundred and Sixty-seven, in the Thirtieth year of Our reign, intituled, "An Act for the Union of Canada, Nova Scotia, and New Brunswick, and the Government thereof, and for purposes connected therewith." after divers recitals it is enacted that "it shall "be lawful for the Queen, by and with the advice of Her Majesty's "Most Honorable Privy Council, to declare, by Proclamation, that "on and after a day therein appointed, not being more than six "months after the passing of this Act, the Provinces of Canada, "Nova Scotia, and New Brunswick, shall form and be One Domi-"nion under the name of Canada, and on and after that day those "Three Provinces shall form and be One Dominion under that "Name accordingly;" and it is thereby further enacted, that "Such Persons shall be first summoned to the Senate as the Queen "by Warrant, under Her Majesty's Royal Sign Manual, thinks fit "to approve, and their Names shall be inserted in the Queen's "Proclamation of Union:"

We, therefore, by and with the advice of

Our Privy Council, have thought fit to issue this Our Royal Proclamation, and We do ordain, declare, and command that on and after the First day of July, One Thousand Eight Hundred and Sixty-seven, the Provinces of Canada, Nova Scotia, and New Brunswick, shall form and be One Dominion, under the name of CANADA.

And we do further ordain and declare that the persons whose names are herein inserted and set forth are the persons of whom we have by Warrant under Our Royal Sign Manual thought fit to approve as the persons who shall be first summoned to the Senate of Canada.

For the Province of Ontario.		For the Province of Quebec.		For the Province of Nova Scotia.	For the Province of New Brunswick.
John Hamilton.	Elijah Leonard.	James Leslie.	David Edward Price.	Edward Kenny.	Amos Edwin Botsford.
Roderick Matheson.	William MacMaster.	Asa Belknap Foster.	Elzear H. J. Duchesnay.	Jonathan McCully.	Edward Barron Chandler.
John Ross.	Asa Allworth Burnham.	Joseph Noël Bossé.	Leandre Dumouchel.	Thomas D. Archibald.	John Robertson.
Samuel Mills.	John Simpson.	Louis A. Olivier.	Louis Lacoste.	Robert B. Dickey.	Robert Leonard Hazen.
Benjamin Seymour.	James Skead.	Jacque Olivier Bureau.	Joseph F. Armand.	John H. Anderson.	William Hunter Odell.
Walter Hamilton Dickson.	David Lewis Macpherson.	Charles Malhiot.	Charles Wilson.	John Holmes.*	David Wark.
James Shaw.	Louis Renaud.	William Henry Chaffers.	John W. Ritchie.	William Henry Steeves.
Adam Johnson Ferguson Blair.	George Crawford.	Luc Letellier de St. Just.	Jean Baptiste Guévremont.	Benjamin Wier.	William Todd.
Alexander Campbell.	Donald Macdonald.	Ulric Joseph Tessier.	James Ferrier.	John Locke.	John Ferguson.
David Christie.	Oliver Blake.	John Hamilton.	Sir Narcise Fortunat Belleau, Kt.	Caleb R. Bill.	Robert Duncan Wilmot.
James Cox Aikins.	Billa Flint.	Charles Cormier.	Thomas Ryan.	John Bourinot.	Abner Reid McClelan.
David Reesor.	Walter McCrea.	Antoine Juchereau Duchesnay.	John Sewall Sanborn.	William Miller.	Peter Mitchell.
	George William Allan.				

Given at our Court, at Windsor Castle, this Twenty-second day of May, in the year of our Lord One Thousand Eight Hundred and Sixty-seven, and in the Thirtieth year of our reign.

GOD SAVE THE QUEEN.

Four Provinces Celebrate Canada's Birthday

. . . it is essential to the welfare of this colony, and its future good government, that a Constitution should be framed in unison with the wishes of the people, and suited to the growing importance and intelligence of the country, and that such Constitution should embrace a union of the British North American Provinces . . .

—British American League, 1849

More important events have taken place in Canada on July 1 than on any other day of the year, but first place will always be retained by Confederation Day, 1867. This was Canada's birthday, although Canada then included only Ontario, Quebec, New Brunswick and Nova Scotia.

Most nations were born of adversity, unhappy occasions, often due to war. Canada was born of diversity, a curious blending of races, geography and economics.

For the most part, her birthday was a happy occasion. In Ottawa, church bells began ringing after midnight, June 30. There was also a 101-gun salute, while 21-gun salutes were fired in other centres. In Saint John and Halifax, however, a number of merchants were so opposed to Confederation that they draped their stores in crepe.

There was a drab ceremony in the Privy Council chamber, in which Lord Monck was sworn in as governor-general by Chief Justice Draper. After the cabinet ministers had taken

The Fathers of Confederation

Architects of Confederation Honored by Queen

their oaths of office, Lord Monck, who hated pomp as much as Macdonald loved it, announced that Queen Victoria had made John A. Macdonald a Knight Commander of the Bath! Six other Fathers of Confederation, Cartier, Galt, Tilley, Tupper, Howland and McDougall, were made Companions of the Bath, which meant they would have no titles. This was a mistake. Cartier and Galt were so angry that they refused the decorations. Later, however, they were made baronets.

The remainder of the day has been summed up beautifully by W. G. Hardy in *From Sea Unto Sea*. He wrote: "The official part of the ceremonies was completed by midday. Then, across the Dominion, but more particularly in what had been the province of Canada, the people went on holiday. In Canada East, renamed Quebec, it was flags and bunting and family parties, and a cricket game at Trois Rivières. Canada West, which had now become Ontario, favored brass bands, regattas, races, and the like. In the more remote centres the farmers gathered in the local fairgrounds or picnic places for a program of sports and a country supper of salads, cold meats, pies and cakes, at tables set up on trestles under the trees. As the soft July night floated down, the villages, towns and cities were bright with Chinese lanterns on the porches and with fireworks and illuminations. The people, the inchoate mass without articulate voice, sensed that something of significance had occurred!"

Other Events on July 1:

1686   Iberville took Fort Rupert, Hudson Bay.

1870   An Order-in-Council authorized a railway to be built to the Pacific if British Columbia joined Confederation.

1873   Prince Edward Island joined Confederation.

1915   Newfoundland troops took Beaumont Hamel in France.

1927   Canada celebrated its Diamond Jubilee of Confederation.
Direct communication was established between governments of Canada and Britain without going through the governor-general.

1941   The Unemployment Insurance Act came into force.

1955   London, Ontario, held its centennial celebration.

1962   Medicare came into force in Saskatchewan.

Fraser at the Black Canyon

Fraser Nears Pacific

Simon Fraser's journey down the mighty river in British Columbia that now bears his name was one of the most dangerous ever undertaken by man.

The Northwest Company wanted to extend its fur trading activities to the Pacific coast, but before this could be done, a route from the Peace River to the Pacific had to be found. Simon Fraser was to find it. He did not have the scientific training of Alexander Mackenzie, the first man to cross the continent, but he was a man of tenacious courage.

Accompanied by John Stuart, Jules Maurice Quesnel, nineteen *voyageurs* and two Indian guides, Fraser left Fort George on May 29, 1808. Down the muddy river, which he thought was the Columbia, they battled rapids and whirlpools, sometimes carrying their canoes down banks so steep that their lives hung by a thread. Near Pavilion, Fraser had the canoes placed on a scaffold, hid most of the supplies and continued on foot. At an Indian encampment (now Lytton), they were shown European goods which could only have come from the Pacific. Nearby, there was a beautiful river of clear blue water flowing into the main river, and Fraser called it the Thompson, after his fellow explorer David

Thompson. Unknown to Fraser, Thompson himself was on the Columbia at that moment.

The journey down from Lytton was even more dangerous. Soon they had to abandon their cedar dugouts and scramble along the river banks. When they reached Black Canyon, one of the Indians climbed to the summit and pulled up the others with a rope hung from a long pole. They made their perilous way past Hell's Gate, creeping above the precipices by hanging onto ropes fastened to trees. In this way they crawled to what is now Spuzzum and Yale!

Near Mount Baker, fierce Cowichan Indians tried to block their way but were kept off through fear of the guns Fraser and his men had managed to carry. On July 2 they reached the Indian village of Musqueam. They were only a few miles from the Pacific and could see the mountains of Vancouver Island. Fraser took a reading for latitude, and discovered that it was 49 degrees; whereas if he had been on the Columbia, as he thought, it would have been 46 degrees 20 seconds. What a disappointment after such a journey! Fraser came so close, but he never saw the Pacific. A tired, discouraged man returned to Fort George on August 5.

Other Events on July 2:

1578 Martin Frobisher discovered Hudson Strait.

1603 Champlain reached the rapids that later became known as "Lachine".

1679 Dulhut (after whom Duluth is called) claimed the Red River area for France.

1851 Lord Elgin laid the cornerstone of the Ottawa Normal School.

1885 Northwest Rebellion ended with the capture of Big Bear.

1955 Charlottetown, Prince Edward Island, celebrated its centennial.

1959 Canada and Japan signed a pact concerning the use of atomic energy.

1963 Canada rushed 50,000 doses of polio vaccine to the Barbados.

Champlain Establishes Colony at Quebec

It was de Monts who fitted out the expedition that was responsible for the founding of Quebec on July 3, 1608. There were three ships; one went to Port Royal to revive the original community, while Champlain took the other two to Quebec. On the way up the St. Lawrence, they had to fight their way past Basque traders at Tadoussac.

Champlain had brought competent workmen and, taking advantage of the abundant timber, they built a habitation of which Champlain left a drawing. The three wooden buildings, each of two stories, with a gallery around the second storey, were protected by a ditch, 15 feet wide and 6 feet deep. Champlain mounted a cannon as a further safeguard because the Indians heard the news of his arrival through their uncanny "woodlands telegraph," and came in thousands to see what was going on. Perhaps they weren't so different from the "sidewalk superintendents" who like to watch new buildings going up today!

Champlain's greatest danger at that time was within his own ranks. While he was working on a garden, a river pilot asked to speak to him alone. He told Champlain that there was a conspiracy to end the French fur trading monopoly. The plan was to sound an alarm at night and shoot Champlain when he appeared. Then Quebec would be handed over to the Basques or to Spain.

Champlain learned who the leaders of the conspiracy were and was amazed to find that even his personal attendant was involved. He invited the conspirators to a festival at which he served wine. He then had them seized and put on trial. Three men were sent back to France to face trial there, and were later executed. Another man, locksmith Duval, was hanged at Quebec. His head was exhibited on a pole as a warning to others who might get ideas.

In 1908 there was a stirring ceremony at Quebec celebrating the tri-centennial anniversary of its founding. Chief among the visitors was the heir to the throne, who later became King George V. British and American warships, decorated by day and lit by night, added to the majesty of the scene, dominated by the stone cliff and Citadel of Canada's oldest city.

Other Events on July 3:

1717   The building of the fortress of Louisburg began.

1754   George Washington, then a British officer, attacked a French force at Fort Necessity and was forced to retreat.

1770   The first ordination of a Presbyterian minister in Canada took place at Halifax.

1797   The Law Society of Upper Canada was established by a statute.

1814   Fort Erie, Ontario, was captured by an American force.

1876   The Intercolonial Railway was completed between Halifax and Rivière du Loup.

Quebec, from a drawing by Champlain

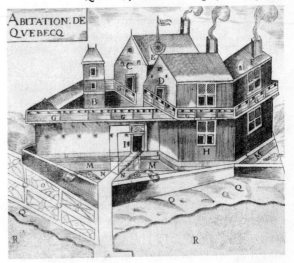

Halifax Greets Liner

In the days of "wooden ships and iron men," the people of Nova Scotia and New Brunswick were the most prosperous, per capita, of all the people in British North America. Shipbuilding yards were turning out vessels, like the *Marco Polo* (see April 17), which became famous in many parts of the world. This prosperity ended when iron ships powered by steam replaced wooden sailing ships. Strangely enough, two Nova Scotians were responsible, and one of them founded the greatest steamship company in the world.

Joseph Howe (see January 1) had helped create the shipbuilding industry in Nova Scotia. The original "Bluenoses" had been encouraged to go in for farming. Howe had other ideas. Nova Scotian soil was not good enough for prosperous farming, and he urged men to take advantage of the timber resources and fine harbours, and go in for shipbuilding. In 1838, however, when Howe was crossing the Atlantic in a windjammer, the steamship *Sirius* came over the horizon and passed his ship "with the speed of a hunter while we were moving with the rapidity of an ox-cart." Howe was so impressed that he urged the Colonial Office in Britain to subsidize fast ships to carry the mail between Liverpool and Halifax.

It was then that the other Nova Scotian, Samuel Cunard, who had made a fortune in lumber and sailing ships, stepped into the picture. He won the contract to carry mail and passengers in fast steamships between Liverpool and Halifax, and joining with some British businessmen, he established the now famous Cunard Line. The first Cunarder, *Britannia*, sailed into Halifax on July 4, 1840, and then went on to Boston. The voyage from Liverpool to Boston was completed in 14 days 8 hours at a speed of 8½ knots. The Liverpool to Halifax run was made in 12 days 10 hours. Cunard himself was received with great enthusiasm everywhere. When he arrived in Boston, he received 1,800 invitations to dinner, within twenty-four hours!

The first iron Cunarder was the *Scotia* (3,871 tons), the largest ship in the world when she was built in 1862. *Scotia* would look like a tug boat alongside the famous Cunarders *Queen Mary* and *Queen Elizabeth*, both more than 80,000 tons.

Among the most famous Cunard liners of all time have been *Lusitania* (sunk by a German submarine in World War I), *Mauretania*, *Berengaria*, and *Aquitania*, which was the flagship of the convoy that carried the First Canadian Division to Britain in World War II.

Other Events on July 4:

1609 Champlain discovered Lake Champlain in New York.

1634 Trois Rivières, Quebec, was founded by a fur trader named La Violette who was later flogged for selling liquor to the Indians.

1793 Alexander Mackenzie left his canoe on the Blackwater River and began walking to the Pacific.

1865 An American consul read the Declaration of Independence at Cordova Bay, near Victoria, British Columbia.

1873 The Montreal *Herald* published letters leading to the resignation of Sir John A. Macdonald.

1886 The first C.P.R. transcontinental train arrived at Port Moody, near Vancouver. It left Montreal on June 28.

1945 Canadians entered Berlin as part of a garrison force.

Montcalm Victorious

Fort Ticonderoga, N.Y.

One of the greatest military leaders who ever operated in Canada was undoubtedly the Marquis de Montcalm, who was killed in Wolfe's attack on Quebec. He was sent to command French forces in Canada in 1756 and at once found himself in a difficult situation.

The governor at that time was the Marquis de Vaudreuil, the Canadian-born son of a former governor. Vaudreuil and his friends did not approve of strict French military discipline, or the superior airs of the French officers. The French, on the other hand, were shocked by the barbarities of the Indians who were allies of the Canadians. French "regulars" did not want to be associated with men who enjoyed cutting up human bodies to be made into soup, or drinking another Indian gourmet delight, "bouillon," a cup of hot blood!

Despite these handicaps, Montcalm went ahead with his plans to crush the British campaign to capture Canada. War was declared soon after Montcalm arrived at Quebec and he immediately went on the offensive. He worked day and night to prepare his forces. In order to attack the British fort at Oswego, New York, he had to move his troops and supplies up the St. Lawrence, a back-breaking task. Oswego fell in twelve days. Montcalm took 1,600 prisoners, whom he managed to transport to Montreal.

In 1757, Moncalm scored another big victory, beating the British at Fort William Henry, at Lake George. This story, an epic of its own, will be told in August.

In 1758 came Montcalm's most remarkable victory. After destroying Fort William Henry, he held Fort Ticonderoga at the other end of Lake George. The British attacked it on July 5, with a force of 16,000 troops, 9,000 of whom were "colonial." Montcalm defended Ticonderoga with 3,000 men. His position seemed hopeless against such odds, but he remained undaunted. He had his men build a breastwork of logs around the fort; the branches, with their full-grown leaves, were left lying on the ground where the trees were cut to retard the British advance. The French could easily see the red coats in the green foliage and fired shattering volleys into them. General Abercromby had to retreat, leaving 2,000 dead or wounded. One of those killed was a brilliant young soldier, Lord Howe, brother of the famous admiral who drove Washington from New York in the American Revolutionary War.

Montcalm became a national hero. He went back to prepare the defense of Quebec after Louisburg fell, knowing in his heart that defeat was inevitable as long as Britain had command of the sea.

Other Events on July 5:

1812   American General Hull arrived at Detroit to invade Canada with 2,500 men.

1814   American forces were victorious at Chippewa, near Niagara Falls.

1827   A general militia order caused riots in Lower Canada.

1866   The first steam engine operated in Prince Edward Island.

1879   Lieutenant-Governor Letellier de St. Just was removed from office by the Federal Government.

1913   Vilhjalmur Stefanson left Seattle to spend five years in the Arctic for the Canadian Government (see February 20).

1958   The Stephen Leacock Memorial Home was opened at Orillia, Ontario.

Luxton and Voss aboard the Tilikum, *1901*

Adventurers Set Sail

The United States has done a wonderful job in making the stories of its heroes and "characters" known to its citizens. Canada has lagged behind in this respect, although the present Lieutenant-Governor of Alberta, Grant MacEwan, has done something to remedy this in his book *Fifty Mighty Men*.

Who, for instance, has heard of Norman Luxton? His father was one of the founders of the Winnipeg *Free Press,* and candidate for mayor in the first city election in 1874. He was defeated by F. E. Cornish. There were 308 names on the voters' list, but 331 ballots were cast! Nobody protested. Cornish, as mayor, fined himself $5 for having been drunk and disorderly during the victory celebration.

Young Norman worked for the Calgary *Herald*, prospected for gold in the Kootenay area of British Columbia and started his own newspaper in Vancouver. As Grant MacEwan explains, when Luxton criticized the ministerial association for not doing enough to counteract vice, "theological buckshot" began to fly at the paper and Luxton's business failed.

The next adventure was an expedition to the South Seas. For $8 Luxton bought a 28-foot Indian dugout canoe which was later called the *Tilikum*. It was 100 years old but he built a cabin on it, and set sail with Captain J. C. Voss, a Norwegian adventurer. They left Nootka on July 6, 1901.

By the time they reached Apia, Samoa, Luxton and Voss hated each other. They needed money so badly that Luxton taught the natives to play poker. The king offered Luxton an estate of coconut trees if he would marry one of his daughters. Refusal would have meant being fed to the sharks but Luxton managed to escape. On another island, they used the old Spanish cannon to save themselves from being made into stew. Eventually they were shipwrecked; Luxton became ill and went to Australia; Voss sailed the *Tilikum* to England, arriving in September 1904.

Luxton returned to Canada and helped found the Winter Carnival and the annual Indian Days Festival at Banff. He played a major part in saving the buffalo from extinction through the creation of Wainwright National Park. In Calgary, the Luxton Museum is a memorial to him.

Other Events on July 6:

1669   La Salle began a journey from Montreal to Niagara; he arrived on September 15.

1795   The Upper Canada Parliament opened a session that passed laws concerning medicine, the Supreme Court, and customs agreement with Lower Canada.

1858   A. T. Galt advocated union of the British North American colonies.

1862   The British Government approved in principle the union of British North America.

1892   A great fire at St. John's, Newfoundland, left 10,000 people homeless.

1896   Quebec was extended to Hudson Bay, thus adding 188,450 square miles to its area.

1906   Parliament passed the Lord's Day Act after a bitter debate.

1961   Robert N. Thompson was elected President of the Social Credit Party.

Indians See First White Woman at Nootka Sound

It was probably on July 7, 1787, that the first white woman arrived in what is now British Columbia. She was the seventeen year old bride of Captain Charles Barkley of the 400-ton *Imperial Eagle*, a British ship operating under an Austrian flag.

Dutch merchants had cornered the East Indies pepper market and doubled its price. British traders struck back by securing a charter awarding them exclusive rights in the East Indies and equipping a number of ships to carry the trade. Charles Barkley was given command of a fine ship called *Loudon*, well-armed with a disciplined crew. Owing to complications in international trade, the *Loudon* was taken to Ostend, Belgium, given Austrian registry and renamed *Imperial Eagle*. All this took about two months, during which time Barkley met Frances Hornby Trevor. They were married in October, 1786, and the *Imperial Eagle* spread her white sails for a voyage around Cape Horn to Nootka, Vancouver Island—quite a honeymoon trip!

Early in July, Barkley entered the strait between Vancouver Island and the mainland and named it Juan de Fuca after an early explorer. After arriving at Nootka, the ship anchored in Friendly Cove near the village of Chief Maquinna. The Indians, who had never seen a white woman before, were amazed by Frances.

There was also a surprise. A small boat came out from shore and a most disreputable-looking white man came on board. He was filthy and wearing otter skins for clothes. It turned out that he was Dr. John Mackay, who had been left there the previous year by an expedition led by James Strange. Mackay had spent the winter with the Indians, studying their habits and their health. He had also planted some garden seeds and grain to see how they would grow. Mackay has the distinction of being the first farmer and doctor on the Pacific coast. He had learned a great deal from the Indians. His garden had grown, but the Indians had stolen his clothes and implements. Mackay was greatly relieved to rejoin some fellow countrymen! Mackay turned out to be a great help to Barkley because he had learned to speak the Indian language. Together, they practically cornered the fur market for a time!

Other Events on July 7:

1613 Sir Thomas Button named the Nelson River, on Hudson Bay.

1620 Champlain began Fort St. Louis on the present site of the Chateau Frontenac Hotel, Quebec.

1821 Lower Canada took over the building of the Lachine Canal from a private company and began construction on July 17.

1870 The British Columbia Government was notified that terms for Confederation had been accepted in Ottawa.

1895 There was a cabinet crisis in Ottawa over the Manitoba separate schools question.

Friendly Cove, Nootka Sound, 1792

Chippewas Cede Territories to Government

Long before the Canadian Government began acquiring land from the Indians in Western Canada, the Indians in Eastern Canada had given up most of their holdings. The Indian treaties for territory west of Thunder Bay began in 1871, but in the East, big deals were being made in the 1820's. For instance, on July 8, 1832, the Chippewas ceded 580,000 acres that are now part of Lambton, Kent, and Middlesex counties in Ontario.

An early land transaction occurred in 1798 when the Chippewas traded St. Joseph's Island for goods worth £1,200, or $6,000 at the old exchange rate of $5 per pound. St. Joseph's Island has 90,000 acres, ranking second in size in Ontario. The deed for the transaction can still be seen in the registrar's office at Sault Ste. Marie. There are nine signatures for the Indians, headed by Okaw, Chippewa Chief, and Wabakangawana, Chippewa Chief of Lake Superior. Okaw's sign was a hand-drawn caribou; the others drew pictures of ducks, cranes, geese, fish, a fox and a wolf. The document concludes by saying that the deal was made after the chiefs heard the terms openly read in their own language. It was fully approved by them.

In return for the island, the Indians received 1,240 blankets, 6,000 yards of cloth, kettles, pipes, tobacco, leather trunks, 25 plain hats, 30 laced hats, and 30 silk handkerchiefs. There were also rifles, ammunition, 60 dozen knives of various types, and scissors. The deal also included one bullock and 50 gallons of rum—for a feast no doubt. Nor were the women forgotten. It is not clear if the plain and laced hats were for them, but there were 6 dozen ivory combs for the girls who wanted to be fancy and 15 dozen horn combs for the others. There were also 15 dozen looking glasses and 30 pounds of thread. Seventy-five pounds of vermillion probably did paint jobs for either sex.

Toronto columnist Scott Young has figured out that if the Indians had taken $6,000 cash instead of goods, and invested it at 5 per cent, they would have about $30 million by July 8, 1972. Mr. Young calculated the earnings until 1972 to avoid a massive reaction on today's stock markets, and said the story contained a lesson for all, especially the Chippewas!

Other Events on July 8:

1760   Captain John Byron defeated a French fleet in the Bay of Chaleur.

1874   The Royal Northwest Mounted Police began their march from Manitoba to Fort Whoop-Up, near Calgary.

1876   Royal Northwest Mounted Police Inspector Denny held a conference with the Blackfoot Chiefs concerning a proposition from Sitting Bull to join in the war against whites in Canada and the United States.

1896   The Conservative Government under Sir Charles Tupper resigned. The Liberals under Sir Wilfrid Laurier took over.

1899   A streetcar strike in London, Ontario, made it necessary to call out troops to quell riots.

1937   The Imperial Airways flying boat *Caledonia* arrived at Montreal from Southampton, England. It was the inauguration of an experimental phase of transatlantic flying.

1958   President Eisenhower was in Ottawa for defense discussions.

Mounties Police West

Many people would fail to identify the maple leaf or the beaver as a symbol of Canada, but most people would recognize a scarlet-coated member of the Royal Canadian Mounted Police.

The famous force was organized by an act of Parliament on May 20, 1873, under the name Royal Northwest Mounted Police. (The name was changed to Royal Canadian Mounted Police in 1920.) The force was assembled at New Fort Toronto, and by June 1874, it was ready to leave for the West. Men, horses, and equipment traveled by United States railway lines to Pembina, just south of the Manitoba border. On July 9, they began their march to the Cypress Hills, Saskatchewan, and the Fort Whoop-Up country, now in the Calgary area.

They were greatly needed. Unscrupulous traders were bringing the proud Blackfoot Indians to a state of degeneration, taking their furs and guns in exchange for a potent drink called "Whoop-Up bug juice." This was made by mixing a quart of whisky, a pound of chewing tobacco, a handful of red pepper, a bottle of Jamaica ginger and a quart of molasses; the mixture was then diluted with water and heated to make "firewater."

There were terrible orgies and massacres among the Indians and the white traders. One of the worst was a battle at Cypress Hills, in May, 1873, between a party of "wolfers" and a tribe led by Chief Little Soldier. The "wolfers" were men who killed animals for their furs by spreading strychnine poison over the ground. They were hated by the Indians and the other white fur traders.

The battle was started when a "wolfer" accused Little Soldier's band of stealing his horse. Later it was found grazing on a hillside, having just strayed away. The "wolfers" rushed the Indian camp, killed Little Soldier and cut off his head, which they mounted on a pole. They then murdered the squaws and their children. It was this type of situation that the Mounties had to keep under control.

N.W. Mounted Police expedition—a halt to cut hay

When the force reached Roche Percée late in July, it divided into two sections. One marched to Fort Edmonton which it reached on October 27, while the other set out for Fort Whoop-Up, which it reached on October 9, after a terrible journey.

Other Events on July 9:

1706 Pierre Le Moyne d'Iberville died at Havana, Cuba.

1793 Upper Canada prohibited the importation of slaves.

1811 David Thompson claimed the area at the junction of the Snake and Columbia Rivers for Britain.

1825 Fort Douglas on the Red River was sold to Robert Logan for £400.

1843 *Prince Albert*, the first iron steamer built in Canada, was launched at Montreal.

1852 A fire in the east end of Montreal destroyed 1,100 homes.

1918 The second airmail flight was flown by Kathleen Stinson from Calgary to Edmonton.

1944 British and Canadian troops launched an attack on Caen, which became important after the opening of the Second Front in Europe.

Maritimes Relieved – Rival "Mosquitoes" Fight

When the American Revolutionary War began in 1775, parts of Nova Scotia had been settled by people brought from the colonial states to replace the Acadians. Naturally, there was a great deal of sympathy for the American cause and an organization was set up to support it.

A delegation to the Congress at Philadelphia gave the names of 600 people who were ready to join the rebellion, and Nova Scotians even attacked Cumberland. They were easily defeated, however, and the uprising in the Maritimes never became serious.

One of the rebel leaders in Nova Scotia gave the Americans advice on how to win the Maritimes, urging them to equip small ships that could run up the tidal waters of Nova Scotia and attack the settlements inland. This was done very successfully. The American raiders sailed close to shore, where heavier British warships could not catch them, and a great many communities were raided and plundered.

Eventually, however, the operation backfired. Many of the American ships in the "mosquito fleet" were little better than pirates, and Nova Scotia soon turned against them. The leading citizens of the fishing village of Lockeport sent a protest to Massachusetts saying: "the scoundrels took 19 quintals of codfish, 4 barrels of salt, 3 salmon nets, 60 pounds of butter, 1 green hide, 5 dressed skins, some cheese and other things . . . These things are very surprising in that we in this harbour have done so much for America, that we have helped three or four hundred prisoners go along to America and have given part of our living to them. If this is the way we are to be repaid we desire to see no more of you without you come in another manner . . ."

They came back in the same manner. However, this time, as most of the menfolk were away, the women and children, living up on a bluff, wore red coats and carried broomsticks which looked like guns. One woman marched up and down with a drum. The raiders thought they were soldiers and departed.

The Government of Nova Scotia organized a tiny navy to oppose the rebels. Rebel strength was further depleted by battles, such as the one on July 10, 1780, between rival members of the "mosquito fleet."

Other Events on July 10:

1920   Sir Robert Borden resigned. He was succeeded by Arthur Meighen.
New Brunswick voted for total prohibition.

1943   A Canadian army invaded Sicily.

1951   Canada ended the state of war with Germany by royal proclamation.

1958   A Canada-United States Joint Committee was established for defense.

1960   Roger Woodward, age seven, survived a 167-foot drop over Niagara Falls.

1963   The Federal and British Columbia Governments agreed on a Columbia River Power Treaty.

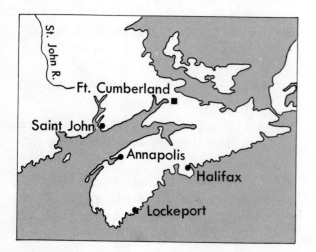

Fire Devastates North

One of the worst enemies of progress in Canada is the forest fire. The average annual loss of timber has been three million acres, valued at about nine million dollars.

The timber industry is not the only one to have suffered the losses owing to fire. In 1911, eight years after the dramatic discovery of silver at Cobalt, Ontario, disastrous fire swept the newly developed mining communities of Northern Ontario.

Fred LaRose, a blacksmith for a construction gang, made the original discovery of silver by accident in 1903. LaRose thought he saw the gleaming eye of a fox, and threw a hammer at it. Instead of killing a fox, he uncovered a vein of silver that turned out to be the richest in the world. LaRose sold his claim for $30,000, but Cobalt produced $300 million in ten years. Still, $30,000 was not a bad prize for a hammer throw!

The mining boom which began at Cobalt spread northward and prospered until 1911. That summer was very hot. On July 11, puffs of smoke could be seen rising from the woods. Gradually, the sun was hidden in a coppery haze. Suddenly, the forests seemed to explode in a crackling, roaring holocaust, driven by a wind of nearly hurricane force. People left their homes and tried to shelter in swamps, lakes and rivers. They waded out as far as they could until only their heads were above water. The strong wind churned up waves and many were drowned.

Others thought they would be safe down the mining shafts, but died when the fire sucked out the oxygen, asphyxiating the helpless people. More than 800 square miles of territory were destroyed, including the communities of South Porcupine, Pottsville, Cochrane, and Goldlands. Other communities like Porquis Junction and Golden City were badly damaged. The Porcupine area was enjoying its own gold mining boom, notably at the Hollinger and McIntyre mines (see July 13).

A raging forest fire in Northern Ontario

The death toll was never known because there were untold prospectors in the woods. It is believed that over 200 people were killed, and more than 3,000 people were left homeless.

Other Events on July 11:

1814 A British force from Nova Scotia captured Eastport, Maine (see August 31).

1865 A convention at Detroit favored continued reciprocity with Canada. Joseph Howe was one of the speakers.

1872 Canada asked the British Foreign Office to take up the Alaskan Boundary question with the United States (see March 25).

1884 Louis Riel arrived in Canada to lead the Northwest Rebellion.

1896 Sir Wilfrid Laurier became prime minister and was in office until October 6, 1911.

1960 The Northwest Territories Council was convened at Resolute Bay. It was the most northerly meeting of any legislative body in the world.

Canada Invaded

We are engaged in an awful and eventful contest. By unanimity and despatch in our councils and by vigour in our operations, we will teach the enemy this lesson: that a country defended by free men, enthusiastically devoted to the cause of their King and constitution, can never be conquered.

—General Isaac Brock, 1812

When the United States of America declared war on Britain on June 18, 1812, the objective was to "liberate" Canada. The Americans had been sending spies into Canada since 1808. One of them was James Fenimore Cooper, later to become a famous author. He reported on the defenses of Kingston, Ontario, which he visited as a member of the crew of an American schooner that pretended to be driven in by a storm.

The first American attack on Canada was almost a comedy. The invasion came from Detroit, but the British knew all about it long before it happened. General Hull, the American commander, announced *even before war had been declared* that his troops were bound for Canada. While they marched from Dayton, Ohio, to Detroit, he sent a large quantity of army stores and baggage by water. When the American schooner entered the Detroit River, it was stopped by a British patrol boat and an examination of its cargo revealed letters and documents outlining the strategy of Hull's campaign! General Hull wasn't worrying. He had 2,500 men; there were only 150 British regulars, 300 militia and 150 Indians on the Canadian side. In any case, Hull expected to be welcomed as a liberator and invited the American soldiers to bring along their wives and children for the joyous occasion!

When Hull crossed the river at Baby's Farm on July 12, 1812, he issued a proclamation stating that the United States offered Peace, Liberty, and Security. The alternative was War, Slavery, and Destruction. He was making his proclamation to the wrong people, because many of them were United Empire Loyalists who had been driven from their homes in the States by persecution!

Shortly afterwards, Hull learned that a combined force of British and Indians from St. Joseph's Island had captured the American fort at Mackinac, Michigan. Another force had captured Fort Dearborn (Chicago). The Indians had run wild at Dearborn and massacred about half the population.

Panic overtook Hull. Chief Tecumseh and some of his Indians were ambushing American soldiers and Hull thought they might attack the wives and children he had brought along to see the "liberation." On August 11, he withdrew his force to Detroit, although it outnumbered the British and Indians two to one.

Other Events on July 12:

1673   Frontenac landed at Cataraqui with 120 canoes.

1744   Indians, incited by Father Le Loutre, attacked Annapolis Royal.

1759   Wolfe bombarded Quebec and repulsed a counter-attack.

1776   Captain Cook sailed from Plymouth on a voyage to Vancouver Island.

1822   Captain Parry sailed north to discover Fury and Hecla Straits.

1849   Twelve people were killed in a riot between the Orangemen and Roman Catholics in Saint John, New Brunswick.

1877   Rioting broke out between the Orangemen and Roman Catholics in Montreal.

1950   Canadian destroyers arrived at Pearl Harbor en route to Korea.

1952   Canada and Ceylon agreed to plan economic aid under the Colombo Plan.

1958   Princess Margaret toured Canada until August 11.

1963   Queen Victoria's monument at Montreal was destroyed by a dynamite explosion.

Porcupine Gold Found

Sure I've got
Warts on my fingers
Corns on my toes
Claims up in Porcupine
And a bad cold in my nose.
So, put on your snowshoes
And hit the trail with me
To P-o-r-c-u-p-i-n-e,— that's me.

—JOHN E. LECKIE, 1910

Some of Canada's most exciting days came through the discovery of gold. The prospectors who found large quantities of it were more lucky than scientific. All they needed in the way of equipment was a pick, shovel and perhaps pans for sifting gold from the sand.

In 1896, George Washington Carmack began the biggest gold rush of all with his discovery on Bonanza Creek in the Yukon. Books, poems, and songs have been written about the Klondike, and Hollywood has produced its own versions. Charlie Chaplin's "Gold Rush" is still worth seeing.

Northern Ontario and Quebec have both had their gold rushes. The development of the rich Porcupine area was due to a lucky strike on July 13, 1909. Thomas Geddes, of St. Thomas, Ontario, and George Bannerman had a hunch about the Porcupine. From North Bay, on the T.N.O. Railway, they traveled north for 220 miles, which was the end of the line. T.N.O. means Temiskaming and Northern Ontario Railway, but in those days people used to say that it meant "Time No Object!"

From the end of the line, they paddled 30 miles west and camped where the river flowed into Porcupine Lake. They began digging on the northern side of the lake and soon uncovered a filigree of gold, as thick as wax dripping from a candle! The news spread like wildfire. Soon the Porcupine area was swarming with prospectors who uncovered Canada's richest gold field and most famous mines.

Among the lucky prospectors were Benny Hollinger and Sandy McIntyre, after whom two great mines have been named. Hollinger borrowed $45 from John McMahon of Haileybury, and found three feet of gold jutting from some moss. Sandy McIntyre's real name was Alexander Oliphant, but he changed it when he fled from Scotland to avoid paying alimony to his wife. He found what is now McIntyre mine but sold his shares for $25 so that he could buy some liquor. In later years, he spent most of his time weeping in saloons while his discovery produced gold worth $230 million.

Is it still possible to be lucky and find gold? Some authorities believe so. In any case it may be worth remembering that July 13 was a lucky day for Geddes and Bannerman.

Other Events on July 13:

1620   The Caën brothers, Huguenots, formed a company to develop Canada.

1789   A British ship, *Princess Royal*, was seized by Spaniards at Nootka, British Columbia.

1922   Canada and the United States discussed the continuing of the Rush-Bagot Treaty prohibiting armaments on the Great Lakes.

1941   Canada approved the Anglo-Soviet Treaty. (Germany had attacked Russia on June 22.)

1949   The first Legislature of Newfoundland as a province of Canada was opened.

1953   The Shakespearian Festival at Stratford, Ontario, opened.

1961   The Right Honorable Duncan Sandys met the government at Ottawa to discuss Britain's proposed membership in the European Common Market.

I wanted the gold, and I sought it;
I scrabbled and mucked like a slave.
Was it famine or scurvy — I fought it;
I hurled my youth into a grave.
I wanted the gold and I got it —
Came out with a fortune last fall,—
Yet somehow life's not what I thought it,
And somehow the gold isn't all.

—ROBERT W. SERVICE, 1907

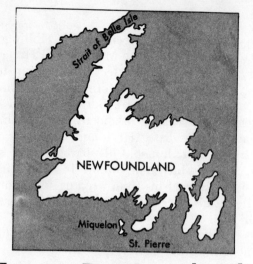

France Retains Islands

Little noticed and seldom visited are the islands of St. Pierre and Miquelon off Burin Peninsula, southwest Newfoundland. They are all that is left of the vast possessions France once held in North America.

France seemed glad to get rid of Canada through the Treaty of Paris signed in 1763, but she kept St. Pierre and Miquelon as bases for French fishing vessels. Fishing rights along the coasts were probably the most valuable thing Canada had to offer in those days. Britain agreed to France's retaining St. Pierre and Miquelon, provided they would be used only as fishing bases. No fort could be built, and the police force was never to exceed fifty men.

France put the Baron de l'Espérance in charge of the islands on July 14, 1763. Although many Acadians had drifted back to Canada after the expulsion of 1755, some of them refused to become British subjects. The Baron de l'Espérance gave them land in St. Pierre-Miquelon, and hoped they would become good settlers.

This was a mistake. The Acadians were farmers and the soil of the island was unsuitable for agriculture. Many of them were so unhappy that they were taken to France. They were unhappy in France too, and decided that the barren soil of St. Pierre-Miquelon was preferable to the tyranny and oppression in France in 1768. So back they came!

A large number made a living by fishing rather than farming. Smuggling was a profitable sideline.

When the American Revolutionary War broke out in 1775, Admiral Montague, Governor of Newfoundland, evacuated nearly 2,000 inhabitants of St. Pierre-Miquelon and sent them to France. Most of them returned at the end of the war and there was peace and quiet until Britain became involved in war again with Napoleon and the French Revolution.

There were even problems during World War II when France was governed by Vichy. It was always possible that Germany would take over France completely, and that St. Pierre-Miquelon could be used as bases for submarines or spies. The inhabitants were allowed to stay on the islands, but a proposal to build a powerful radio station was cancelled.

Gradually, St. Pierre-Miquelon, through their direct link with old and new France, are becoming increasingly attractive to tourists. The tourist trade will probably become the islands' most important source of revenue.

Other Events on July 14:

1643　Charles La Tour sailed from Boston to attack Charnisay, his rival for Nova Scotia.

1696　Iberville and Bonaventure captured the British ship *Newport* near St. John's, Newfoundland.

1760　General Murray left Quebec with 2,500 troops to attack Montreal.

1789　Alexander Mackenzie reached the Arctic Ocean the same day as the fall of the Bastille (see June 3).

1915　Sir Robert Borden was the first Dominion Prime Minister to attend a British cabinet meeting.

1940　A. G. L. McNaughton was made lieutenant-general and placed in command of a British corps as well as Canadian troops in Britain.

River Mouth Reached

David Thompson taking an observation

On July 15, 1811, David Thompson reached the mouth of the Columbia River only to find that John Jacob Astor's fur company had established a post there late in March. This was a great disappointment to Thompson, who had hoped to claim the territory for Britain. Nevertheless, this is an opportunity to present a few highlights in the life of the man who was probably the greatest geographer in the world.

David Thompson was of Welsh extraction and came from a poor family. He was only fourteen years of age when he was apprenticed to the Hudson's Bay Company and sent to Fort Churchill, Hudson Bay, in 1784. He spent thirteen years there and at other company posts in Saskatchewan, and also a winter with Indians at the present site of Calgary. Surveying, which he studied with Philip Turnor, became his favorite hobby.

In 1797 he transferred to the Northwest Company and made a 4,000 mile journey of exploration that included the headwaters of the Mississippi. Later he was made a partner in the company. Years were spent tracing the crazy course of the Columbia River, which curves back and forth between Canada and the United States, almost entwining itself with the Kootenay. Thompson was the first man to travel the full length of the Columbia and back again. He began his final assault on the Columbia in 1810. He manufactured snowshoes and sleds and started from the Athabaska River on December 29 in weather 21 degrees below zero! He traveled through the Rockies under these conditions to the junction of the Canoe and Columbia Rivers.

After Thompson finished his work in the West, he went to live at Terrebonne, near Montreal, where he prepared a map of Western Canada which is now in the Ontario Archives. His maps were not like those of the early explorers. They were accurate.

When Thompson arrived at Churchill in 1784, the map of Canada was blank from Lake Winnipeg to the west coast of Vancouver Island. When he departed from the West in 1812, he had mapped the main travel routes through 1,700,000 square miles of Canadian and American territory! It is tragic to remember that David Thompson died in 1857, in poverty and nearly blind.

Other Events on July 15:

1710   A British force attacked Port Royal, Nova Scotia.

1870   Manitoba became the fifth Canadian province (see May 12).
A royal proclamation stated that all territory between Ontario and British Columbia belonged to Canada.

1889   The C.P.R. was given a contract by Britain to carry mail from Halifax or Quebec to Hong Kong.

1896   The Canadian yacht *Glencairn* won an international race.

1930   The Federal Government allowed Manitoba to control its own natural resources.

Sir John A. Macdonald (1815-1891)

Sir John Goes West

On this day in 1886, Sir John and Lady Macdonald were crossing Canada on the new C.P.R. transcontinental. It was the first time the great architect of Canada had been west of Ontario!

Sir John and Lady Macdonald began their trip on July 11. It must have been an amazing experience for the Prime Minister, then seventy-one years old, to see the West for the first time. Although his son Hugh, by his first marriage, lived at Winnipeg, Sir John had never been out there. On the trip west, Sir John and his wife spent three days in Winnipeg with him.

They continued across the prairies and stopped at Regina for a week-end with Governor Dewdney. It was less than a year after the hanging of Riel in the Regina jail, an issue that was to plague Sir John for the rest of his career. When the train stopped at Gleichen, Alberta, the old Indian leader Crowfoot was introduced. He was wearing his oldest clothes, a sign of mourning for his nephew Poundmaker, who had died after being put in prison for his part in the Northwest Rebellion.

Sir John and Lady Macdonald really saw the Rockies! They rode on what was called the "buffer bar" or "cowcatcher" of the engine while they were going through Kicking Horse Pass. Vancouver had been burned to the ground only a few weeks before they arrived, so the Macdonalds went over to Victoria. Strangely enough, Sir John had been a member of Parliament for the capital of British Columbia, although he had never seen it. He was given a seat there when he was defeated in his own constituency in Kingston in 1878.

This was Sir John's first view of the Pacific! He and Lady Macdonald enjoyed two weeks rest at Driard House, and then the Prime Minister drove the last spike of the railway between Esquimalt and Nanaimo. The ceremony took place at Shawnigan Lake, now the site of a famous boys' school.

Without being critical of Sir John, it might have been a good thing for Canada if he had gone west with Hugh in 1870, or even before the Northwest Rebellion in 1885. Circumstances made such a trip almost impossible before it actually took place.

Other Events on July 16:

1647   Lake St. John, Quebec, was discovered by Father de Quen.

1783   Royal grants of land were given to the United Empire Loyalists.

1885   Lord Revelstoke saved the C.P.R. financially. The mountain and community in British Columbia are named after him.

1925   Saskatchewan voted for government control of liquor, repealing the Prohibition Act of 1916.

1965   Lucien Rivard was arrested more than four months after escaping from Bordeaux Prison.

Americans Lose Fort Mackinac to the British

On July 17, 1812, a small British force from St. Joseph's Island captured Fort Mackinac (Michilimackinac) from the Americans. Strangely enough the British had also captured it on the same date in 1777, during the American Revolutionary War.

The capture of Fort Mackinac in 1812 was a colorful affair. The British had only 45 regular soldiers on St. Joseph's Island, but they recruited 180 Canadians and 400 Indians and traveled to Fort Mackinac in canoes! It was a journey of 50 miles, but they made it in good time and managed to get a cannon up the island's cliffs without being detected. The 60 American "blue coats" in the garrison surrendered immediately, giving up seven cannons and valuable supplies. This action and the subsequent massacre at Fort Dearborn (Chicago) were responsible for General Hull's retreat to Detroit after his invasion of Canada on July 12.

Two great figures in Canadian history then came on the scene. They were General Isaac Brock, and Indian Chief Tecumseh. George M. Wrong, in his book *The Canadians*, says that Brock ranks in fame next only to Wolfe. Some of his exploits will be recounted in future stories. Tecumseh was an American Shawnee chief and had an almost equally famous brother known as "the Prophet." They had a plan to combine all the Indians from Canada to Florida to resist encroachment on their hunting grounds. Tecumseh and "the Prophet" tried to do this peacefully by making a deal with the United States that no purchases of land would be made without the consent of the Indian tribes affected. The Americans would not agree to this and General Harrison defeated "the Prophet" in the Battle of Tippecanoe in 1811.

Now Tecumseh wanted revenge but waited until war broke out between Britain and the United States. Tecumseh, who was commissioned a brigadier-general in the British army, was the symbol of all the Indians' hopes of recovering their lands. When he joined the British on the Canadian side of the Detroit River, hundreds of Indians followed him. They played a vital and colorful part in the capture of Fort Meigs, and in all the skirmishes around the Detroit area.

Other Events on July 17:

1673   The Dutch attacked Ferryland, Newfoundland.
      The second census of Canada showed the population as 6,705. It grew to 17,125 by 1706.

1777   Fort Mackinac surrendered to the British.

1817   The first sod for the Lachine Canal was turned.

1874   Lord Carnarvon offered to mediate the dispute between the Federal Government and British Columbia.

1909   The Juvenile Delinquent Act came into force.

1959   An Emergency Measures Organization was formed to deal with atomic attack.

Dummy models depict American surrender in North Blockhouse of Fort Mackinac.

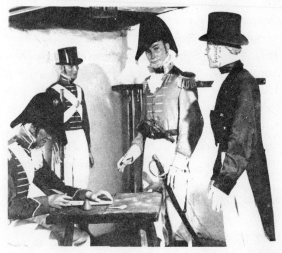

Ex-President of Confederacy Visits Montreal

One of the greatest welcomes ever given to an American citizen visiting Canada occurred July 18, 1867, a few days after Confederation, when Jefferson Davis appeared in Montreal. He had been President of the Confederate States during the American Civil War and had just been released from Fortress Monroe where he had been held for two years as a war criminal. He had been bound with chains, insulted, and ill-treated, but had finally been released on bail. After his release Davis traveled to Montreal where his wife had found shelter for her two children with her mother, Mrs. William Burr Howell, whose home was on St. Catherine's Street, where the Henry Morgan store now stands.

The occasion for the ovation was a performance of Sheridan's play *The Rivals* at the Theatre Royal on Coté Street. It was a benefit performance for the Southern Relief Association which was helping Southern states devastated by the Civil War. When Davis and his family appeared in the theatre the crowd cheered for half an hour; the band played *Dixie* and someone shouted "We shall live to see the South a nation again" to which the audience answered, "Amen."

Montreal had been a hotbed of Confederate spy activity during the Civil War, and many escaped prisoners of war found shelter there. A group of them raided St. Albans, Vermont, during the Quebec Conference on Confederation in 1864, and raised fears that a Northern army might retaliate by invading Canada (see October 19). The welcome in Montreal on July 18, 1867, aroused more hostility among the "Yankees." The New York *Herald* said in an editorial: "The fuss made over the arch-rebel on this occasion proves that the Canadians are in a very bad condition of mind. They won't recover their equanimity until they are formally annexed to us."

Davis and his family stayed in Montreal in a home on Mountain Street bought for them by friends. It later became the office and home of Dr. Henry Drummond, famous for his poems about the *habitants*.

Other Events on July 18:

1628 David Kirke captured French supply ships in the St. Lawrence.

1739 A census of Canada showed a population of 42,701.

1817 The first treaty with western Indians was made by the Earl of Selkirk on behalf of King George III.

1905 The Dominion Act created the provinces of Alberta and Saskatchewan; it was to take effect on September 1.

1910 Grand Trunk Railway employees went on strike until August 2. They received a 15 per cent wage increase.

1913 The immigration of Sikhs from India caused riots in Vancouver.

1921 United Farmers won an election in Alberta.

1929 A plebiscite in Prince Edward Island upheld prohibition.

1932 Canada and the United States signed an agreement to build the St. Lawrence Seaway.

1959 The Federal Government placed oil, gas, and international electric power under a National Energy Board.

Kirke Brothers Raise British Flag at Quebec

In these days when efforts are being made to bring about church unity, it is interesting to look back on the bitterness that existed for many years.

When Champlain persuaded the Duke of Montmorency to help him (see February 25), the Duke reorganized the Company of New France and gave the brothers Guillaume and Eméry de Caën a monopoly. They were Huguenots (Protestants) and their appointment caused a terrific row. They were supposed to support six Récollet priests in Quebec. Instead they left them to starve and brought out Protestant workmen who jeered at the priests and sang heretical hymns that shocked the Catholics!

Strained feelings between England and France eventually led to war. This was unfortunate for Champlain. The Company of New France tried very hard in 1628 to send him settlers and supplies. There were twelve ships for fishing, and four others laden with merchandise. A Scottish trader at Dieppe, Lewis Kirke, saw the convoy prepared and notified his sons, David and Lewis Kirke Jr. They obtained Charles I's permission to equip three armed ships to capture the supplies going to Champlain.

The Kirke brothers intercepted the French convoy between Gaspé and Tadoussac. According to history, there was a fierce battle for twelve hours, but no one was killed on the English side and only two on the French. The fighting could not have been very serious! The French ships were captured, however, and the Kirke brothers took the supplies and 600 prisoners. As a result, Champlain, who had 100 people to feed, was left without supplies for a year. Most of the settlers had to leave Quebec and live with the Indians in order to survive.

On July 19, 1629, the year following the capture of the supply ships, the Kirke brothers arrived back in Quebec. Champlain had only sixteen men in the garrison, but he tried to bluff the Kirkes into believing that he could blow their ships out of the water. They weren't fooled; they entered Quebec easily and raised the British flag. Quebec was captured by Britain 130 years before Wolfe's campaign.

There was a catch. The Kirkes took Champlain to England, but had to release him because the war had ended! Quebec was returned to France and back went Champlain.

Other Events on July 19:

1695 The first sawmill in New Brunswick was built at the mouth of the Nashwaak River.

1701 The Iroquois deeded hunting grounds north of Lake Ontario and west of Lake Michigan to England.

1817 Selkirk settlers returned to the Red River after being driven out by the Northwest Company.

1846 Toronto received news that had been sent by telegraph from New York to Buffalo, and then by steamer to Toronto.

1875 The Parliament of Canada Act defined the powers and privileges of its members.

1886 Captain Scott was fined at Digby, Nova Scotia, for seizing an American fishing vessel. The fishing agreement with the States had ended July 1, but the Americans were allowed to continue fishing until the end of the season.

1921 Prohibition came into effect in Ontario.

1958 Prime Minister Nkrumah of Ghana visited Ottawa and addressed a joint session of Parliament.

John Sebastian Helmcken

B.C. Joins Canada

Canada from sea unto sea became a reality on July 20, 1871, when British Columbia entered Confederation. The extension was not achieved easily and Prince Edward Island and Newfoundland were yet to come. Alberta and Saskatchewan were in Confederation, but as Northwest Territories they did not become separate provinces until 1905.

Between 1867 and 1871 there was a great deal of support in British Columbia for a movement to join the United States. Nevertheless, in May, 1870, three delegates left Victoria for Ottawa to discuss terms for joining Canada. One of them was Dr. J. S. Helmcken who had been the leader of the movement for joining the United States! He began to change his mind when the delegates were traveling through the United States to Ottawa by the Union Pacific Railway. He saw how that railway had been put through the Sierra Mountains and realized that it might be possible to build a railway through the Rockies. Surveyor Pallister disagreed.

When the delegates arrived in Ottawa they were received by Sir George Etienne Cartier, because Sir John A. Macdonald was ill. The negotiations were easy. Some of the British Columbia delegates thought they might have to settle for a wagon road through the mountains, but Canada promised to begin building a transcontinental railway within two years and to have it completed within ten. Canada also agreed to take over British Columbia's debt. The province would have the same form of government as the others and send three senators and six M.P.'s to Ottawa.

In recent years there has been a good deal of co-operation between British Columbia and Quebec. After completing the Columbia River Power agreement, the Government of British Columbia under Premier W. A. C. Bennett lent Quebec $100 million, saving the province $750,000 which would have been paid in legal fees and brokers' commissions if the money had been raised through the usual channels.

This friendship may stem, in part, from the negotiations in Ottawa in 1870, when Joseph Trutch of British Columbia said: "We must all remember in British Columbia that to Sir George Cartier and his followers in Lower Canada, we owe the position we are now in—and especially the Canadian Pacific Railway."

Other Events on July 20:

1814   Eight Canadian traitors were hanged at Ancaster (Hamilton), Ontario.

1877   The University of Manitoba was established.

1883   The first rail for the Pacific section of the C.P.R. was laid at Port Moody, British Columbia.

1885   The trial of Louis Riel began at Regina. He was sentenced September 18.

1945   The first family allowance cheques were sent to Canadian mothers.

1963   Scientists gathered in Canada to study the eclipse of the sun.

1965   Prime Minister Pearson outlined a medicare plan to provincial premiers.

Mine Sold for $12.50

How would you like to buy a gold mine for $12.50? That is what Eugene Sayre Topping, writer, sailor and miner, paid for "Le Roi" on July 21, 1890. It turned out to be one of the richest mines in the world!

Topping also happened to be deputy recorder of deeds at Nelson, British Columbia. One day he was approached by two prospectors, Joe Bourgeois and Joe Moris. Bourgeois and Moris had staked four claims on Red Mountain, with protecting posts on a fifth, which they called "Le Wise." The reports on the samples they brought to Nelson were disappointing and they did not feel like paying the recording fee of $2.50 for each of their five claims. So they agreed with Topping that he could have "Le Wise" if he would pay the $12.50 for all five claims.

Topping agreed, registered the claims, and went to see his property. He liked it, and changed the name to "Le Roi." Then he left by train for Spokane, Washington, where he hoped to be able to raise enough money to work his property. He found the money before he arrived at Spokane, because on the train he met Colonel R. W. Redpath, a financier, and George Forester, a lawyer, who after seeing samples, guaranteed to spend $3,000 on development before June, 1891. For this they were to receive shares in the company.

"Le Roi" was a success from the start. It paid $725,000 in dividends in eight years. British Columbia found itself in another mining boom. There was more than gold. In 1891, silver, zinc and lead were discovered in the Slocan area. A mine called "Slocan Star" paid out $300,000 in five years, and "Payne", contrary to the sound of its name, paid out nearly $1.5 million in seven years. Gold and copper deposits were discovered along the British Columbia-United States border. The most famous mine was Granby, which in 1908 shipped out more than 23 million pounds of copper. Coal was found in

First train of ore from Le Roi Mine, B.C.

Crow's Nest Pass, and the great smelter was built at Trail. The sparkplug of this terrific boom was one investment of $12.50!

Other Events on July 21:

1667   France regained Acadia through the Treaty of Breda.

1730   The population was estimated as 33,682.

1759   Colonel Guy Carleton led an expedition 21 miles up the St. Lawrence during Wolfe's attack on Quebec.

1836   The Champlain and St. Lawrence Railway opened, connecting Laprairie on the St. Lawrence with St. John's, Quebec, on the Richelieu River. The railway was horse-drawn for the first year and was the only passenger railway in Canada until 1847.

1899   A new suspension bridge over the Niagara River between Queenston and Lewiston was opened.

1932   An Imperial Conference opened at Ottawa; R. B. Bennett was then prime minister.

1936   Mount Waddington in British Columbia, 13,200 feet, was climbed for the first time.

1961   Prime Minister Diefenbaker opened the government-built town of Inuvick in the Arctic.

Mackenzie records his achievements, 1793

Mackenzie Ends Trip

On July 22, 1793, Alexander Mackenzie painted a message on a large rock at Bella Coola, British Columbia: "Alexander Mackenzie, from Canada, by land, the twenty-second of July, one thousand, seven hundred and ninety-three." It marked the end of one of the most remarkable journeys in Canadian, or any other, history.

Mackenzie set out in search of the Pacific on May 9, 1793, after special training in navigation and astronomy in England. Mackenzie wrote later that words failed to express the anxiety, suffering, and dangers of the journey across 500 miles of mountains. From the beginning, he and his companions were often fortunate to escape being dashed to pieces in the turbulent waters of the Peace and Fraser rivers.

Mackenzie went down the Fraser as far as Alexandria, but the Indians there told him that he would not be able to continue. So the expedition went back 60 miles until it reached the junction of what is now the Blackwater River. After they had worked their way up the Blackwater for some distance, Mackenzie decided they should try to get to the Pacific on foot. Each man carried

a gun and a 90-pound pack. The canoe and the rest of their supplies were hidden.

The expedition walked westward for two weeks. Each night Mackenzie had to sleep next to the Indian guide to prevent him from sneaking away. Finally they came to an Indian camp on the Bella Coola River. Here they traded goods for boats dug out of logs and continued down the river, passing through forests whose trees were bigger than any they had ever seen. By July 20, they found themselves paddling through salt water. Two days later they saw the waters of the Pacific. Mackenzie's quadrant told him that they were at Latitude 50° 20′ 48″ N. He inscribed his famous message on the rock using a paint made from the vermilion he had brought for the Indians.

The small party had not been there long when a party of obviously hostile Indians approached and made signs that they had been fired on by white men. It had probably happened when some of Captain Vancouver's men had explored that part of the coast. Mackenzie and his men retreated quickly, despite their jubilation.

Other Events on July 22:

1635   Champlain held a council with the Indians at Quebec. He died late that year.

1812   General Brock issued a proclamation countering the one issued by General Hull (see July 12).

1847   The Imperial Act gave Canada control of taxation.

1884   The boundary of Ontario was defined by the Imperial Privy Council.

1915   Sir Sandford Fleming, engineer and railway builder, died. He also originated the system of "standard time" (see November 18).

1944   Royal Canadian Mounted Police patrol boat *St. Roch* left Halifax for Vancouver by way of the Northwest Passage. The trip was made in 86 days.

Prince Edward Island Divided by Lottery

There are often suggestions that hospitals, medicare, and other public services in Canada should be financed by State lotteries, as they are in Ireland (Eire) and other countries. There are a number of precedents for public lotteries in Canada. Many of the United Empire Loyalists drew their holdings from a hat, as did the early settlers of Lunenburg, Nova Scotia, and Edmonton, Alberta.

The most spectacular lottery for land was in Prince Edward Island and it took place in London, England, on July 23, 1767. The results were not satisfactory because many of the people who received holdings in Prince Edward Island never went there. One of its worst problems for years was "absentee" landlords. If it had not been for the lottery, however, Prince Edward Island might have been a feudal kingdom, ruled by lords, with its people living little better than serfs.

When Prince Edward Island was ceded to Britain by the Treaty of Paris in 1763, it was placed under Nova Scotia. The Earl of Egmont, First Lord of the Admiralty, asked King George III to grant him the island forever! He proposed to be the "Lord Paramount" while under him there would be 40 "Capital Lords," 400 "Lords of the Manor," and 800 "freeholders." The lords would have castles, surrounded by moats, and the castles would be armed with cannons, capable of firing four pound balls. If there was any danger, the castle being attacked would fire its cannon; this would be heard by the next castle which would also fire, and so on around the island until everyone had been alerted. The Earl of Egmont claimed that the entire island could be armed in fifteen minutes!

King George referred the matter to the Board of Trade and Plantations, which turned down Egmont's request as being adverse to the principles of settlement in the other colonies. Instead, it was decided to hold the lottery and divide Prince Edward Island among people who had claims for military or other public service. One of the lucky winners of the lottery, Captain Walter Patterson, became the first governor.

Other Events on July 23:

1627   Lord Baltimore brought colonists to Ferryland, Newfoundland.

1629   William Alexander granted part of Acadia (Nova Scotia) to Charles La Tour and his son.

1689   Father Sebastian Râle was sent on a mission to the Abenaki Indians.

1840   The Act of Union, based on the Durham report, united Upper and Lower Canada. It went into effect on February 10, 1841.

1892   Manitoba voted for prohibition. It was not put into effect.

1927   Edward, Prince of Wales, Prince George, and Prime Minister Stanley Baldwin sailed for Canada in the *Empress of Australia*.

1944   The Canadian Army began operations in Normandy as a separate force.

1952   The International Red Cross opened its conference at Toronto.

Captain Walter Patterson, first Governor of P.E.I.

Battle of Lundy's Lane, 1814

War at Lundy's Lane

Canada's most popular patriotic song, "The Maple Leaf Forever," includes the phrase "At Queenston Heights and Lundy's Lane our brave fathers side by side . . . firmly stood and nobly died." The battle of Lundy's Lane began on July 24, 1814, and continued throughout the next day between Twelve Mile Creek (St. Catharines) and Chippewa on the Niagara Peninsula. It was one of the most bitterly fought battles of the War of 1812. General Drummond threw into action 1,900 British regulars, 390 Canadian regulars, and 800 Canadian militia—a total of 3,090 men. General Brown countered with 2,700 regulars, 1,350 volunteers from New York and Pennsylvania, and 150 "Canadian Volunteers" led by a traitor, Willcox.

It was a confused battle, fought first in moonlight, and then in the heat of day. Although they could hear the roar of Niagara, the troops had no water. When the end came, they dropped to the ground and slept where they had stood. The British-Canadians had 84 men dead, 559 wounded, and 235 missing. The Americans said they lost 171 men, but the British-Canadians buried 210 the following morning. The Americans also had 572 wounded and 110 missing. Warfare was becoming more modern. Most of the American deaths were due to British

shrapnel, and what were called rocket missiles. The leading generals on both sides were among the wounded.

Who won the battle? As in many other cases, perhaps neither side won outright. The Americans eventually withdrew after burning Chippewa Bridge and hurling a good deal of their supplies and tents into the Niagara, so the British-Canadians were probably justified in claiming victory. The battle certainly benefited the British, for it relieved the pressure on Canada and enabled British sea-power to harass the Atlantic coast of the United States. The best thing that can be said about the battle is that it was the last time Americans and Canadians killed each other.

Other Events on July 24:

1534 Jacques Cartier planted a cross at Gaspé.

1762 St. John's, Newfoundland, was taken by the French under De Ternay. It was recaptured by the British, led by Lord Colville, on September 18.

1790 Spain agreed to pay reparation for the British ships seized at Nootka, British Columbia.

1846 The electric telegraph was demonstrated at Toronto.

1848 *James Ferrier,* the first locomotive imported from Britain, was used on the Montreal-Lachine railway.

1860 The Prince of Wales (later King Edward VII) arrived in Newfoundland. He continued to Halifax on July 30; Saint John, August 2; Charlottetown, August 9; and Quebec, August 18.

1933 The World Grain Exhibition was held at Regina.

1967 President Charles de Gaulle of France delivered "Quebec Libre" speech in Montreal. Two days later he cancelled his official visit to Ottawa and returned to France.

Where Is The Railway?

Of all the conditions usually attached to a union of this colony with Canada, that of early establishment of railroad communication from sea to sea is the most important. If the railroad scheme is utopian, so is Confederation. The two must stand or fall together.

—BRITISH COLUMBIAN, 1870

British Columbia became part of Canada in 1871 (see July 20). The terms included a stipulation that a transcontinental railway would be started within two years, and completed in ten years. There was, however, a private agreement among the negotiators that British Columbia would not insist on a literal fulfillment of the deal if it caused too great a strain on Canadian finances. Some of the Ontario members wanted to include the clause: "within ten years if the financial ability of the Dominion will permit." This amendment might have led to the defeat of the government, and so the gentlemen's agreement was made and outlined to a caucus of Conservative members.

Two years went by and nothing had happened, except a symbolic turning of the sod at Esquimalt on Vancouver Island on July 19, 1873, one day before the deadline! Rumblings of trouble began to be heard. It was forgotten that the agreement did not have to be adhered to strictly if it imposed financial strain. In fact that part of the agreement had been given very little publicity.

The rumblings gradually grew into a roar, beginning with an official protest on July 25, 1873. By the end of the year, Sir John A. Macdonald's government had been beaten and cautious Alexander Mackenzie (no relation to the explorer) had become prime minister. He wanted more time and asked for it. By 1874, many British Columbians were so angry that they invaded the Legislature (see February 7).

De Cosmos was the premier, and the people suspected that he was willing to change the terms of the agreement with the Federal Government. As a result, his career in provincial politics came to an abrupt end.

By 1878 the discontent had grown to such an extent that the British Columbia Legislature passed a resolution by fourteen to nine to secede from the Dominion if the railway were not started by May 1879. Future stories will describe the various developments and how they were solved.

Other Events on July 25:

1680   Dulhut rescued Father Hennepin from the Sioux Indians.

1715   Acadians appeared again before the Council of Nova Scotia at Halifax, and refused to take the oath of allegiance. Their deportation followed later in the year.

1759   Wolfe issued a warning to Canadians at Quebec to keep out of any fighting.

1787   Captain John Dixon named the Queen Charlotte Islands.

1871   Anthony Musgrave left British Columbia. He was the last colonial governor.

1917   Finance Minister Sir Thomas White introduced income tax legislation as a "temporary war-time measure."

1956   The Prime Minister of Australia, the Right Honourable R. G. Menzies, and his wife were guests of Canada until July 29.

1958   An agreement was signed to develop the South Saskatchewan River.

Kingston, Ontario

Annexation Proposed

One of the early, important steps towards Confederation took place at Kingston, Ontario, on July 26, 1849. It followed the rioting in Montreal over the Rebellion Losses Bill (see April 25).

The Tories, who had opposed the Rebellion Losses Bill so violently, arranged to hold a convention at Kingston to discuss the ills of the country. The heavy losses caused by the rebellions in 1837 and 1838 now had to be paid for. Adding to the country's financial difficulties was Britain's adoption of free trade in 1846. Before free trade, Canadian wheat had paid a lower duty on entering Britain than wheat from the United States. As a result, the Americans were sending their wheat to Canada to be ground into flour, and then exporting it to Britain under the Canadian preference. This led to the creation of a large number of flour mills in Canada and increased business for the shipping industry, transportation and longshoremen.

When Britain adopted free trade, the Canadian preference ended. The milling and shipping business was ruined and there was a depression with unemployment. Canadians were moving to the United States where conditions were better.

There were many dismal speeches at the Kingston convention. The Kingston *Whig* correspondent reported a Scottish lady as saying: "I couldna hae conceived I had been sae truly miserable hadna I been told it."

It was at this meeting that the Tories drew up a manifesto urging annexation to the States. It was probably the strangest document ever signed by responsible people in Canada, including J. J. Abbott, who later became prime minister. He dismissed his action later by saying that it was "the outburst of a moment of petulance." John A. Macdonald, then a young member of Parliament, refused to sign the document and said later: "Some of our fellows lost their heads."

Sir John always minimized the negative side of the Kingston meeting and emphasized the positive. One of its achievements was the creation of the British American League, which reaffirmed the connection with Britain and advocated the confederation of all the British North American provinces. Even so, Sir John voted against Confederation at the meeting in Quebec in 1864 (see June 22). The streams of politics are difficult to fathom!

Other Events on July 26:

1664   The Sovereign Council fixed prices of commodities.

1757   Montcalm defeated the British at Lake George, New York.

1811   Selkirk Colonists led by Miles Macdonell sailed from Scotland for the Red River. They arrived in August the following year.

1881   The C.P.R. was completed as far as Winnipeg.

1923   President Harding of the United States visited Vancouver. He was the first American President to visit Canada during his term of office.

1936   Edward VIII (the late Duke of Windsor) unveiled the Vimy Memorial.

1953   An armistice was signed in the war in Korea.

First Permanent Colony Founded at Port Royal

One of the happiest meetings in Canadian history occurred off the shore of Nova Scotia on July 27, 1606. De Monts, Champlain and party had spent their first winter in Canada on Dochet Island in the St. Croix River, not far from the wealthy summer resort of St. Andrew's, New Brunswick. Dochet Island proved to be unsatisfactory as a base, so the party moved to Port Royal, now Annapolis Royal, in Nova Scotia, where they spent the winter of 1605.

This was a pleasant experience. The winter was mild, and Champlain directed the building of houses surrounded by a ditch that carried running water. He even designed two reservoirs—one of fresh water to hold trout, and the other, salt water for fish from the sea. There was a safe harbor big enough to hold 2,000 ships.

De Monts had returned to France, seeking to have his monopoly renewed by Henry IV. He left instructions that if he had not returned by July 16 the colony was to be abandoned and the settlers were to return to France. As it happened, Henry IV would not renew de Mont's monopoly. It was a sad day for the Port Royal colonists when July 16 came, heralding no ship from France. They loaded their supplies into small pinnaces, the only boats they possessed, and sailed along the south shore, hoping to find fishing vessels that would take them back to France.

De Monts never saw his colony again, but the Sieur de Poutrincourt had managed to buy the rights to Port Royal. On July 24, as his ship *Jonas* was sailing along the south shore of Nova Scotia, it sighted the pinnaces from Port Royal. The colonists were told the good news and returned to Port Royal with the *Jonas*. On July 27, the entire group gathered at the first permanent French colony in Canada, described by Mark Lescarbot, a young historian in Poutrincourt's Party, as "a marvelous sight." The future of New France seemed to be assured (see May 11).

Other Events on July 27:

1758   Louisburg fell to Amherst and Wolfe (see June 2).

1812   The Parliament of Upper Canada met until August 5. It passed laws for defense.

1853   The Grand Trunk Railway was completed from Sherbrooke, Quebec, to the American border.

1891   A railway between Calgary and Edmonton was completed.

1898   The first locomotive operated on the White Pass and Yukon Railway (see February 18).

1927   The World Poultry Congress was held in Ottawa until August 4.

1957   American Secretary of State John Foster Dulles arrived in Ottawa for talks with Prime Minister Diefenbaker and members of the Government.

Champlain's view of Port Royal

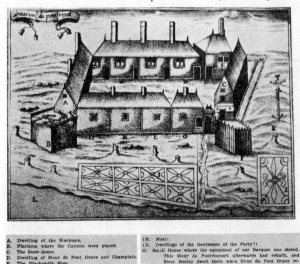

A.   Dwelling of the Workmen.
B.   Platform where the Cannon were placed.
C.   The Store-house.
D.   Dwelling of Sieur de Pont Grave and Champlain.
E.   The Blacksmith Shop.
F.   Palisade of Pickets.
G.   The Bakery.
H.   The Kitchen.
(I.   The Gardens).

(M.   Moat).
(N.   Dwellings of the Gentlemen of the Party?)
O.   Small House where the equipment of our Barques was stored. This Sieur de Poutrincourt afterwards had rebuilt, and Sieur Boulay dwelt there when Sieur du Pont Grave returned to France.
P.   Gate to our Habitation.
Q   (K).   The Cemetery.
R   (L).   The River.

Frontenac's journey

Frontenac Builds Fort

Count Frontenac, part of whose story was told on January 11, first came to Canada as governor in 1672. His biggest problem apart from the intrigues among the civil servants at Quebec and Montreal, was to keep the Iroquois under control. The French were inclined to treat them with contempt, and there is a French word "iroquois" that means a boor, peasant, or clown. It was not an accurate description of a proud race whose discipline and strategy in war can be admired even today.

In June, 1673, Frontenac set out from Quebec to survey his domain, and to build a fort where Lake Ontario flowed into the St. Lawrence. The 185-mile trip to Montreal was not too difficult. Then came the hard task of transporting 400 men and supplies up the river to Lake Ontario. Frontenac had two flat-bottomed boats built at Montreal on which were loaded the equipment and cannon for the fort. The men traveled in 120 canoes, taking turns dragging the flat-bottomed boats against the current. Getting through the rapids was back-breaking. The men pulling the boats had to wade along the shore, sometimes up to their necks in water.

Meanwhile, Frontenac had sent La Salle ahead to summon a conference of Iroquois. The historic meeting took place where Kingston, Ontario, now stands. Frontenac put on a great show to impress the Indians. Sixty chiefs were invited to his tents, which they reached by passing through a double rank of soldiers. Frontenac spoke to them through an interpreter. The evil days of strife were ended, he said, and the Indians' enemies henceforth would be France's enemies. He was building a fort so that the Indians would not have to go all the way to Montreal to trade. The Iroquois took it all with a grain of salt. They could make better trade deals with the English and the Dutch in the heart of their own territory.

What did impress them was the speed with which the French built the fort. It was ready by July 28, 1673, obviously impregnable to attack. Frontenac, who was anything but modest, called it "Fort Frontenac," and raised over it the *fleur-de-lis* of France.

Other Events on July 28:

1755   The Council of Nova Scotia made a decision to deport the Acadians.

1819   Richard John Uniacke was tried for murder as the result of a duel. He was led into court by his father who was Attorney-General of Nova Scotia.

1847   Canada, Nova Scotia, and New Brunswick Railroads were incorporated.

1858   The Macdonald-Cartier government was defeated on the motion that Ottawa would not be the capital of Canada.

1914   The Montreal and Toronto stock exchanges closed for three months.
The export of vital materials was prohibited, except to Britain, France, Russia, Japan and the United States.

1930   The general election resulted in a victory for the Conservatives under R. B. Bennett: Conservatives 138, Liberals 87, United Farmers 10.

Icelanders Arrive

When Manitoba became Canada's fifth province in 1870, it had a population of about 12,000. Of these, approximately 1,500 were English-speaking. The remainder spoke French (the language of the Métis), or Indian. The situation changed greatly within six years through an influx of settlers. Basically, Manitoba had been bilingual (English and French) in 1870. In 1876 it was multilingual, as it is today.

The most important language additions in the six years were German and Icelandic. The German was due to Mennonite settlers, who, although they came from Russia, spoke Low German. They were given land, religious freedom and exemption from military service, all of which they had lacked in their own homeland. More than 6,000 Mennonites had arrived in Manitoba by 1879.

Among the most remarkable settlers were the Icelanders. Their homes had been destroyed by a volcanic eruption in 1873 and they came to Canada at the suggestion of Governor-General Lord Dufferin. The first party arrived at Quebec on July 29, 1873, and went to the attractive Muskoka area of Ontario. They found it difficult to settle there, however, and after exploring various possibilities, chose a more suitable location at Willow Point on Lake Winnipeg. They liked it so well that they called it Gimli which, in Icelandic, means "Paradise."

The first party numbered only 285, and traveled in flat-bottomed boats down the Red River and across Upper Lake Winnipeg to the bay of white sand beaches, where fish were plentiful, and trees provided lumber for building. They had few possessions apart from tools and books. As they had a great love of literature and language, they learned to speak English more quickly than any other race, many of them being fluent in six months, without a trace of an accent!

Icelanders arriving at Point Edward, Ont., 1875

During one period, more than 2,000 Icelanders arrived in the area. They might have felt that they deserved a place in Canada. It is generally believed that the Norsemen were the first Europeans to land in North America. Others claim that the Irish were first. It is possible that neither theory is correct and that the honor should go to the ancestors of these Icelandic immigrants.

Other Events on July 29:

1704 A New England force under Benjamin Church attacked Beaubassin and Grand Pré in Acadia.

1848 The last plank was laid on the Niagara Suspension Bridge.

1895 The Territorial Exhibition opened in Regina.

1911 The Canadian Northern Railway was completed between Montreal and Port Arthur, Ontario.

1912 The Imperial Privy Council upheld authority to make marriage laws.
The Roman Catholic Church had declared marriage laws invalid in 1907.

1965 A seven day postal strike ended in most cities.

"War Clouds" for Gen. Simcoe, 1792

Land Cleared for York

As Toronto is Canada's second largest city, it is difficult to believe that it was once possible to catch Atlantic salmon in the Don and Humber Rivers flowing through it, or to shoot waterfowl on the bay between the city and its protecting island. Yet it was so on July 30, 1793, when John Graves Simcoe, Lieutenant-Governor of Upper Canada, began clearing the site for the capital.

When Simcoe was appointed in 1791, the capital was at Newark, now Niagara. It was protected by Fort Niagara on the American side of the river, still held by the British as insurance that the United States would carry out the terms of the peace treaty. Detroit was also held by Britain for the same reason.

Simcoe felt sure that there would be another war between Britain and the United States and was anxious to find a new location for the capital because the present site was too close to the border. In February, 1793, he began a memorable tour of the country he governed, traveling by sleigh over the backwood trails. When Simcoe stopped for the night he always had the members of the company sing "God Save the King." His first stop, after three days, was at a Mohawk village on the Grand River, where he attended church with Chief Brant. He then continued to Detroit.

Although his first choice for the new capital was the site of London, he had to settle for the Toronto Bay area because it provided immediate transportation facilities. On May 4 he heard that Britain and France were at war, and feeling certain that the Americans would side with France, he decided to move as quickly as possible.

The building of what is now Toronto began on July 30. While it was under construction, Simcoe and his family lived in a huge tent that had belonged to Captain Cook who, with Simcoe's father, had served with Wolfe in the campaign to capture Quebec in 1759. Simcoe called the new capital "York" in honor of the Duke of York's victories in Europe.

Other Events on July 30:

1609   Champlain helped the Hurons and Algonquins attack the Iroquois near Crown Point.

1711   Sir Hovenden Walker sailed from Nantucket to capture Canada. This was one of the biggest fiascos in Canadian history (see August 22).

1865   Sir Etienne Taché, who formed a government with Sir John A. Macdonald during negotiations for Confederation, died.

1886   The first tea train left Vancouver for Montreal.

1898   The Imperial Privy Council upheld the right of Manitoba to abolish separate schools.

1900   Japan prohibited emigration to Canada.

1927   The Prince of Wales, Prince George, and Prime Minister Stanley Baldwin arrived at Quebec on a tour of Canada.

1954   Field Marshal Alexander, former governor-general, opened the British Empire Games in Vancouver.

1962   Britain agreed to buy 24 million pounds of uranium from Canada.

Murder Suspects Arrested Near Rimouski, Quebec

Many visitors to London, England, go to see Madame Tussaud's famous waxworks. In the "Chamber of Horrors" is the figure of Dr. Crippen, one of the most publicized murderers of all time.

Dr. Crippen wanted to get rid of his wife so that he could marry an attractive typist, Ethel Le Neve. He used his knowledge of medicine to destroy most of her body, and buried the remains under the concrete floor in the cellar. He then announced that she was visiting relatives in the United States and, later, that she had died there. The death notice was published in the paper. Dr. Crippen also raised a good deal of money selling her jewellery and other valuables.

He might have got away with the crime if a suspicious neighbor had not asked Scotland Yard to investigate. Inspector Drew called on Dr. Crippen and asked routine questions which caused Crippen to panic. He went to Brussels with Ethel Le Neve, disguised her as a boy, and booked a passage to Canada on the *S.S. Montrose*. It sailed from Antwerp on July 20, 1910.

Captain Kendall of the *Montrose* became suspicious of the pair about two hours after they had been at sea. Ethel Le Neve was supposed to be Crippen's son, but he saw them holding hands on the boat deck. Captain Kendall then turned detective, and his written account is amusing. He noticed that Dr. Crippen's "son" ate like a lady, and not like a young boy. Furthermore, "his" trousers were very tight around the hips, and a split in the back had been fastened with pins! He made Dr. Crippen laugh so that he could see if he had false teeth.

After two days at sea, Captain Kendall radioed Scotland Yard that he felt certain Dr. Crippen and Ethel Le Neve were among the passengers (the first time wireless was used to track down a criminal). Inspector Drew and Sergeant Mitchell were rushed across the Atlantic in the *S.S. Laurentic*, and boarded the *S.S. Montrose* at Father Point, off Rimouski, Quebec. Crippen and Miss Le Neve were arrested on July 31 and taken back to London for trial. Crippen was convicted and hanged at Pentonville Prison, although protesting his innocence to the end. Ethel Le Neve was defended by a famous British lawyer, Lord Birkenhead, and was acquitted.

Other Events on July 31:

1687   Fort Niagara was built by Denonville at the mouth of the Niagara River.

1759   Wolfe attacked Quebec, but was repulsed.

1763   Pontiac defeated the British at Bloody Run (see May 7).

1837   A meeting at Quebec formed a "Committee of Vigilance" with W. L. Mackenzie, the representative for Upper Canada. It proposed to form provisional governments in both provinces.

1868   The Imperial Parliament passed the Rupert's Land Act authorizing Canada to acquire the Northwest Territories.

1874   The first party of Mennonites arrived at Quebec and settled in Manitoba (see July 29).

1907   A plant to develop electric power from coal was opened at Maccan, Nova Scotia. Famous inventor Thomas Edison, who was a member of a family from Digby, Nova Scotia, was one of the founders.

1913   Alys McKey Bryant made the first solo flight by a woman in Canada at Vancouver racetrack. The first woman in Canada to get a pilot's licence was Eileen Vollick of Hamilton, Ontario, in 1928.

1957   DEW (distant early warning) radar line went into operation.

"Let us open the windows and the doors of the provinces. Let us look over the walls and see what is on the other side. Let us know one another and that will lead to understanding . . .

Fraser River Valley, B.C.

Montreal, P.Q.

"I pray God that we may all go forward hand in hand. We can't run the risk of this great country falling into pieces."

—GOVERNOR-GENERAL VANIER, 1967.

British Airship *R-100* Arrives at Montreal

For many years after 1930, there was a steel tower 200 feet high at St. Hubert's airfield, which was the airport for Montreal until Dorval was opened. It was a mooring mast for the *R-100,* a British airship that crossed the Atlantic and arrived at Montreal on August 1, 1930. It was pioneering a plan to provide an airship service throughout the British Commonwealth.

Eight non-stop flights had been made over the Atlantic by British and German airships when the *R-100* made its flight to Canada in 1930. The trip was carefully prepared, with work on the mooring mast at St. Hubert starting in November, 1927. The venture was financed jointly by Britain and Canada, with Lieutenant-Commander A. B. Pressy of the Royal Canadian Navy in charge of the mooring mast.

The flight of the *R-100* across the Atlantic was one of the marvels of the age. It left Cardington, England, on July 29 at 3.30 a.m. and arrived over Montreal on the night of July 31; it had to cruise around until dawn until it could connect with the mooring tower. The flight took 78 hours and 52 minutes. Modern aircraft fly from London to Montreal in less than 7 hours.

The "dirigible," as airships were called, had been damaged by a storm while coming up the St. Lawrence, but was repaired quickly so that it could go on a demonstration flight. What excitement there was when it flew over Ottawa after dark, and was illuminated by searchlights from the Parliament Buildings! It appeared over Niagara Falls at 6 a.m. and then flew over Hamilton and Toronto while people were going to work.

It looked as though airships were going to be the mode of travel for the future, but they were too vulnerable to the elements. Two months after the flight of the *R-100* to Canada, the *R-101* crashed on a flight to India, killing forty-six people, including every British authority on airship operation. In April, 1933, the U.S. *Akron* crashed into the Atlantic off the coast of New Jersey with seventy-three lives lost. The U.S. *Macon* was another casualty.

The experiments with airships ended in 1937 when the giant *Von Hindenburg* exploded and burned while landing at Lakehurst, New Jersey. Meanwhile, conventional aircraft were beginning to span the Atlantic.

Other Events on August 1:

1703   The Marquis de Vaudreuil was appointed Governor of Canada and Acadia.

1824   John Galt proposed the formation of the Canada Land Company for settlement in Ontario.

1834   British Columbia abolished slavery.

1914   Governor-General the Duke of Connaught offered Canadian troops to Britain.

1950   The R.C.M.P. took over the policing of Newfoundland and Labrador.

1952   The Social Credit Government of British Columbia took office under Premier W. A. C. Bennett.

The R-100 *moored at Cardington*

Goodwill Ambassadors Leave for Saint John

Modern political leaders seldom go anywhere without taking along public relations experts, or having the way prepared by them. It's all part of the policy of creating a "good image" as the advertising people call it.

One of the first big public relations campaigns in Canada began on August 2, 1864. It was also one of the most successful. D'Arcy McGee, member of Parliament for Montreal West (see April 7), was the organizer. Delegates from Canada were to attend the Charlottetown Conference, in September, in which representatives of the four Atlantic colonies were to discuss a union among themselves. The Canadian delegates wanted to popularize the idea of Confederation beforehand.

McGee felt that Canadians and Maritimers had never become acquainted, and it would be helpful if Canadians other than political leaders visited the Atlantic colonies. He enlisted the support of Sandford Fleming, and together, they organized a tour of members of Parliament, business and newspaper men. In all they numbered approximately 100.

The party left Montreal on August 2 and traveled by train to Portland, Maine, where they boarded a paddlewheeler. This took them to Saint John, where a crowd of 15,000 was waiting to welcome them.

The Canadians looked in wonderment as they were taken to their hotels in carriages, drawn through deeply rutted dirt streets, lined with livery stables, blacksmith shops, general stores, oyster houses and taverns. Saint John had a population of 42,000 and was then the largest city in the Atlantic colonies, almost as big as Quebec and Toronto.

Major Donald J. Goodspeed, a Canadian army historian, has written that the Canadians were a little shocked by Saint John. The men dressed informally, but wore new-style bowler hats on the backs of their heads. They smoked big Havana cigars even on Sundays! They chewed tobacco on the streets! The women were smartly dressed, but somewhat flashy according to Canadian standards. In Goodspeed's words they had "tightly-corseted figures swelling incredibly at the bosom, their hair brushed up in short curls on the top of their heads, and their long skirts swirling and flirting over rustling crinoline petticoats." It was the beginning of a wonderful tour, more of which will be described in future stories.

Other Events on August 2:

1786   Captain James Strange claimed Vancouver Island for Britain.

1858   New Caledonia became British Columbia (mainland).

1862   Victoria, British Columbia, was incorporated as a city.

1871   Treaty No. One was concluded with the Northwest Indians at Lower Fort Garry. It was revised in 1875.

Saint John, New Brunswick, 1864

Gilbert Reaches Nfld.

Newfoundland, Britain's oldest colony, now Canada's tenth province, was officially claimed for Britain by Sir Humphrey Gilbert, who sailed into St. John's Harbor on August 3, 1583. Two days later, on the spot where Newfoundland's war memorial now stands, he planted the cross of St. George.

Newfoundland was discovered long before, probably by Norsemen, Icelanders and adventurers from Ireland. There are no definite dates for their landings, however, so John Cabot usually receives the credit. He sighted Newfoundland in 1497 and shouted "Bona Vista," which is how Cape Bonavista got its name. Cabot was given £10 by King Henry VII for his discovery.

Cabot reported that, a few days before sighting Newfoundland, he sailed over waters where codfish were so thick that a boat could hardly be rowed through them! Soon fishermen from Europe were in the area, catching cod by the ton and drying them on the shore. Britain decided to claim the new land and sent out Sir Humphrey Gilbert in 1578. One of Gilbert's two ships was attacked and sunk by Spaniards, so he returned to Britain.

Sir Humphrey then sold half of his estates, and fitted out five ships with 250 men, including carpenters, blacksmiths, masons and musicians! One of the ships deserted for the more profitable trade of piracy, but the others arrived at St. John's on August 3, 1583.

The ceremony claiming Newfoundland for Britain was attended by all the inhabitants. Sir Humphrey wore leather top boots, velvet surtout (cloak) with a lace collar about his neck, and a breastplate of armor. He proclaimed the Church of England as the official church of Newfoundland. Any man who spoke disrespectfully of the Queen would lose his goods, and his ears! A piece of turf with a twig was presented to Sir Humphrey as a sign that "The Newfoundlande" was now British.

Sir Humphrey was lost about a month later when his fleet was caught in a storm. The last

Gilbert claims Newfoundland, 1583

that was seen of him was when he was reading the Bible on the lurching deck of the *Squirrel,* to which he had transferred. He shouted, "Cheer up, boys, we're as near to Heaven by sea as on land!" The *Squirrel* went down in the storm, while the *Golden Hind* managed to return to Britain.

Other Events on August 3:

1610 Henry Hudson discovered Hudson Bay.

1751 The first printing press in Canada was set up in Halifax by Bartholomew Green.

1847 The first electric telegraph service between Montreal and Toronto was inaugurated.

1860 Joseph Howe was elected Premier of Nova Scotia.

1878 Canada refused to accept the arbitration award for the northwest boundary of Ontario.

1900 There was a general strike in the C.P.R. shops.

1914 Regulations were issued for money and banks. Bank notes were issued instead of Dominion notes.

1961 The Honorable T. C. Douglas, former Premier of Saskatchewan, was elected President of the New Democratic Party.

British Columbia Buys Its Own Navy

Every war has its humorous incidents. Nearly everybody in London had a favorite bomb story during the blitz in 1940. During World War I, when the soldiers were living like rats in mud and being eaten by lice, Bruce Bairnsfather produced some famous cartoons.

One of the best stories about Canada in World War I concerned British Columbia, and it happened at the outset. It didn't seem funny at the time, but British Columbia had its own navy for a few days! Its total strength was two submarines.

There was great alarm in Victoria and Vancouver late in July and early in August, 1914, because Germany had a naval squadron in the Pacific under Admiral von Spee. The story circulated that it would bombard the cities and then capture British Columbia with the help of former German citizens living there. Some very respectable citizens of German extraction were given a rough time.

The old cruiser *Rainbow*, stationed at Esquimalt since 1910, was ordered to protect grain ships from the German cruisers *Nürnberg* and *Leipzig*. There were no real guns or ammunition to protect Victoria and Vancouver, except a few old relics.

The British Admiralty sent out a "warning telegram" on July 29. A group of businessmen in Victoria learned that a Seattle shipyard had built two submarines for the Government of Chile, and informed Premier McBride. The premier urged the commander-in-chief at Esquimalt to get in touch with Naval Service Headquarters in Ottawa, who referred the matter to the Admiralty. In the meantime, Premier McBride did not wait. He knew that the United States would put neutrality laws into effect as soon as war was declared, and the submarines would not be allowed to leave Seattle. Captain W. H. Logan, Lloyd's representative in Victoria, was sent to Seattle to buy the submarines under the greatest secrecy and have them delivered near Trial Island, just outside Canadian territorial waters. They made their way to the island in fog and darkness. Having been inspected and found satisfactory by a retired officer of the Royal Navy, they were taken over by Commander Bertram Jones on August 4.

The chief janitor of the Parliament Buildings, Premier McBride's personal messenger, was sent to Seattle with a cheque for $1.5 million to pay for the submarines.

There was near panic when the submarines appeared off Victoria on the morning of August 5. The shore battery had not been notified, owing to the secrecy, and might have fired on the submarines with its old guns if word to hold off had not been received in the nick of time.

There was more comedy in finding crews for the submarines, but British Columbia had its own navy until August 7 when the Federal Government took over for the British Admiralty. Fortunately Admiral von Spee's fleet sailed south and British Columbia was not attacked during the war.

Other Events on August 4:

1693   Two hundred canoes with furs arrived at Montreal, reopening trade from the West.

1769   Prince Edward Island was made a separate colony from Nova Scotia.

1786   James Strange named Queen Charlotte Sound, British Columbia.

1864   The Canadian Parliamentary party was at Saint John, New Brunswick, en route to Charlottetown (see August 2).

1915   The Ottawa School Board was replaced by a commission of three members when the board refused to insist that teachers should be qualified to speak English.

1960   The Bill of Rights was approved by the House of Commons.

Iroquois Retaliate with Massacre at Lachine

Some stories of Indian massacres have already been related, but the worst one of all happened at Lachine, a suburb of Montreal, on August 5, 1689.

There are two sides to every story, and sometimes more. It was the Iroquois who massacred the residents of Lachine, but there had been provocation two years before. Governor Denonville had been asked by Louis XIV to capture some Iroquois and send them to France as galley slaves. The Récollet priests had a mission for the Iroquois at the Bay of Quinte, west of Fort Frontenac on Lake Ontario. The Iroquois at the mission were invited to visit Fort Frontenac with their wives and children, but when they arrived they were seized by Denonville's Intendant, Champigny. Récollet Father La Hontan was horrified to see fifty members of his mission tied to posts, but could do nothing about it. They were flogged, and insects were put on their skins, while Hurons forced their fingers into hot pipes of tobacco. They were then sent to be galley slaves in France, where most of them died. Governor Denonville returned to Montreal as a great hero.

On the night of August 4, 1689, a violent summer hailstorm swept across Lake St. Louis. As the householders got up to make sure windows were closed, they heard the screeching war cry of the Iroquois rising over the noise of thunder and hail. Within minutes, swarms of naked Iroquois, armed to the teeth, came running down the lane, their faces smeared with warpaint. There were 1,500 of them, taking advantage of the storm to cross the lake unseen.

It is said that those who died in the first few minutes of the onslaught were fortunate. Men and women were cut down by tomahawks, and the brains of little children were dashed out against doorframes and bedposts. One hundred prisoners were taken to the Iroquois villages in the Finger Lakes area, tied to stakes and burned or tortured.

The prisoners might have been saved if soldiers 3 miles away had been allowed to take action. Unfortunately, their commanding officer, Subercase, was in Montreal attending a reception for Denonville. Returning to the camp, Subercase cursed his men for not having gone to Lachine without him. When they arrived, the horror of the scene was beyond description, but the surgeon, who had managed to hide, told Subercase that the Indians had taken a large quantity of brandy. Subercase knew this was the time to attack, but just as he was about to follow the Iroquois, word came from Governor Denonville that he must hold his troops to guard Montreal. The Indians stayed on the rampage, capturing new communities and taking more prisoners, none of whom could be rescued by the French.

Other Events on August 5:

1583 Sir Humphrey Gilbert claimed Newfoundland for Britain (see August 3).

1756 Montcalm transported his army to Sackets Harbor, New York.

1774 Perez and Martinez of Spain cruised off Vancouver Island.

1789 The first conference of the Protestant Episcopal Church was held at Quebec.

1812 General Brock left Niagara to capture Detroit.

1822 The Imperial Trade Act regulated trade between Upper and Lower Canada.

1833 The *Royal William* left Quebec on one of the first voyages across the Atlantic using steam.

1963 The premiers of Canada met at Halifax.

1965 The Canadian Wheat Board announced a sale of 27 million bushels of wheat to Russia.

Sir Edmund Walker Head (1805-1868)

Macdonald Dupes Brown

No, friends, the "double-shuffle" was not an old-fashioned dance like the "Montreal toddle"! It was a cute political trick pulled by John A. Macdonald on his old rival, George Brown. After a few days of fast foot-work, it reached a climax on August 6, 1858.

John A. Macdonald and George Etienne Cartier formed a government dependent on the support of Cartier's French-Canadian followers. In December 1857, Queen Victoria announced her choice of Ottawa as the capital of Canada. This displeased a number of centres. On July 28, 1858, with Parliament meeting in Toronto, Clear Grit leader Brown saw an opportunity to defeat the Macdonald-Cartier government. He proposed a motion that the City of Ottawa should not be the permanent seat of government. As expected, enough French-Canadian members voted for the motion to defeat the Government.

Brown then proposed a motion to adjourn, which would have meant the resignation of the government, but the French-Canadian members voted against it. Macdonald and Cartier could have taken this as authorization to stay in power, but decided instead to trap Brown. They took the stand that their government had been defeated on a matter of policy and should resign. Governor Sir Edmund Head then called on George Brown to form a ministry. It was sworn in on August 2 at noon, and defeated that afternoon by a majority of forty. Brown·then asked Governor Head to dissolve Parliament and call an election. Governor Head refused and asked A. T. Galt to form a ministry. When he failed, George Etienne Cartier was invited to try.

The new Government formed on August 6 was the old Macdonald-Cartier ministry with the positions reversed. In those days when a member of Parliament joined the cabinet, he had to resign his seat and run in a by-election. Macdonald used a law that had been passed the previous year, avoiding the necessity of a by-election if a cabinet minister resigned his post but took a new one within a month. He had been attorney-general. Now he became postmaster-general for one day and then he and Cartier reverted to their former posts!

George Brown yelled "trickery" and "collusion," but to no avail. After the "double-shuffle," the Macdonald-Cartier government remained in power until May, 1862.

Other Events on August 6:

1691 Henry Kelsey claimed the Red River area for Britain.

1812 Governor Prevost of British North America and General Dearborn of the States signed an Armistice to end the war. It was revoked by Congress.

1827 The convention of 1818, between Britain and the States on the question of the Oregon boundary, was renewed indefinitely.

1866 An Imperial statute established union between Vancouver Island and the mainland of British Columbia.

1884 A public school system for the North-west Territories, including separate schools, was established by ordinance.

Peace Bridge Opened

Because of his close ties with Canada, the late Duke of Windsor gained the affectionate regard of many Canadians. As Edward, Prince of Wales, he was attached to the Canadian Expeditionary Force in France during World War I. After the war he dedicated the Canadian memorial at Vimy Ridge. Probably the most appreciated of the prince's actions was his purchase of the E. P. Ranch near Calgary, where he spent several enjoyable holidays.

One of his four memorable tours was in 1927 when he came to Canada with his brother George, and Prime Minister Stanley Baldwin. It was the first time a British prime minister had visited Canada during his term of office. He and Edward did not get along well together, and it was Prime Minister Baldwin who insisted in 1936 that Edward must abdicate if he married Mrs. Wallis Warfield Simpson, an American divorcee.

The Prince of Wales, Prince George, and Prime Minister Baldwin arrived at Quebec on July 30, 1927, to begin a country-wide tour. It was the occasion of Canada's Diamond Jubilee and there were celebrations everywhere. The Prince of Wales dedicated the Memorial Chamber of the Peace Tower of Parliament while the new carillon played *God Save the King, O Canada* and *The Maple Leaf*. They were heard throughout the world over the relatively "new-fangled radio." Even American isolationist Charles Lindbergh, then a great hero, flew his *Spirit of St. Louis* to Ottawa.

Another important event on the Prince's itinerary occurred on August 7, when the Prince of Wales, with Prime Ministers Mackenzie King and Stanley Baldwin, opened the Peace Bridge between Fort Erie, Ontario, and Buffalo, New York. Vice-President Dawes represented the United States.

Of course feminine hearts throbbed from coast to coast wherever the royal brothers appeared. There were rumors of romance, especially when Miss Valerie Jones was

King Edward VIII, Duke of Windsor

brought to Ottawa from Brockville to be the Prince of Wales' partner at a dance!

Edward and his young brother George got along well together and tried to be informal whenever circumstances allowed. There was hearty laughter in Vancouver where Edward was supposed to speak at a luncheon. He suddenly introduced his brother as the speaker instead. George was taken by surprise but rose to the occasion very well.

Other Events on August 7:

1679   La Salle launched *Griffon*, the first ship on the Great Lakes above Niagara (see January 8).

1803   Selkirk's settlers from Scotland arrived at Prince Edward Island.

1858   George Etienne Cartier put Confederation on the party platform.

1930   R. B. Bennett became Prime Minister of Canada.

1950   The government announced its decision to create an armed force for the United Nations. Brigadier Rockingham was appointed Commanding Officer.

Canadian troops in France

Canada's 100 Days

The beginning of the end of "the war to end wars" was on August 8, 1918. It is known in history now as "the 100 Days of the Canadian Army." From the enemy's point of view, August 8, 1918, was "the black day of the German army," a phrase used by General Erich Ludendorff.

For three weary years, the Allies and the Germans had opposed each other in muddy trenches, sometimes only 50 yards apart, along a front of 300 miles from the sea coast to the frontier of Switzerland. Trench warfare ended in March, 1918, when the Germans broke through at Amiens, inflicting heavy losses on the British. They nearly got through to Paris, but could not keep up the pace.

The Canadians had been held in reserve until August 8, and now, with the Austra-

lians, they were used in a move that fooled the enemy. A small part of the Canadian and Australian armies was sent to Flanders as a decoy. Their main forces were moved to Amiens only a few hours before zero hour.

The decoy worked. When the Canadians and Australians began their attack on Amiens, supported by nearly 500 tanks, they found that the Germans had left only six reduced divisions to defend the city. Tanks were comparatively new in warfare, having been used for the first time in the Battle of the Somme in 1916.

A mist helped to hide the attacking Canadians and Australians at Amiens, and with firm ground they were able to move forward 8 miles on a front which was 15 miles wide. The tide of battle had been turned, although there was a great deal of hard fighting ahead. By October, the Canadians had lost 16,000 men in the drive, but, helped by four British Divisions, they destroyed nearly fifty German divisions, one-quarter of the German force on the Western Front.

Other Events on August 8:

1619 The first Lutheran service in Canada was held at Icy Cove, Hudson Strait, during the Jens Munck expedition.

1665 Father Allouez named Lake Superior "Lake Tracy" after the Marquis de Tracy.

1686 Fort Albany, Hudson Bay, surrendered to Iberville after a siege.

1774 Spanish explorer Perez discovered Nootka Sound, Vancouver Island.

1863 Angus McAskill, famous Cape Breton giant, died.

1865 The Confederation committee that had gone to Britain reported to the Belleau-Macdonald government at Quebec.

1963 Canada signed an atomic test agreement with Russia, Britain and the United States.

Fort William Henry Yields to General Montcalm

On July 5, the story was told how General Montcalm defeated the British at Ticonderoga, New York, in 1758. The next step was to attack Fort William Henry at the end of Lake George. The fort was commanded by a tough Scottish soldier, Colonel Munro, who had 2,500 troops. Montcalm, however, had 8,000 men, whom he started moving towards Fort William Henry on August 3. Brigadier Lévis, with Indians leading the way, approached the rear of the fort while Montcalm's main force made a frontal attack.

When Munro heard that Montcalm was coming, he sent an urgent message to General Webb at nearby Fort Edward to send reinforcements. Webb in turn was pleading with Governor Loudon of Massachusetts to send reinforcements to him and did nothing to help Fort William Henry. A message was sent to Munro saying that Webb did not think it was "prudent" to send help until he was reinforced. The messenger was killed and scalped by Indians who brought the message to Montcalm. Montcalm in turn relayed it to Munro and urged him to surrender.

On August 9, after several days of bombardment, Munro had to surrender. Montcalm agreed to allow the British troops to march to Fort Edward provided they undertook not to fight again for 18 months. They were allowed to take one cannon with them in recognition of their gallant defense.

Montcalm has often been blamed unjustly for a great tragedy which then occurred. He warned the British to get rid of all their liquor so that it would not be consumed by the Indians. This was not done and the Indians invaded the hospital where they scalped the patients, many of whom were suffering from smallpox. The infected scalps later spread the disease through Indian villages, resulting in many deaths.

The march to Fort Edward began early the next morning. Montcalm posted a number of French regulars along the route to protect the British from the Indians, should they go on the rampage. Some of the British had filled their canteens with rum instead of water, and gave drinks to the Indians, hoping to make friends with them. The rum had the opposite effect. Many of the soldiers were ill and could not keep up with the rest. They were killed. Men, women, and children were attacked and taken prisoner. Of the 2,200 who began the march from Fort William Henry, only 1,400 reached Fort Edward.

Many of the French soldiers did not care if the Indians killed the British and did nothing to stop the slaughter. However, Montcalm, Lévis, Bourlamaque and other French officers did their best. At one point Montcalm shouted: "Kill me, but spare the English who are under my protection." This helped to bring some order out of chaos.

The episode was dramatized years later in the book *The Last of the Mohicans* by James Fenimore Cooper, who once acted as an American spy in Canada.

Other Events on August 9:

1656   Oliver Cromwell granted Acadia to Charles La Tour.

1759   Lower Town Quebec was destroyed by British gunfire.

1836   The Chippewas ceded 1.5 million acres, now parts of Bruce, Grey, Huron, and Wellington counties, Ontario.

1842   The Ashburton-Webster Treaty was signed, settling the boundary differences between Canada and the States.

1864   Canadian Parliamentarians arrived in Nova Scotia en route to Charlottetown.

1878   The British Columbia Legislature voted to secede from Canada.

1941   Winston Churchill arrived at Argentia, Newfoundland, for a meeting with American President Roosevelt.

Indians and French Attack New England

Recent stories about Indian atrocities can be topped by many more. It is important to remember that the Indians often had provocation, and were sometimes urged to do their worst by the French, English and Dutch. Furthermore, their atrocities were not unique. Heretics were being burned at the stake in Spain, and enemies of the Church and State were torn to pieces in France and hanged on gibbets all over the countryside of Britain. It was a cruel age.

Some of the worst atrocities took place in the New England States, as part of Governor Frontenac's campaign to impress the Indians that France was far from finished in North America. The French inflamed the Abenaki Indians to massacre many settlements, including Wells on August 10, 1703.

The pattern of attack was nearly always the same. The French and Indians would swoop into a settlement during the night, or early in the morning; kill most of the men, women and children; take some prisoners, and burn their homes.

Haverhill, in Massachusetts, produced an amazing story. A Mrs. Dunstan had just given birth to a baby. The Indians smashed the baby against a tree and forced Mrs. Dunstan, Mrs. Neff and a small boy to go back to Acadia with them. It was a walk of 250 miles, which Mrs. Dunstan was in no condition to undertake. Nevertheless she kept going for more than 100 miles. One night their party of two warriors, three squaws, and seven children were sleeping close to the fire, while Mrs. Dunstan, Mrs. Neff, and the boy were trying to keep warm as best they could away from the fire. The two women took up hatchets and quickly killed ten of the twelve Indians. The other two were helpless. They ate the Indians' food, scalped the bodies, and walked back to Haverhill with the bloody scalps swinging from their hands!

The attacks on Wells, Scarborough, and many other settlements produced similar stories. One woman scalded an attacking Indian to death by throwing boiling water on him. The other Indians thought so highly of her trick they took her prisoner instead of killing her. On the march to Acadia she gave birth to a baby. Its crying annoyed the Indians, so they dropped red-hot coals in its mouth.

The attacks on the New England settlements did not achieve any lasting benefit. On the contrary, they helped stir up the anger that led eventually to the capture of Louisburg, the expulsion of the Acadians, and finally the loss of France's North American possessions.

Other Events on August 10:

1760 General Amherst sailed from Oswego, New York, to capture Montreal.

1764 Governor Murray assumed office and established civil government.

1838 Lord Durham's ordinance banishing rebels without trial was disallowed by the British Government.

1850 Laws were passed to regulate currency. The Bytown and Prescott Railway was incorporated.

1876 Alexander Graham Bell conducted the first long distance telephone conversation between Brantford and Paris, Ontario—a distance of eight miles.

1943 Allied leaders including Churchill, Roosevelt, and Mackenzie King held a conference at Quebec.

1953 The Liberals under Louis St. Laurent won the general election: Liberals 171, Conservatives 51, Co-operative Commonwealth Federation 23, Social Credit 15.

1954 Ground was broken for the St. Lawrence Seaway Power Development at Cornwall, Ontario.

Heads of State Meet

Early in August, 1941, two Canadian destroyers, H.M.C.S. *Assiniboine* and H.M.C.S. *Restigouche,* were patrolling the North Atlantic when they received a thrilling message in code. They were to rendezvous with the new battleship H.M.S. *Prince of Wales* at a position given in longitude and latitude.

What could a lone British battleship be doing at sea at that time? The *Assiniboine* and *Restigouche* had to go full steam ahead to make the rendezvous on schedule, and sighted the *Prince of Wales* amidst rain and fog at 9:25 on the morning of August 6. Then they were told why they were there. The battleship flashed a message to the destroyers: "We have the Prime Minister, the First Sea Lord, the Chief of Imperial General Staff, and the Chief of the Air Staff on board and are proceeding to rendezvous with the President of the United States." *Restigouche* and *Assiniboine* were to act as an anti-submarine screen for the battleship to Argentia, in Placentia Harbor, Newfoundland.

Although the sea was rough, the battleship raced ahead at 30 knots. It was difficult for the destroyers to keep pace. Their egg-shell hulls could not stand the pounding a battleship could, and they asked the Admiral to slow down. Reluctantly, he agreed to reduce speed to 29 knots!

Assiniboine and *Restigouche,* passing through a lane of American destroyers, entered Placentia Harbor with the *Prince of Wales* on August 9. President Roosevelt was on board the U.S.S. *Augusta* with his naval and military advisers, and Secretary of State, Cordell Hull. The United States was not involved in the war until December 1941, when the Japanese attacked Pearl Harbor and the Philippines. Nevertheless, President Roosevelt was battling the isolationists in the United States and giving the nations of the British Commonwealth all the aid he could.

Prime Minister Churchill and President Roosevelt held conferences alternately on the *Prince of Wales* and the *Augusta* and issued

Prime Minister Churchill and President Roosevelt

what was known as the Atlantic Charter on August 14. It emphasized that neither Britain nor the United States sought any other nation's territory. They respected the rights of all people to choose their own form of government and intended to see that sovereign rights were restored to nations from which these had been taken. The charter also said there should be trade on equal terms for all nations, including the enemy, and access to raw materials. It concluded with a strong plea for disarmament.

While Churchill and Roosevelt were drawing up the Atlantic Charter, their military experts were making plans. They included an agreement about convoy escorts that gave Canadian and American destroyers a larger area of responsibility. *Assiniboine, Restigouche,* and many other units of the Royal Canadian Navy played outstanding roles in the Battle of the Atlantic.

Other Events on August 11:

1585   John Davis entered Davis Strait on his Arctic voyage.

1791   Edward, Duke of Kent, arrived in Halifax to command the 7th Royal Fusiliers.

1854   The Act of Union was amended to make the Legislative Council elective.

1960   The Medical Research Council of Canada was established.

1965   Canada sold another 187 million bushels of wheat to Russia.

Yukon Gold Rush

Gold Rush Begins

The man who started one of the biggest gold rushes in the world missed making a fortune because he didn't like Indians! Gold had been discovered along the Yukon River in 1896, and a few prospectors were making a little money. One of them was Robert Henderson. In one of the creeks running into the Yukon River, Henderson and four other men panned gold worth $750. Henderson called it "Goldbottom," and went to a settlement called Ogilvie for supplies.

On the way back, he met George Washington Carmack, an American who wanted to be an Indian and who was known as "Siwash George." Carmack was fishing for salmon with two Indians, "Tagish" Charlie and "Skookum" Jim. Henderson urged him to try Goldbottom Creek. However, he added that he didn't want Indians staking claims.

Carmack didn't like Goldbottom Creek, and was angered when Henderson refused to provide tobacco for his companions. Carmack and his friends left Henderson and on the way back, on August 12, they panned some gravel on Rabbit Creek and immediately found four dollars worth of gold.

They staked claims, which Skookum Jim was left to guard, while Carmack and Tagish Charlie rushed to record them at Constan-

tine's Post on Forty Mile. On the way there, Carmack told everyone about their discovery. They wouldn't believe him until he poured gold dust out of an empty shotgun shell. Henderson, however, was not informed, although he claimed later that he told Carmack to try Rabbit Creek.

Then the rush started. It was the Klondike Gold Rush, the biggest and most exciting in the world. Huge fortunes were made. "Big Alex" MacDonald staked half of Claim 30 on Eldorado for a sack of flour and made $20 million. He spent it almost as quickly and died penniless in a log cabin. One of the prospectors brought his bride along. Whenever she needed money, she just panned the muck the men were digging up and nearly always found a few nuggets! Poor Robert Henderson, whose dedicated work started it all, had to settle for a pension of $200 a month from the Government.

Other Events on August 12:

1615 The first mass in Ontario was celebrated by Father Le Caron in Huron Village near Thunder Bay.

1768 An Order-in-Council confirmed the border between Canada and New York.

1787 Prince William Henry (later King William IV) arrived at Quebec as captain of the H.M.S. *Pegasus*.

The first Anglican Bishop in the British Empire, Charles Inglis, was appointed for Nova Scotia and Quebec.

1842 An Imperial statute created the Amalgamated Assembly of Newfoundland.

1856 The Legislature of Vancouver Island opened. It was the first west of the Great Lakes.

1882 The Grand Trunk and Great Western Railways were amalgamated.

1889 An Imperial Act defined the boundaries of Ontario and Manitoba.

Early Halifax

Canadians Warmly Received in Halifax

On August 2, the story was told about the Canadian goodwill tour of the Maritimes organized by D'Arcy McGee and Sandford Fleming in 1864. Several days were spent in Saint John, banqueting and speech-making. Then the delegates set out for Halifax.

Halifax was greatly different from Saint John; it had been a British military and naval base for more than 100 years. Here, there was great formality, and class distinction: the larger homes had servants' quarters at the rear, with separate entrances; smart landaus and four-wheel coaches were driven along the streets by liveried coachmen. Scarlet-coated British soldiers and blue-jacketed sailors of the Royal Navy lent color to the scene. When night came, the lamp-lighters turned up the gas jets in their square glass cages along the streets. All night long, the watch patrolled the street calling out the hour: "Three o'clock and all's well!"

The Canadians stayed in Halifax for six days. One of the happiest times was a "hodge-podge and chowder party" at the Royal Halifax Yacht Club on August 13. There were kilted pipers and Highland dancers. The afternoon was hot, so the delegates took off their black broadcloth coats and stove-pipe hats. Bearded senators and members of the legislature played leap-frog on the lawn!

Before the visit ended and the delegates returned to Canada, many warm friendships had been made. Joseph Howe, soon to oppose Confederation strongly, made a speech in which he said: "I am not one of those who thank God I am a Nova Scotian merely, for I am a Canadian as well . . . I have looked across the broad continent and studied the mode by which it could be consolidated . . . and why should union not be brought about? Is it because we wish to live and die in our insignificance?"

In one of his speeches, Howe also made a prediction: "I believe that many in this room will live to hear the whistle of the steam-engine in the passes of the Rocky Mountains and to make the journey to the Pacific in five or six days." It seemed incredible, but it came true. Howe did not live to make that trip, but many of his peers did.

Other Events on August 13:

1812   General Brock met Indian Chief Tecumseh to plan a campaign to drive General Hull back into the States.

1863   John Sandfield Macdonald became Prime Minister of United Canada until March 14, 1864.

1913   Troops were called out to quell rioting at Nanaimo, British Columbia.

1963   An Anglican Congress at Toronto drew 1,000 delegates from 78 countries.

Buffalo in Wainwright Park, Alberta

Buffalo Protected

One of the great tragedies of Canada was the disappearance of the buffalo. If it had not been for decisive, last minute action, the buffalo would have become extinct. Yet, before the arrival of white men on the North American continent, the buffalo were probably the most abundant large animal in the world.

Buffalo were the staff of life for the Indians on the Prairies. They slaughtered them indiscriminately, but could not deplete their numbers. Even when the Indians joined with the Métis and had rifles, the buffalo survived. Gradually the pressure became too great. American freebooters came onto the Prairies and the slaughter increased. As many as 50,-000 buffalo robes were shipped across the border in a year. The slaughter in the United States was worse. When the buffalo became scarce, the Blackfoot, Cree and Piegan Indians began to starve.

On August 14, 1877, the Northwest Council took action. It issued an edict prohibiting hunters from driving buffalo into pits and ravines where they could easily be cornered and killed. Destroying buffalo for amusement, or for the purpose of taking their tongues and other choice cuts, was also forbidden. There was to be a closed season from November 15 to August 14. The "Mounties" drove out the American freebooters, but the Indians and Métis paid little attention to the laws. By 1880 the buffalo had practically disappeared from the Prairies. There was no population count of buffalo in Canada, but in 1900 the United States estimated that there were only 250 left on this side of the border.

A few people like Norman Luxton (see July 6) took action. Luxton suggested to Frank Oliver, founder of the Edmonton *Bulletin*, that Canada should buy a herd of buffalo sheltered by Michael Pablo in Montana. This was done through the Government and the buffalo were brought to Wainwright, Alberta. They became the foundation of the great buffalo preserve in the national park. The buffalo will not become extinct now, but neither can they be allowed to roam the Prairies. It is part of the cost of civilization.

Other Events on August 14:

1756   Oswego, New York, surrendered to Montcalm.

1848   The Act of Union was amended, repealing the clause that English be the only official language in Canada.

1855   The Imperial Merchant Shipping Act provided for lighthouses.

1861   Montreal was badly flooded. One quarter of the city was under water.

1956   Parliament was prorogued after 152 days, its longest session since 1903.

1957   The Fourteenth Congress of the Universal Postal Union opened in Ottawa until September 25.

1961   The provincial premiers held a conference in Charlottetown.

Medical College Granted Charter at Kingston

When the American Revolutionary War ended, Canada benefitted from an influx of 50,000 United Empire Loyalists. They changed the entire complexion of the British North American colonies, especially Upper Canada.

The newcomers faced severe problems. They also created problems for the communities in which they settled. A rapidly increasing population made it necessary to provide streets, schools and other public services.

There was a great shortage of doctors. As late as 1815, there were only forty qualified medical men in Upper Canada! The result was that there were a great many hucksters touring the countryside, selling "wonder medicines" from wagons. They were colorful and entertaining, but their drugs were often little more than colored water, with perhaps some unpleasant flavoring to make them seem effective.

Sometimes the hucksters would bring an entertainment troupe with them and put on shows. During each performance, there was a pause while the huckster extolled the virtues of his medicines. Sales were good, but the few medical men were furious!

In 1838, an editorial in the Toronto *Patriot* said: "Quacks are an intolerable nuisance in any city where empiricism and radicalism go hand in hand. It is a monstrous grievance that our government should allow the province to swarm with these pestilent vagabonds, every one of whom is a Yankee loafer."

Attempts had been made to regulate the practice of medicine. Dr. John Rolph tried to form a medical school in Toronto in 1824, but became involved in politics. After taking part in the Rebellion of 1837, he had to flee to the United States. He was pardoned in 1843 and returned to Toronto, where he resumed his school. It became part of the University of Toronto in 1887.

The outcry against "quacks" became so great that the legislature passed an act in 1839 incorporating the College of Physicians and Surgeons in Upper Canada. It examined candidates for licenses to practise medicine in the province. In this way the situation was gradually brought under control. On August 15, 1866, the Royal College of Physicians and Surgeons received a charter at Kingston, Ontario.

Other Events on August 15:

1534   Cartier began his return to France after his first voyage to Canada.

1689   Fort Pemequid, near Kennebec, Maine, was attacked by the Abenaki Indians under French leadership.

1696   Fort. Pemequid surrendered to Iberville and the Indians.

1766   The first issue of the Nova Scotia *Gazette* was published.

1818   Robert Gourlay was tried for sedition.

1866   Ottawa College became the University of Ottawa.

1890   A conference of the Church of England at Winnipeg established the union of all synods.

1955   A ceremony at Grand Pré, Nova Scotia, commemorated the expulsion of the Acadians in 1755.

First Medical College, Toronto

First Medical College, U.C., Toronto 1844

Meeting of Brock and Tecumseh, 1812

Hull Loses Detroit

General Hull's invasion of Canada was described on July 12. He retreated to Detroit when he heard about the capture of Mackinac and Fort Dearborn a few days later. In the meantime, General Brock, who had the difficult job of guarding both the Niagara and Detroit sectors, rushed to Amherstburg to join forces with Indian Chief Tecumseh.

Tecumseh, who radiated cheerfulness, energy and decision, impressed Brock and the British officers. He wore a neat uniform with a tanned deerskin jacket, and ornamented leather moccasins. Suspended from his nose was a strange ornament of three small crowns.

It was known that Hull had 2,500 troops, some of whom were mounted. Brock had 300 regulars, 400 militia and Tecumseh's 600 Indians. It was a desperate undertaking to cross the river with such a small force and attack a much stronger army in a fortified position. Tecumseh was greatly pleased when Brock decided to do it, and said to the other chiefs: "This is a man!"

Tecumseh's warriors crossed the river in canoes during the early morning hours of August 16. When daylight came the guns at Sandwich and those of the armed schooner *Queen Charlotte* opened fire on Detroit. One of the first mortar shells killed three officers on Hull's staff. British troops had now crossed the river and were approaching Detroit, with Brock and Tecumseh riding side by side. The 600 Indians hidden in the woods began screaching their eerie war cries. The shells continued to explode in the fort.

Hull had his son, married daughter and two small grandchildren with him. Many of his men had brought along their wives and children. As the redcoats began to form for the attack, Hull decided to surrender. The white flag went up and half an hour later the fort was in British hands. The Americans were allowed to return home on condition that they would not fight again in the war. Great quantities of supplies were captured.

Brock took off his tasseled scarlet sash and put it around Tecumseh in the presence of the troops and Indians. Tecumseh then returned the compliment, wrapping his gaudy arrow-patterned sash around Brock, who wore it until he was killed two months later.

Other Events on August 16:

1637 The Duchess of Aiguillon donated 22,400 livres to the Hôtel Dieu (Hospital), Quebec.

1750 Three hundred German settlers arrived at Lunenburg, Nova Scotia.

1777 The British were defeated at the Battle of Bennington.

1784 New Brunswick was made a separate colony from Nova Scotia. Thomas Carleton (brother of Sir Guy) became the first governor.

1827 The first stone of one of the Rideau Canal locks was laid by Captain John Franklin, the famous Arctic explorer.

1858 The first cable message from the States to Britain was sent via Newfoundland.

Steamer Crosses Ocean

On August 17, 1833, the *Royal William* sailed from Pictou, Nova Scotia, to London, England. This may have been the first time any ship had crossed the Atlantic entirely under steam power.

That distinction is disputed by the United States and Holland. The Americans claim that the *Savannah* was the first steamship to cross the Atlantic. The *Savannah,* however, also used sails. There is more reason to believe that the honor should go to the Dutch ship *Curaçao*, which is believed to have crossed the Atlantic under steam power in 1827, on a voyage from Antwerp to Dutch Guiana. If the Dutchmen were first, then our *Royal William* was second, taking a more difficult course across the North Atlantic.

Royal William was built at Quebec in 1830 with the aid of a government subsidy. Its purpose was to provide a regular service between Quebec and Halifax. The engines were installed in Montreal and sails were added in case of a breakdown. She was described as "a smoke-belching, paddle-wheeling, clanking steam kettle." The label probably came from a die-hard who believed in sails alone!

The Quebec-Halifax run did not prove to be profitable. *Royal William* also tried picking up trade to and from Boston, and was the first British steamship to enter an American port. That run did not work out well either, so finally the ship was sold to interests in England. She left Pictou on August 17, 1833, after picking up a load of coal for fuel. The trip to London took 25 days. Eventually *Royal William* was converted into a warship and sold to Spain.

Although *Royal William's* career in Canada was not successful, her advent on the St. Lawrence marked an era of progress, especially for Montreal. Until that time, Quebec had been the important city. In 1830, Montreal

The Royal William *leaving Pictou*

took steps to move into the lead. A harbor commission was formed to improve the docks and to put navigation aids along the river.

Other Events on August 17:

1760   Two French barques, *Actaquaise* and *Iroquois*, were captured by five British rowing galleys at Point au Baril, near Brockville, Ontario. They were the last French ships on the Great Lakes.

1889   The Canadian College of Music opened in Ottawa.

1903   The congress of the Chambers of Commerce of the British Empire opened in Montreal.

1913   The Ontario Department of Instruction ruled that French was not to be used in schools beyond Grade 1.

1923   The Federal Pension Appeal Board was appointed.

1940   Prime Minister Mackenzie King and President Roosevelt held a conference at Ogdensburg, New York.

1954   Prince Philip attended the British Empire Games at Vancouver.

1965   Four treasure hunters were killed at Oak Island, Nova Scotia, where Captain Kidd's treasure is supposed to be buried.

Fort Garry in 1872

Sioux Begin Slaughter

Before the days of Sitting Bull and the Northwest Mounted Police, the people in the Red River-Fort Garry area suffered a real scare. Little Crow appeared at Fort Garry with eighty of his followers, demanding food and ammunition.

Little Crow was an amazing Indian. He attended the Episcopal Church every Sunday wearing a good suit, white collar and dark tie. He looked like any other American or German farmer from the area, except for his gleaming black hair and beaded moccasins.

In 1851 the American Government persuaded the Sioux to live in two reservations. The Indians felt they had been tricked into the deal, and cheated of a down payment of $275,000. Furthermore, the $45,000 they received every month for supplies often arrived late, and when it came the storekeeper would sell the Indians spoiled, wormy food. When the payment due in August, 1862, failed to arrive, Little Crow went to storekeeper Myrick and asked him for food supplies on credit. Myrick replied, "If your people are hungry, let them eat grass."

Next Sunday Little Crow went to church as usual. Then he called a council of war. He told his followers that their golden opportunity had come. Most able-bodied men were fighting in the American Civil War. Nothing could stop the Sioux from regaining their freedom.

On Monday, August 18, storekeeper Myrick was found dead, his mouth stuffed with grass.

Forty-eight hours later, 2,000 people had been killed, and Fort Garry and the Red River settlement were isolated. When Little Crow went to see Governor Dallas at Fort Garry, he brought along medals and flags that had been presented to the Sioux. He reminded the governor that the Sioux had fought for the British in 1812 and had been promised the protection of "the red flag of the north." Governor Dallas agreed to provide food, but no ammunition or guns. The Sioux could not exist on that basis, so Little Crow disbanded them and headed south with his sixteen year old son, Wowpinapa. A few days later, an unknown white man saw them picking berries. Believing the adage "The only good Indian is a dead Indian," he shot and killed them.

Other Events on August 18:

1620   The Duke of Montmorency was appointed Viceroy of Canada, and Champlain, his lieutenant.

1670   Jean Talon arrived at Quebec as Intendant, bringing Récollet priests to break the Jesuit monopoly.

1704   French and Indians from Placentia, Newfoundland, raided Bonavista and burned four ships.

1843   George Brown published *The Banner*, a paper for the Presbyterian Free Church.

1876   A conference was held among the Northwest Territories, Manitoba, Canada, and the Indians.

1914   Parliament held a special war session until August 22.

1927   Prime Minister Stanley Baldwin sailed for Britain after accompanying Edward, Prince of Wales, and Prince George, to Canada.

1956   The Alexander Graham Bell Museum was dedicated at Baddeck, Nova Scotia.

1962   The tricentenary of the founding of Placentia, Newfoundland, was celebrated.

Canadians Suffer Heavy Casualties at Dieppe

One of the most controversial battles in which Canadian troops ever fought was the Dieppe raid on August 19, 1942. Books and articles have been written about it; television and radio programs produced, but many missed the purpose and significance of Dieppe.

During the summer of 1942, the Russians were fighting the Germans practically alone, suffering terrible losses with their backs to the wall. They insisted that the Allies take action in Europe to relieve the pressure on them. The United States had barely entered the war and had few forces in Britain. It was impossible for the British, Canadian, Australian, New Zealand and other forces in England to attack Europe alone, in what was called "the second front." Yet something had to be done. After lengthy consultations the Allies decided to mount a heavy offensive on Dieppe, as a morale-builder and test of German defenses. It was a rehearsal for the "second front" which actually opened on June 5, 1944, almost two years later.

Nearly all the writers and producers who have dealt with the Dieppe raid have failed to bring out that it was a *combined operation*, not just an attack by the 2nd Canadian Division. Dieppe, for the first time, co-ordinated army, navy, and air force. The navy did an incredible job, escorting more than 100 troop-carrying ships to harbors along the coast of the south of England and then sweeping them safely through the German minefields in the darkness. Before and during the assault, the air force tangled overhead with German bombers and fighters, inflicting severe losses on the Luftwaffe at a time when it was trying to conserve its strength.

The bravery and fighting ability of the six battalions of the 2nd Division and the Calgary Tanks that formed the ground attack cannot be described here. Two of their members won the Victoria Cross: Lt.-Col. C. C. I. Merritt of the South Saskatchewans, and Reverend J. W. Foote, chaplain of the Royal Hamilton Light Infantry, who worked as a stretcherbearer on the centre beach. Captain P. A. Porteous, a British Commando, also received the Victoria Cross. There were many other deserved decorations in all ranks.

The cost was heavy. Of the 5,000 Canadians who took part in the raid, 3,367 were killed, wounded or taken prisoner. This was more than the entire Canadian Army lost in the first year of fighting in France after D-Day, 1944. The heavy casualties were due in some measure to bad luck. The element of surprise was lost when a commando unit leading the attack ran into a German convoy moving along the coast in the dark. The shooting alerted the shore defenses.

Valuable lessons were learned from Dieppe which prepared the way for the successful assault on June 5, 1944, which led to the end of the war. Dieppe, with its strong historic link with Canada, deserves a proud place on Canada's battle flag.

Other Events on August 19:

1652 The Iroquois killed Governor Duplessis at Trois Rivières.

1954 The Right Honorable C. D. Howe was awarded the Guggenheim medal for his part in the development of Canadian aviation.

Calgary Tanks at Dieppe, 1942

Bigot Goes to Quebec, Leads Group of Swindlers

One of the biggest "crooks" who ever operated in Canada was François Bigot, who was the Intendant or business manager at Louisburg before it fell to Pepperell in 1745, and at Quebec before it was taken by Wolfe.

Louisburg fell easily to Pepperell's amateurs from New England, partly because it was not as strong as it was supposed to be. Inferior materials had been used in the walls. The soldiers who did the work were supposed to be paid, but they received no money. Provisions sent to the soldiers were sold to officers and there was dissension among the ranks while Bigot lined his pockets.

Despite his record, Bigot was sent to Quebec on August 20, 1748, and organized a ring of "crooks" to help him. One of them was Joseph Cadet, son of a local butcher, who was made Commissar-General and looked after supplies. He made enough money to become the Baron de la Touche D'Arrigny, with an estate in France.

Under Bigot's evil genius, the group plundered Canada and the treasury of France. People were overcharged for goods from France. Canadian farm products were bought at low prices, stored and then released to the troops when the highest prices could be charged. King Louis would buy presents for the Indians which they seldom received as Bigot and his gang would sell them. On one occasion, when Louis needed supplies for his armies in Europe, Bigot made a profit of 12 million francs!

The fall of Quebec, like Louisburg, was due in part to inferior or scarce supplies resulting from Bigot's activities. When they returned to France, there was an investigation of all the officials who had served at Quebec.

Governor Vaudreuil was acquitted and received a pension. Twenty-seven judges heard the charges against Bigot and his accomplices. The trials lasted for more than a year and Bigot's testimony covered 1,200 pages. He pictured himself as the victim of evil associates! Somehow he escaped the guillotine and was banished from France with a heavy fine. Other members of the gang were sent to the Bastille, but some of them had enough money to buy an easement of their sentences. Cadet's daughters married into the nobility of France!

Other Events on August 20:

1691   Henry Kelsey of the Hudson's Bay Company was the first white man to see what is now Saskatchewan.

1820   The coronation of George IV was celebrated in Canada, eleven months before the ceremony in London, July 10, 1821!

1823   J. C. Beltrane and Major Long of the United States explored the Red River area with the idea of acquiring it for the United States.

1882   The first train arrived at Regina.

1883   The first session of the Legislative Council of the Northwest Territories was held at Regina.

1907   The University of Saskatchewan was founded.

1955   Governor-General Vincent Massey opened the Boy Scout World Jamboree at Niagara-on-the-Lake.

1962   Manitoba celebrated the fiftieth anniversary of its founding.

Gold Discovered at Barkerville

On August 21, 1860, gold was discovered in the creeks running into the Quesnel River in British Columbia, and prospectors swarmed into the area later known as Barkerville. Billy Barker, from Cornwall, England, decided to sink a shaft rather than pan for gold. He tried Williams Creek, and by August, 1862, had sunk a crude shaft 40 feet into the bedrock. By this time Barker was almost broke, and other prospectors told him that he was crazy to go on. Determination paid off. Before the end of the month, Billy Barker struck rich pay dirt. His claim was only 600 feet long, but he took gold worth $600,000 from it.

Then Barkerville grew up almost overnight. It became a town of log shanties, saloons, and false-fronted stores built on stilts along narrow, muddy streets. People flocked there from all parts of the world. There were not only miners, but clerks and card-sharpers, bankers and barbers, poets and priests, dudes and dancing girls. There was real inflation in Barkerville; boots sold for $50 a pair, and soap for $1.25 a bar. Entertainers, including strolling Shakespearean players, were paid in gold dust!

Disaster came in 1868 when Barkerville was destroyed by fire. Fortunately, when the gold petered out, many Barkerville residents stayed in British Columbia to share the wealth of other, less fickle, natural resources. Billy Barker was one of the many, although he didn't benefit much. He married a very expensive girl who spent money as naturally as she breathed! Barker ended his days in the Old Men's Home in Victoria.

Barkerville was a ghost town for many years, but was rebuilt almost in its original form in 1958, when British Columbia celebrated its 100th anniversary. Now it is a historic park, and during Barkerville Days in the summer, thousands of visitors enjoy the sights and entertainment of the gold rush days.

Other Events on August 21:

1820   Robert Gourlay was banished from Canada.

1847   The Canada Life Insurance Company was established.

1860   Edward, Prince of Wales (later King Edward VII) arrived at Montreal during a tour of British North American colonies.

1872   Chebucto Head Lighthouse, Halifax, began operation.

1902   Doukhobors in the Yorkton area of Saskatchewan turned horses and cattle loose on the prairies.

1903   Croatian Fraternal Union of British Columbia was formed.

British Fiasco Saves French Canada

Britain might have captured Canada from France in 1711 instead of 1763 if it had not been for the amazing foul-up of an expedition under Sir Hovenden Walker. The leadership of the strongest military force that had ever sailed from Britain was incredible. Sir Hovenden Walker was an Admiral of the Royal Navy, but there is no record of how he obtained that rank. His second-in-command was General Jack Hill, who would be called a playboy today. He was appointed because his sister, Abigail Hill, was Lady of the Queen's Bedchamber.

The Walker-Hill expedition totalled 9 warships, more than 60 transports, and 12,000 troops, many of whom were highly trained soldiers who had fought under Marlborough. It looked as though the final hour had come for France in North America.

The fleet sailed from Nantucket on July 30, 1711. One of the British ships captured a French ship in the St. Lawrence. Its captain was a French officer, Paradis, who knew the river well and accepted a bribe to pilot the fleet up the St. Lawrence. On August 22, while near Anticosti Island, Admiral Walker believed they were sailing near the south shore. Although the captain of the flagship reported that land had been sighted (the river is 70 miles wide at that point), Walker's argument persisted; they were near the south shore. He ordered the fleet to stop for the night, with bows pointing north. Then he went to bed.

Before he fell asleep, an officer came into his cabin and reported that there were breakers on all sides. Walker ordered him out. Soon the officer returned and urged the Admiral to look for himself. Walker appeared in dressing gown and slippers, and called the pilot Paradis. It was soon established that the fleet was off the north shore, in treacherous water near Sept-Iles. The warships were saved, but 10 transports and service ships were wrecked. About 500 men were rescued, but after a conference with General Hill, Walker decided to return to Britain. There were still 50 ships and 11,000 men available to fight!

Walker was dismissed from the service on half pay, while General Hill went back to being a "man about town." The incident is known in Canadian history as "the magnificent fiasco."

Other Events on August 22:

1776   Governor Carleton was instructed by the British Government to attend to civil duties. General Burgoyne was made Commander of Forces in Canada. This led to Carleton's resignation.

1884   The Calgary Agricultural Society was organized; it was the forerunner of the Calgary Stampede.

1901   The sod was turned for the Cape Breton Railway.

1919   Edward, Prince of Wales (the late Duke of Windsor), opened the Quebec Bridge.

1935   The Reverend William Aberhart formed the world's first Social Credit Government in Alberta.

1950   A nation-wide railway strike began, causing Canada's worst transportation crisis.

1954   The Duchess of Kent and Princess Alexandra (widow and daughter of Prince George in the story of August 7) arrived at Quebec for a Canadian tour.

1955   Prime Minister Garfield Todd of Rhodesia visited Ottawa.

Kelsey Hunts Buffalo

Henry Kelsey sees buffalo on the Western Plains

It was not until 1926 that historians could be certain that Henry Kelsey really did reach as far west as Saskatchewan in 1691. He was an employee of the Hudson's Bay Company and his career was distorted by witnesses who criticized the company during a parliamentary investigation in 1749. The story of his journey to Western Canada came to light in 1926 when his diary was found in the library of Castle Dodds, at Carrickfergus, Northern Ireland.

The Hudson's Bay Company was granted its charter in 1670 on the understanding that it would explore the enormous territory under its control, and try to find the Northwest Passage. Kelsey, although only twenty years old, was working at the Hudson's Bay Company post at Fort Nelson, Hudson Bay. He volunteered to accompany a party of Stone Indians to their hunting grounds, and left with them on June 12, 1690.

Many of the great explorers, Cartier, Champlain, Mackenzie, Fraser, and Thompson kept diaries. Fortunately Kelsey did too, but much of his writing was in poor verse. He described his departure thus:

Then up ye River I with heavy heart
Did Take my way & from all English part
To live among ye natives of this place
If God permits me for one two years space.

Kelsey's writings are entertaining but do not give a clear account of where he went. It is known now that he reached The Pas, which he named Deering's Point after a director of the company. He was the first white man to see the Prairies, musk oxen, and a buffalo hunt; he actually took part in a buffalo hunt on August 23, 1691.

Kelsey was given the name *Mis Top Ashish* by the Indians. It meant *Little Giant* because he saved an Indian in a fight with two fierce grizzly bears.

Before any other white man penetrated the Prairies (La Vérendrye and his sons did so in 1738), Kelsey had spent nearly forty years on Hudson Bay, including the two years

exploring the interior. He was captured by Iberville in 1694 when the great French-Canadian military leader attacked York Factory.

Other Events on August 23:

1541 Cartier reached Stadacona (Quebec) on his third trip to Canada.

1714 High prices caused riots at Quebec. The Comte de St. Pierre lost his charter to develop Ile St-Jean (Prince Edward Island).

1829 Sir John Colborne was appointed Lieutenant-Governor of Upper Canada.

1871 The Paris rowing crew of Saint John, New Brunswick, defeated the Renforth crew from Tyne, England, in a stirring race at Saint John. James Renforth, the Tyne stroke, died.

1882 Pile O'Bones was named Regina when the C.P.R. tracks arrived there.

1898 A Joint High Commission met at Quebec to consider disputes between Canada and the United States.

1956 The Northwest Territories Council opened a session at the new town of Aklavik.

Canada: Two Provinces

On August 24, 1791, the British Parliament passed the Constitutional Act. It divided Canada into two provinces, Upper and Lower, each having its own lieutenant-governor and legislature. This system was kept in effect until the Act of Union in 1840.

Britain has been criticized for not taking the opportunity to unite all the British North American colonies, as they were in 1867. Confederation was suggested as early as 1784 by Colonel Robert Morse of the Royal Engineers, whose letter on the subject is in the National Archives. He predicted "a great country may yet be raised up in North America." Confederation was also urged by a New York Loyalist, William Smith, who later became Chief Justice of Quebec, and Jonathan Sewell, another Chief Justice of the same province.

William Pitt, who sponsored the Canada Act, and other British statesmen who supported it, were of the opinion that the Confederation suggestions were ahead of their time. They felt it would be better if Confederation was worked out by Canadians themselves rather than by Britain.

This Act was made necessary by the great influx of United Empire Loyalists after the American Revolutionary War. The new English-speaking settlers did not want to live under French law, despotic governors, or the Roman Catholic Church. In order to help the Protestants, the act provided that every eighth acre of land should be set aside to provide revenue for the clergy. These were called "the clergy reserves." When Pitt was asked what he meant by the "Protestant clergy," he replied that it was the clergy of the Church of England. This caused great problems later on because many of the new settlers were Presbyterians, Methodists, Baptists and Congregationalists.

Actually, Pitt wanted to make Canada like Britain, with a hereditary nobility. He said there was "something in the habits, customs and manners of Canada that peculiarly fitted it for the reception of hereditary honors." Some of the governors had similar ideas, and it used to be a joke in Ontario that Lord So-and-So was busy getting in the hay!

Other Events on August 24:

1814   British troops captured Washington, D.C., and burned public buildings in reprisal for the American sacking of Newark and York.

1852   Nanaimo, British Columbia, was established by Governor Douglas. The Hudson's Bay Company took possession of the coal deposits.

1870   The Wolseley expedition arrived at Fort Garry and Riel fled.

1885   The first census of the Northwest Territories showed the population as follows: Assiniboia 22,000, Saskatchewan 10,700, and Alberta 15,500.

1957   H.M.C.S. *Labrador* was the first deep draught ship to go through Bellot Strait.

Red Fife ready for threshing

Missionary Crowned World Wheat King

The first Canadian to win the title "World Wheat King" was John Brick, a Church of England clergyman, who did some farming in the Peace River area of Alberta as a hobby!

Brick came from England with his wife and four children and studied theology in Ontario. Fascinated by stories of the West, he received permission to start a mission at Dunvegan on the Peace River. When he had built his church, Brick decided to do some farming. After five years he returned to Toronto where he raised $5,000 for his mission. The Federal Government was interested in his farming experiment, and contributed $2,000.

When Brick returned to Peace River in 1888, the Edmonton *Bulletin* reported on August 25 that "Reverend John Brick, the Church of England missionary, is now on his way to Peace River. He is bringing up a large outfit, including a portable grist mill, agricultural and carpenter's tools. Also a thoroughbred Durham bull, two Holstein heifers and an Ayrshire cow, Berkshire and Yorkshire pigs and some poultry."

Brick's farm made great progress. In the spring of 1892, he planted a bushel of a new type of wheat seed, Red Fife, and harvested an amazing 72 bushels to the acre. The crop had to be cut with a sickle and threshed with a flail on the floor of the church!

Somebody suggested to Brick that he send a sample of his wheat to the World's Fair at Chicago, which he did more as an advertisement for Peace River than in the hope of winning an award. In order to ship it, he had to make the ten-day journey to Edmonton when the temperatures dropped as low as 60 below zero along the way!

Then the news came. Wheat from Peace River had won the World Championship! Where was Peace River? Finally the newspapers located it and there was more astonishment. John Brick and the people of Peace River did not hear the news until many weeks later.

There is now a bronze tablet at the town of Peace River commemorating the great achievement of the parson with the wheat crown.

Other Events on August 25:

1758   Colonel Bradstreet captured Fort Cataraqui (Kingston, Ontario) with a force of 3,000 British soldiers.

1760   Fort Lévis, above the St. Lawrence rapids, was taken by General Amherst.

1955   Russian farm experts toured Canada until September 10.

Resolution and *Discovery* Enter Hudson Bay

Usually the title "Maritime Province" is reserved for Nova Scotia, New Brunswick, or Prince Edward Island. Manitoba is grouped with Saskatchewan and Alberta as a "Prairie Province," but Manitoba was actually discovered from the sea, and has a coastline on Hudson Bay.

While Champlain was colonizing Nova Scotia and Quebec, he was also hoping to find a route to China through the continent. At the same time, and even before, British and Danish sailors were trying to locate the supposed "Strait of Anian" through the Arctic. Among them were Hudson, Davis, Frobisher, Baffin and Munck. On August 26, 1612, two British ships, *Resolution* and *Discovery*, came sailing down Hudson Bay under the command of Thomas Button. He was searching for the Anian Strait, but all he had seen was shoreline stretching north and south. He decided to stop in the estuary of a great river flowing from the southwest to rest his crew and make repairs. Suddenly the weather

Sir Thomas Button (d. 1634)

turned cold and the ships were closed in by ice. Button knew that he would have to stay for the winter and had his men build dykes to prevent the ice from crushing the hulls of his ships. They were the first Europeans to spend a winter in Manitoba. Button called it "New Wales," in honor of his homeland.

It was a hard winter. Many men died from scurvy, among them Francis Nelson, sailing master of the *Resolution*; Button named the river after him. There were only enough men left to handle one ship, so the *Resolution* was abandoned and they sailed back to Britain in the *Discovery,* the ship from which Henry Hudson had been put overboard by a mutinous crew.

Although Button had not found the Northwest Passage, he was still hopeful. His encouraging reports led Gibbons, Bylot and Baffin to make further attempts to discover it. Still, it wasn't until 1632 that other explorers proved there was no route to China through Hudson Bay, 56 years after Martin Frobisher began the search in 1576.

Other Events on August 26:

1731   Pierre La Vérendrye and his sons arrived at Grand Portage and discovered that the north route was the best to the West.

1784   Cape Breton was separated from Nova Scotia and made a colony. It was returned to Nova Scotia in 1820.

1793   Governor Simcoe named York (see July 30).

1876   Treaty Number Six was signed at Fort Carleton with the Crees, Assiniboines, and Chippewas.

1961   Prime Minister Diefenbaker opened hockey's Hall of Fame in Toronto and granted $5 million to aid Canadian amateur sport.

British Dominions Asked to Help in Middle East

Sir Winston Churchill became such a great hero to Canadians in World War II that it was forgotten or forgiven that his name had been anathema to many people before and after World War I.

In the great naval controversy between Liberals and Conservatives from 1911 to the outbreak of war in 1914, Churchill, who was then First Lord of the Admiralty, had openly supported the Conservatives' position: that Canada should not try to create a navy, but should spend the money strengthening the Royal Navy.

In 1922 Churchill burst upon the Canadian political scene again. This time W. L. Mackenzie King and a Liberal government were in power. Turkey, as an ally of Germany, had been defeated in the war. Under the Treaty of Versailles, the Allies had kept control of the Dardenelles, the Sea of Marmara, and the Bosporus, dividing Europe and Asia. An international commission, on which Sir Robert Borden represented British interests, gave Gallipoli and Smyrna to Greece. A young Turkish officer, Mustapha Kemal, organized a government of his own to free Turkey. On August 27, 1922, Canadians read that Kemal had launched an all-out attack on the Greeks in Smyrna. Within two weeks, Smyrna had been captured and the British garrison at Chanak, headquarters of the army of occupation was trapped. Would Kemal go on and attack the British?

Winston Churchill, who had become Colonial Secretary, and Lord Chancellor Birkenhead, issued a press statement, without Cabinet approval, that Britain had invited the British Dominions to send troops to help defend the British position at Chanak. Prime Minister Mackenzie King read of the cabled request in Toronto newspapers, while absent from Ottawa.

During the war, Prime Minister Sir Robert Borden and Prime Minister Smuts of South Africa had established the position that as the Dominions had made such a big contribu-

tion, they must be consulted in decisions about foreign affairs in which they would be involved. So Prime Minister Mackenzie King replied that he could not commit Canada without the approval of Parliament.

Fortunately it all blew over without Britain's or Canada's going to war. A peace conference settled the situation in the Middle East. The importance of the "Chanak Crisis" was that Prime Minister King established Canadian relations with Britain on an orderly basis.

Other Events on August 27:

1670 Fort Jemseg on the Saint John River surrendered to de Soulange.

1836 King William IV granted £2,000 to St. Andrews and the Quebec Railway as a first instalment of the payment of £10,000.

1851 Richard Blanshard appointed a council to govern Vancouver Island.

Sir Winston Churchill (1874-1965)

Radisson and Groseilliers Form Partnership

This is an opportunity to describe something of Radisson's career, because it was on August 28, 1661, that he and his brother-in-law Chouart des Groseilliers began their great partnership that led to the founding of the Hudson's Bay Company.

Pierre Radisson's adventures began as a young boy at Trois Rivières, Quebec. He was captured by a band of Iroquois while hunting ducks and taken to their village in the State of New York. Somehow he managed to attract the attention of a squaw who had lost a son of about the same age and she adopted him. Radisson gained some knowledge of the language and customs of the Iroquois which helped him save a Jesuit mission after he escaped (see March 19).

Radisson and Groseilliers formed a fur-trading partnership. They went as far west as Lake Superior, where they were very successful. There is some possibility that they were the first white men to see the Mississippi River.

Soon after, Radisson and Groseilliers were fined for fur-trading infractions and decided to offer their services to the British. They met Sir George Carteret, a good friend of King Charles II. Carteret took Radisson and Groseilliers to England to tell their stories to Charles. The king, and especially his cousin, Prince Rupert, were greatly impressed by Radisson and Groseilliers, although they could not pronounce their names. They were usually called "Radishes and Gooseberry."

They fitted out an expedition to Hudson Bay to bring back furs. Groseilliers so impressed King Charles with his fur-laden cargo that Charles formed the Governor and Company of Adventurers of England Trading into Hudson's Bay on May 2, 1670.

Even so, Radisson and Groseilliers were displeased because King Charles only gave them a "gold chain and medall." They returned to Canada and, working for both the French and Dutch, later led an expedition to drive the English out of Hudson Bay. The story of Radisson's life becomes complicated and is difficult to follow, especially as most of it was written by Radisson himself. In any event, he returned to England in 1684, and was given shares in the Hudson's Bay Company. When he died the company gave his widow £6 in recognition of his work!

Other Events on August 28:

1781 Annapolis Royal (formerly Port Royal) was raided by American privateers.

1792 Captain George Vancouver arrived at Nootka Sound, British Columbia, to arrange a territorial deal with Spain (see March 23).

1833 Slavery was abolished in British Columbia.

1846 The British Possessions Act gave the provinces power to enact their own tariff and other agreements.

1873 Henry Thibert discovered gold in the Cassiar region of British Columbia.

1891 All railways in Quebec, New Brunswick and Nova Scotia were declared to constitute an Intercolonial Railroad.

1904 The Archbishop of Canterbury arrived at Quebec for his visit to Canada.

1910 The Queen's Own Rifles arrived at Aldershot, England, for maneuvers.

1950 Parliament was called into a special session to deal with the railway strike (see August 22), and Korean war.

Quebec Bridge Falls

People sailing to Canada for the first time are always thrilled to pass under the Quebec Bridge. When completed in September, 1917, it was the biggest bridge in the world, although it no longer holds that distinction. The plan to build a bridge across the St. Lawrence, eight miles above Quebec, was first proposed in 1853. Before it was completed in 1917, the Quebec Bridge had fallen down twice, with the loss of seventy-three lives.

The original plan would have cost $3 million, but no engineer would undertake its construction. In 1882, the idea was revived when the famous Firth of Forth bridge was built in Scotland. Sir James Brunless, who built the Firth bridge, was brought over to Canada as a consultant, but work progressed slowly. Finally the job was entrusted to a New York firm.

On completion day, August 29, 1907, with thousands watching, the southern cantilever suddenly collapsed. The crash killed sixty workmen and injured eleven others, as tons of twisted steel sank to the bottom of the St. Lawrence. There was a dramatic sight as a priest administered the last rites to a man caught inside a girder. There were no devices capable of cutting metal quickly enough in those days, and he drowned as the water rose inside the girder.

The Laurier government then stepped in and put the Department of Railways in charge. The contract was awarded to the St. Lawrence Bridge Company with two Canadian steel companies supplying the materials. On September 11, 1916, another large crowd assembled to see the centre span raised into position. It was floated down the St. Lawrence on six steel barges. Thousands watched from the shores or from small boats in the river. There was great cheering and waving of handkerchiefs as the giant cranes began to lift the span from the barges. As it rose to approximately 15 feet above the water, there was a crack like a rifle-shot and the span

The Quebec Bridge, 1917

plunged into the river. Thirteen men were killed.

Another center span was built and floated down the river. The huge cranes began lifting it on September 15, 1917, and it was in its place by September 20. The Quebec Bridge had finally been completed!

Other Events on August 29:

1708   French and Indians from Acadia massacred the settlement at Haverhill, Massachusetts.

1758   Wolfe, instructed by Amherst, left Louisburg to destroy settlements along the lower St. Lawrence, including Gaspé and Miramichi.

1849   The Toronto, Sarnia and Lake Huron Railroad was chartered. In 1858 it became part of the Northern Railroad.

1864   Macdonald, Cartier and other Canadian delegates left Quebec for a conference at Charlottetown (see September 1).

1883   The first Salvation Army service in Canada was held at London, Ontario.

1914   The Princess Patricia Canadian Light Infantry (the Princess Pats) sailed from Montreal for Britain. The main Canadian Expeditionary Force followed on October 31.

1917   The Compulsory Military Service Act caused a demonstration by 5,000 people in Montreal.

Currency To Change

One of the big events in Britain in 1965 was the decision to change the system of currency from the complicated pounds, shillings and pence, to the decimal system. Canada might have been stuck with pounds, shillings and pence in the 1850's if it had not been for a hard battle by Finance Minister Hincks and others.

When the United States adopted the decimal system in 1808, Canada tried unsuccessfully to do the same. Britain wanted to keep Canada in the "sterling bloc," using its currency. Various measures were passed by the Parliament of Canada after the Act of Union in 1840 but were disallowed by the British Government. Finally a compromise was reached on August 30, 1851, but it was not until January 1, 1858, that the decimal system of currency became effective. Problems were created when New Brunswick and Nova Scotia joined Canada in 1867, and other provinces after that.

Some unusual forms of currencies were used in Canada over the years. Even playing cards were used as paper money (see April 18). When Britain took Canada from France in 1763, there were 800,000 livres of unredeemed paper money in circulation, and many people were big losers.

Then Spanish silver dollars gained wide acceptance, many of them coming into circulation through illicit trade. These dollars had different values in different places. In New York a dollar would be worth eight shillings, but only five in Halifax. In Quebec silver dollars were called "Halifax currency", while Montreal called them "York currency." One problem was to get metal coins small enough to make change. Merchants used to cut the Spanish dollars into smaller pieces known as "four bits", and "two bits", expressions still in use today, meaning 50 or 25 cents.

Currency complications continued as late as 1881, as new provinces joined Confederation. Their currencies were taken out of circulation gradually and redeemed. Even in the 1920's, a paper bill, known as a "shinplaster" (worth 25 cents), was often seen.

Other Events on August 30:

1746 A force from Trois Rivières under Major Riguad de Vaudreuil attacked Crown Point.

1812 Selkirk settlers reached Fort Douglas (Winnipeg).

1851 The Legislative Council of British Columbia held its first session.

1954 The Duchess of Kent opened a new generating station at Niagara Falls.

1971 Alberta Conservatives led by Peter Lougheed defeated Social Credit government which had been in power since 1936.

British Attack Maine

When the United States declared war on Britain in 1812 with the intention of capturing Canada, many people in the New England States were opposed to the war and there was a movement to secede from the Union. This was one of the reasons why the Maritime Provinces were not attacked, except by raiders from the sea.

The Maritimers did not feel the same about attacking the States. They contended that the New Brunswick-Maine border should be the Penobscot River, south of the St. Croix. The United States claimed certain islands in Passamaquoddy Bay that Maritimers felt should belong to Britain.

Late in May 1814, the garrison at Halifax received the news that Napoleon had been beaten and sent to exile. Plans were put into effect to capture Maine, and a force was sent to Shelburne. It was reinforced by more troops from Bermuda brought by Captain Thomas Hardy, one of Nelson's great officers.

There was no problem capturing Eastport. It was defended by only 80 bored soldiers, who were glad to pull down the Stars and Stripes in surrender. Sir John Sherbrooke, the soldier-governor of Nova Scotia, attacked the fort at Castine on August 31, 1814. He had a naval squadron and 1,800 troops. There was little opposition and the British were able to get up the river to Bangor easily. Another force took Machias.

With eastern Maine in British hands, a number of citizens took the oath of allegiance to Britain, so that they could resume trade with British ports all over the world. Castine became the chief customs house, and by the end of the year more than £13,000 had been collected.

When Maine was returned to the States at the end of the war, the money was taken to Halifax and placed in a special account called the "Castine fund." It was used later to found Dalhousie University.

The States made no effort to drive the British troops out of Maine and they lived

Sir John Sherbrooke (1764-1830)

with the Americans in harmony. By this time, both sides were eager to end a war that should never have begun. Negotiations were then taking place at Ghent in Belgium.

Other Events on August 31:

1670   Hudson's Bay Company officers arrived at Fort Nelson to establish posts.

1674   The Council ordered beggars to leave Quebec as the result of a drive by five women.

1694   The British ship *William and Mary* defeated seven French warships at Ferryland, Newfoundland.

1696   The British recaptured Fort Nelson, Hudson Bay.

1825   Tea brought directly from East Indian ports was sold for the first time in Montreal. This helped to check smuggling from the United States.

1859   British Columbia put the Gold Fields Act into force.

(above) The annual Grey Cup game in late fall attracts the attention of thousands of enthusiastic football fans across Canada. The classic matches the best team of the Eastern and Western Conferences in a gruelling, all-or-nothing contest.

(right) During the last few years, Canada has climbed into prominence in international skiing competition, both as a host of major events and as a new threat to European skiing supremacy. Spirited by Nancy Greene, winner of the 1967 World Cup for women, the Canadian team promises to be strong competition in the 1968 Winter Olympics.

(below) The NHL Stanley Cup play-offs climax an exciting year of hockey in Canada and the United States. The increased popularity of hockey in the United States resulted in the expansion of the NHL from six to sixteen teams.

Charlottetown Conference, 1864

Canadians Present at Charlottetown Conference

Negotiations for the Confederation of the British North American colonies really got under way in 1864. Canada's cradle was the Charlottetown Conference that began on September 1, and rocked to the sound of circus music!

Delegates from New Brunswick and Nova Scotia arrived at Charlottetown on August 31. Their original purpose had been to meet with representatives of Prince Edward Island to discuss the possibility of forming a maritime union. Newfoundland was not represented. The Canadians asked for permission to attend the conference so that they could present a plan to join the Maritimes in a federal union, or Confederation.

When Premïers Tilley of New Brunswick and Tupper of Nova Scotia arrived at Charlottetown with their delegations, there was little room for them in the inns. The islanders had flocked to Charlottetown to watch their first circus in twenty years. Even the cabinet ministers were there, and the only official available to greet them was William Pope, Colonial Secretary. He managed to find accommodation for them at the Mansion House Hotel, one of twenty inns in Charlottetown. Then *they* went to the circus!

The Canadians, led by Macdonald, Cartier, Brown, Galt and McGee, sailed from Quebec on August 29. They had a fine trip down the St. Lawrence, although they were awed by Brown's habit of getting up early in the morning for a cold salt-water bath, and then having a brisk walk around the decks of the *Queen Victoria*. They reached Charlottetown early in the morning of September 1, and once again only faithful William Pope was on hand. He went out to the *Queen Victoria* in a small boat rowed by a fisherman. Pope was sitting on an oyster barrel and when they drew alongside the chief steward asked them about the price of oysters!

The conference was held in the Council Chamber of Province House, and the scene has been preserved, with the actual tables and chairs used by the delegates still in place. It began on the afternoon of September 1, and the visiting Canadians were invited to speak first. Macdonald and Cartier outlined their plans during the first two days, and the meetings continued until September 7. Then the conference adjourned to meet at Halifax three days later.

Other Events on September 1:

1917 The Canadian Press Company was formed. It is a co-operative news gathering agency owned by the newspapers.

Alberta and Saskatchewan Join Confederation

Alberta and Saskatchewan were made provinces of Canada on September 1, 1905. As the official ceremonies took place in Edmonton on September 1 and in Regina on September 3, it should be justifiable to tell the story on September 2.

When the area was bought from the Hudson's Bay Company in 1869, Alberta and Saskatchewan were included in the Northwest Territories, and became "districts" within them later. When they became provinces in 1905 they were greatly enlarged. Alberta now covers more than 255,000 square miles, is 800 miles long and averages 300 miles in width. Saskatchewan covers about 252,000 square miles, is 700 miles long and averages 335 miles in width.

Prime Minister Sir Wilfrid Laurier made his first trip west to open the two new provinces, and attended the ceremonies at Edmonton and Regina with Governor-General Earl Grey. Photographs of the ceremonies at Edmonton show the Governor-General and the Prime Minister on the speakers' stand, against a background of scarlet-coated Mounties on horseback, and Indians from the Hebbema Reserve. Thousands of people from far and wide went to Edmonton and Regina for the great occasions.

When Alberta and Saskatchewan were made provinces they did not have the power they have today. The Federal Government retained all public lands, mines, minerals, and resources. The provinces did not even have complete control of education. R. B. Bennett, who was Leader of the Opposition in Alberta, and who became Prime Minister of Canada in 1930, strongly attacked the arrangement whereby the provinces did not have control of their own resources.

One of the interesting things about the development of Alberta and Saskatchewan is that they, more than other provinces in Canada, broke away from the old political parties, the Liberals and the Conservatives. Alberta elected a United Farmers government in 1921. A Social Credit government elected in 1935 remained in power until 1971 (see August 30). Saskatchewan elected a Co-operative Commonwealth Federation (Socialist) governent in 1944, and it won successive elections in 1952 and 1956. Both provinces contribtued heavily to the Progressive Party which played a big part in the Federal Parliament until 1930, when the Conservatives under R. B. Bennett swept the country.

Other Events on September 2:

1535   Jacques Cartier explored the Saguenay River on his second voyage to Canada.

1670   Port Royal, Acadia, was returned to France following the Treaty of Breda.

1683   La Salle left Canada in disguise to seek the protection of the king.

1726   The Marquis of Beauharnois was made Governor of Canada.

1750   St. Paul's Church, Halifax, was opened. It is the oldest Protestant church in Canada.

1858   James Douglas was appointed Governor of British Columbia.

1870   A. G. Archibald arrived at Winnipeg to be Lieutenant-Governor of Manitoba.

1945   The formal terms of surrender were signed by the Japanese civil and military envoys on board the *U.S.S. Missouri* in Tokyo Bay.

1962   The Sons of Freedom Doukhobors began a 400-mile march from Shoreacres to Agassiz, B.C.

1964   The Royal Commission into the Protestant School Board of Greater Montreal land transactions made its report.

Treaty Ends War

They passed down the silent rivers which
flow to the mighty lake;
They left what they'd made for England
(but those who have made can make),
And founded a new dominion for God
and their country's sake.

—CLIVE PHILLIPPS-WOLLEY, 1917

There are two Treaties of Paris in Canadian history—the treaty of 1763 by which France ceded Canada to Britain and the treaty of 1783 which ended the American Revolutionary War. The second treaty is also known as the Peace of Versailles, but as a treaty of that name ended World War I, it certainly does not clear up the confusion!

The treaty of 1783 was signed on September 3. When the time came for the final negotiations, Britain was in a strong position (see May 8) and determined to retain Canada. By the treaty, Britain held the Maritimes, the part of old Canada south of the St. Lawrence, the region north of the St. Lawrence above Montreal, and the Great Lakes. It was surprising that Benjamin Franklin, chief negotiator for the States, did not claim the northwest territory of the Hudson's Bay Company. He may have felt that it was worthless, but his oversight paved the way for Canada's expansion to the Pacific.

One of the tragedies of the treaty, from Canada's point of view, was Britain's failure to obtain better terms for the United Empire Loyalists. Many Americans felt bitterly about the Loyalists. Governor Clinton of New York said that he would rather roast in hell than show mercy to Loyalists after they had destroyed some property while under British protection in New York City. The only concession Britain gained for the Loyalists was a promise by Benjamin Franklin that he would ask the various States to be liberal to them. It was a worthless promise.

Franklin was a wily trader. When he was trying to persuade Britain to cede Canada to the States, he said he still loved "dear old England." Now that they were going separate ways, they should trade together in peace and harmony. In order not to risk a future conflict it would be better if the Maritimes and Canada were part of American territory! He nearly got away with it!

Other Events on September 3:

1814   The American vessel *Scorpion* was captured at Nottawasaga.

1825   The Halifax Banking Company opened for business.

1841   The Canadian Parliament passed resolutions for responsible government.

1864   Canadian delegate Galt discussed financial plans at the Charlottetown Conference on Confederation.

1894   Labor Day was celebrated for the first time in Canada.

1957   Prime Minister Diefenbaker welcomed 1,500 scientists at Toronto for the meeting of the International Union of Geodesy and Geophysics.

1962   The Trans-Canada Highway was officially opened.

Loyalists landing at Saint John, N.B.

Benedict Arnold (1741-1801)

Arnold "Sells Out"

Benedict Arnold has been regarded for years as the biggest traitor in American history, yet he was one of the most brilliant American soldiers of all time. His achievement in leading a force across the wilds of Maine to attack Quebec is considered by some to be even greater than Wolfe's endeavor.

Arnold's resentment gradually mounted when he was passed over in promotions, and constantly harried by charges of misconduct. In 1780, he decided to work for the British and sent them information about West Point, the gateway to the Hudson River. The British officer carrying the information was caught and Arnold barely managed to escape into British lines before his wrongdoing was discovered.

He was made a brigadier-general in the British army and was paid more than £6,000 compensation for the loss of his property. He helped the British in the attacks on Richmond

and New London, but could not find satisfactory employment when he went to London.

In 1787 he went to live in Saint John, New Brunswick, but even the Loyalists treated him with contempt. He began a trading business with the West Indies, and contempt turned to anger when his warehouse burned to the ground. His partner, Munsen Hoyt, said that Arnold had set it on fire to collect insurance. There was a court case in which Arnold charged Hoyt with slander, and "blackening my character." Hoyt replied: "It is not in my power to blacken your character because it is as black as can be." Arnold was awarded 20 shillings damages. A crowd gathered on King Street and burned him in effigy. The mayor had to read the riot act to disperse the crowd.

On September 4, 1791, Arnold advertised in the *Royal Gazette* that he was selling "excellent feather beds, mahogany fourposter bedsteads, an elegant set of Wedgwood gilt ware, cabriole chairs covered with blue damask, and a lady's elegant saddle and bridle." He left Saint John after the sale and went back to London where he fitted privateers for the war against France. He died in 1801, after ten melancholy years.

Other Events on September 4:

1535 Cartier landed at the Ile au Coudres and celebrated the first mass in Canada.

1812 Lord Selkirk took possession of the Red River area.

1860 The Duke of Newcastle would not allow the Prince of Wales to visit Kingston, Ontario, because of an Orange celebration.

1876 Edward Hanlon of Toronto won the world rowing championship at Philadelphia (see November 15).

1916 Canadian forces took over a sector of the Somme.

1929 Lignite was discovered at Abitibi River, Ontario.

France Claims Victory

France won her greatest naval victory against Britain on September 5, 1697, in an action fought off Hayes River, Hudson Bay.

At dawn on September 5, Pierre Le Moyne d'Iberville, who had been ordered by Louis XIV to clear the English out of Hudson Bay, saw three British ships tacking towards his anchorage in Hayes River. He had no wish to be left without room to manoeuver so he put out to sea at once, leaving some of his men on shore. Many of his crew were ill below decks, suffering from scurvy. Only 150 were left to man the *Pelican's* guns and sails. The three British ships, *Hampshire, Deering* and *Hudson's Bay,* had 124 guns and 600 men between them. Iberville had only 44 guns and 150 men. The odds seemed hopeless, but Iberville decided to fight.

The three British ships sailed towards him in battle formation, with the mighty *Hampshire* in the lead. Iberville pretended that he was trying to board the *Hampshire,* which veered off. Then he blasted the *Deering* and shot off her mainsails. Another fast manoeuver enabled him to hit the *Hudson's Bay.*

The *Hampshire,* commanded by Captain Fletcher, poured heavy fire into the *Pelican.* There were many casualties on board. The battle continued for three hours, with Iberville preventing Fletcher from getting within range to take advantage of superior gun and manpower. Fletcher became impatient, and sailed close enough to shout to Iberville to surrender. In the courtly manner of the day, Fletcher called for wine and held up a glass in a toast to his valiant enemy. Iberville did the same on the bridge of the *Pelican.* As the *Hampshire* came round for the kill, it heeled over in a sudden gust of wind. Iberville then poured in a broadside that gashed the *Hampshire's* side, and it sank quickly, with Captain Fletcher going down with his ship. The *Hudson's Bay* and *Deering,* both damaged, got away. The *Pelican,* also badly damaged, went aground on a shoal. Nevertheless, it was a great naval victory for Iberville.

Pelican *and* Hampshire *firing broadsides*

Other Events on September 5:

1534   Cartier returned to France after his first voyage.

1755   Acadians were told officially that they were being deported.

1854   Parliament met at Quebec.

1883   Methodist churches in Canada were united.

1906   The Grain Growers' Company was opened in Saskatchewan.

1945   Igor Gouzenko left the Russian Embassy in Ottawa and passed on information that uncovered a Russian spy network in Canada and the United States.

1962   Canada contributed $5 million to the "food bank," sponsored by Canada and the United States.

Robert Campbell (1808-1894)

Campbell Seeks Bride

One of the little-known but amazing characters of Canadian history was Robert Campbell, a Hudson's Bay Company factor. Among many exploits, he traveled 9,700 miles to get married, although he didn't know who the girl would be. Three thousand miles of the journey were on snowshoes!

Robert Campbell came from Perthshire, Scotland, and arrived at Red River in September, 1830. One of his first jobs was to try to get some sheep from Kentucky. His party traveled more than 1,500 miles before they were able to buy 1,370 sheep and lambs. Then they had to drive them overland to the Red River. It took four months to reach Red River and only 251 sheep survived the journey.

By 1850, Robert Campbell had become Chief Factor of the Hudson's Bay Company, and had been in the Yukon for twenty-seven years. There is a bit of confusion about who decided that he should get married. One version is that the head office in London made the suggestion and offered to send him a bride. The other is that Campbell said he wanted to come out to get married, and rejected the mail-order offer.

He set out from White River in the Yukon on September 6, 1852, ascended the Pelly River, crossed the mountains to the Liard, and arrived at Fort Simpson on October 21. A typical entry from his diary says: "Breakfasted on Little River. Left our Indians far in the rear and came up to party that had preceded us. Camped on a small river with a few willows to make a fire. They had killed a deer of which we had the head for supper." Actually Campbell ate anything he could get, even squirrels and skunks.

From Fort Simpson he traveled on snowshoes over frozen Great Slave Lake, Lake Athabaska, and Ile à la Crosse to Carlton House. Then he went on to Fort Pelly, Fort Garry, Pembina, Crow Wing, Minnesota, and Chicago. When he arrived in Scotland he had traveled continuously for 9,700 miles. After all this labor for love, the girl he chose as his bride was too young, and they had to wait for six years until she journeyed 6,000 miles to meet him in Canada!

Other Events on September 6:

1727 Acadians were summoned before the Council of Nova Scotia to swear allegiance. They did at this time, but their refusal after 1748 led to their deportation.

1806 The Mississauga Indians ceded 85,000 acres which are now Halton and Peel counties, Ontario.

1952 Canada's first television station opened at Montreal.

1957 The Honorable Louis St. Laurent resigned as Leader of the Liberal party. He was succeeded by Lester B. Pearson.

Hunt Flies Homemade Airship over Edmonton

This is the anniversary of perhaps the biggest hoax in Canadian aviation, and it was uncovered only recently. J. A. D. McCurdy had flown the first airplane in Canada on February 23, 1909, at Baddeck, Nova Scotia. Later in 1909 it was announced that Reginald Hunt of Edmonton had accomplished an even more remarkable feat. Working alone, and without financial backing, he had built his own airplane and flown it over Edmonton for half an hour on September 7. Newspapers published stories and pictures of Hunt's exploit.

Actually, Hunt had made a balloon shaped like an airship, and not an airplane. However, airplanes were so little known in 1909 that reporters called the airship an airplane, and the mistake was not discovered until years later when the National Research Council investigated. There was also a picture of Hunt standing beside an airplane, but it turned out to be a French Farman, and not the balloon Hunt had flown.

McCurdy's *Silver Dart* was built in the Curtiss bicycle workshop in Hammonsport, New York. The honor of building the first airplane in Canada should go to William Wallace Gibson who was brought up on a farm near Regina. He began building model airplanes in 1903 after reading that the Wright brothers had flown in the United States. He devised a motor from the spring of a window-blind roller!

Gibson moved to Victoria, British Columbia, when he was twenty-seven and found a gold mine which he sold for $10,000. He used this money to build a full-sized airplane, making every part by hand and using his own plans, although he had never had a lesson in drafting or engineering. He even designed an unorthodox 50 horsepower engine and had it built by a Victoria machine shop. It weighed 210 pounds. There were two propellers, one behind the other. The pilot's seat was an ordinary horse saddle! Gibson's plane took to the air on September 8, 1910, flew 200 feet and crashed into an oak tree! It was no mean feat. The Wright brothers had flown only 210 feet in their first try, and A. V. Roe in England flew less than one hundred.

Other Events on September 7:

1535 Cartier reached the Island of Orleans on his second voyage; he named it Bacchus.

1619 Jens Munck, a Dane, discovered the Churchill River, Hudson Bay.

1763 King George III issued a proclamation inviting his subjects to settle in Canada.

1816 The first Canadian steamer on Lake Ontario, *Frontenac*, was launched.

1864 The Charlottetown Conference adjourned and delegates arranged to meet again in Halifax.

1910 The Hague Tribunal defined American fishing rights on the North Atlantic coast.

1927 Edward, Prince of Wales, and Prince George returned to Britain after their tour of Canada.

1958 Duplessis, Premier of Quebec for eighteen years, died.

Twelve thousand delegates from 51 nations attended the World Power Conference at Montreal.

1961 The armed forces were increased by 15,000; plans were announced to train 100,000 civil defence workers.

1965 Prime Minister Pearson dissolved Parliament and called an election for November 8.

Lord Jeffery Amherst (1717-1797)

Montreal Surrenders

After the fall of Quebec, General Amherst spent the winter at Oswego, New York, gathering an army of 10,000 soldiers and 1,350 Indians. He also had another force at Crown Point, Lake Champlain, ready to march on Montreal from the south. Brigadier Murray's regulars at Quebec were to come up the river as soon as Lévis had been driven off (see April 28).

When the arrival of the British fleet forced General Lévis to lift the siege at Quebec, he led his troops to Montreal as quickly as he could, leaving part of the force at Jacques-Cartier to try to block Murray coming up. He stationed another contingent at Ile-aux-Noix to check the British coming from Crown Point and a third at Fort Lévis below Fort Frontenac (Kingston) to delay Amherst coming down the river.

Murray easily side-stepped the blockade at Jacques-Cartier, and Bougainville could not stop the British from Crown Point. Amherst had left Oswego with his huge force on August 9, and made good progress until he met the French under Captain Pouchot at Fort Lévis. Pouchot fought cleverly, delaying Amherst until August 29. Then river pilots were picked up to maneuver Amherst's boats through the rapids. On September 7, a British army of 20,000 men surrounded Montreal.

The French position was hopeless. Governor Vaudreuil was willing to capitulate and sent Amherst a list of conditions under which he would surrender. One of them was that the French were to be allowed to march out of the city with honors of war, meaning their flags and guns.

Amherst would not agree but insisted that all the French troops in Canada must lay down their arms and not serve again during the war. General Lévis was so angry that he burned the French banners that were in his keeping and threatened to hold out on St. Helen's Island.

On September 8, 1760, the British army marched into the city and the French surrendered at the Place d'Armes. The *fleur-de-lis* was lowered from the flagstaff and the red cross of Britain was raised in its place. That night, for the first time, British drums beat the sunset tattoo in the streets of Montreal.

Other Events on September 8:

1842　Parliament met at Kingston.

1869　Governor Musgrave toured British Columbia to study the possibility of Confederation.

1930　Parliament opened with R. B. Bennett as the new prime minister.

1961　The University of Montreal was host to delegates from French-speaking universities from many parts of the world.

Riots In Vancouver

One of the most interesting stories about William Lyon Mackenzie King happened in 1907 when he was Deputy Minister of Labor.

On September 9, Ottawa heard that there had been a race riot in Vancouver. People in British Columbia were greatly disturbed because thousands of Asiatics were coming to live there. In a single year, 8,000 Japanese, 2,000 Sikhs and 1,500 Chinese arrived. The Japanese were feared because they were very proud of their homeland which had become strong enough to defeat Russia in a war. It suspected that the Japanese settling in Canada were the advance guard of a full-scale invasion.

Vancouver citizens formed the Asiatic Exclusion League, and on Saturday, September 8, attacked the Chinese and Japanese sections of the city. The Chinese showed only passive resistance, but the Japanese put up a fight and drove out the attackers with sticks, bottles and knives. The fighting continued on Sunday, September 9.

Prime Minister Laurier decided to send Deputy Minister of Labor Mackenzie King to Vancouver to assess Chinese and Japanese claims for losses through the rioting and, more important, to study the reasons for the recent influx of Japanese. The Government moved cautiously because it was trying to work out a trade agreement with Japan.

When Mackenzie King was in Vancouver, he raided the office of the Japanese immigration agent. Later he told Governor-General Lord Grey that he had gone to Vancouver prejudiced in favor of the Japanese, but had changed his mind after studying documents he took from the immigration agent's office. It was clear that the Government of Japan knew immigration quotas were being exceeded, and that there was a definite danger of an invasion.

Mackenzie King's official report on the situation has never been published, but Rodolphe Lemieux, Minister of Labor, went to Japan and managed to work out a satisfactory im-

Rodolphe Lemieux (1866-1937)

migration agreement. The anti-Asiatic feeling in British Columbia simmered down over the years. Today Vancouver is delighted with its Chinese citizens and its "Chinatown," which is second only in size to San Francisco's. The Japanese were evacuated during World War II, but those who remained have become expert fishermen and market gardeners.

Other Events on September 9:

1912 Vilhjamur Stefansson returned after four years in the Arctic (see February 20).

1959 It was announced that Canada's first nuclear power station, costing $60 million, would be built near Kincardine, Lake Huron.

1963 A federal-provincial conference was opened in Ottawa.

1965 The Fowler Committee published its recommendations for improvements in broadcasting.

British Lose to Captain Perry on Lake Erie

September 10, 1813, was a black day for British forces in Canada. The key to the situation was the naval strength on Lake Erie; the British needed superiority there in order to supply Colonel Procter's force (see October 5). The job was entrusted to Captain Robert Barclay. His opposite number for the Americans was Captain Perry.

Five of the American ships were at Black Rock, near the entrance to the Niagara River, but they could not get out because they would have been shelled by British guns at Fort Erie. Perry's ships at Presqu'Isle (now Erie, Pennysylvania) were also in a bad position. There was a sandbar at the entrance to the harbor and the heavy warships could not sail over it unless they were buoyed up by barges on either side. They would be easy targets for British warships outside the harbor.

Then came the turning point. The British gunners had to leave Fort Erie to help repel an American invasion of the Niagara Peninsula. This enabled Perry's ships to leave Black Rock. Captain Barclay, for some mysterious reason, relaxed his guard at the entrance to Presqu'Isle and Perry took advantage of the lapse to get his warships over the sandbar. The American warships were united and free to operate on Lake Erie.

Colonel Procter was in a desperate situation. Barclay, knowing he had to provide supply ships for him, had no other alternative but to attack Perry's fleet. He had only six ships to the Americans' nine. He did not even have proper guns, but had to take what he could from Fort Malden and install them on his ships, although they were not suitable.

Barclay knew he had little chance of success, but he had to try. The rival fleets met on the morning of September 10 and after three hours of skilful, desperate fighting, the Americans won a complete victory. Two days later, Perry was able to send his famous message scribbled on the back of an old letter: "We have met the enemy and they are ours." The defeat made it impossible for Procter to hold the Detroit sector.

Other Events on September 10:

1621 King James I granted William Alexander all the territory between the St. Lawrence and the sea which lay east of the St. Croix River.
Acadia became Nova Scotia.

1755 The expulsion of the Acadians from Nova Scotia began.

1895 The Sault Ste. Marie Canal was opened.

1939 Canada declared war on Germany.

1951 Canada and Pakistan signed a technical assistance pact, with Canada providing $10 million aid in the first year. The foreign ministers of Great Britain, France, and the United States met in Washington, D.C., for a conference on measures to contain Soviet aggression.

1959 The Honourable Paul Sauvé was chosen to succeed the late Maurice Duplessis as Premier of the Province of Quebec.

1960 Halifax International Airport was opened.

1962 The bank rate was reduced from 6 per cent to 5½ per cent and exchange reserves were increased as a result of the emergency austerity program.

1964 The House of Commons consented to appoint a special committee to consider and report upon the flag question.

Quebec Hosts Conference of Allied Leaders

During World War II the Allied leaders met as often as possible to plan for the future. Prime Minister Churchill of Britain and President Roosevelt of the United States met three times in Canada. The first conference was at Argentia, Newfoundland, where the two drew up the Atlantic Charter (see August 11). They met twice at Quebec; the first conference being in August, 1943, and the second, on September 11, 1944.

When the second Quebec Conference took place in 1944, Germany was on the way to defeat. Prime Minister Churchill crossed the Atlantic in the *Queen Mary,* accompanied by Mrs. Churchill and his chiefs of staff. They landed at Halifax and traveled by train to Quebec, where President and Mrs. Roosevelt were already waiting, with their famous little dog "Falla." Governor-General the Earl of Athlone, his wife Princess Alice, and Prime Minister Mackenzie King were there to extend Canada's greetings, but Canada's part in the conference was only that of any other allied nation.

This conference, the eighth attended by Churchill, was completely different from the others, which had been held in the critical days of the war. Now, as Churchill said, everything the Allies touched was turning to gold.

Churchill missed Harry Hopkins, one of Roosevelt's chief aides, who had done a great deal to overcome difficulties between the British and Americans. He was ill in London and cabled that he did not feel able to tackle another Battle of the Plains of Abraham "where better men than I have been killed."

Hopkin's jest contained a great deal of irony. Although the Allies were winning in Europe, the problem now was to defeat Japan. The British had needed and welcomed American help to defeat Germany, and now they wanted to help the Americans defeat Japan. The American military leaders tried to keep the British out of the Pacific sector as much as possible. Churchill offered to send a British fleet to the Pacific to serve under American command, but American Admiral King turned down the offer! He was overruled by Roosevelt.

Other Events on September 11:

1541   Cartier reached Lachine rapids above Montreal on his third voyage to Canada.

1738   Pierre La Vérendrye left Lake of the Woods to explore the West, and founded Portage La Prairie.

1754   Anthony Henday was the first white man to enter what is now Alberta.

1847   A hurricane off Newfoundland caused the loss of 300 lives.

1861   The Yonge Street railway was opened at Toronto.

1898   The city of New Westminster, British Columbia, was destroyed by fire.

1916   The centre span of Quebec Bridge fell (see August 28).

1958   Camillien Houde, mayor of Montreal, died. Though he openly espoused Italy's cause in World War II, he was re-elected mayor six times.

Churchill at second Quebec Conference, 1944

Maritimers Convene

This question has now assumed a position that demands and commands the attention of all the colonies of British America. There may be obstructions, local prejudices may arise, disputes may occur, local jealousies may intervene, but it matters not — the wheel is now revolving and we are only the fly on the wheel; we cannot delay it — the union of the colonies of British America under the Sovereign is a fixed fact.

—Sir John A. Macdonald, 1864

We don't know each other. We have no trade with each other. We have no facilities, or resources, or incentives, to mingle with each other. We are shut off from each other by a wilderness, geographically, commercially, politically and socially. We always cross the United States to shake hands. Our interests are not identical, but the very opposite — they are antagonistic and clashing.

—Halifax Acadian Recorder, 1866

The cradle of Confederation, which "rocked" to circus music at its opening, September 1, 1864, closed with graceful waltz music on September 7. There was a ball in the Legislative Assembly Hall, which was decorated with flags, flowers, evergreen boughs, mirrors and special lighting effects designed by the superintendent of the Charlottetown Gas Works. The spirit of the conference was reflected in the gaiety of the party that continued until five in the morning. John A. Macdonald predicted that Confederation would make Canada, "at least the fourth nation on the face of the globe."

An agreement was made to meet at Halifax, where the Maritime delegates wanted to have a meeting of their own. This took place on Monday, September 12, and the Canadians were told later that the representatives of the Maritimes would meet them at Quebec on October 10. This was the turning point in the negotiations. The Maritimers had rejected the original plan of forming a union of their own and were prepared to advocate Confederation with Canada.

The official Canadian party then retraced some of the steps taken by D'Arcy McGee's goodwill mission in August. They went to Saint John and Fredericton for three days. One of the highlights of the Saint John visit was a dinner at Stubb's Hotel at which George Etienne Cartier stood up alone and sang *God Save the Queen* in both French and English.

Confederation had been well launched, although details still remained to be worked out at Quebec. It was the culmination of a number of coincidences. The end of the American Civil War posed a threat to British North America: unite or be absorbed by the U.S.A. The Maritimes' need for a railway to Canada was almost as important from their point of view. Construction began in 1868 and was completed in 1876. It is now the Canadian National route between Montreal and Halifax.

There was opposition to Confederation, and some of the merchants in Halifax and Saint John draped their stores with crepe on July 1, 1867. However, the opposition was disorganized and never became strong enough to prevent the movement that gathered momentum from the time of the Charlottetown conference.

Other Events on September 12:

1672 Count Frontenac was made Governor of Canada for the first time.

1696 Iberville arrived at Placentia for a campaign to capture Newfoundland.

1759 Admiral Saunders bombarded Beauport as a cover for Wolfe's assault on Quebec.

1760 General Amherst sent 200 men from Montreal to capture Detroit.

1858 Gold was found at Tangier River, Nova Scotia.

1943 Ex-Premier Mussolini, who had been held a prisoner near Rome, was rescued by German troops. Three days later, he proclaimed the establishment of a Republican Fascist Party.

Wolfe Reaches Plains

Death of Wolfe

The world could not expect more from him than he thought himself capable of performing. He looked on danger as the favourable moment that would call forth his talents.

—HORACE WALPOLE, 1763

Valour gave them a common death, history a common fame, posterity a common monument.

JAMES C. FISHER, 1828

Do you remember the old adage about "for want of a nail, a shoe was lost. For want of a shoe a horse was lost. For want of a horse a battle was lost"? It has a sequel. For want of a proper guard at the top of the cliff at Quebec on September 13, 1759, France lost Canada.

General Montcalm was not to blame. He had stationed the Guienne Regiment on top of the cliff, but it had been moved for some other duty. When Montcalm ordered it back, Governor Vaudreuil cancelled the order and said he would see about it the following day. It was a day too late. Vaudreuil's action punctured a clever defense that "old fox" Montcalm had sustained since June 27, when Wolfe began his campaign.

Wolfe deserved the lucky break that enabled him to get his troops up the cliff to the Plains of Abraham. Women had been seen washing clothes along the river bank. Later the clothes were seen drying on top of the cliff. Obviously there must be a path, and Wolfe decided to use it.

The Royal Navy provided enough row boats to carry 1,800 troops from the warship *Sunderland* which had taken up a position in the river at Sillery, above Quebec. When a signal light flashed at 1.30 a.m., they drifted quietly down the shore until they reached the path. Wolfe was the first to land and then twenty-four trained men scaled the cliff by clinging to roots and branches. The small guard at the top was taken by surprise and captured. Then the path was cleared and the main force climbed up quickly. By dawn there were 5,000 British troops in battle formation on the Plains of Abraham. In the meantime, Admiral Saunders had been threatening a landing at Beauport below Quebec, drawing attention away from Wolfe's operation.

The battle was over by noon. General Wolfe was one of the 655 British soldiers who were killed. General Montcalm was one of the French casualties estimated as high as 1,200 by the British and as low as 150 by the French. Governor Vaudreuil escaped to Montreal, and Quebec was surrendered on September 18.

Other Events on September 13:

1710   Cadillac was appointed Governor of Louisiana.

1775   Benedict Arnold led a force from Boston to attack Quebec.

1886   The Canadian Pacific Telegraph system was opened.

1893   The Montreal Presbytery found Professor Campbell guilty of heresy.

1959   The second centennial anniversary of the Battle of the Plains of Abraham was commemorated.

1963   George Drew resigned as High Commissioner to Britain.

Sir George Stephen (1829-1921)

C.P.R. Agreement Signed

The building of the C.P.R. transcontinental is one of the most fascinating stories in Canadian history, and many books have been written about it. The present C.P.R. is the *third* company by that name. The agreement creating it was signed in London, England, on September 14, 1880.

The first C.P.R. was organized by Sir Hugh Allan of Montreal, but was disbanded when it was discovered that he had contributed a large sum of money to Sir John A. Macdonald and other members of the Government for an election campaign. The Macdonald government had to resign and was out of office for five years. Strangely enough, the man who struck the final blow forcing the Macdonald government to resign was Sir John's old friend Donald A. Smith, who had been his emissary

in dealing with Louis Riel during the Red River uprising (see January 19).

When the present C.P.R. company was formed in 1881, Donald Smith could not be included among the board of directors because he had defeated the Macdonald government. He and George Stephen of the Bank of Montreal had made a fortune from the St. Paul and Pacific Railway in the United States, although it had gone bankrupt. George Stephen was president of the new C.P.R. and one of the directors was John Rose, a lifelong friend of Macdonald's. When they were young they had put on shows in the United States in which Rose acted as a dancing bear while Macdonald provided musical accompaniment. There was more profit in railway building.

The House of Commons passed the C.P.R. bill on February 1, 1881. It gave the company $25 million, and 25 million acres of land for development. The C.P.R. was also given 710 miles of railway that had been built by the Government at a cost of nearly $38 million.

The transcontinental was completed on November 7, 1885, at Craigellachie, British Columbia. Once again Donald A. Smith got in the final blow. By this time he had become one of the directors, and as such, he was given the honor of driving home the last spike (see November 7).

Other Events on September 14:

1535   Cartier discovered Stadacona (Quebec) on his second voyage up the St. Lawrence.

1758   The British were defeated at Grant's Hill.

1763   The British were defeated at Devil's Hole by the Seneca Indians.

1853   Lady Head turned the first sod of the European and North American Railway designed to serve Nova Scotia, New Brunswick, and Maine.

1926   The Liberal government, led by Mackenzie King, defeated the Conservatives under Arthur Meighen.

Niagara Falls in 1860

Edward Prince of Wales Visits Niagara Falls

This is not the most important thing that has happened in Canada on September 15 over the years, but it is perhaps one of the most colorful. Edward Prince of Wales came to Canada in 1860 representing Queen Victoria (see August 21). He opened Victoria Bridge in Montreal, laid the cornerstone of the original Parliament Buildings in Ottawa, and presided at a number of important functions. When Queen Victoria died, he became King Edward VII.

Edward was only a young man when he came to Canada in 1860, and efforts were made to see that he had a good time, despite his dour guardian, the Duke of Newcastle. One of the entertainments was a visit to Niagara Falls on September 15, where he saw an astonishing performance by the great French tightrope walker Blondin, whose real name was Jean François Gravelet.

A tight-rope was stretched across the river, over the roaring cauldron of the falls, and Blondin crossed to the other side carrying a man on his back! When he returned, he amazed everyone by getting on stilts and walking across on them! The Prince was so delighted that he gave Blondin a purse of $400. They became great friends and Blondin eventually went to live in London, where he died in 1897 at the age of eighty.

Blondin walked the tightrope over Niagara Falls a number of times. It was 1,100 feet long, and 160 feet above the water. The first time, in 1859, he went across blindfolded. Then he crossed in a sack. On another occasion he pushed a wheelbarrow. Perhaps his greatest achievement was that of carrying a small stove to the half way mark, and balancing there while he cooked and ate an omelette.

Blondin kept stunting in other parts of the world until he was seventy-nine, and he never had a serious accident. His final performance was in Belfast, Ireland.

Other Events on September 15:

1688 Governor Denonville acceded to demands by the Iroquois and abandoned and destroyed Fort Niagara.

1916 Canadian troops fought in the Battle of the Somme where tanks were used for the first time.

1959 Major-General Georges P. Vanier was appointed governor-general, succeeding Vincent Massey.

Columbia Power Agreement Signed

A secret meeting between President Kennedy of the U.S.A. and Premier W. A. C. Bennett of British Columbia in Seattle in November 1961 paved the way for the Columbia River Treaty, which initiated large-scale development of water and electric power in Canada. Some of this power will be made available to the U.S.A., since the need for more natural resources becomes greater in the U.S.A. every year. The abundance of many resources in Canada provides Ottawa with another important bargaining lever (see May 16).

The development of the Columbia River was discussed by leading Canadians and Americans for many years and five U.S. presidents participated in the talks. Agreement was near in 1961, but British Columbia would not accept the terms proposed by the Conservative government in Ottawa, led by John Diefenbaker. B.C. Premier Bennett felt that he had a better plan and held out until 1963, when Liberals led by L. B. Pearson took over the federal government and accepted his terms. Premier Bennett said at the time that:

> "Not only will this revenue build the High Arrow Dam, Duncan Lake Dam, and the dam at Mica Creek, but it will also provide two million horse-power of electricity to British Columbia without cost to British Columbians."

The Columbia River Treaty was signed by President Johnson of the U.S.A., Prime Minister Pearson of Canada and Premier Bennett of British Columbia at the Peace Arch on the British Columbia-Washington boundary on September 16, 1964. President Johnson handed Premier Bennett a cheque for $273,291,661.25 and quipped to the crowd, "The Canadians went for that last twenty-five cents." It was the largest cheque ever received by a premier of a Canadian province and Bennett insisted that it be delivered before 2 p.m. so it could be deposited in a bank in time to earn interest that very day.

A few weeks later British Columbia lent Quebec $100,000,000. Premier Bennett had turned the tables on his political opponents because his "funny money" Social Credit government had come to the financial rescue of the orthodox Liberal government of Canada's oldest province.

The Columbia River is the fourth largest river in North America. It is eventually expected to provide forty million kilowatts of installed capacity. The Duncan Dam was completed in 1967 and the Arrow Dam, renamed the Hugh Keenleyside Dam, began operation in 1968.

Other Events on September 16:

1842   Baldwin and Lafontaine formed a government (see June 14).

1858   Andrew Bonar Law was born at Rexton, New Brunswick. He became Prime Minister of Britain, the first person from the Commonwealth to do so.

1893   Calgary, Alberta, was incorporated as a city.

1901   The Duke and Duchess of Cornwall and York (later King George V and Queen Mary) began a visit to Canada.

1957   A four-month strike ended at the Aluminum Company of Canada plant at Arvida, Quebec.

1960   A Royal Commission was appointed to investigate all aspects of federal government administration.

1962   The International Nickel Company of Canada gave $2.5 million to Laurentian University, Sudbury, Ontario.

1963   Canada sold wheat worth $500 million to Russia. It was the largest sale of wheat in history.

1964   Prime Minister Pearson and President Johnson, in a ceremony at Blaine, Washington, formally signed the Columbia River Treaty.

Sir John A. Returns

Until 1939, the battlegrounds of election campaigns were the big public meetings at Vancouver, Winnipeg, Toronto and Montreal. Political writers and commentators could usually judge who was going to win an election by the reception given the Conservative or Liberal leaders in those places.

One of the greatest political campaigners was Sir John A. Macdonald. He really began the tariff issue by introducing what was called "The National Policy" before the election on September 17, 1878. His government had been forced to resign in 1873 owing to a campaign fund scandal. Macdonald sat back quietly for almost five years and watched Liberal Prime Minister Alexander Mackenzie struggle with a severe depression.

As the time for the next election drew nearer, the question was whether or not Mackenzie would try to improve economic conditions by making a reciprocal trade deal with the United States. When Mackenzie committed himself to reciprocity, Macdonald trotted out his "National Policy" of higher tariffs for prosperity. Years later, D'Alton McCarthy, who was Macdonald's chief aide in Ontario, admitted that if Mackenzie had based his campaign on higher tariffs, Macdonald would have advocated reciprocity. Nevertheless, the high-low tariff battle continued until 1939 when World War II made it clear that nations do better through economic co-operation than through competition.

Macdonald was also largely responsible for the old system of spectacular public meetings. It has been said that he made after-dinner speeches popular. In the 1878 campaign he introduced the "political picnic." Tables were set under the trees. There were plates of cold chicken, tongue, ham, frosted cakes and mounds of strawberries, and jugs of iced lemonade and raspberry cordial. People came from miles around in their horse-drawn carriages, dressed in their Sunday-best. After a

> *Not only is this country made a slaughter market by being overwhelmed by the sweepings of the United States, but it has sometimes been made a sacrifice market by ruinous proposals for the purpose of suppressing any given trade. We all remember what the salt manufacturers of the United States did when the salt manufacturers first opened work in Goderich. The salt manufacturers of Syracuse and Salena sent in their salt with instructions to undersell Canadian salt on the Canadian market, to crush this infant industry. The shoe trade was dealt with in the same way by the leather manufacturers of the United States.*
>
> —SIR JOHN A. MACDONALD,
> Advocating the
> National Policy

delightful luncheon, Macdonald would speak from a specially built platform to a well-nourished, warm-hearted audience. One such picnic at Belleville, Ontario, was attended by 15,000 people.

Macdonald won the election of 1878, despite the fact that he was defeated in his own constituency. A safe seat had to be found for him in Victoria, B.C. Sir John remained prime minister until his death 13 years later. Political picnics and public meetings lasted far longer than that.

Other Events on September 17:

1705   The Marquis of Vaudreuil was made Governor of New France.

1792   The first Legislature of Upper Canada opened at Newark, now Niagara.

1814   The Americans were repulsed at Fort Erie, Ontario.

1859   Victoria Bridge at Montreal was completed. It was the first bridge over the St. Lawrence and was opened by the Prince of Wales in 1860.

1949   L. B. Pearson represented Canada at the first NATO meeting in Washington.

1951   The first election was held in the Northwest Territories.

D'Haussonville Surrenders St. John's to Amherst

Two cities in Canada share the distinction of being real "war veterans": St. John's, and Quebec. They have been bombarded, besieged and bothered more than any others. Quebec was captured only twice, by the Kirke brothers in 1629 when Champlain was out of supplies, and by Wolfe in 1759. It withstood heavy attacks by General Lévis in 1760, and by the Americans under Arnold and Montgomery in 1775. There was also an attack by a British force from New England in 1690, but Governor Frontenac repulsed it easily.

St. John's was raided by the Dutch, but the worst attacks were by the French, who had a base in Placentia. Iberville took it in 1696 (see May 19) and destroyed the fort and settlement. The French attacked again under Subercase in 1705 and under St. Ovide de Brouillion in 1708. Once again St. John's was destroyed.

The last attack by the French was in 1762 when St. John's was captured by d'Haussonville. This was a tactical move. France knew that the Seven Years' War was ending, and felt that by capturing Newfoundland it would be in a better position to bargain at the peace table. D'Haussonville was sent from France with four ships which eluded British warships outside Brest in a thick fog. He reached the Bay of Bulls on June 24, and then marched to St. John's, which he captured.

The British struck back as soon as possible. Colonel William Amherst was sent from New York, and a fleet under Lord Colville sailed from Britain to deal with the four French warships at St. John's. The French position was strong but Amherst captured it easily after a three-day march from Torbay. The attack amounted to a series of letters. Amherst wrote to d'Haussonville urging him to surrender. D'Haussonville replied that he would not surrender until he had no more powder to fire. Amherst replied that if d'Haussonville blew up the fort when he left it, every man in the garrison would be put to the sword. After another exchange of letters, Amherst wrote: "I don't thirst after the blood of the garrison, but you must determine quickly or expect the consequences." D'Haussonville then surrendered quietly on September 18, 1762.

Other Events on September 18:

1608 Pontgravé sailed for France, leaving Champlain with twenty-eight men to hold Quebec.

1663 A Sovereign Council was formed for the Government of Canada.

1679 La Salle sent his ship *Griffon* to Niagara, laden with furs. It was never seen again (see January 8).

1787 Prince William, later King William IV, visited Montreal.

1839 Joseph Howe published his famous letters to Lord Russell on the subject of responsible government.

1867 A Conservative government under John A. Macdonald won its first federal election after Confederation. Nova Scotian provincial elections were held on the same day and practically all the Confederation supporters were defeated.

1875 The Supreme Court of Canada was organized.

1885 Compulsory vaccination caused riots in Montreal.
Louis Riel was due to be hanged; his hanging was postponed until November 16.

1961 An electronic survey was completed, outlining the legal limits of Canada, including the polar continental shelf.

1963 Princess Alice arrived in Canada for an official visit.

British Occupy Quebec

Although Wolfe won the Battle of the Plains of Abraham on September 13, 1759, the city was not occupied until September 19.

Wolfe had died on the field of battle, but Montcalm, fatally wounded but still mounted on his black horse, was brought back into Quebec supported by two men. Before dying, he had time to send a message to General Townshend asking him to be kind to the French sick and wounded, and to carry out an agreement for an exchange of prisoners. His body was placed in a crude wooden box and buried in a convent. A British shell had come through the roof and blasted a hole in the ground large enough to make a grave.

Wolfe's death may have been due to the fact that he wore a new uniform, against the advice of his officers. He was a marked man when he led the Louisburg Grenadiers in the attack. Wolfe was wounded in the wrist and groin before the fatal bullet pierced his lungs.

By the middle of October it was time for the ships to sail for Britain or be frozen in the St. Lawrence for the winter. Admiral Saunders sailed, taking Townshend with him and leaving General Murray in charge. Murray was Governor of Canada until 1766, when he was recalled, although he continued to be paid as governor for eight years after that date.

The first winter in Quebec was miserable because the city had been so badly damaged by nearly ten weeks of bombardment. Food and fuel were scarce. Murray had nearly 7,000 troops to look after, as well as 4,000 citizens who chose to remain in Quebec and take the oath of allegiance. Murray was very strict with his troops. Any soldier found guilty of robbing a French citizen was hanged. Officers were instructed to lift their hats whenever a religious procession went by. If they did not want to do that, they had to get out of sight until the procession passed.

Actually, the British soldiers got on well with the French and worked with them in the fields, helping to bring in the harvest. They

Montcalm wounded after battle

were not equipped for winter, however. Their hands froze to their shovels when they tried to clear the snow and Scottish soldiers in kilts suffered when they had to go into the forests to get wood for fuel. There was so much sickness that Murray's forces had been reduced to half by the middle of winter.

Other Events on September 19:

1654 The first marriage on record in Canada took place at Quebec.

1860 Edward, Prince of Wales, left Canada for a visit to the United States.

1864 Canadian delegates arrived at Quebec after attending the Charlottetown Conference.

1891 A tunnel under the St. Clair River was opened, connecting Canada and the United States by railway.

1949 The Canadian dollar was devalued 10 per cent following the devaluation of the British pound on September 18.

1960 The new University of Alberta was opened at Calgary with a 320-acre campus.

1963 Plans were announced to develop Confederation Square at Ottawa at a cost of $100 million.

Marquis of Lorne and Wife Arrive in Victoria

British Columbia has contributed some of the most unusual stories to Canadian history. How Victoria became the capital was recounted on April 2, the use of camels on the Cariboo Trail, on May 29. In 1859 George Barston was elected member of the legislature for Nanaimo, but only one vote was cast. Guess who voted? The story of Topping's buying one of the world's richest gold mines for $12.50 was told on July 21. The Hudson's Bay Company's purchase of Vancouver Island for seven shillings a year was related on January 13. Here is yet another remarkable story from beyond the Rockies.

On September 20, 1882, Governor-General the Marquis of Lorne arrived in Victoria to attempt to solve the serious railway problem. There was not only the delay in getting the C.P.R. through to the Pacific, but also the question of who would build a railway on Vancouver Island. There was great unhappiness in British Columbia as suggestions were received that the province should secede from Canada and join the States.

The Governor-General's visit was almost too successful. The vice-regal tour was supposed to last two weeks, but the Marquis and his wife, Princess Louise, daughter of Queen Victoria, stayed three months. While her husband was touring the interior of British Columbia, watching Andrew Onderdonk build the railway through Fraser Canyon,

Arch erected for Marquis of Lorne and his wife, 1882

Princess Louise remained in Victoria. She would walk along the streets visiting bazaars, examining needlework displays, and shopping. On one occasion, a baker, not knowing who she was, ordered her to come out from behind a counter where she was looking at something.

When the Governor-General arrived back in Victoria, he found that a telegram from William Van Horne of the C.P.R. had arrived, stating that a route had been found through Kicking Horse Pass, and that the railway would be completed from Montreal to the Pacific by January 1, 1887.

The announcement was not greeted with as much joy in Victoria as might have been expected. Instead, Premier Beaven asked if Vancouver Island could become a separate kingdom with Princess Louise as its Queen!

Many people on Vancouver Island were beginning to fear that the completion of the railway would make the mainland too strong, to their disadvantage. Of course no such step was considered, but Vancouver Island was promised that it could have a railway of its own and a dry-dock at Esquimalt.

Other Events on September 20:

1697   The Treaty of Ryswick was signed. France returned Hudson Bay and Newfoundland to Britain, in return for Acadia.

1758   General Monckton landed troops at the present site of Saint John, New Brunswick.

1816   A stage coach ran between York and Niagara.

1854   The *Canadian*, the first ship of the Allan Line, sailed from Liverpool for Canada.

1917   Parliament gave votes to women who had close relatives in the armed forces.

1956   George Drew resigned as leader of the Conservative Party.

Liberals Defeated

Sir Wilfrid Laurier's days as Prime Minister of Canada ended with a general election on September 21, 1911. It was one of the most astonishing upheavals in Canadian political history and surprised even the Conservatives who thought they had no chance of winning.

The election of 1911 was called "the reciprocity election." The Elgin-Marcy Treaty signed in 1854 (see May 16) had brought ten years of prosperity to Canada and many people hoped another deal could be made. In January, 1911, Canadian Finance Minister Fielding met American President Taft secretly in Albany, New York, and worked out a reciprocal trade agreement. Canadian raw products could be sold in the States, while Canada would reduce tariffs on American manufactured products.

When news of the deal became known, Conservative leader Sir Robert Borden was so despondent that he wanted to resign. It seemed impossible that the Liberals could be defeated in the next election, but Borden was persuaded to stay on and fight it out.

Then the tide suddenly turned. Laurier's right hand man, Sir Clifford Sifton of Winnipeg, was opposed to reciprocity and joined seventeen other Liberals in signing a manifesto against it. It was amusing, perhaps startling, that while Sifton opposed reciprocity, his newspaper, the Winnipeg *Free Press,* supported it. Other wealthy Liberal supporters deserted Laurier, including Sir William Van Horne of the C.P.R. who said that he was "out to bust the damn thing." He wanted trade moving east and west, not north and south.

It was the Americans themselves who cooked Laurier's goose. President Taft said that Canada was at the parting of the ways with Britain. Champ Clark, Speaker of the House of Representatives, said he had no doubt that Britain would joyfully see all her North American possessions become part of the United States, and added: "We are preparing to annex Canada!"

William S. Fielding (1848-1929)

That was enough ammunition for the Conservatives. They waved the British flag in every campaign speech. When the votes were counted, the Conservatives had 133 seats and the Liberals 86, exactly the reverse of the position before Laurier called the election. Laurier never became prime minister again.

Other Events on September 21:

1812 Gananoque, Ontario, was raided by an American force.

1818 Lord Selkirk was tried for breaking into the Northwest Company headquarters at Fort William and arresting the partners (see June 12).

1928 Canada introduced airmail stamps.

1963 Place des Arts was opened at Montreal.

Blackfoot Sign Treaty

If the Police had not come to the country, where would we be all now? Bad men and whiskey were killing us so fast that very few indeed of us would have been left today. The Police have protected us as the feathers of the bird protect it from the frosts of winter. I wish them all good, and trust that all our hearts will increase in goodness from this time forward.

—CROWFOOT, 1877

One of the most pathetic stories in Canadian history is about the signing of Treaty Number Seven with the Blackfoot Indians on September 22, 1877. Chief Crowfoot insisted that the meeting take place at Blackfoot Crossing on the Bow River, near present-day Cluny. Four thousand Indians came: Blackfoot, Blood, Piegan, Stoney and Sarcee. Some wore little more than war paint and a breachcloth. They sat on the ground with the chiefs in front, then the head men, and braves, with squaws and children in the rear.

Canada was represented by David Laird, Lieutenant-Governor of the Northwest Territories. The negotiations took five days, and the treaty which resulted was better than those which preceded it. Each chief was promised a horse, wagon and harness. There was a medicine chest for each band and a grant

The signing of Treaty Number Seven, 1877

of $1,000 for three years for provisions to those Indians who engaged in farming. An important additional clause assured the Indians of aid in times of pestilence or famine.

Crowfoot, the leader, was one of the greatest Indians who ever roamed the prairies. When he died, Will Rogers said he was sure there would be a horse and saddle waiting for him in Heaven. While the negotiations were taking place, the Indians were fed by the Government, but Crowfoot would not take anything. He did not want it said that he had been influenced by gifts of food or tea. Finally he made a speech to Governor Laird: "I hope you will look upon the people of these tribes as your children and that you will be charitable to them." He thanked the Northwest Mounted Police who, he said, "have protected us as the feathers of the bird protect it from the frosts of winter."

When the Indians were paid their treaty money, they bought what they wanted from the traders and went to the reserves that had been created for them. Within three years, the buffalo had disappeared and the once proud owners of the plains were reduced to killing their horses for food and to eating gophers and mice.

Other Events on September 22:

1830   Robert Campbell arrived at the Red River to begin his service with the Hudson's Bay Company (see September 6).

1851   Quebec became the capital of Canada.

1930   The House of Commons passed the Unemployment Relief Act.

1959   Two Canadians, Dr. Wilder Penfield and Dr. E. W. R. Steacie, were made members of the U.S.S.R. Academy of Science. They were the first Canadians to be honored in this way.

1961   An aerial survey of wildlife on the Arctic islands was completed.

Labor Union Formed

It is in obedience to foreign agitation carried on by paid agents who have nothing to lose as the result of their mischievous counsels that the printers of this city have succumbed.
—Toronto *Globe*, 1872

We may destroy our happiness by inoculating our industrial system with the maladies of a distant country [England] and an alien state of society.
—Toronto *Globe*, 1872

Never in the history of Canada have labour unions shown so much activity; never have they been so well organized, and never has that organization made such determined, and in many cases unreasonable, efforts to secure for labour the domination of Canadian factories, and to wrest from the employer his inherent rights, to control the policy of his business and manage it as he thinks best.
—Canadian Manufacturers' Association, 1903

Labor can do nothing without capital, capital nothing without labor, and neither labor or capital can do anything without the guiding genius of management; and management, however wise its genius may be, can do nothing without the privileges which the community affords.
—W. L. Mackenzie King, 1919

Labor Day was celebrated for the first time in Canada on September 3, 1894, but the birthday of the labor movement was September 23, 1873. It was then that forty-five delegates from unions in Toronto, Hamilton and Ottawa formed the Canadian Labor Union.

The first known trades union in Canada was formed by printers in Quebec City in 1827. While it tried to regulate wages, it was more of a mutual aid society to care for the sick, and to provide social and recreational opportunities for its members. Labor unions had a hard time in the eighteenth and nineteenth centuries because they were held down legally; they were judged to be "in restraint of trade." However, labor began to make progress in Britain after the 1820's, and in 1871

the British Parliament adopted a "Magna Carta of Trades Unionism" which had an immediate effect in Canada and the States.

In July, 1872, the Trades Assembly in Toronto began a campaign for shorter hours and printers went on strike for seventeen weeks, demanding a nine-hour day. Twenty-four of them were thrown into jail, but public indignation led to their release. Prime Minister Sir John A. Macdonald introduced an act repealing such harsh measures. It was passed quickly by Parliament, and shortly afterwards the Canadian Labor Union was formed, representing fourteen unions in Toronto, and five in both Hamilton and Ottawa. Its members were assessed five cents every three months!

The Trades and Labor Congress of Canada was formed in 1886, but it cannot be said that the labor union movement grew quickly. In 1914, out of a labor force of 850,000, only 166,000 were union members. Industrialists organized more quickly. Between 1909 and 1911 nearly 200 manufacturing companies were united in 41 combinations. Their capital rose from $125 million to $335 million. Interlocking directorates put great power into the hands of a few individuals, although Parliament passed a Combines Investigation Act in 1910 to regulate monopolies and price fixing.

As early as 1907 there was also legislation to deal with industrial disputes. The Lemieux Act prohibited strikes and lockouts until disputes had been examined by a mediation board.

Other Events on September 23:

1787 The site of Toronto was purchased from the Mississauga Indians.

1844 Governor Metcalfe dissolved Parliament and forced an election. John A. Macdonald was elected for the first time, representing Kingston, Ontario (see March 29).

1908 The University of Alberta was opened at Edmonton with thirty-seven students.

C.P.R. Opens Branch Line to Coal Banks, Alberta

By 1885 the C.P.R. had pushed its way beyond Winnipeg. It had passed Pile O'Bones (Regina) and entered Calgary, a "rootin, tootin" cowboy town.

Moving supplies to the workers was a tremendous problem. There was a lucky break when coal was discovered near Fort Whoop-Up, and a company was formed to mine it. The C.P.R. then built a branch line from Dunsmore, on the main line, to Coal Banks, now Lethbridge, and that problem was solved. The branch line was opened on September 24, 1885. One year later, Lethbridge had a population of more than 1,000.

One of the most successful suppliers of beef for the construction crews was Pat Burns, the "cattle king." He was born at Oshawa, Ontario, in humble circumstances, and went to school at Kirkfield. Pat and his brother John decided to go out west. In order to earn money to travel they worked in the bush, but were paid two oxen instead of money. They slaughtered the oxen and sold the meat, earning more money than if they had been paid wages.

This taught Pat Burns a valuable lesson, and when he reached the West, he gradually developed a business, buying cattle (on time) from farmers, and selling the beef to construction gangs. He then began his famous meat packing firm in Calgary.

There are countless stories about Pat Burns. It is said that he was one of the few people who never made an enemy while making a million dollars. One story tells how he was driving in a parade in Calgary when he saw a little pig walking beside a float as a mascot. It was obviously becoming exhausted so Burns stopped his limousine and took the dejected pig in with him.

Another story tells how he sent men from his Calgary plant to paint his little church at Midnapore. The new paint made the other church at Midnapore look bad, so Burns said "paint that church too."

Prime Minister R. B. Bennett made him a senator on the occasion of a testimonial dinner in 1931. It was Burns' 75th birthday, and 700 people were there. A two-ton birthday cake was cut into 15,000 pieces to send to his friends.

Other Events on September 24:

1669 Father Galinée and La Salle, going west, met Joliet near the present site of Hamilton, Ontario. Joliet had been trying to find copper in the Lake Superior area.

1897 An arch bridge was opened over the Niagara River. It was the third bridge. The first was the suspension bridge built in 1855. The second was a cantilever built in 1883.

1956 Canada, Britain and the United States signed an atomic energy agreement in Washington.

1959 External Affairs Minister Howard Green addressed the United Nations on disarmament.

1962 The Garden of the Provinces was opened at Ottawa by Prime Minister Diefenbaker.

1963 A Canadian delegation, headed by Privy Council President Lamontagne, left for London to attend the Commonwealth Conference on Finance and Trade, preceding the International Monetary Fund Meeting.

1965 *Ojibwa*, the Royal Canadian Navy's first 2000-ton Oberon class submarine, was commissioned at Chatham, England, by Canadian High Commissioner Chevrier.

Major General B. F. Macdonald was appointed to command the newly-formed UN India-Pakistan Observation Mission.

Allen Taken Prisoner

Among the great Indian chiefs who fought for the British was Joseph Brant, whose name is commemorated in a number of places in Canada, notably Brantford, Ontario. His dedication to the British cause came about through a spectacular development.

Early in the American Revolutionary War, General Washington sent a column under Benedict Arnold to capture Quebec, while another under General Montgomery moved against Montreal. One of Montgomery's officers was Ethan Allen, who led the Green Mountain Boys from New Hampshire.

Allen was impetuous and would not wait for Montgomery's campaign to develop. Instead he made a sweep against Montreal with his own Green Mountain Boys. They arrived at a point across the river from Montreal and sent a message to the city demanding that it surrender at once. A loyal force led by Major Cardin, who had been one of Wolfe's officers, crossed the river and engaged Allen at Long Point. There was sharp fighting on September 25, 1775, in which Cardin was killed, but Allen and eighty of his mountain boys had to surrender. They were taken to Montreal and Allen was shipped to Britain where he spent two years in prison.

Aboard the same ship was Joseph Brant, a young Mohawk chief, who was invited to visit England by the British garrison in Montreal. In Britain, Brant was treated as though he were royalty. He was the honored guest in every drawing room of society. His portrait was painted by Romney, one of the great artists of the day. The famous biographer, Boswell, became one of his friends. He was given a remarkable gun for the age; it could fire fifteen shots from a single loading!

When Brant returned to his own country in 1776, he was convinced that no nation could defeat the British, even though the Americans had captured Montreal while he was away. The Mohawks, members of the Iroquois nations, fought loyally with the British, although it was a losing cause.

Joseph Brant (1742-1807)

Other Events on September 25:

1726   Acadians signed a British oath of allegiance, on condition that they did not have to fight against the French.

1759   The ship *Tilbury of St. Esprit* was lost off Cape Breton with 200 lives.

1872   The Interoceanic Company was organized for the construction of the C.P.R.

1888   Ottawa Exhibition opened for the first time.

1911   Conservative leader Sir Robert Borden was drawn through the streets of Ottawa after winning the reciprocity election (see September 21).

1950   A federal-provincial conference was held in Quebec City.

1956   The first three-way telephone service was opened between Ottawa, London and New York.

Nelson Enchanted by Quebec—and Mary Simpson

Prince William, later King William IV, visited Canada as a frigate captain and not unlike many sailors, had a girl in every port. One of his friends, and fellow-captain of a frigate, was Horatio Nelson. He had a girl in one Canadian port, Quebec, and there is a romantic but sad story about them.

During the summer of 1782, Nelson was attacking American privateers along the coasts of Nova Scotia and Cape Cod. His crew began to suffer from scurvy, so Nelson took his ship *Albermarle* to Quebec for a refit in September. This is one of the most delightful months of the year along the St. Lawrence, with the maple leaves changing to red and gold, and Nelson was enchanted. He referred to "fair Canada" in letters home.

Nelson was in Quebec for most of September and fell in love with Mary Simpson, the daughter of the provost marshal of the garrison. She was only sixteen years old, but Nelson was determined to marry her. Prince William had predicted earlier that Nelson was going to do great things, even though he was probably the youngest captain in the Royal Navy. Nelson's Quebec friends agreed, and felt that marriage to an obscure Canadian girl would hurt his career. They tried to talk him out of it and there were some tempestuous scenes. There is even a story, unverified, that Nelson had to be tricked into sailing from Quebec.

It was mid-October before he left. He never returned to Canada, or Mary Simpson, again. Peace talks had already begun, and the British evacuated New York in May, 1783. The war against the United States ended in September, but Britain was also fighting France, Spain, and Holland so there was plenty of action to occupy Horatio Nelson.

Other Events on September 26:

1659   Bishop Laval called a conference to deal with the problem of supplying liquor to the Indians.

1667   René Gaultier de Varenne and Marie Bouchard of Trois Rivières were married. They were the parents of the famous explorer Pierre de la Vérendrye.

1862   Milton and Cheadle began to explore a route through the Rockies.

1904   Earl Grey was appointed governor-general.

1917   Compulsory military service went into effect.

1951   David M. Johnson was appointed Canada's permanent representative to the United Nations.

1959   A. R. Mosher, Honorary President of the Canadian Labour Congress and chief founder of the Canadian Brotherhood of Railway Employees, died.

1960   Prime Minister Diefenbaker spoke to the United Nations Assembly.

1963   The Progressive Conservative Government of Premier John Robarts returned to power in Ontario.

King William IV

Canadian Pacific Railway Engine 374, Countess of Dufferin

Stephenson Demonstrates His Locomotive

On September 27, 1825, George Stephenson demonstrated his locomotive in England. It drew six small freight cars and a coach at 15 miles per hour while a man rode ahead on horseback, waving a red flag, to warn people. He couldn't keep ahead of the train for long, and then it was every man for himself.

Strangely enough, the fireman on that first locomotive was a Mr. Whitehead, whose son Joseph was destined to bring the first locomotive into Winnipeg, in October, 1877. The *Countess of Dufferin*, now on display outside the C.P.R. station in Winnipeg, was bought from an American railway line. It traveled under its own steam from St. Paul to Fargo, North Dakota, where it was loaded on board a barge with six flat cars. The 65,000 pound *Countess* made a triumphant journey down the Red River. It was draped with flags and bunting, while Joseph Whitehead kept up steam pressure so that its whistle could be sounded along the way. Forts along the river fired their cannons in salute. It was the dawn of a new era for Western Canada. Just as the river boat had ended the days of the Red River carts hauling supplies between Winnipeg and St. Paul, so the railway ended the days of the river boats.

Governor-General and Lady Dufferin were in Winnipeg when the new train arrived. There was a public holiday, and the railway barge was greeted by the city fathers wearing morning coats and top hats.

Winnipeg wanted to look its best for the visit of the vice-regal party. It had only been incorporated for three years and was in the process of being built. The citizens went into the woods and cut hundreds of spruce trees which were set in post holes along the streets. They looked great until a strong wind blew up. When Lord and Lady Dufferin arrived, the trees were leaning at an angle of 45 degrees.

The *Countess of Dufferin* was put to work immediately on the construction of a railway line south to Emerson, where it connected with an American line. Thousands of settlers came by this route until the C.P.R. reached Winnipeg in 1882.

Other Events on September 27:

1918   British and Canadian troops broke the Hindenburg Line, leading to the end of World War I in November.

1962   Canada's Twenty-fifth Parliament was opened.

N.W.T. Gets Lieut.-Gov.

The opening of the prairie lands would drain away our youth and strength. I am perfectly willing personally to leave the whole country a wilderness for the next half century, but I fear if the English do not go in, the Yankees will, and with that apprehension, I would gladly see a crown colony established there.

—Sir John A. Macdonald, 1865

Although John A. Macdonald said in 1865 that he did not think the Prairies were of any use to Canada, he changed his mind quickly after Confederation. The United States bought Alaska from Russia in 1867 for $7,200,000. In those days some people called the deal "Seward's folly," because American Secretary of State Seward had negotiated it. They had to eat their words later on. The United States took about $100 million worth of gold out of Alaska, not to mention other assets. The U.S. was now looking at the northwest. If Alaska could be picked up for $7.2 million, why not get the territory in between? Prime Minister Macdonald decided Canada should get there first.

The Senate Foreign Relations Committee reported: "The opening by us of a North Pacific railroad seals the destiny of the British possessions west of Longitude 90 (the head of Lake Superior). They will become so American in interest and feeling . . . the question of annexation will be but a matter of time."

James W. Taylor, American Treasury agent in St. Paul, wrote to the Hudson's Bay Company offering $5 million for Rupert's Land. He said: "I know that President Grant is anxious to make a treaty with England which transfers the country between Minnesota and Alaska to the United States in settlement of the *Alabama* controversy and as consideration for the establishment of reciprocal trade with Canada."

Ottawa obtained secret copies of those documents, and immediately informed the Hudson's Bay Company that it would have to sells its territory to Canada. The Government then created the Northwest Territories out of Rupert's Land, to be administered by a lieutenant-governor and council. William H. McDougall was appointed lieutenant-governor on September 28, 1869, and left immediately for Fort Garry. The consequences of the hurried arrangements were severe and will be the subject of future stories.

The British Government put pressure on the Hudson's Bay Company to surrender its territory to Canada, and the price was set at £300,000, equivalent then to $1.5 million. The money was supposed to be paid on October 1, but Canada was unable to raise a loan in London and the deal was delayed until December 1, 1869.

Other Events on September 28:

1813 The British were defeated by the Americans at York Bay (Toronto).

1857 A railway between Galt and Guelph, Ontario, was opened.

1892 New Brunswick abolished its legislative council.

1950 Indonesia became the sixtieth member of the United Nations. Fourteen additional applicants failed to gain the unanimous support of the Security Council, a prerequisite for membership.
The meetings of the Constitutional Conference of Federal and Provincial Governments at Quebec, for devising a method of amending the Constitution, came to an end.

1951 The International Monetary Fund lifted restrictions on the selling of gold.

1955 A joint Canada-United States Committee on Trade and Economic Affairs met in Ottawa.

1960 Skyway Bridge between Prescott, Ontario, and Ogdensburg, New York, was opened.

Ceremonies Open For Building of Rideau Canal

The Rideau Canal between the Ottawa River and Lake Ontario is now used only by pleasure boats. The lift from the Ottawa River to the canal is through a series of picturesque locks between the Parliament Buildings and the Chateau Laurier Hotel. The first stone of one of the locks was laid by Sir John Franklin, the famous explorer.

The project that eventually led to the building of the Rideau Canal began on September 29, 1783, immediately following the end of the American Revolutionary War. British military leaders wanted a route from the St. Lawrence to Lake Ontario that would not be exposed to the American border. Lieutenants Jones and French were assigned to survey what was then wild territory and reported that a canal was feasible by using the Rideau River and a chain of lakes.

Nothing was done until after the War of 1812, when the building of the canal again became an issue. In 1824, Upper Canada became impatient with the delay and had another survey made by Samuel Clewes. The British Government offered to lend Upper Canada £70,000 to build the canal, but Upper Canada would not go through with it. In 1826, the British Government sent Colonel John By to build the canal. He built the eight locks up the steep cliff from the Ottawa River and reserved the land on either side for military purposes.

By coincidence, the opening ceremonies for the building of the canal in 1827 were on the same date that Jones and French began their survey, September 29. People came from near and far, on foot, in canoes and by ox-teams. It was an Indian summer; the forests were rich in color, with scarlet maples and golden birches. During the opening ceremony, in which Governor Dalhousie turned the first sod, frogs in nearby marshes provided their "musical" accompaniment. The first steamer, *Rideau,* made the journey from Kingston to Bytown in 1832. The route was busy until nearly 1900 when railways made it unnecessary.

Other Events on September 29:

1788 The first ship built on the Pacific coast, the *North West America,* was completed by Captain Meares at Nootka, Vancouver Island.

1962 Canada's spacecraft Alouette was launched at Vandenburg Base, Calif.

View of Rideau Canal Locks, 1879

The Silver Dart *piloted by J. A. D. McCurdy*

Aerial Experimental Association Established

Everyone knows that Alexander Graham Bell invented the telephone but few realize that he ranks with the Wright brothers as an inventor of the airplane. Alexander Graham Bell did his developmental work on the airplane at Baddeck, Nova Scotia, and established the Aerial Experimental Association there on September 30, 1907, helped by money contributed by his wife.

There is a charming story about how the Bells found Baddeck. While they were on a summer cruise their ship put into Baddeck. Bell visited the local newspaper office where the editor had installed one of those newfangled telephones. This one wasn't working properly and the editor, not knowing who Bell was, complained that there wasn't anyone nearer than Halifax who could fix it. Bell took off the mouthpiece and removed a dead fly, after which the telephone worked perfectly. The incident led to the Bells establishing a summer home at Baddeck. It was while watching seagulls there that Bell told an incredulous newspaper reporter that men would fly within ten years. (The Wright brothers flew exactly ten years later.)

Bell first experimented with rocket propulsion, then with kites. In 1908, he developed the kite *Cygnet,* big enough to carry Thomas Selfridge who lay face-downward in it. The kite took off from the water, towed by the steamer *Blue Hill,* and rose 160 feet into the air. Selfridge brought it down gently but was nearly run down by the steamer.

Then came experiments with gliders taking off from the ice. Bell was helped by Selfridge, F. W. Baldwin, J. A. D. McCurdy and Glen Curtiss who were members of the Aerial Experimental Association. Curtiss, an American motorcycle expert, studied Bell's models to see if a motor could be installed. In March, 1908, "Casey" Baldwin went along the ice at 20 miles per hour, pulled a lever, and flew 318 feet. Tests were made with other "drones" until they were ready for the first public flight in the British Commonwealth. J. A. D. McCurdy flew the *Silver Dart* for half a mile on February 23, 1909. It was one of the great steps forward in aviation. McCurdy eventually became Lieutenant-Governor of Nova Scotia and attended the fiftieth anniversary of his flight in 1959 at Baddeck.

Other Events on September 30:

1749 Indians massacred settlers at the present site of Dartmouth, Nova Scotia.

1947 Canada was elected to the United Nations Security Council for a two-year term.

1953 McGill University announced the development of a radar defence system for North America.

Laval Chosen Bishop

Visitors to Quebec City are always intrigued by the huge statue of Bishop Laval, standing with arms outstretched in welcome and blessing on top of the cliff. He was officially named Bishop of Quebec on October 1, 1674, by Pope Clement X, although he had been acting as such since June, 1659.

Laval belonged to a great and wealthy family, but he gave his share of the family estate to his brother and joined an order that went through the country barefoot and lived on food supplied by the people. He was in the thick of dispute from the beginning—when he was appointed there was a struggle for power between his order, the Jesuits, and the Sulpicians. His appointment was a triumph for the Jesuits.

The Pope appointed Laval "vicar-apostolic" of Canada rather than Bishop, because he would have come under the king if he had been bishop of Canada, while a vicar-apostolic came under the Pope. So Laval was in the middle of another controversy between Church and State.

Laval insisted on absolute equality between the governor and himself. On one occasion the governor and the bishop were present at a catechism in a school. When the governor entered, resplendent in plumed hat, velvet doublet and jewelled sword, two boys stood up and saluted, which they did not do for Laval. They were whipped the next morning.

However, on the other side of the ledger, when Laval was in his eighties he was suffering from arthritis and could not sleep. One cold, winter night he hobbled out for a walk and found a small boy who had been turned out of his home. The youngster was shivering, not being dressed for cold weather. Laval took him back to his own quarters, gave him a warm bath, put him in his own bed and sat there watching him while he slept. The next day he made arrangements for his permanent care.

Statue of Bishop Laval, Quebec City

During his career at Quebec, from 1659 to 1706, Laval was given crown lands that became very valuable. He made arrangements secretly that when he died the revenue from them was to be used for education. Laval University is one of the many memorials to his service.

Other Events on October 1:

1754　Anthony Henday stopped with the Blackfoot Indians at the present site of Red Deer, Alberta.

1764　A proclamation of 1763 came into force, replacing military by civil rule.

1853　The Toronto *Globe* was issued as a daily newspaper.

1916　The second war loan was oversubscribed by $100 million.

1930　An Imperial conference was opened in London. Prime Minister R. B. Bennett represented Canada.

1958　Canada House at New York was officially opened.

The coat-of-arms of Charles Lawrence

Parliament Meets

When the Acadians were deported from Nova Scotia in 1755, "planters" from New England were brought in to take their place. As a result, Nova Scotia opened the first Parliament in what is now Canada on October 2, 1758.

Governor Cornwallis, the builder of Halifax, had been given instructions to "summon and call general assemblies of the Freeholders and Planters according to the usage of the rest of our colonies and plantations in America" but had done nothing about it. He was succeeded by a tough soldier, Colonel Lawrence, who might also have done nothing except that his hand was forced by the settlers from the American colonies. They were accustomed to self-government and demanded it for Nova Scotia.

On February 7, 1758, Governor Lawrence and his council passed resolutions providing for the election of sixteen members for the province at large, with four from Halifax, and two from Lunenberg. As soon as any community had a population of fifty, it could elect two members. Nobody could complain about lack of representation when there was a Member of Parliament for every twenty-five people!

The first Parliament in Canada met in the Court House at the corner of Argyle and Buckingham Streets in Halifax on October 2, 1758. It remained in session until April 11, 1759, with breaks for the usual holidays. The members voted to serve without pay. The total expense of the first session was £250, of which £100 went to the clerk.

The Church of England was formally established, but Protestant dissenters were allowed freedom of worship and conscience. The same privileges were denied "members of the popish religion." The British criminal code was adopted, including penalties of the stocks, pillory, flogging, branding, cutting off ears and hanging. As late as 1816, a man was sentenced to have his ears cut off. The use of profane language was a criminal offence.

Nova Scotia's Parliament was conducted with great ceremony. Charles Dickens, who visited Halifax in 1840, said it was like looking at the British Parliament through the wrong end of a telescope!

October 2, 1758, was commemorated by the Canadian Club of Halifax which erected a memorial tower along the picturesque Northwest Arm of the city.

Other Events on October 2:

1535   Cartier landed at Hochelaga, the site of Montreal.

1847   A telegraph service was opened between Montreal and Quebec.

1871   The sod was turned for the Prince Edward Island Railway.

1887   A sturgeon, 11 feet 9 inches long and weighing 822 pounds was caught at Ladner, British Columbia, and towed to New Westminster.

1895   The Mackenzie, Yukon, Ungava and Franklin districts were formed.

1955   The Canadian Unemployment Act came into force.

1960   The first Canadian conference on children was held at St. Adèle, Quebec.

First Convoy Embarks

For the first contingent, our recruiting plans were, I think, different from anything that had ever occurred before. There was really a call to arms, like the fiery cross passing through the Highlands of Scotland or the mountains of Ireland in former days.

—SIR SAM HUGHES, 1916

Britain declared war on Germany on August 4, 1914, and Prime Minister Borden had already promised to send a Canadian army. It was something of a miracle that the first contingent of 33,000 men was ready to sail from Quebec on October 3, 1914.

The incredible Minister of Militia Sam Hughes (see February 13) was largely responsible. He had many critics, but said: "My critics will stop their yelping as a puppydog chasing an express train gives up its job as a useless task." He was the express train. Sir Sam, as he became, personally supervised the embarkation from Quebec of 33,000 men and 7,000 horses. The horses would not walk the gangplanks to get into the ships, so they had to be lifted on board in slings. Sir Sam was a great man for getting things done in a hurry, but when the first convoy sailed, 800 horses and nearly 5,000 tons of ammunition and supplies had been left behind.

There were thirty troop transport ships escorted by three battleships and six cruisers, most of them twenty years old. As there was great danger from German submarines and surface raiders, the landing point in Britain was changed several times while the convoy was crossing the Atlantic. It arrived at Plymouth on October 14 and was met by General Alderson, commander of the Canadian forces, who had preceded them.

The British naval officer in charge of the escort was Admiral Wemyss. As soon as the troops were landed safely, he went to the Admiralty in London. Wemyss was boiling mad. In his opinion, the convoy had been a dreadful risk. If the first Canadian contingent had suffered heavy casualties at sea, what would have been the effect on troops coming to Britain from other parts of the Commonwealth? The senior officer replied, "Oh you must take some risks in wartime," but Wemyss replied, "Only justifiable risks."

Wemyss felt it would have been safer if the ships had sailed on their own, not bunched together, with the sea lanes protected as much as possible by the warships. Many ship captains felt the same way in World War II.

Other Events on October 3:

1836   The Assembly of Lower Canada declined to vote money for government expenses.

1871   The Manitoba Government issued an order-in-council for defense against the Fenians.

1874   Edward Blake outlined the "Canada first" program.

1927   Prime Ministers Mackenzie King of Canada and Baldwin of Britain opened the transatlantic telephone service.

1955   A federal-provincial conference was opened at Ottawa.

Canada's first contingent sets sail on October 3, 1914

"Yankee Gale" Claims American Fishermen

Canada's smallest province, Prince Edward Island, has three nicknames, which is more than any other province can claim. It is known as "the Garden of the Gulf," "the Cradle of Confederation," and "the Cradle in the Waves." The cradle has rocked too sharply at times.

The famous Canadian sailing ship *Marco Polo* was wrecked on Cape Cavendish (see April 17). The S.S. *Queen Victoria,* which took the Canadian delegates to the Charlottetown Conference in 1864, was lost in a hurricane on October 4, two years later. By coincidence the worst storm of all was also on October 4, but in 1851, when a large number of American fishermen lost their lives off Charlottetown. Estimates range from 150 to 300 lives.

The storm is known in history as the "Yankee Gale." There were more than 100 American fishing vessels off the north shore of Prince Edward Island when a freak storm suddenly blew up. It lasted from Friday afternoon until Sunday evening, when watchers on the shore could see 70 fishing vessels wrecked on the beaches and sand dunes. Nearly all of them were from the New England states. The bodies of a great many victims were never recovered, but 70 were buried in various cemeteries along the shore.

The real cause of the disaster was not the storm, but the lack of a clear-cut fishing agreement between the British North American colonies and the United States. The situation had been confused since the War of 1812. In 1818, it was agreed that Americans could fish outside the three-mile limit of Newfoundland and the Maritimes, but the problem was "three miles from what?" The Americans said the treaty meant three miles from the winding of the coast, so that they could fish inside the wider bays. Newfoundland and the Maritimes claimed that it meant three miles from the headlands, and American fishing vessels entering that boundary were taken into custody. When the storm struck Charlottetown on October 4, 1851, the American fishing fleet tried to ride it out rather than risk running into the harbor. The result was the great loss of life.

There was so much anger on both sides that Britain sent a number of Royal Navy ships to patrol the fishing grounds. There was even a danger of war. The dispute was settled by the Elgin-Marcy Treaty signed in 1854 which gave Canada a beneficial reciprocity treaty with the States, and the Americans better fishing rights (see May 16).

Other Events on October 4:

1764 An ordinance regulated foreign currency.

1860 Church union began at Pictou, Nova Scotia.

1909 Governor-General Earl Grey laid the cornerstone of the Parliament Building, Regina.

1913 A new customs agreement between Canada and the States went into effect.

1922 A hurricane led to a forest fire and the loss of forty-one lives at Haileybury, Ontario.

1927 Airmail service was begun to northern mining communities.

1950 An oil pipeline was opened between Edmonton and Regina.

1954 Delegates from seventeen nations in the Colombo plan met at Ottawa.

1963 A strike of 1,300 longshoremen began in the St. Lawrence River ports.

Tecumseh Dies

Commodore Perry's victory over British ships on Lake Erie (see September 10) set off a chain reaction of events which had serious consequences for Canada. General Procter, who was responsible for defending the area from Detroit to Burlington, had sent men and guns to Barclay's fleet, and now they were lost. He was left with only 900 regular troops, and about 1,200 Indians under Tecumseh. Most of the Canadians in the militia had gone to their homes to harvest their crops.

Procter could be cut off from the British force at Burlington, and it was important to retreat, quickly. He ordered his troops at Detroit to burn the fort there, and return to the Canadian side of the river. Tecumseh was disgusted. He did not really understand how the situation had been changed by Barclay's defeat on Lake Erie, and he and his Indians wanted to stand and fight the Americans as they came. Tecumseh told Procter he was like a dog running away with his tail between his legs, and asked the British to give their rifles to his Indians. Feelings ran high, but finally Procter persuaded Tecumseh to move up the Thames Valley towards the present site of London. From there, if necessary, they would be able to use Dundas Street, the old military road built by Simcoe, to join British troops at Burlington.

The Americans, especially the cavalry, advanced with great speed. When Procter reached Moraviantown, 6 miles beyond Chatham, Tecumseh refused to move farther. He had been wounded in rearguard fighting, and his Indians were deserting in large numbers. He insisted on making a last-ditch stand at Moraviantown, and placed his Indians in a swamp. Procter, who would not desert him, placed his men as effectively as possible. There were only about 900 fighting men left in the combined British-Indian force.

The battle took place on October 5, 1813, and was over in a few minutes. Tecumseh was killed, but his body was hidden so that it could not be mutilated by Americans seeking

revenge. They liked to take strips of skin from bodies, make them into razor-strops, and present them to members of Congress. Fortunately, the Americans did not follow up their advantage after winning the battle at Moraviantown.

Other Events on October 5:

1793 Captain Vancouver left Nootka, Vancouver Island, and explored the coast as far north as Alaska.

1835 Citizens of St. Andrew's, New Brunswick, held a public meeting in support of the building of a railway to Quebec.

1871 Fenians tried to capture the Hudson's Bay Company post at Pembina, on the Manitoba border.

1878 The Marquis of Lorne was appointed Governor-General of Canada.

1903 Alberta College (Methodist) was founded at Edmonton.

1955 The Canadian Government announced a plan to build a large power plant in Pakistan as part of the Colombo plan.

Technicality Favors U.S.—Astoria Is Returned

If a British naval captain had not been so wide awake, to put it politely, Canada might now own what is American territory as far south as Portland, Oregon. The Columbia River would be the "St. Lawrence of the West."

Fort Astoria, near the mouth of the Columbia River, had been established by John Jacob Astor in 1811. The fort's only link with the outside world was a ship which visited the fort while on trading trips to Vancouver Island and dropped necessary supplies. Unfortunately the captain was a rough character, and on one occasion struck an Indian chief who came on board to trade. The next day members of the tribe came on board, ostensibly to trade, drew their knives and killed the captain and most of the crew. The ship's clerk, mortally wounded, crawled down to where the ammunition was stored, and set off a blast that killed the Indians and sent the ship to the bottom.

As a result, the people at Fort Astoria were isolated and without supplies. They were starving when a party of Nor'Westers appeared, after traveling David Thompson's route down the Columbia, and they were glad to sell the post to the North West Company. They would be assured of supplies, and also protection from any British naval unit that might appear.

In the meantime, such a unit had been sent to capture Fort Astoria. It was H.M.S. *Raccoon* under the command of Captain William Black. After sailing all the way from Britain he was greatly disappointed to find that Fort Astoria was already British territory, through purchase by the North West Company rather than through a brilliant naval action of his own. So Captain Black put on a show. On December 12, 1813, he hauled down the British flag and raised it again, while the Americans and Indians watched the performance.

When the War of 1812 ended, it was agreed that all territory taken by military action would be returned. Britain claimed Fort Astoria because it had been purchased from the Astor Company. "Oh no," said the Americans, "The fort was taken by military action by the captain of H.M.S. *Raccoon*." They had witnesses to prove it, and their case held good. The fort was returned to the States on October 6, 1818, and Canada lost the territory from the British Columbia border to Portland, Oregon.

Other Events on October 6:

1744   A force from Louisburg abandoned the attempt to capture Annapolis Royal.

1868   Prime Minister Macdonald proposed better terms for Nova Scotia for joining Confederation. This led Howe to join Macdonald's government.

1890   The United States put the McKinley high tariff plan in effect against Canada.

1911   The Laurier government resigned after having been in power since 1896.

1948   A Newfoundland delegation arrived in Ottawa to discuss terms for entering Confederation. The agreement was signed on December 11.

Fort Astoria

Disaster at Miramichi

One of the most famous fishing and hunting areas in Canada is the Miramichi Valley in New Brunswick. Sportsmen from all parts of the continent fish the Miramichi River and its many tributaries every year for Atlantic salmon.

Among the keenest fishing fans was Ted Williams, one of the greatest batters in baseball for many years. As soon as the baseball season finished at the end of September, Williams would be out of his Red Sox uniform and heading for the Miramichi. It was just as well—for his fishing—that the Red Sox got into the World Series only once during his career, for his team's absence from the championship enabled him to reach Miramichi before the season closed.

The entire Miramichi area was almost destroyed by one of the worst forest fires in Canadian history on October 7, 1825. In the afternoon the wind was moderate and shifting. A broad cloud of smoke was seen to rise vertically, northwest of Newcastle. At seven o'clock in the evening the breeze freshened, and the air suddenly darkened. Ashes and cinders came down so heavily that people were blinded and could hardly breathe. About an hour later a loud roaring noise was heard in the woods, and the wind began to blow with hurricane force. Suddenly sky and earth were illuminated by a sheet of flame which enveloped Newcastle and Douglastown. Houses were blazing within three minutes.

People in Newcastle ran into a marsh about half a mile away, and tried to escape from the flames and heat by burrowing into the mud and water. Others rushed to the river and clambered into boats, or hung onto rafts and logs. Many simply stood or swam in the river and tried to protect themselves from the scorching heat.

Cattle and other animals, wild and domestic, followed the people into the river. At one place a bear was seen sheltering in the river with some cows, but did not try to

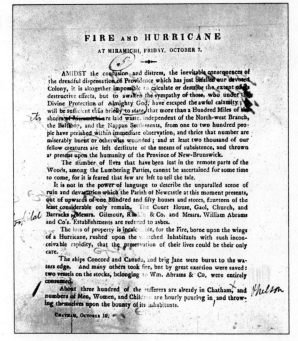

Old document of the fire, 1825

harm them. Even the salmon were terrified of the flames. They rushed from pool to pool, and many were bruised to death on the rocks.

New Brunswick is famous for its folk songs, and the story of the great Miramichi fire is still told in songs and verse.

Other Events on October 7:

1663   Jean Baptiste Le Gardeur de Repentigny was chosen as the first mayor of Quebec.

1763   The Treaty of Paris went into effect. King George III issued a proclamation annexing the Island of St. John (Prince Edward Island) and Cape Breton to Nova Scotia. The territory of Quebec was defined.

1876   The Northwest Territories were organized with a government and a capital.

1963   Eleven members of the F.L.Q. (Quebec separatist movement) pleaded guilty to terrorism. Their sentences ranged from six months to twelve years.

Hotel Dieu Hospital Opens at Montreal

While Madeleine de Verchères and Laura Secord are generally regarded as the outstanding heroines of Canada, there were many others whose bravery and devotion to duty equalled that of any man.

Among them was Jeanne Mance, who came to Canada with Maisonneuve. She called on a Jesuit father in Paris and told him she had a divine call to serve in Canada. After she had been questioned by the Queen, Anne of Austria, and other ladies of the court, money was provided for her to accompany Maisonneuve and found a hospital, the Hôtel Dieu Hospital, which was opened on October 8, 1642.

As was expected, the Iroquois were bitterly opposed to the building of a settlement at Montreal, and they attacked mail and supply boats going between Montreal and Quebec. It was not even safe to go outside the palisade to cut wood. On one occasion three men were killed and three others were carried off and tortured to death. Louis XIII sent out a ship, *Notre Dame de Montréal*, with supplies and a number of expert workmen to reinforce the settlement. One of the workmen was a leading engineer, Louis d'Ailleboust, who was accompanied by an unwilling wife. Madame d'Ailleboust was soon so impressed by Jeanne Mance that she became one of her most faithful helpers.

D'Ailleboust strengthened the defense of the settlement and then turned his attention to building the hospital, for which he had brought an additional gift of money. The worst problem was lack of room inside the palisade, and so the hospital had to be built on the other side of the St. Pierre River, a small stream that flowed through Montreal. D'Ailleboust chose high ground to protect the hospital from the spring floods. The ground was easier to defend than the settlement itself, and Maisonneuve would have been the wiser if he had built there at the outset.

In 1653, the hospital was attacked by 200 Iroquois when Jeanne Mance was there alone with her patients. A brave soldier, Lambert Close, went to the rescue with 16 men, fought the Iroquois for twelve hours, and managed to drive them away. There were many such adventures ahead for Jeanne Mance.

Other Events on October 8:

1804　The schooner *Speedy* was lost on Lake Ontario with distinguished passengers aboard.

1904　Edmonton was incorporated as a city.

An Anglo-French convention settled the question of shore rights for French fishermen. France surrendered these rights in return for cash indemnities and territorial concessions in Africa.

1906　A federal-provincial conference opened at Ottawa.

1907　The transatlantic wireless opened for public service.

1951　Princess Elizabeth and Prince Philip began a tour of Canada which lasted until November 12.

1960　The Federal-Provincial Constitutional Conference of Attorneys-General, which had met in Ottawa to discuss amendment of the BNA Act, came to an end.

1964　Chief Justice G. S. Challies of the Quebec Superior Court was named commissioner to inquire into the fatal crash of the TCA aircraft at St. Thérèse, Quebec, November 29, 1963.

The eighteenth Olympiad commenced in Tokyo, Japan. The gold medal for coxless pair rowing was won by George Hungerford, Vancouver, and Roger Jackson, Toronto.

Sifton Reaches Yukon

*This is the law of the Yukon, that
   only the Strong shall thrive;
That surely the Weak shall perish,
   and only the Fit survive.
Dissolute, damned and despairful,
   crippled and palsied and slain,
This is the Will of the Yukon;—
   Lo, how she makes it plain!*
— ROBERT W. SERVICE, 1907

*I am the land that listens, I am the
   land that broods;
Steeped in eternal beauty, crystalline
   waters and woods.
Long have I waited lonely, shunned as
   a thing accurst,
Monstrous, moody, pathetic, the last
   of the lands and the first.*
— ROBERT W. SERVICE, 1907

Canada lost Pacific coast access to the Yukon in the boundary decision of 1905 (see March 25). Canada might have lost the entire Yukon during the 1897 gold rush if Minister of the Interior Sir Clifford Sifton and the Northwest Mounted Police had not taken prompt action.

During the gold rush the boundary question had not been decided, so Canadians were able to reach the Yukon through Skagway and Dyea. When the prospectors reached the Yukon they had to buy licences costing $10, and the annual renewal fee went as high as $100 for a time. They also had to pay royalties on the gold they obtained, and one man could stake only one claim in the Klondike. American prospectors had to pay 35 per cent import duty on goods they brought with them. They were very angry about the taxes and restrictions, but Canada pointed out that it was costing $390,000 a year to keep law and order in the Yukon. The Mounties did keep law and order in their usual remarkable manner. No one was allowed to carry a gun, gambling establishments were closed on Sundays, and criminals were sent out of the country.

The position of the Yukon boundary was so unsettled that Sir Clifford Sifton decided to look into it himself. He traveled from Ottawa with a group of officials and landed at Skagway on October 9, 1897. One of the members of the party was Major Walsh of the Northwest Mounted Police who had kept Chief Sitting Bull in check (see May 6). Major Walsh set up posts in the Lake Bennett-Lake Tagish area, and Sifton ordered another detachment of Mounties under Major Steele to police the entrances at the summits of the passes. This was done in February 1898.

The police arrived just in time because the United States was planning to send troops into the Yukon. If the Americans had gone in to police the area, it is likely that they would have remained and the Yukon would have been lost to Canada.

Other Events on October 9:

1682   Joseph le Febvre de la Barre and Jacques Demeulle were appointed Governor and Intendant of Canada, replacing Frontenac and Duchesneau who were recalled. Demeulle created "card money" (see April 18).

1811   The first Selkirk settlers for Red River landed at York Factory, Hudson Bay.

1820   A proclamation rejoining Cape Breton to Nova Scotia was issued. They had been separated in 1784.

1838   Lord Durham resigned as Governor of British North America.

1899   The Soulanges Canal was opened. This completed a waterway from Quebec to Lake Superior.

1909   The Grand Falls Paper Mill opened in Newfoundland.

1918   Canadian troops were in action at Cambrai, leading to the end of World War I.

1961   Mrs. Franklin D. Roosevelt opened Memorial University at St. John's, Newfoundland.

1963   Canada and the United States agreed to store nuclear missiles in Newfoundland.

Champlain's arrival at Quebec

Champlain Wounded

After Champlain founded Quebec in 1608 he wanted to explore inland. In order to do this he had to be on friendly terms with the Montagnais Indians in the Montreal area, and their allies, the Algonquins and Hurons farther inland. This meant joining those three tribes in their wars against the Iroquois. It was a decision that cost France dearly in years to come as the Iroquois were far better fighters.

Champlain made a big hit with his Indian allies in 1609 when he accompanied them to what is now Crown Point, Lake Champlain, and used firearms on the Iroquois for the first time. He even drew a picture of the scene. His Indians won a great victory over the dreaded Iroquois and Champlain was "in" solidly. The trouble was that his Indians wanted repeat performances, and arranged a really big campaign for 1615. When he returned from a trip to France they met him at Tadoussac, and urged him to go to the Huron country between Lake Simcoe and Georgian Bay. He would lead 2,500 Hurons in an invasion of Iroquois country.

Champlain was delighted to have the opportunity to explore so far and arrived at the chief Huron village of Cahiagué (now Hawkestone) in September. He had traveled up the Ottawa River to the Mattawa, and then on to Lake Nipissing. From there he turned south until he came to a body of water so large that he could hardly believe his eyes. He called it Mer Douce, or Fresh-Water Sea. It was Georgian Bay.

The plan was to attack the Onondagas, and wipe them out. The Hurons were confident that they could do it with the help of Champlain and his men, armed with guns. The attack on October 10, 1615, was a failure. The Indians had no leader of their own and could not be controlled. They were so overconfident that they would not travel quietly, and the Iroquois at Onondaga knew they were coming. They would not use their usual shields when they attacked and the Iroquois mowed them down with their arrows. Champlain and his men used their guns, but the Onondagas were brave and accepted their losses. The battle was over in three hours. Champlain was wounded, having been hit in the leg by an arrow, and had to be carried away. The Hurons were supposed to take the French back to Quebec, but they refused to do so. Champlain had to spend the winter at Cahiagué. It was an uncomfortable, sometimes disgusting experience, but Champlain learned a great deal about Indian lore during the winter months, and wrote a book about his sojourn there (see January 9).

Other Events on October 10:

1792 Alexander Mackenzie left Lake Athabaska for a trip to the Pacific (see July 22).

1864 Delegates from Canada and the Atlantic Provinces gathered at Quebec to draw up a framework for Confederation. The conference lasted until October 28.

1878 The Liberal government under Alexander Mackenzie resigned after their election defeat. The Conservatives under Sir John A. Macdonald came into power.

1911 Sir Robert Borden succeeded Sir Wilfrid Laurier as prime minister.

1950 Canada and the United States ratified the Hydro Power Treaty.

Riel Makes Debut

Whereas, it is admitted by all men, as a fundamental principle, that the public authority commands the obedience and respect of its subjects. It is also admitted that a people, when it has no Government in preference to another, to give or to refuse allegiance to that which is proposed.

—Proclamation of the Provincial Government of the Northwest, Dec. 8, 1869, signed by John Bruce and Louis Riel.

If ever, in time to come, we should have the misfortune to become divided — as foreigners have sought before — that will be the signal for all disasters which we have until now so happily avoided. But let us hope that the lessons of the past will guide us in the future!

LOUIS RIEL, 1870

One of the most dramatic scenes in Canadian history took place in Manitoba on October 11, 1869. Canada was in the process of taking over the huge Northwest Territory. The half-breed settlers, known as Métis, who had lived and hunted there for many years, were greatly disturbed because they did not know what would happen to their lands. They had no legal papers showing that they owned anything. They simply had "squatters rights."

The Métis were led by twenty-five-year-old Louis Riel. His grandmother had been the first white child born in the Red River settlement, and his father had played a leading part in breaking the Hudson's Bay Company monopoly. Young Riel had been educated in Montreal, and was known to be brilliant, but vain and unstable.

When Sir John A. Macdonald's government decided to take over the territory, it moved quickly, for a number of reasons. Ottawa had received secret information that the United States was planning to take over the area and had agents working there (see September 28). Although a number of local organizations had been formed to provide some control, the sooner Canada could take over, the better it would be.

The greatest difficulty was that the Métis and other settlers were badly informed. Practically no official information was given to the few newspapers. The Canadian Government had no intention of depriving the Métis of their holdings, but it was necessary to survey the area, so that fair shares could be allocated to all claimants. Public Works Minister William McDougall sent out survey parties to do the preparatory work, without explaining their purpose to the settlers.

On October 11, one of the survey crews began working on land claimed by André Nault, a cousin of Louis Riel. Nault tried to stop them, but they waved him away, so he saddled a horse and rode for help. In a short time he came back with sixteen Métis whose leader put a moccasined foot on the surveyors' chain and said "You go no further."

So, Louis Riel appeared on the stage of national affairs, and the part he played has not been forgotten, even today. It was the beginning of the Red River uprising, which still influences the political life of Canada.

Other Events on October 11:

1676   Public markets were established at Quebec, Trois Rivières, and Montreal. Trade elsewhere was prohibited.

1776   Sir Guy Carleton defeated the Americans at Lake Champlain but General Benedict Arnold escaped.

1875   The first Icelanders arrived at Winnipeg.

1910   The Ontario Hydro Electric system was opened at Berlin (now Kitchener), Ontario.

1917   An order-in-council prohibited strikes and lockouts during the war.

1958   Prime Minister Walter Nash of New Zealand visited Ottawa.

1960   The Federal Government announced a program to help low income families obtain rental housing.

1962   Two hundred Canadian *Starfighter* aircraft left for Germany.

Samuel Vetch (1668-1732)

Port Royal Taken

It is sometimes difficult to judge when to use "Acadia" and when to use "Nova Scotia." The best date is 1713 when the Treaty of Utrecht was signed. Although France kept Cape Breton, the treaty gave all "Nova Scotia, or Acadia . . . to the Queen of Great Britain and to her crown forever."

The change from Acadia to Nova Scotia was brought about by Samuel Vetch, a Scotsman, who became a successful trader in Boston. His ambitions, however, went far beyond earning money; he wanted to drive Spain and France from the continent, and make Queen Anne "sole Empress of the vast North American continent." Vetch went to London and persuaded the Government to provide a fleet and troops to capture Acadia, and eventually Canada. The New England merchants were keen to capture Acadia because Port Royal had become a base for privateers who were attacking their ships. In 1708, they had

captured or destroyed thirty-five vessels. The next year one privateer left Port Royal and in twelve days captured four ships laden with wheat and corn.

The expedition was put in charge of another remarkable man, Colonel Francis Nicholson, who during his career served as Governor of Virginia, New York, Maryland, and Carolina. The British force arrived in Boston in July, 1710, but did not sail into Port Royal Harbor until late in September. The military force included a regiment of Royal Marines, and four battalions of troops from New England. Vetch was adjutant-general, and was to become Governor of Acadia if the campaign were successful.

There were no more than 250 French soldiers to defend Port Royal, and they were there only because Subercase, the commander of the fort, had paid them with money he had borrowed; France had sent no supplies for two years. Subercase was a stubborn fighter, but his small force was no match for Nicholson's 2,000 men. He surrendered on October 12, 1710, and the French flag was replaced by the British. Port Royal was renamed Annapolis Royal in honor of the queen, and from then on Nova Scotia, except for Cape Breton, would belong to Britain.

Other Events on October 12:

1689 Frontenac arrived at Quebec for his second term as governor.

1841 Alexander McLeod was acquitted in the *Caroline* case that almost caused war between Britain and the States.

1887 Sir Richard Cartwright, a prominent Canadian political leader, supported unrestricted reciprocity with the United States.

1907 The Canadian Government agreed to pay for damages caused by mobs raiding the Chinese and Japanese sections of Vancouver (see September 9).

1957 The Honorable L. B. Pearson, Minister of External Affairs, was awarded the Nobel Peace Prize.

Canada Recognizes China

At the beginning of the 20th century, Britain was still guiding Canada's foreign relations. Later in the century, Canada was often accused of following the lead of the U.S.A. in foreign affairs, despite Ottawa's refusal to join the Organization of American States. But there was consternation in Canada, the U.S.A. and some other parts of the world on October 13, 1970, when Mitchell Sharp, Minister of External Affairs, announced in the House of Commons that Canada was giving official recognition to the Republic of China.

The move should not have come as a surprise. Negotiations had been taking place for twenty-two months. In fact, the first steps dated back to 1960 when Communist China bought 200,000,000 bushels of wheat from Canada. This deal was negotiated by the Conservative government led by John Diefenbaker.

Relations became closer when Pierre Elliott Trudeau became Prime Minister in 1968 (see April 6). Trudeau had paid extensive visits to China in 1949 and 1960. The second visit was as a member of the first group of white Westerners to be admitted since the revolution and the visit lasted six weeks. In 1966, Trudeau was a member of the Canadian delegation to the United Nations and he was in favour of the Communist government's admission as the official representative of China at the U.N. He also told his colleagues that Canada should recognize Communist China.

Canada's delay in recognizing Communist China is believed to have been due to unwillingness to embarrass the U.S.A. By 1970, the U.S.A. probably welcomed Canada's move. The New York Times reported that most Americans approved; only the most bitter anti-Communists were opposed.

Canada's move was soon followed by the establishment of an embassy from Peking in Ottawa. Communist China was admitted to United Nations as the official representative of China, and President Nixon of the U.S.A. announced that he was going to China to visit the Communist leaders.

There is little doubt that Canada's recognition of China in 1970 helped to break the dangerous log jam in international affairs.

Other Events on October 13:

1755   A large number of Acadians were deported to South Carolina.

1812   General Isaac Brock was killed in battle at Queenston in the war of 1812. His troops went on to victory, driving the Americans back across the border.

1899   Canada organized a contingent to fight in the South African war.

1917   The first class were called to military service under the new conscription act.

1957   Queen Elizabeth made her first television broadcast.

1961   The Canadian Maritime Union was formed to compete with the Seafarers International Union.

1962   A bad storm on the Pacific coast killed forty-six people in British Columbia and the United States.

Brock Monument, Queenston, Ontario

Jerry Potts (1840-1896)

Fort Macleod Begun

It is said that "the Mounties always get their man." One of the best men they got was Jerry Potts, but he was not a criminal. He served as police scout and guide for twenty-two years. No gallery of famous characters in Canadian history would be complete without a picture of Jerry: round-shouldered, bow-legged, pigeon-toed, and scarred from head to foot from fights with Indians.

Jerry was half Indian himself and could get along with Indians or with white men equally well. Some of his adventures are described in Grant MacEwan's book, *Fifty Mighty Men*. The Mounties discovered him when they were making their long march west in 1874.

They were trying to get to Old Man River to establish a base, but they became lost when they reached Sweet Grass. Colonel Macleod made a side trip to Fort Benton on the Missouri River, and heard about Jerry Potts. He persuaded him to help the new police force, and they went to Sweet Grass together.

Needless to say, the Mounties were not impressed by Potts at first, but they soon learned that there was no better man on the prairies to help them out of trouble. When water was needed, Jerry could find a spring. When food was scarce Jerry could find a buffalo. He was never lost, even in the dark. On one occasion when he was looking for a pile of stones as a landmark, Colonel Macleod asked, "What's the matter? Are you lost?" Potts answered, "No, stones lost!" He seldom spoke when he was traveling, but concentrated on looking for the landmarks that would show him the way. He guided the first force from Sweet Grass to Old Man River where they began building Fort Macleod on October 14, 1874.

In one of his early Indian fights, Jerry Potts received a gun pellet in the flesh below his left ear, but always refused to let it be taken out. It was his good-luck charm. Somehow the pellet worked its way out in 1896 and he was greatly disturbed. He died later in the year, and was buried at Fort Macleod with full military honors.

Other Events on October 14:

1747   Admiral Hawke defeated a French fleet bound for Canada.

1841   A Royal charter was issued for the University of Kingston (Presbyterian).

1844   John A. Macdonald was elected to Parliament as member for Kingston.

1935   The Liberals won a general election with 173 seats, Conservatives 40, Social Credit 17 (first time), C.C.F. 7, Reconstruction Party 1.

1952   The Honorable L. B. Pearson, Minister of External Affairs, was elected President of the United Nations Assembly.

Tracy Takes New York Territory For New France

The State of New York was taken over by Canada on October 15, 1666, but the New Yorkers knew nothing about it then, and refuse to recognize it now!

France was making a determined effort to defeat the Iroquois, and drive the English and Dutch out of North America. The famous Carignan-Salières Regiment under the Marquis of Tracy was sent out to Quebec to do the job. Tracy and his soldiers, who had fought with distinction in the Turkish War, made a magnificent impression when they arrived at Quebec, their blue coats piped with white, plumed hats, long leather boots turned back half-way over the calves, muskets carried in slings over their shoulders. People cheered when they marched from Lower Town to the summit of the cliff.

Yet these famous soldiers had to learn a new type of fighting. They were taken on a winter expedition against the Iroquois by Governor Courcelles and it was a complete failure. When they returned, Tracy had them trained in forest fighting, and taught them how to look after themselves on the long marches through Indian country.

By September, 1666, Tracy decided that the regiment was ready to invade what is now New York State, home of the Iroquois. One of the members of the invasion force was a Sulpician priest who had been given a special name for the invasion: Monsieur Colson. Actually, he was François Dollier de Casson, who had been a well-known soldier in France. He became a priest because he was disgusted with the cruelties of warfare. De Casson was very strong, and often called "the Samson of New France." On one occasion two "Annies", as the French called the Iroquois, tried to take him by surprise, stealing up behind and attacking him. He lifted them in the air, knocked their heads together till they were unconscious, and threw them aside.

It was a tough march to the Iroquois settlements but their conquest was easy; the troops burned them, and destroyed the crops. Then, on October 15, 1666, Tracy raised a cross bearing the lilies of France, and proclaimed the territory as belonging to New France.

Other Events on October 15:

1851 Lady Elgin turned the sod for the Northern Railway.

1864 Premier Tilley of New Brunswick, at the Quebec Conference, demanded that a railway be built between Canada and the Maritimes as a condition of Confederation.

1884 The first issue of *La Presse* appeared in Montreal.

1953 The Trans-Mountain oil pipeline was completed between Edmonton and Vancouver.

1954 Hurricane Hazel killed eighty-two people and caused $24 million damage.

1959 The provinces demanded a greater share of taxes at a federal-provincial conference.

Marquis de Tracy (c. 1596-1670)

Phips' Armada Confronts Frontenac at Quebec

Britain made a number of attempts to destroy French power in North America before Amherst and Wolfe staged their successful campaigns from 1758 to 1760. One of them was in 1690, and its leader was William Phips, a former ship's carpenter and sailor. He did not learn to read or write until he was thirty, when he went to live in Boston. Then he got lucky. He married a wealthy widow, and found a sunken Spanish ship which had a treasure of £300,000 of which he was allowed to keep £16,000.

Phips was now a great figure in the public eye, and early in 1690 was put in charge of an expedition to capture Port Royal in Acadia. He was completely successful, made the inhabitants of that part of Acadia swear allegiance to William and Mary, and plundered them unmercifully. He became an even greater hero.

In 1690, Phips was put in charge of an expedition against Quebec. He accepted the task—modestly for him—saying, "The plan is well formed and I am the best man to handle it." Actually he knew practically nothing about military tactics, and in this campaign he was up against a wily warrior, Count Frontenac. When his armada of 32 ships arrived off Quebec on October 16, 1690, Frontenac was prepared.

Phips sent a young officer ashore to demand Frontenac's surrender. Frontenac had him blindfolded, and rushed through the streets to the summit. The young officer was made to climb over barricades and other obstacles, and was breathless when he appeared before Frontenac. The young officer said that he came in the name of William and Mary, King and Queen of England, to demand instant surrender. Frontenac replied that he knew no William, a lawful king, but only William the usurper. Then he added, "Ma défense se fera par la bouche de mes canons."

Phips bombarded Quebec for a few days, and tried to land troops at Beauport. Although he had a far superior force, he did not have the military experience to cope with Frontenac, and had to give up the battle after a week of frustration. The chapel at Quebec, *Notre Dame des Victoires*, commemorates the occasion.

Other Events on October 16:

1679 A meeting of the Quebec Council voted that liquor should not be taken to Indian villages.

1820 Cape Breton was returned to Nova Scotia following the proclamation of October 9.

1869 Joseph Howe left Fort Garry after a fact-finding trip for the Government.

1911 Winnipeg received the first electric power.

1914 The first contingent of Canadian troops for World War I landed at Plymouth.

1918 Canada and the States made a reciprocal trade arrangement whereby the States took wheat and flour from Canada.

1942 R.C.M.P. patrol vessel *St. Roch* completed a voyage from Vancouver to Halifax via the Arctic. The ship left Vancouver June 2, 1940.

Sir William Phips (1651-1695)

T.C.A. Organized

The Douglas DC-8

Occasionally a politician emerges who likes to get things done and is prepared to bulldoze his measures through the House of Commons, if necessary. The Right Honorable C. D. Howe, Member of Parliament for Port Arthur, Ontario, was such a man.

One of Howe's greatest achievements was the creation of Air Canada, originally called Trans-Canada Airlines. Parliament passed the act establishing it in April, 1937. When the airline was organized it was designed to serve major communities spread across more than 4,000 miles of mountain, forest, and prairie. Today it operates over 40,000 miles, serving the States, the Caribbean, Britain, and continental Europe. The more appropriate name *Air Canada* was adopted in 1964.

Trans-Canada Airlines inaugurated its first commercial flight on September 1, 1937, between Vancouver and Seattle. It had only two 10-passenger Lockheed aircraft and a Stearman bi-plane, acquired when it bought out Canadian Airways Company on the Pacific Coast.

Airports and navigational aids were more advanced in Western Canada; so headquarters were established at Winnipeg. By October 17, 1938, after extensive training of pilots and ground crews, T.C.A. was ready to carry mail and freight between Montreal and Vancouver. Passenger service was inaugurated on April 1, 1939. The journey from Montreal to Vancouver took eighteen hours. Now it is made in six hours by DC-8 jetliners.

The original pilots still with the company include George Lothian, Herbert Seagrim, J. L. Root, W. E. Barnes, J. A. Jones, L. K. Lewis, J. A. Wright and M. B. Barclay. They used to employ a number of tricks to gain enough altitude to fly over the Rockies. Pilots flying from Lethbridge to Vancouver would turn east rather than west to catch the air current which flowed over the mountains and hit the ground. The pilots would ride the rising air to gain altitude! Passengers had to wear oxygen masks when flying over the mountains and occasionally on other routes when it became necessary to fly at an altitude of more than 10,000 feet to escape bad weather.

Since 1937 Air Canada has grown from 72 employees and three aircraft to an international carrier employing 12,000 men and women, with a fleet of seventy-eight turbine aircraft. It is now one of the world's largest commercial airlines, and has assets worth nearly $300 million.

Other Events on October 17:

1760   Sappers under "Foul-weather Jack" Byron, grandfather of the poet, destroyed fortifications at Louisburg, Nova Scotia. The work took two years.

1777   The Americans defeated the British under General Burgoyne at Saratoga.

1794   Captain George Vancouver sailed from Nootka Sound after his third voyage.

1877   Chief Sitting Bull refused to return to the United States (see May 6).

1878   Sir John A. Macdonald became Prime Minister again and remained in office until his death in 1891.

1910   The first cruiser of the Royal Canadian Navy, H.M.S. *Niobe,* arrived at Halifax.

1963   Old Age Pensions were increased to $75 a month.

1971   Premier Alexei Kosygin of Russia arrived in Canada for a nine-day state visit.

Sir William Alexander (c. 1567-1640)

King Offers Baronetcy

One of the greatest gifts in the history of the world was made by King James I of England in 1621. He gave William Alexander territory now known as Newfoundland, Nova Scotia, New Brunswick, Maine, and part of Quebec!

Alexander was tutor to King James' son, Prince Henry, and had some reputation as a poet. One of his works was *Doomes-Day*, eleven thousand lines which were very dull. King James, who authorized the revision of the Bible used by most Protestant churches today, wanted to rewrite the Psalms himself, in metric form. Alexander helped him, for the poetry tutor had an unusually good eye for business. The continent of America already contained a New England, New France, and New Spain; so he persuaded King James to give him territory that could be developed as New Scotland, or Nova Scotia.

Alexander became "Sir William" and was authorized to offer grants of land 3 by 6 miles along the sea coasts "to all such principal knights and esquires as will be pleased to be undertakers of the said plantation and who will promise to set forth six men, artificers or laborers, sufficiently armed, apparelled and victualled for two years." Alexander was to "erect cities, appoint fairs, hold courts, grant lands and coin money." He certainly would "coin money" if he owned that territory today!

The knights and esquires were slow to take up the grants of land, however, so King James provided an additional incentive on October 18, 1624, by creating an order called "Knights Baronet of Nova Scotia." Any man could be a "Baronet of Nova Scotia" if he went to live on his grant of land, or paid a sum of £150. He would have the right to wear about his neck "an orange tawney ribbon from which shall hang pendant in an escutcheon agent a saltire azure with the arms of Scotland."

The scheme never developed to any great extent, but there are descendants of the Baronets of Nova Scotia still alive today. Headquarters of the order is in the castle of Clackmannanshire in Scotland.

Other Events on October 18:

1646   The Iroquois broke their peace agreement and killed Fathers Joques and Lalande.

1748   By the Treaty of Aix-la-Chapelle, Louisburg was restored to France in exchange for Madras, India.

1951   Canada agreed to maintain an army and air force in Europe under NATO.

1957   The Montreal *Herald* stopped publication after 146 years.

1963   Longshoremen marched on Ottawa protesting the appointment of trustees to oversee their affairs.

1965   Abraham Okpik became the first Eskimo member of the Council of the Northwest Territories.

War Measures Act Passed

Canadians were shocked on October 19, 1970, when the House of Commons passed the War Measures Act. They knew that the federal and Quebec governments had been struggling with the Front de Liberation du Quebec (F.L.Q.) since October 5, when British Trade Commissioner James Cross had been kidnapped and held for ransom.

Quebec Labor Minister, Pierre Laporte, was kidnapped next on October 10, and his body was discovered eight days later. He had been murdered by his abductors, a cell of the F.L.Q.

The nation was greatly concerned for the safety of Cross and was horrified by the murder of Laporte. Suddenly everyone realized that the Province of Quebec, and perhaps all of Canada, was threatened by a subversive movement. Prime Minister Trudeau, Opposition Leader Stanfield, and other leading members of the House of Commons appeared on television to explain why wartime measures were necessary. The situation was clarified later in the book *The October Crisis*, written by cabinet minister Gerard Pelletier (see story for April 6). In his words:

> "History shows that major political upheavals are often brought by the action of a handful of resolute men who will stop at nothing and who reject the rules of legal protest. If they succeed and the majority of the people follow them, we have a change of regime which can only survive by preventing others from using the very methods that brought it into power. If they succeed without the support of the people, we have a dictatorship of the military type."

The F.L.Q. had been working for eight years to separate the Province of Quebec from Canada. It had planted nearly one hundred bombs in the Montreal area, some of which caused death and injury. It had staged a number of holdups to get explosives, military weapons, and other equipment.

The purpose of the kidnapping of British

Troops patrol downtown Montreal near Notre Dame Church, where funeral of slain Quebec cabinet member Pierre Laporte was held.

diplomat Cross was to blackmail the governments for $500,000 (later waived) and to publish the F.L.Q. manifesto (which was broadcast by the C.B.C.).

The War Measures Act enabled the governments to send troops to Montreal to help the Quebec Provincial and Montreal City Police who were exhausted after two weeks of constant duty. Eventually, a deal was made whereby Cross was released unharmed and his kidnappers were allowed to go to Cuba. Those responsible for the murder of Laporte were caught and sent to trial.

Other Events on October 19:

1690 Phips' attack on Quebec was repulsed at Beauport.

1787 The Mississauga Indians in Ontario were given a grant of land and £2,000. They owned the very valuable land between Toronto and Hamilton, and other areas.

1864 Confederate soldiers in the American Civil War attacked St. Albans, Vermont, from Canada.

1869 The Red River Metis organized themselves on hearing the news that Canada was taking over Hudson's Bay Company territory.

1869 The last spike of the European and North American Railroad was driven at Vanceboro (near the Maine-New Brunswick border).

Manitoba Railway Conflict Almost Causes "War"

"Danger! Railway Crossing" is a familiar sign. On October 20, 1888, a railway crossing nearly caused civil war in Manitoba. The provincial government had broken the C.P.R. monopoly and arranged to have a railway built from Winnipeg to the American border where it would connect with the Northern Pacific Railway. It was hoped that the competition would lead to lower freight rates, and the C.P.R. was determined to fight the measure to the last ditch to prevent this.

One track of this new Red River Valley railway was to go to Portage la Prairie, and would have to cross C.P.R. tracks. As the Red River Valley workers got close to Headingly, where the crossing was to be made, they saw a derailed locomotive blocking the way. It had been placed there by order of C.P.R. superintendent William Whyte. There were also five railway cars nearby carrying about 250 workmen who had been sworn in as special constables.

There was consternation in Winnipeg. Fifty-three men were sworn in as special constables. A train carrying the constables and another 200 citizens left the city at 3:30 p.m. and stopped about 1 mile south of St. James' Bridge, where the two railways were supposed to cross. The situation was tense. Chief Clark of the Provincial Police told the C.P.R. men that their appointments as special constables had been cancelled. Alderman T. Nixon, a justice of the peace, promptly swore them in again.

Meanwhile the Red River Valley track-layers were getting closer to the crossing. The Winnipeg citizens were determined that the C.P.R. men should not stop them, and a special train was sent to Winnipeg to bring back soldiers.

The expected "war" did not take place because the Red River Valley track-layers were still several hundred yards from the crossing when darkness fell. Most people went back to Winnipeg for the night, and cooler heads had prevailed by morning. The matter was referred to the Supreme Court of Canada which ruled that the Legislature of Manitoba had the power to charter railways within the bounds of "old Manitoba." The new railway was allowed to go through.

Other Events on October 20:

1686 An Ursuline convent, founded in 1639, was burned at Quebec.

1818 The Convention of London regulated the North American fisheries and the boundary west of Lake of the Woods.

1855 The Government moved to Toronto.

1867 Ottawa was proclaimed as the seat of government of Canada.

1887 A conference of premiers endorsed reciprocity with the United States.

1899 Britain and the United States failed to agree on the Alaska boundary.

1919 United Farmers won the Ontario election; E. C. Drury became premier.

1920 British Columbia ended prohibition by voting for government control.

1922 Bonar Law became the first man born outside Britain to become British Prime Minister. He was born at Rexton, New Brunswick.

1960 Sir John A. Macdonald Hall, the new law school of Queen's University, was officially opened by Prime Minister Diefenbaker, and Dr. John Bertram Stirling was installed as the University's eighth Chancellor.

1964 Charges of police brutality at demonstrations during the Royal Visit to Quebec were termed exaggerated in the report of Acting Attorney-General Wagner.

Wheat Shipped East

You have been blessed with an abundant harvest, and soon I trust will a railway come to carry to those who need it the surplus of your produce, now — as my own eyes have witnessed — imprisoned in your storehouses for want of the means of transport.

LORD DUFFERIN at Winnipeg, 1877

Perhaps the most important contributing factor in the development of Canada has been the growing of wheat. The first shipment of wheat from Manitoba to eastern Canada took place on October 21, 1876. It was 857 bushels of Red Fife grown in Kildonan, Springfield and Rockwood. The order had been for 5,000 bushels, but it was not possible to gather that much so late in the season. The first shipment of wheat overseas took place in 1884, and went from Brandon, Manitoba, to Glasgow, Scotland.

Red Fife was developed originally by David Fife, near Peterborough, Ontario. There is a memorial to him on the highway between Toronto and Peterborough. Fife had been sent a sample of wheat by a friend in Glasgow. He thought it was wheat to be planted in the autumn and harvested the following summer, but only three plants grew. Two of them, it is said, were eaten by a cow. Fife kept the remaining seed and planted it the following April. This time it grew far more successfully. It was harder than other spring wheats and ripened nearly two weeks faster than other seed of its type, thus lessening the risk of being spoiled by early September frost. He called it Red Fife.

Fife's first market for the new wheat was the Middle West of the United States. In 1868 the Red River crops were destroyed by a plague of grasshoppers and the settlers had to buy seed from their neighbors across the border. That was the way Red Fife came to be tried on the Canadian Prairies, and it was a tremendous success. It not only proved to be the most suitable wheat for the soil already under cultivation, but it enabled wheat to be grown much farther north.

Of course improvements were made on Red Fife. The introduction of the wheat, followed by the production of better harvesting machinery and better milling processes, soon made "Canadian Number 1 Hard" the finest wheat in the world. It led to the great immigration to western Canada that brought more than 2 million new settlers to Canada in 15 years.

Other Events on October 21:

1755 Another large group of Acadians was sent to British colonies in the south.

1852 Robert Campbell began the 3,000 mile snowshoe walk of his 9,000-mile journey to find a wife (see September 6).

1880 A contract was signed with the present Canadian Pacific Railway Company to build the transcontinental railway.

1886 Canada protested the seizure of United States fishing vessels in the Bering Sea.

1887 Premiers met at Quebec to discuss grievances against the Federal Government. Premier Mercier of Quebec mentioned the possibility of his province's leaving Confederation and becoming the "Laurentian State."

1963 The House of Commons concurred in a report of the Committee on Privileges and Elections to give precedence in the House to the Thompson Social Credit Party. It also recognized the Caouette Social Credit Rally.

Canada and Britain agreed to develop heavy water reactors using a Canadian nuclear process.

1965 Governor - General Vanier officially opened the Concordia Bridge, linking Montreal Island with the man-made islands of the Expo '67 site.

Fourteen-Year-Old Girl Saves "Fort Dangerous"

This day belongs to Madeleine Jarret de Verchères, a fourteen-year-old girl who became Canada's outstanding heroine. She lived at Verchères, about 20 miles from Montreal, in "Fort Dangerous," so called because it was on a route used constantly by the Iroquois and was liable to be attacked.

The summer of 1692 had been quiet, and Madeleine's father and mother decided that they could go away for a few days on business. The Iroquois had been waiting for such an opportunity, and they suddenly attacked the fort on the morning of October 22. Men and women were working in the fields, bringing in a bountiful harvest of pumpkins, melons, and fruit. Most of them were killed immediately. Madeleine was playing on a wharf when the massacre began, and she barely

Madeleine de Verchères

managed to elude one of the Indians as she dashed back to the fort and closed the gate.

There was panic inside. Two soldiers, who had been left to guard the fort, were prepared to blow it up rather than be captured and tortured by the Indians. Madeleine told them they were cowards and made them go to their posts.

Then she put on a soldier's hat to show that she had taken command, gave guns to her brothers, who were only twelve and ten years old, and told them to fight for their home and their religion. She rallied the people in the fort through her courage, and ordered the women to stop wailing and crying, which would only encourage the Indians. At her command a cannon was fired to warn the neighbors of the attack.

For eight days and eight nights, with little food or sleep, Madeleine organized a skillful defense of her home. She had the people moving around in the fort, shouting to each other as if they were soldiers. This led the Indians to believe that there were more people in the fort than was actually the case.

When help came from Montreal, Madeleine met the commanding officer at the gate, said, "I surrender my arms to you," and collapsed!

Most holders of the Victoria Cross would have taken off their hats to this brave girl, had they seen her courageous action. King Louis XIV granted a pension to her father in recognition of her bravery.

Other Events on October 22:

1690   Phips abandoned his attack on Quebec and sailed down the St. Lawrence.

1846   The first telegraph company was formed to serve Toronto, Hamilton and Niagara.

1958   Blanche Margaret Meagher was appointed Ambassador to Israel, the first Canadian woman to hold such a post.

Talon Begins Second Term as Intendant

One of the most remarkable men who ever came to Canada from France was Jean Baptiste Talon. He was the Intendant, or business manager, from 1665 to 1668, and served a second term from October 23, 1670, until 1672.

Jean Talon believed in seeing things for himself. When he first arrived at Quebec, there was a message from the nuns expressing the hope that he would protect them. Later that day a man called at the Hôtel Dieu and said he was the Intendant's valet. He wanted to know what the nuns needed in the way of protection. The nuns quickly realized that their visitor was no valet, but Talon himself. He often disguised himself in this way and went from door to door in Quebec and Montreal, learning about living conditions.

Talon enjoyed the confidence of Louis XIV and worked directly with him, rather than through the governor or the bishop. He was largely responsible for bringing out "the king's girls" (see April 5) in 1671. Before the end of the following year 1,100 babies had been baptized!—a big increase in a population of only seven thousand.

The new families needed homes, and Talon must have been Canada's first town-planner. A big problem was to provide every home with enough property to grow crops. Yet the houses could not be far apart or they would be attacked by the Indians. Talon solved the problem by shaping the new communities like pies. The homes were in the center, close together, but the properties stretched out behind them in the triangular shape of wedges of pie.

Talon sent survey parties throughout the country, and as far south as the lower Mississippi, to look for precious metals. He built the first iron foundry, tannery, brewery, and fish-processing plants. He also started a ship-building industry and developed trade with the West Indies.

When he finally returned to France in 1672, the king made him secretary of his cabinet, and gave him the title of Comte d'Orsainville, a name derived from his estate in Canada.

Other Events on October 23:

1785   The Government of New Brunswick was moved from Saint John to St. Anne's Point, now Fredericton.

1837   A meeting at St. Charles on the Richelieu River, Quebec, marked the beginning of the rebellion in Lower Canada.

1847   A telegraph service was opened between Montreal and Albany, New York.

1952   Canadian troops fought in the battle of "Little Gibraltar Hill," Korea.
Canada's new consumer-price index, constructed to replace the cost-of-living index, was released.

1958   An explosion in a coal mine at Springhill, Nova Scotia, killed seventy-four miners.

1963   The Maritime Union Trustees Act received royal assent. It appointed a three-man board to oversee maritime unions.

1964   Quebec Superior Court Justice Adrien Meunier was sentenced to imprisonment for two years on three perjury counts. This conviction of a judge in Quebec was believed to be without precedent.

Alexander Graham Bell (centre) with two friends

Bell Memorial Unveiled

The inventor of the telephone, Alexander Graham Bell, did some of his most important experimental work at Brantford, Ontario. His profession was teaching deaf people to lip-read, and curing impediments of speech. He also liked to play the piano.

One day he was visiting the home of Mabel Hubbard in Boston. He was playing the piano and suddenly said to her father, "Mr. Hubbard, sir, do you know that if I depress the *forte* pedal and sing "do" into the piano, the proper note will answer me, like this?" He pressed the pedal and sang "do"; the piano responded like an echo. Then he went on to explain that if two pianos in two different places were connected by a wire, and a note was struck on one, the same note would respond in the other! It was the beginning of what was known as the "multiple telegraph" from which Bell developed the telephone. Mr. Hubbard became one of his backers, and Bell married his daughter.

American publications often do not mention Bell's work in Canada on the development of the telephone. When the Bell Memorial was unveiled in Brantford, Ontario, on October 24, 1917, Alexander Graham Bell said that the telephone had been conceived in Brantford in 1874 and born in Boston in 1876. Brantford could justly claim the invention of the telephone and the first transmission of the human voice over real live wires.

In 1876, using the wires of the Dominion Telegraph Company, Bell installed a telephone transmitter in Paris and a receiver in Brantford, eight miles away. This was the first telephone call in history. Transmission went one way only but voices came through so clearly that Bell knew that his father was one of the speakers although he had not expected him to be there. The transmitter was in Paris, the receiver in Brantford, and the electric battery that enabled the sound to travel through wires was in Toronto, 68 miles away!

Alexander Graham Bell had wire strung all around Brantford, using stove pipes for poles. He was known as "Crazy Bell", and no inventor was more persecuted. After he invented the telephone a Boston newspaper insisted that he should be arrested for leading people to believe that it was possible to talk through a wire. Altogether, he had to face 600 lawsuits from others who claimed that they had invented the telephone. One of the claimants was a man called Reis. When his "telephone" was demonstrated in court, it failed to transmit speech. His lawyer explained, "It can speak, but it won't!" The patent for the telephone turned out to be the most valuable in the history of the world.

Other Events on October 24:

1705 An Act of Parliament provided for uniform circulation of card money (see April 18).

1852 The Toronto Stock Exchange was opened.

1903 The Grand Trunk Pacific Railway received a charter to build a line between Quebec and Winnipeg.

1945 Canada officially joined the U.N.

Steamship *Sophia* Hits Reef and Founders

One of the worst sea disasters on the Pacific coast took place on October 25, 1918. The Canadian Pacific Steamship *Sophia* left Skagway, Alaska, bound for Victoria and Vancouver. On board were 343 people "going outside" for the winter. Some of them were characters from Klondike gold rush days, and they formed a happy crowd of travelers. They gathered in the *Sophia's* lounge to sing the old dance hall songs and listen to the stories of William Scouse of Seattle, who had hoisted the first bucket of gold at Eldorado Creek twenty years before.

The ship was commanded by Captain Louis P. Locke, formerly of Nova Scotia. As the *Sophia* steamed through the night, it suddenly struck a hidden rock known as Vanderbilt Reef. The ship did not sink, but was listing badly. Captain Locke sent out an S.O.S. which brought the U.S. steamer *Cedar* and a number of small boats to the *Sophia's* assistance during the day. Unfortunately the wind was gale force and it was impossible to take off the passengers; so the captain of the *Cedar* decided to stand by until the wind moderated. The passengers were brave, and as happy as possible under the circumstances. They continued their songs around the piano, defying the storm and their thoughts of dying.

Suddenly, about five o'clock in the afternoon, *Sophia* began to founder. Captain Locke sent out a wireless signal: "For God's sake, come and save us." *Cedar* tried to come close but could not make it because of the high seas and a snowstorm that reduced visibility to nil.

The last that was heard from *Sophia* was a wireless message: "Just in time to say goodbye. We are foundering." All the passengers and crew, 343 in all, were lost. When the bodies were recovered many of them were carrying valuables. One negro woman had $80,000 in bills sewn into her clothing. Another victim was carrying $40,000. Several had gold dust with them, while another woman was carrying diamonds and rubies in a bag tied to her neck. The only survivor was a brown and white English setter that somehow swam to shore. It came into Tec Harbor two days later, its coat greasy with oil.

Other Events on October 25:

1666 Radisson and Groseilliers had an audience with King Charles II who promised them ships for an expedition to Hudson Bay (see August 28).

1768 Port La Joie, founded by the French, was renamed Charlottetown in honor of the wife of George III.

1780 Sir Frederick Haldimand, Governor of Quebec, protested that laws favored merchants and not the inhabitants.

1798 A boundary commission made the St. Croix River the southern border between New Brunswick and Maine.

1920 Plebiscites in Alberta, Saskatchewan, and Nova Scotia resulted in large majorities for prohibition.

The helpless Sophia *sinks on Vanderbilt Reef*

Victory at Chateauguay Saves Montreal

It seems strange that films showing cowboys fighting Indians should be so popular on American television. Perhaps cowboys fared better than soldiers in the Indian wars, but certainly the Canadian Indians terrified American troops during the War of 1812.

A great French-Canadian military leader, Colonel Charles de Salaberry, probably saved Montreal from being captured in 1813 by using the Indians to scare off a strong American force. While General Wilkinson was moving 8,000 American soldiers down the St. Lawrence towards Montreal, General Wade Hampton was preparing to attack from Lake Champlain, with 4,000 regular infantry, a squadron of cavalry, and 10 guns. After two days of heavy going through woods and marshes, his troops came to the Chateauguay stream in Canadian territory.

The British knew of the American plan and had sent De Salaberry to Chateauguay with four companies of his own Voltigeurs, Canadian militia, and 170 Indians. De Salaberry established a strong defensive position where the only road through the woods led to a ford across the river.

The attack began on October 25 and continued through the following day. Colonel de Salaberry had his Voltigeurs defending an advance position and also the ford. At the same time he sent a company of militia, some Indians, and all his buglers into the woods across the river. As De Salaberry expected, the Americans made a frontal attack on the forward position, while sending another force to try to take the ford. They ran into strong opposition from the Voltigeurs in their defensive positions, who were deadly shots with their muskets.

Then the sound of bugles and the war cries of the Indians were heard, giving the impression that a military force was coming from Montreal. The Americans were in such a state of panic that they began firing at each other. General Hampton ordered them to withdraw, spent three days considering what his next move should be, and then decided to retreat. Four thousand American soldiers had been turned back by 400 French-Canadians and their Indian allies.

When General Wilkinson heard that General Hampton had withdrawn, he also decided to give up. Montreal had been saved.

De Salaberry at Chateauguay, 1813

Other Events on October 26:

1678   The "Brandy Parliament" met to discuss the sale of liquor to the Indians.

1774   Congress invited the people of Canada to join the thirteen American colonies opposing Britain.

1848   Ottawa University was opened.

1850   Captain McClure of the Royal Navy discovered the Northwest Passage while searching for the Franklin expedition.

1934   The Honorable H. H. Stevens resigned from the Bennett government and formed his own Reconstruction Party.

1950   Canada and the United States announced agreement on six economic principles for joint defense production.

Holland Claims Acadia

During World War II, when Holland was occupied by the Germans, Princess Juliana and her three children were evacuated to Ottawa. The princess was due to give birth to another child, and since the baby would be in the direct line of succession to the throne of Holland, it was desirable that the birth should take place on Dutch territory. Prime Minister Mackenzie King arranged to have a room in the Ottawa Civic Hospital ceded to Holland, and the baby was born there.

It was not the first time that Holland had claimed territory in Canada. In the seventeenth century the Dutch were as active as the British, French and Spanish in the establishment of colonies. They had founded New York in 1626, calling it New Amsterdam, and invaded Newfoundland several times. In 1674, Captain Aernoutsz, who was based in the West Indies, decided to capture Acadia, which then belonged to France. He obtained the help of Captain John Rhoades of Boston, an experienced pilot, and organized an expedition which captured Governor Chambly and a number of small forts. Aernoutsz then claimed the territory for Holland, and on October 27, 1676, the Dutch West India Company appointed one Cornelius Steenwijck as governor of the newly-acquired province.

Aernoutsz tried to enforce a blockade so that the ships of other nations could not trade in Acadia. This annoyed the New Englanders who enjoyed a good trade there, and when some of their ships were seized by the Dutch, countermeasures were organized. An armed fleet sailed from Boston and intercepted some of Rhoades' ships in the Bay of Fundy. There was a sea battle in which Rhoades was captured, and then taken to Boston where he was tried for treason and piracy. Found guilty, he was fortunate not to have been hanged. The Dutch claim to Acadia ended abruptly, before Steenwijck had ever set foot there.

Cornelius Steenwijck (d.1684)

There is warm friendship today between Holland and Canada, because Canadian troops helped to drive out the Germans in 1944-1945. Every year Holland sends thousands of tulip bulbs to Ottawa, and their display in Ottawa is one of the outstanding attractions of the capital.

Other Events on October 27:

1812 The second party of Selkirk colonists arrive at the Red River.

1835 The legislature of Lower Canada opened an important session that dealt with a measure to light Montreal with gas.

1856 The Grand Trunk Railway was opened between Montreal and Toronto.

1883 Sir John A. Macdonald appealed for financial help for the C.P.R., then almost bankrupt.

1961 The Victoria Rifles of Canada celebrated its centennial. It is the oldest regiment in Montreal.

1962 A new agreement averted a strike of 6,000 employees of the C.P.R.

Blueprint for Confederation Drawn Up at Quebec

By October 28, 1864, the Quebec Conference (see October 19) had drawn up a blueprint for Confederation. Seventy-two resolutions had been discussed. When the delegates and their wives left for Montreal by special train, all but three resolutions had been approved, and these were dealt with at Montreal.

There was great jubilation because the delegates did not realize how difficult the days ahead would be—Confederation still had to be approved by the five provinces, then submitted to the British Parliament, and this was to take another two and a half years.

After their meeting at Montreal the delegates toured the chief cities of Upper and Lower Canada. They went first to Ottawa, the new capital chosen by Queen Victoria, and had lunch in the new Parliament Buildings, although they were only half-finished. Then they went on to Toronto, making stops at Kingston, Belleville, and Cobourg, where they were greeted by cheering crowds and brass bands. There was a torchlight procession in Toronto as they went from the station to the Queen's Hotel and four brass bands played along the route. Then the tour went on to Hamilton and St. Catharines. Everywhere, there was sight-seeing, speech-making, and a great deal of eating and drinking. The men did the eating and drinking, while their ladies, in true Victorian style, sat in the galleries and watched!

The most difficult problems solved by the seventy-two resolutions included that of striking a balance between federal and provincial powers—the American Civil War had shown how important it was to have a strong federal government. It was agreed that all powers not expressly assigned to the provinces should be reserved for the Federal Government, which could also disallow provincial legislation.

The provinces would lose a great deal of revenue by not being able to impose customs duties; so it was decided that the Federal Government would pay each province 80 cents for every member of its population. It was agreed to build the Intercolonial Railway between Canada and the Maritimes. The seventy-two resolutions also made provision for the Northwest, British Columbia, and Vancouver Island, should they decide to join the Confederation at a later date.

Other Events on October 28:

1790 The Nootka Convention concluded, ending Spain's claim to what is now the Pacific coast of Canada.

1851 The Hincks-Morin government came into power.

1891 The Supreme Court declared the Manitoba Separate School Acts unconstitutional.

1926 The Queen of Roumania visited Ottawa.

1950 Governor-General Alexander's term of office was extended for one year.

1954 R.C.M.P. patrol boat *St. Roch,* which went through the Northwest Passage both ways, ended its career in Vancouver where it is now on display.

1958 Prince Philip visited Ottawa until October 31 as President of the English-speaking Union.

Prime Minister and Mrs. Diefenbaker began a tour of European and Commonwealth countries.

1960 The Banting and Best Department of Medical Research, University of Toronto, received a gift of one million dollars for medical research from Garfield Weston, Canadian industrialist.

Stock Market Crash Rocks the World

October 29, 1929, was one of the most depressing days in Canadian history. Prices suddenly crashed on the world's stock markets, and Canada was plunged into ten years of poverty. One year after the crash there were 400,000 unemployed in Canada, and many people who had jobs were earning less than subsistence pay. Thousands of men looking for work traveled through the country by hiding in freight cars, or even "riding the rods" under them! Countless families, forced to live almost at starvation level for several years, were held together only by the courage, character, and self-sacrifice of parents and children.

People who could not find work went "on relief." Payments varied from place to place. A family of seven in Toronto received food vouchers worth $7 a week; in Saskatchewan a family of five was given $10 a month and a 98-pound sack of flour. Money was not to be spent on fruit, or any vegetables except potatoes and dried beans. Children often went to school without shoes or proper clothing.

The stock market craze in the years before the crash was worse than it is now. Brokers' offices were popular meeting places in town. Even little old ladies sat there and watched the magic figures on the boards, buying and selling with everyone from leading executives to office boys. They bought shares "on margin," paying perhaps 10 per cent of their value and owing the rest. When market prices suddenly collapsed the brokers called on them to pay what was owing, and they did not have enough money. The brokers could not collect the money owed to them by their customers, and they could not pay money they owed to banks and other lenders. People who, on the morning of October 29, were rich in terms of stocks and shares, found that these were worthless by evening. Conditions became so bad that hotel clerks would jokingly ask a man registering for a room, "Sleeping or jumping, sir?"

It was not until 1937 that economic conditions began to improve to any extent, and it was only the outbreak of war in 1939 that got factories and farms into full production, and provided employment at better wages.

Other Events on October 29:

1653   Radisson escaped from the Iroquois and went to Europe.

1899   The first Canadian contingent for the South African war sailed from Quebec.

1923   *Bluenose* defeated *Columbia* by one minute in an international challenge race (see March 26).

1925   General election: Conservatives took 116 seats, Liberals 101, Progressives and Independents 28, Labor 2. Nevertheless, Liberal Leader Mackenzie King formed a government by obtaining the support of the Progressives.

1952   An international joint commission approved the joint Canada-United States application for permission to develop the St. Lawrence River power.

1955   The latest type destroyer H.M.C.S. *St. Laurent* was commissioned at Montreal.

1964   The final report of the Special Committee on the Canadian Flag was presented to the House of Commons.

Henry Asbjorn Larsen, the noted Arctic explorer and RCMP superintendent, who captained the *St. Roch*, died.

Carleton Fails to Rescue Preston at St. Jean

The American Revolutionary War began in April, 1775, and by July a large force had been sent to Lake Champlain with orders to attack St. Jean on the Richelieu River, and then to capture Montreal. The commander of the American Army from New York was General Philip Schuyler and his instructions permitted him to capture any other part of the country provided that it would not be disagreeable to the Canadians! Many of the Americans believed Canadians would welcome an invasion to relieve them from "British tyranny." Indeed, some French-speaking Canadians and English-speaking businessmen did support the American cause. They even managed to send a Canadian battalion to help American General Montgomery.

Before trying to capture Montreal the Americans had to defeat a British force stationed at St. Jean, at the end of the navigable part of the Richelieu, the route from Lake Champlain. Its commander was Major Charles Preston who had 600 troops, most of them regulars, including a platoon of Scottish Loyalists. Although Montgomery surrounded the fort with a much larger force and urged Preston to surrender, the British commander held out through September and October.

Meanwhile, Governor Carleton had arrived in Montreal from Quebec and was trying to raise a force to rescue Preston at St. Jean. He had 200 regulars, and some of the seigniors persuaded about 1,200 habitants to join up. They did not like the war, or being taken from their farms when they should be doing their fall plowing. Scores of them deserted every night.

Carleton tried to take a force across the St. Lawrence on the night of October 30, but it was unable to land because of American gunfire. Major Preston had to surrender on November 3, and the way was now open for the Americans to march to Montreal. Carleton's only hope was to try to save Quebec, and to get there he made a spectacular trip down the river in disguise, under the noses of American patrols. He arrived just as General Arnold was beginning his attack on the city, and he maintained Quebec's defense until the following May, when the siege was lifted by the arrival of units of the Royal Navy.

Other Events on October 30:

1773   A meeting at Montreal petitioned King George III for an Assembly.

1846   The Great Western Railway was authorized to extend from Hamilton to Toronto.

1869   The British Government urged British Columbia to join Confederation.

1917   Montreal and Toronto stock markets put a minimum price system into effect.

1929   Ontario voted for continuation of the Liquor Control Act.

1962   Canada voted not to allow Red China to join the United Nations.

1963   A member of the Quebec F.L.Q. separatist group was sentenced to three years in prison for his part in a bombing incident.

Sir Guy Carleton (1724-1808)

Métis Stop MacDougall

In 1869, the Métis stopped the surveyors who had been sent from Canada to mark out the land that was being taken over from the Hudson's Bay Company (see October 11). The next act of the drama followed on October 31.

William McDougall, Minister of Public Works in the Macdonald government, had been appointed the first lieutenant-governor of the territory. Although Canada was not entitled to take over the territory until December 1, McDougall left Ottawa by train early in October. On the day that Riel stopped the survey party, McDougall was at St. Cloud, in Minnesota, preparing to complete the journey to Fort Garry by Red River cart. He was traveling like a king with his family, four assistants, and enough goods and chattels to fill sixty carts.

McDougall's progress towards the border was being reported to Riel by agents along the way. He reached Pembina on October 30 and was in the United States' Customs house when a Métis handed him a note. It was written in French and said that the National Committee of Métis of Red River ordered him not to enter the Northwest Territories without special permission of the committee.

McDougall was furious! Who were these upstarts ordering him not to enter the territory of which he had been appointed governor! The next day he sent his secretary, J. A. N. Provencher, into the territory to investigate. Provencher was traveling just ahead of Captain D. R. Cameron, who had recently married a daughter of Sir Charles Tupper. He found that the Métis had erected a barrier at the Rivière Sale. However, he made an effort to be friendly and attended mass. Then Captain Cameron came along with his bride and two servants. On reaching the barrier, he put a monocle in one eye, gazed coldly at the Métis, and roared, "Remove that blawsted fence!"

William McDougall (1822-1905)

Provencher and Cameron were escorted back to Pembina, and Sir Charles Tupper himself had to intervene to regain his son-in-law's baggage. McDougall had to stay at Pembina until December 1, when he crossed the border and read a proclamation that he had forged, announcing that Canada had taken over the territory (see December 1).

Other Events on October 31:

1685 La Salle began his exploration of the Mississippi.

1780 The schooner *Ontario* was lost on Lake Ontario.

1873 The International Bridge was opened at Niagara.

1902 Sandford Fleming sent the first cable to Australia.

1919 Werner Horn was sentenced at Fredericton to ten years in prison for attempting to blow up a bridge across the St. Croix River on February 2, 1915. It was wartime sabotage organized by a German spy ring operating in the United States.

1950 A 1,000-mile pipeline was completed between Edmonton and the Great Lakes.

The Katimavik (Eskimo word for "Meeting place"), a huge inverted pyramid, turned out to be the focal point of the Canadian Pavilion at the 1967 World Exhibition. The Canadian Government began its construction on June 18, 1965, and the pavilion, built on twenty-one acres of the largely man-made Ile de Notre Dame, was the largest at Expo.

Saskatchewan Opens Dept. of Municipal Affairs

In 1905, when Alberta and Saskatchewan became provinces, thousands of people were flocking to the Prairies. In the first ten years of the century, Winnipeg's population grew from 42,000 to 136,000; Regina's from 2,250 to 30,000; Edmonton's from 2,600 to 25,000; Calgary's from 4,400 to 44,000; and Saskatoon's from 113 to 12,000!

Because of this rapid growth the provincial governments and municipalities were under pressure to provide public services. On November 1, 1908, the Government of Saskatchewan established a Department of Municipal Affairs. Saskatchewan and Manitoba were the first provinces to do so.

The majority of newcomers were taking up holdings on the land, and their huge wheat-growing areas meant that homes were widely separated. Alexander Graham Bell's new-fangled telephone had been fully accepted after a long struggle, and was a blessing to the western farmers. In fact it was so essential to their welfare that a Rural Telephone Act was passed, making it possible for groups of five people to construct, maintain, and operate a rural telephone system. In his book *Saskatchewan: the History of a Province*, J. F. C. Wright has an amusing story of how the rural telephone systems provided entertainment before radio. One prolonged ring on the line was a signal for all subscribers to lift their receivers and listen. There might be an announcement of an auction sale, dance, or public meeting, or perhaps serious news about a fire or other tragedy.

Telephone conversations were seldom private, and were made with the knowledge that probably most of the other subscribers were listening. Their clocks could be heard ticking, or perhaps the shout of a child at play, or a sudden snore from grandfather asleep in his chair. However, no one ever "let on" that he or she was listening. If someone heard that a neighbor was going to town, he or she would allow an interval to elapse, then phone the neighbor and say "Do you happen to be going to town today? If so, I wonder if you would mind bringing back some groceries for us?" Radio was a blessing in later years but it never provided the intimate entertainment of the country telephone system!

Other Events on November 1:

1696   Iberville began a march across the Avalon Peninsula to take St. John's (see May 19).

1788   Bishop Inglis opened an academy at Windsor, Nova Scotia, which later became King's College.

1813   American General Wilkinson began a move down the St. Lawrence from Lake Ontario to attack Montreal.

1838   Lord Durham sailed for London after resigning as governor.

1847   A Normal School was opened in Toronto. T. J. Robertson was headmaster.

1850   Joseph Howe sailed for London to try to raise money to build a railway.

1893   A statue of Sir John A. Macdonald was unveiled at Hamilton, Ontario.

1895   The Independence of Canada Club adopted a platform.

1915   The Government launched the first Victory Loan Campaign.

1945   The United Nations Food and Agricultural Organization held a conference at Quebec with twenty nations represented.

1950   Restrictions on consumer credit were put into effect.

1955   The Honorable L. B. Pearson, then Minister of External Affairs, opened the "Canada Dam" at West Bengal, India.

Sir Alexander Tilloch Galt (1817-1893)

Galt Joins Sir John A.

Sir John A. Macdonald changed his mind about important matters of policy, and he was also good at persuading other people to change their minds. In 1864, Sir John voted against Confederation, and then became its leading architect. In 1865, he said that the Prairies were "of no present value to Canada" although he agreed that the Northwest should be kept from the United States. Four years later, Macdonald acquired the territory for Canada.

Among the important people Macdonald persuaded to change their minds were two leading Liberals, A. T. Galt and Joseph Howe, both of whom joined his government. Howe was probably sorry later because he was only given a minor job in the Macdonald cabinet, and the move angered his former friends and supporters in Nova Scotia—some would even cross the street when they saw him coming.

The winning over of Galt was amusing, but it also helped to pave the way for Confederation. The Liberals were known as the Rouge party in Quebec, and Galt was one of its most powerful members. He was, above all, a businessman, and made a great deal of money in the railway building boom. George Brown, leader of the Clear Grits, passed some critical comments on politicians who made fortunes from the railways, even if they were his allies. Galt was obviously annoyed, and Macdonald quickly took advantage of the situation. On November 2, 1857, he wrote to Galt: "My dear Galt: You call yourself a Rouge. There may have been at one time a reddish tinge about you but I observe it becoming by degrees fainter. In fact you are like Byron's Dying Dolphin, exhibiting a series of colors—the last still loveliest—and that last is true blue, being the color I affect. Seriously you would make a decent Conservative . . . so pray do become true blue at once: it is a good standing color and bears washing."

Galt joined the Macdonald government immediately after the "double-shuffle" in 1858 (see August 6) on condition that Confederation of the five eastern provinces and acquisition of the Northwest be included in the party platform. This was the first real sign that the railway and business interests of Lower Canada were likely to throw their weight in favor of federal union.

Other Events on November 2:

1796   Six Nations Indians authorized Chief Brant to sell their land.

1809   King George III made a gift of a communion plate to the Metropolitan Church Cathedral at Quebec.

1833   W. L. Mackenzie was expelled from the Upper Canada legislature for the third time.

1869   Louis Riel entered Fort Garry to take charge.

1885   The first passenger train for Winnipeg left Montreal.

1911   The citizens of Montreal contributed $1.5 million to McGill University.

1947   Food rationing was ended in Canada.

1960   Canada's first national theatre school was opened in Montreal.

St. Helen's Island Granted to Charles Le Moyne

St. Helen's Island, Montreal, site of Expo '67, was given to a member of the Le Moyne family of fighting brothers on November 3, 1672. As Ste. Hélène was one of the most famous of the Le Moyne brothers (see February 9), it might be thought that the island was called after him, but this was not the case. The island was named by Champlain in honor of his wife whom he married in Paris, in 1610, when she was only twelve years old! Champlain was forty-three.

Since Hélène was so young, the marriage contract stipulated that she must remain with her parents for two years before going to Canada. Instead she did not set out until 1620, when she was twenty-two years old. By this time she had become an attractive, mature woman accustomed to the gracious living of Paris. She arrived at Quebec with trunk loads of the latest Parish fashions. The style of the day was dainty dresses with rebato collars, wrist cuffs of pointed lace, graceful slashed sleeves, barred petticoats, and polonian shoes.

Champlain had neglected his home, *L'Habitation,* and it was listing like a ship in a heavy sea! It was draughty, cold, and the roof leaked. It did not take him long to realize that things had to be improved; so he took some of the men working for the Récollet fathers and made his home dry and warm.

Life in Quebec did not live up to Hélène's expectations. Champlain himself was now fifty-three, and no longer able to take the adventurous journeys into the wilderness that had made him such a hero in his wife's eyes. He had not attempted to revive the Order of the Good Time that had been so successful at Port Royal (see May 11), and on the long, winter nights, all Hélène could do was climb the trail to the summit and visit the friendly stone home of the Héberts.

The marriage was not successful. Champlain only mentioned it twice in his diary: the day his wife arrived, and the day she went back to France four years later. Hélène wanted to enter a convent, but Champlain would not agree. After he died she became a nun and founded a convent of her own.

Other Events on November 3:

1667   The Treaty of Westminster restored Acadia to France although the actual transfer did not take place until the Treaty of Breda in 1670.

1894   The first issue of *Le Temps,* Ottawa, was published.

1957   One of the most advanced atomic energy reactors in the world opened at Chalk River, Ontario.

St. Helen's Island, Montreal

Nelson Claims Presidency of Lower Canada

Some of the saddest stories in Canadian history date from the rebellions in Upper and Lower Canada in 1837 and 1838. The chief issue was the right of the people, English-speaking or French, to have self-government. King William IV was completely opposed to any concessions, and told Lord Gosford, the Governor from 1835 until shortly before the outbreak of the rebellion: "By God, I will never consent to alienate the crown lands or to make the council elective." Faced with such an attitude, many Canadians felt that their only hope was to use violence.

The rebellion in Upper Canada was ended quickly, and its chief leader, W. L. Mackenzie, fled to the United States in December, 1837. Louis Joseph Papineau, one of the greatest French-Canadian orators, was the political leader of the rebellion in Lower Canada. Here the situation was complicated because there was racial bitterness as well as a demand for self-government. There was some sharp fighting in the Montreal area in the autumn of 1837 during which a British officer, Lieutenant Weir, was brutally murdered. Loyal troops, who found Weir's mangled body near St. Denis, burned the village and slaughtered a number of its inhabitants. "Remember Weir" was their slogan.

Papineau, who said later that he had never intended rebellion, fled to the States. So did a number of other French-speaking leaders, including Conservative George Etienne Cartier, and Liberals Hippolyte Lafontaine and Augustin Morin, who later became prime ministers of Canada, receiving honors from Queen Victoria.

The rebellions might have ended in 1837 if the leaders who escaped to the States had not received financial help from the Americans and formed the Hunters' Lodges (see January 5). With this help Robert Nelson, an English-speaking rebel leader in Lower Canada, arrived at Napierville, Quebec, on November 4, 1838, and proclaimed himself President of the Republic of Lower Canada. Three thousand *habitants* volunteered to join his "army" although many of them were armed only with clubs and pikes. What happened to them will be. told on November 9.

Other Events on November 4:

1775   The Halifax garrison was reduced to 390 men. George Washington missed a chance to capture the Maritimes.

1809   The steamer *Accommodation*, the first on the St. Lawrence, carrying John Molson as a passenger, arrived at Quebec from Montreal. The trip took 66 hours at a speed of five knots but 30 hours was spent at anchor. The fare was $8.

1838   Sir Francis Hincks founded the Toronto *Examiner*.

1873   The famous clash between Sir John A. Macdonald and Donald A. Smith took place in the House of Commons.

1879   It was ruled that the Queen or the governor-general had the sole right of appointing Queen's Counsels.

1889   Large deposits of coal were discovered in Nova Scotia.

1952   Canada advised the United States of its intention to build the St. Lawrence Seaway.

1959   The province of Alberta banned trading stamps and similar promotion schemes.

An agreement on the exchange of science experts was signed in Moscow by the President of the National Research Council of Canada and the President of the Soviet Academy of Science.

1960   A fifteen-year program for the rehabilitation of inmates in federal prisons was announced by Justice Minister Fulton.

Scandal Topples Tories

November 5, 1873, was one of the blackest days in the life of Sir John A. Macdonald. He was charged with having accepted bribes in connection with the award of the Pacific Railway contract, and his government was forced to resign.

Two important groups had been trying to win the contract. One was led by a friend of Macdonald's, David L. Macpherson of Toronto, who had the backing of the Grand Trunk Railway. The other group was led by Montreal financier Sir Hugh Allan, who had strong backing from a number of railway promoters and financiers in the States.

If Macdonald had had his way the contract would have gone to Macpherson. Cartier, who was solicitor for the Grand Trunk Railway, would also have used his influence in Macpherson's favor. Allan took vigorous steps to deal with this situation. He was so successful in undermining Cartier's support in his own constituency in the election campaign of August, 1872, that Cartier had to agree to support Allan. Allan also paid out $350,000 for campaign funds to ensure the re-election of the Conservatives. Macdonald made the mistake of sending Allan a telegram asking for $10,000.

Allan was awarded the contract after the return of the Conservatives, on condition that he dropped his American associates. George McMullen, representing the disgruntled Americans, released to the press correspondence indicating that Allan's company was financed by Americans who had advanced large sums of money to Macdonald, Cartier, and others so that they would get the charter. McMullen also made available a copy of Macdonald's telegram to Allan.

A Royal Commission was appointed, and agreed that the Government had received and used money from Allan. On the night of November 4 there was a vote of confidence in the Government—if it were defeated, the Government would have to resign. Everything depended on Sir John's old colleague, Donald

Sir David Lewis Macpherson (1818-1896)

A. Smith, who had been rushed from Fort Carlton to vote; he was a Conservative and it looked as though the Government might ride out the storm. Instead Smith announced that he could not conscientiously vote for the Government. Macdonald jumped to his feet and roared that he "could lick that man Smith quicker than hell could frizzle a feather." The Macdonald government had to resign.

Other Events on November 5:

1653   A peace treaty between the French and the Iroquois was signed at Quebec.

1814   American forces destroyed their own base at Fort Erie, Ontario.

1889   The Province of Quebec paid the Jesuits $400,000 and the Protestant Board of Education $80,000 under the Jesuit Estate Act.

1917   The use of grain was prohibited in the manufacture of liquor during the war.

1956   Major-General E.L.M. Burns of Canada was made commander of the United Nations International Force.

1963   Seafarers International Union leader Hal Banks was charged with conspiracy.

The Battle of Passchendaele, 1917

Canadian Corps Triumphs at Passchendaele

Many Canadians still recall November 6, 1917, as a day of horror. On this day the Allies fought the bloody and disheartening Battle of Passchendaele, a ridge only a few miles from Ypres where Canadians had made their first gallant stand in 1915 (see April 22). They had fought a second Battle of Ypres in 1916, and had clinched their reputation as shock troops at Vimy Ridge and the Somme.

Passchendaele was to be the worst of all. Field-Marshal Haig was determined to attack the Germans with all his strength. He was prepared to keep the attack going for six months, if necessary, although he was strongly opposed by members of the War Cabinet.

British, Australian, and New Zealand troops fought the first part of the battle, and assaults were maintained during August, September, and October. Rain fell heavily most of the time, including one period of four days and nights. A record could not be kept of the casualties, but a British estimate was 500,000 of their own men to 270,000 for the Germans. By the end of October the British, Australians, and New Zealanders were worn out and half-destroyed. The Canadian Corps, under its new commander, Sir Arthur Currie, then moved into the battle.

Kim Beattie, historian of the 48th Highlanders of Canada, described conditions: "The mud sea . . . was awful beyond words. Derelict guns, bodies, bloated horses and broken limbers were scattered wherever they looked . . . on the day that the 1st Division attacked, half of the battalion was detailed to the task of stretcher bearing . . . at Passchendaele, where a man could only move a yard or so at a time without sinking to his thighs, and where shells fell always about them and burst in the mud, it was work that defies description."

The Canadians fought in those conditions for nearly a month, and took the village of Passchendaele on November 6, 1917. This was accounted one of the war's great victories, but yielded only 2 square miles of ground.

Other Events on November 6:

1662　Pierre Boucher returned from France with 100 soldiers and 300 colonists.
The French also settled Placentia, Newfoundland.

1867　The first session of Canada's First Parliament opened. Members received $6 per day.

Last Spike of C.P.R. Driven at Craigellachie

The third company with the name of Canadian Pacific Railway Company was headed by George Stephen of Montreal who, with Donald A. Smith, had already made a fortune in railway building. The new C.P.R. did not include Smith on its board of directors at first, however, because he had brought about the defeat of Sir John A. Macdonald's government in 1873 (see November 5).

The contract to complete the building of the transcontinental was signed on October 21, 1880. In the meantime, work had already started in British Columbia under the direction of an American engineer, Andrew Onderdonk. He completed his work in October, 1885, after bringing in thousands of laborers from China.

The tracks from east to west had been laid at a prodigious rate, thanks to the organizing ability of another American, William Van Horne, although he was never quite sure whether he would be able to complete his task. Time and again the C.P.R. ran out of money, and was several times on the verge of bankruptcy. On one occasion the situation was so desperate that George Stephen went to Britain to raise money. When he succeeded he sent his colleagues a cable reading: "Stand fast, Craigellachie." This was the battle cry of the Grant clan to which he and his cousin Donald Smith belonged, and it brought hope that the railway could go forward under their direction. The Northwest Rebellion of 1885 really saved the situation. The transport by rail of a military expedition from Ottawa to Winnipeg in six days, in contrast to the two months this journey normally took, was a spectacular demonstration of the railway's value. The Government readily lent the company enough money to finish its work.

On November 7, 1885, in the Gold Range of the Rockies, the tracks from the East met the tracks from the West. A special train had brought out a group of C.P.R. executives in frock coats and top hats. A railway worker held an iron spike; Donald Smith picked up a hammer and drove it home. Canada's first transcontinental railway had been completed. The place where Donald Smith (later Lord Strathcona) drove the last spike was named Craigellachie.

Other Events on November 7:

1816   A police constable and twelve men tried to arrest Lord Selkirk at Fort William but Selkirk arrested the constable!

1850   The Upper Canada School of Medicine was affiliated with the University of Toronto.

1873   The first session of government under Alexander Mackenzie began after the defeat of the Macdonald government owing to C.P.R. bribery charges.

1900   The Liberals under Sir Wilfrid Laurier were sustained in a general election, which led to the retirement of Sir Charles Tupper as Conservative leader. Sir Robert Borden succeeded him.

1950   The first contingent of Canadian troops for the Korean war landed at Pusan.

Donald A. Smith driving the last spike of the C.P.R.

Carleton Evacuates Montreal, Heads for Quebec

Canada was in turmoil on November 8, 1775. Governor Carleton was preparing to evacuate Montreal, since he could not stop the American army after the break-through at St. Jean (see October 30). He and the people of Montreal did not know that General Benedict Arnold had just marched an American army across Maine and was ready to attack Quebec. Neither did the people of Quebec know about the situation in Montreal.

Carleton made an amazing run from Montreal to Quebec. After gathering supplies, ammunition, and about 130 officers and men, and loading them into a few small ships, he began his trip down the river. Soon after leaving Montreal, they were held up by head winds, and most of them were easily captured by American riflemen and *congressistes,* the Canadians who had joined the American invaders.

Carleton only managed to escape because one of the sloop captains, known as the "Wild Pigeon," offered to guide him through some treacherous channels at night in an open boat. Carleton was disguised as a Canadian *habitant,* wearing a blanket coat and sash, red bonnet, and moccasins. When the boat passed between Ile St. Ignace and Ile du Pas, the "Wild Pigeon" made his men stop rowing and paddle with their hands, so that they could pass the American guns undetected. Carleton reached Quebec on November 19, to find it besieged by Arnold's army, but he managed to get into the city safely.

Arnold's march through Maine and crossing of the river to Quebec was a great military achievement. It was a journey of 200 miles through rugged terrain. The troops had to drag their supplies in heavy boats, or carry them along trails made by hunters and trappers. Towards the end of October it began to snow and at times they had to wade in icy water up to their waists. The trip took thirty-one days, and nearly half of Arnold's force died of exhaustion or exposure, or deserted, before he reached the St. Lawrence.

Arnold surpassed Wolfe's feat, with help from Canadians and Indians, by ferrying 700 men across the river in canoes and small boats. He had his men drawn up on the Plains of Abraham on the morning of November 14, and, in the role of "liberator of oppressed Canadians," demanded the surrender of Quebec, which was refused. This was only the beginning of a long battle.

Other Events on November 8:

1603   Pierre Du Gua, Sieur de Monts, received a royal commission to colonize *L'Acadie* (Acadia).

1631   Cape Breton was given to Sir Robert Gordon to form the province of New Galloway.

1832   Robert Campbell left on an expedition to buy sheep in Kentucky (see September 6).

1861   Captain Wilkes took Confederates from the British ship *Trent* and nearly caused a war in which Canada would have been attacked (see May 20).

1873   Winnipeg was incorporated as a city.

1919   Prime Minister Sir Robert Borden left for a peace conference in Paris.

1902   A railway was completed between Calgary and Edmonton. It was the first railway to reach Edmonton.

1951   Broad disarmament proposals, which the United States offered to Russia on November 7, were formally presented to the United Nations General Assembly by Secretary of State Dean Acheson.

1965   The Liberal Government was re-elected as a minority government in a general election. The Liberals won 131 seats, Conservatives 97, New Democratic Party (N.D.P.) 21, Creditistes 9, Social Credit 5, others 2.

Nelson Deserts His Men

During the uprisings in Canada in 1837-1838, the rebels received financial aid from a secret American organization, the Brotherhood of Hunters (see November 4). The sequel was very sad, and was perhaps one of the most pathetic stories in Canadian history.

Robert Nelson had obtained the services of the two French soldiers-of-fortune, Hindenlang and Touvrey. They were to lead the army of 3,000 *habitants* to Montreal, where it was Nelson's intention to seize the banks. He also planned to capture wealthy citizens and hold them for ransom. If Nelson had been successful there might have been war between Britain and the States, because the rebels were receiving aid from Americans.

When Nelson proclaimed himself President of the Republic of Canada on November 4, 1838, he made Hindenlang commander of the military force with the rank of brigadier-general. A force of 500 men was sent to the American border to obtain a supply of arms and ammunition from a Hunters' depot.

In the meantime, Sir John Colborne had crossed the St. Lawrence from Montreal with about 5,000 regular troops and loyal volunteers. The small rebel force going to get arms at the border was cut off and decimated in a fight that lasted half an hour. Most of the survivors fled into the States, leaving their guns and wounded companions on the field. When the news became known, Hindenlang's army dwindled rapidly until he was left with only 1,000 men. As he had been cut off from his supply base, Hindenlang knew he could not attack Montreal, and decided to try to get his men across the border.

Their way was blocked at the Odelltown crossroads on November 9, by 200 loyal militia who had taken up a position in a Methodist church. Hindenlang ordered an attack, but many of his men refused to fight and dropped to their knees in the snow to pray. Of those who did attack, about 100 were killed or wounded. Robert Nelson deserted his followers and managed to escape into the States.

Sir John Colborne (1778-1863)

Hindenlang was captured and hanged with 11 others. Fifty-eight other rebels were sent to convict settlements in Tasmania. The political leaders escaped scot-free. Two of those who escaped, Cartier and Lafontaine, later became Prime Ministers of Canada!

Other Events on November 9:

1613 An expedition from Virginia under Captain Argall left Port Royal, Nova Scotia, after destroying French settlements.

1864 The first shipment of lumber from British Columbia to Australia marked the beginning of a big export trade.

1872 An Order-in-Council authorized the building of the Intercolonial Railway between Montreal and Halifax.

1928 The Imperial Privy Council ruled that gold and silver in land still held by the Hudson's Bay Company (seven million acres) belonged to the Dominion government and not to the company.

1942 Canada broke off diplomatic relations with Vichy France.

1943 Canada signed the United Nations Relief and Rehabilitation Agreement known as UNRRA.

Storm on Great Lakes Kills 251 Seamen

November 10, 1913, was a tragic day on the Great Lakes and in many homes in Canada and the United States. A storm that started on Friday, November 7, and raged through the weekend had cost the lives of 251 seamen. Lakes Superior and Michigan were hit first. Twenty-six ships were lost within 48 hours. The toll was worse on Lakes Huron and Erie where 41 ships were sunk or wrecked with a loss of 194 lives.

It was nearly the end of the navigation season. A storm warning had been issued by the American Weather Bureau to all ports on the Great Lakes, but there was no indication that a wind approaching hurricane force would develop. On the morning of Saturday, November 8, the centre of the storm was at Sault Ste. Marie. The barometer was dropping rapidly, and there was heavy rain over the lower Great Lakes. The Weather Bureau issued another warning. Then the wind intensified and moved into Lake Huron. Waves began to rise to frightening heights, but in 1913, few ships had wireless, and they kept plodding along their courses. By Sunday morning the full fury of the storm was sweeping southward through Lakes Huron and Erie. Winds were gusting up to 90 miles an hour. The skippers on Lake Huron had to decide whether to head into the wind and hold on, or run before it into the more narrow southern area. There were sand bars and rocky reefs along the way, not leaving much running room.

It was in the pocket of Lake Huron, from Goderich to Sarnia, that many ships were wrecked. On Sunday morning the wind suddenly changed from northwest to northeast, and crews were amazed to see the huge waves driving in the opposite direction from the wind. Some huge ships just crumpled and disappeared. One of them was the *James Carruthers*, 550 feet long, and 7,800 tons. She was never seen again after leaving Sault Ste. Marie.

Altogether, the loss and damage to ships and property exceeded $100 million. The four days of horror are still remembered by veteran Great Lakes seamen from Sarnia to Tobermory.

Other Events on November 10:

1678　Quebec Council allowed the sale of liquor to Indians to check the increasing flow of furs to English traders.

1696　An English settlement at Ferryland, Newfoundland, was destroyed by Iberville.

1727　France excluded all foreign commerce from French colonies.

1852　Hugh and Andrew Allan established the Montreal Ocean Steamship Company for service between Canada and Britain.

Parliament was dissolved at Quebec owing to an outbreak of cholera.

1853　The Great Western Railway was opened from Niagara Suspension Bridge to Hamilton, a distance of 43 miles. It reached London on December 31.

1856　A telegraph line was opened between Newfoundland and New York.

1898　A Joint High Commission meeting at Washington failed to settle the Alaska Boundary.

1916　Prices were controlled by Order-in-Council.

1925　A wheat yield of 423 million bushels was the largest in history up to 1925.

1960　The deepest oil or gas well in Canada was completed at Fording Mountain, British Columbia.

Armistice Day scene outside Buckingham Palace, 1918

Signing of Armistice Ends World War I

November 11, 1918, is still a vivid memory to many Canadians who fought in World War I. Germany had asked for an armistice, and hostilities ended on the 11th hour of the 11th day of the 11th month of the year. The toll of dead and wounded since August, 1914, was the worst the world had ever known. Not counting civilians, more than 8,000,000 had been killed, 21,000,000 wounded, and 7,800,-000 had been listed as captured or missing.

Canada's contribution had been amazing, especially for a nation of 12 million. More than 595,000 had enlisted, of whom 422,000 served overseas. Casualties were 35,684 killed in action, 12,437 dead from wounds. Another 155,839 were wounded, many of whom died later, or suffered for years.

Canadian troops played a great part in the final drive that forced the Germans to stop fighting. It began on August 8, 1918, which General Erich Ludendorff later called "the black day of the German Army." By October, the Canadians had suffered 16,000 casualties but had taken Cambrai, Douai, and Mons. When they were rested on October 26, Field Marshal Sir Douglas Haig said they had covered themselves and their country with glory.

The armistice was signed at 11 a.m. Paris time, when most people in Canada were still asleep. They were wakened by the sounds of bells ringing and whistles blowing. There were joyful celebrations in every community throughout the day. The centre of rejoicing in the English-speaking world was London, England. King George V and Queen Mary appeared on the balcony of Buckingham Palace to acknowledge the cheers of a huge crowd that had gathered outside. There was no radio in those days, but the king spoke from the balcony and said: "With you I rejoice. Thank God for the victories the allied armies have won, which have brought hostilities to an end. Peace is in sight."

Following World War II, the name "Armistice Day" was changed to "Remembrance Day", and the 11th hour of the 11th day of the 11th month now commemorates all the men and women who died for Canada in the Boer War, two World Wars, the Korean War and in other actions for the United Nations.

Other Events on November 11:

1813   Americans were defeated at Crysler's Farm.

1872   A railway was completed between Halifax and Saint John, New Brunswick.

1916   The Duke of Devonshire became Governor-General of Canada.
Sir Sam Hughes resigned as Minister of Militia (see February 14).

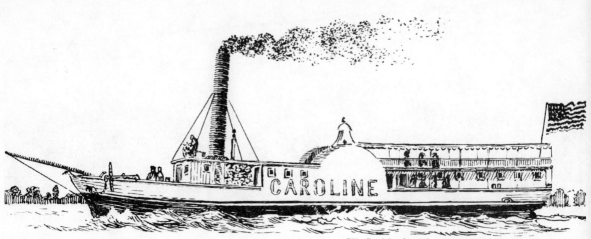

W. L. Mackenzie's supply ship, Caroline, *1840*

Raiding Party Sends *Caroline* Over Niagara

Although Britain and the United States have not fought each other since the War of 1812, there have been a number of occasions since then when war was narrowly averted. One of them resulted from an incident on November 12, 1840, which seems trivial today.

After the collapse of the Upper Canada Rebellion in 1837, W. L. Mackenzie established a base on Navy Island above Niagara Falls and raided Canada. Allan MacNab, who later became Prime Minister of Canada, led a raiding party to the American shore, captured Mackenzie's supply ship *Caroline,* and sent it over the falls. An American was killed in the fighting, and this caused great anger in the State of New York.

The Brotherhood of Hunters, who were responsible for aiding Mackenzie, took their revenge by attacking and burning a Canadian ship in the St. Lawrence River; but feelings were still inflamed in 1840, when a Canadian, Alexander McLeod, boasted in a New York saloon that he had killed the American on the *Caroline.* He was promptly arrested and put on trial for murder. The Foreign Secretary, Lord Palmerston, held that the raid on the *Caroline* had been legal because in aiding the rebels in Canada, it was committing an act of piracy. McLeod had done his duty, acting under military instructions.

The dispute became so heated that Palmerston instructed the British ambassador in Washington to tell the American Government that "war, immediate and frightful in its character," would follow if McLeod were executed. Palmerston's note was so severe that it might have provoked the States to declare war and attack Canada. McLeod was acquitted and released and Britain made a mild apology to the States for the raid on the *Caroline.*

Other Events on November 12:

1774 British citizens in Quebec protested the Quebec Act which restored French civil law.

1820 The Presbyterians of Quebec and Montreal petitioned for a share of the clergy reserves.

1856 The Grand Trunk Railway was opened from Quebec to Toronto.

1921 Sir Robert Borden, who had resigned as prime minister in July, 1920, represented Canada at a conference in Washington to limit armaments.

1962 The International Exhibition Bureau approved Montreal as the site for the World's Fair in 1967 (Expo '67).

Birge's Plan Fails

Sir John A. Macdonald's place in Canadian history is that of architect of Confederation and the first prime minister. It is easy to forget that he was also a practising lawyer from Kingston, Ontario.

Macdonald lost one of his most important law cases as the result of an incident that took place on November 13, 1838, during the rebellions in Upper and Lower Canada. An American leader of the Brotherhood of Hunters, John Birge, raised a force of 400 men to attack Prescott, Ontario, and thus drive a wedge between Upper and Lower Canada. In recruiting speeches throughout the State of New York, Birge claimed that nine-tenths of the population of Upper Canada, and four-fifths of the militia were "oppressed" and ready to join his invasion force.

The invasion force sailed from Sackets Harbor on November 11, 1838, but as it came nearer to Prescott, Birge developed a convenient stomach ache, and asked to be put on shore at Ogdensburg. About half the force deserted with him. Command then fell on a former Polish officer, Von Schultz. He was a brave, competent soldier, and under his direction, the invaders managed to capture a windmill on the river bank below Prescott and some stone houses, which they made into forts. They unfurled a Patriot flag, made by the ladies of Onondaga County, New York, on which was embroidered a star, an eagle, and the words, "Liberated by the Onondaga Hunters." Von Schultz expected help from the Canadians whom Birge had claimed would join them. Instead, a British naval detachment from Kingston arrived on the scene on November 13. It was followed by Canadian militia which, far from being disloyal, attacked the windmill. Von Schultz and his deluded men fought bravely, but had to surrender after three days. British and Canadian troops had seventy-six men killed or wounded, while the Hunters lost thirty-seven.

The invaders were taken to Kingston where the leaders were defended by the young

Sir Alexander Campbell, Sir John A.'s law partner

lawyer, John A. Macdonald. Von Schultz was the only one who pleaded guilty. He said he had thought that Canadians wanted to be liberated, but he had been misled by the Hunters. Eight of them, including Von Schultz, were hanged, although Macdonald did his best for them.

Other Events on November 13:

1637 Newfoundland was granted to Sir David Kirke.

1689 The Iroquois massacred the settlement at La Chesnaye, 20 miles down the river from Montreal.

1705 Negro slaves were declared to be "moveable property."

1775 American troops under General Montgomery occupied Montreal.

1849 The capital of Canada was shifted to Toronto owing to riots in Montreal.

1929 There was a second sharp stock market crash (see October 29).

1953 The American President and Mrs. Eisenhower visited Ottawa.

1956 Prime Minister St. Laurent announced the creation of the Canada Council.

Calgary *Eye Opener*

People are always ready to admit a man's ability after he gets there.
—ROBERT C. EDWARDS, 1912

It is well that there is no one without a fault for he would not have a friend in the world.
—ROBERT C. EDWARDS, 1915

It's as easy to recall an unkind word as it is to draw back the bullet after firing a gun.
—ROBERT C. EDWARDS, 1916

The difference between a friend and an acquaintance is that a friend helps where an acquaintance merely advises.
—ROBERT C. EDWARDS, 1921

If you want work well done, select a busy man — the other kind has no time.
—ROBERT C. EDWARDS, 1922

Bob Edwards, who died on November 14, 1923, was not what might be called a man of distinction, yet he was voted the most colorful pioneer in western Canada. Edwards, who was born in Edinburgh, Scotland, arrived in Canada in 1894, and founded a newspaper at Wetaskiwin in the Northwest Territories which, according to him, had "287 souls and three total abstainers." He wanted to call his paper *Wetaskiwin Bottling Works* because it was sure to be a "corker" but settled for *Wetaskiwin Free Lance.* It was the first paper to be published between Calgary and Edmonton.

Edwards' most famous publication, *Eye Opener,* originated at High River in 1902. Soon he moved it to Calgary and it began to gain a national circulation. Bob Edwards had no respect for people in high places. His definition of a statesman was "a dead politician, and what this country needs is more of them." The *Eye Opener* often contained a column of social notes the whole country waited to read. A typical item would be "The family of Mr. and Mrs. W. S. Stott, 11th Avenue West, all had mumps this week. A swell time was had. Mr. Stott will not be able to deliver his address today at the Rotary convention, much to the relief of those who have heard him speak."

Another was "Mrs. Alex F. Muggsy, one of our most delightful West End Chatelaines, has notified her friends that her usual Friday musicale is called off for this week. Her husband, old man Muggsy, has been entertaining his own friends with a boozical for a change and is in an ugly mood."

Edwards was a heavy drinker, and it is said that liquor interests offered him money to support their cause before Alberta voted on prohibition in 1915. The prohibitionists also went to see him and asked for his support. Edwards asked how much money they would pay, but they replied that they did not have any money. He replied, "That settles it. I'll be with you. The next issue of the paper will be for your cause."

He fought for many worthwhile causes ahead of his time. They included provincial rights, conservation of soil, trees, and water, votes for women, senate reform, and even hospital benefits and old age pensions.

Other Events on November 14:

1684 Bishop Laval sailed for France to resign.

1775 Benedict Arnold tried to force Quebec to surrender.

1954 French Premier Mendes-France visited Quebec and Ottawa.

1955 A four-month strike ended at the De Havilland Aircraft plant, Toronto.

1957 Prime Minister Diefenbaker announced a $125 million power development for the Maritimes.

1962 Sioux Rock, depicting Indian legends, was found at Port Arthur, Ontario.

Ned Hanlan Wins World's Sculling Championship

Canadian athletes have always been among the world's best in winter sports, especially hockey and skating. They have also won world titles in skiing and bob-sledding. Boxing is another sport in which Canadians have excelled (see February 23). The first Canadians to win world renown were oarsmen.

It was natural that Canadians should take to boats like ducks to water. Regattas were great social occasions, and were held in Toronto Bay as early as 1848. The first crew of oarsmen to win distinction came from Saint John, New Brunswick. In 1855, in an eight-oared boat, they defeated the American champions for a purse of $2,000. In Confederation year, a four-oared crew from Saint John went to Paris and won the World's Championship. It became known as the "Paris crew."

More modern rowing, using sliding rather than fixed seats, was introduced in 1868 when Dick Tinning won the Canadian Championship. He was beaten later by Thomas Loudon, and then the two of them helped to train perhaps the greatest sculler the world has ever seen, Edward Hanlan of Toronto. On May 30, 1876, Hanlan gained prominence by winning the Philadelphia Centennial Race of three miles. Then he was invited to meet the world champion, E. A. Trickett of Australia, in a race in Britain.

It was held on November 15, 1880, on the famous Thames River course of about 4½ miles from Putney to Mortlake. The event drew international attention and betting was heavy, most of the money backing Trickett. In fact, bookmakers found it difficult to persuade bettors to place money on Hanlan. They must have made a fortune because the race was no contest. Hanlan drew ahead so quickly that he stopped rowing every now and then to thank the people on the banks of the river for applauding him. Towards the end of the course, he lay down in his shell and rested until Trickett caught up with him! Then he easily beat him to the finish line.

Edward Hanlan won the World's Championship six times, earning $50,000 in prize money. Hanlan's Point on Toronto Island is named after him.

Other Events on November 15:

1765 An ordinance admitted French-speaking jurors to courts and permitted lawyers to plead in French.

1877 The Northwest Council passed laws to conserve the buffalo.

1948 W. L. Mackenzie King resigned as prime minister and was succeeded by Louis St. Laurent (see April 21).

The Paris Crew

The execution of Louis Riel

Louis Riel Hanged

Where did Sir John A. Macdonald really stand on the question of Louis Riel? After the Red River uprising and the shooting of Thomas Scott in 1870, Protestant Ontario was bitterly demanding that Riel be arrested and tried for murder. Sir John would say, "Where is Riel? I wish I could get my hands on him." Privately he was sending him money, on the understanding that he would leave the country.

After the Northwest Rebellion in 1885, Riel was tried in Regina. Once again there was an uproar in Quebec, especially after Riel was declared guilty and sentenced to be hanged. The date of the execution was postponed several times, as pressure on Macdonald continued to mount. Pleas for clemency came from many parts of the world. Conservative members of Parliament from Quebec told Sir John that they would not be responsible for the consequences if Riel were hanged. There was a flood of threatening anonymous letters.

The Government was adamant, however, and Sir John said, "He shall hang though every dog in Quebec bark in his favour." Riel was hanged on November 16.

Yet it is possible that Sir John tried to help Riel, as he did after the Red River uprising. It seems clear that there was a scheme to free Riel before the day of the execution. One story is that the Northwest Mounted Police on guard were to turn their backs for half an hour while Riel was taken from his cell. A relay of fast horses would carry him across the American border. If this story were true, then it would have taken someone in high authority, possibly Sir John, to have arranged it. The present-day Royal Canadian Mounted Police, successors to the Northwest Mounted Police, say they have nothing in their records to substantiate the story. It may have been that the escape was planned by Gabriel Dumont, a friend of Riel, who had found refuge in the States (see December 10).

In any case, the escape became impossible when an enemy of Riel heard about it and "spilled the beans." The hangman was another enemy. When he put the noose around Riel's neck, he asked, "Do you know me, Louis Riel? It is my turn today."

Other Events on November 16:

1686 Britain and France signed the Treaty of Neutrality governing possessions in North America in the event of war in Europe.

1837 Warrants were issued for the arrest of Papineau and other rebellion leaders.

1869 A convention of Métis at Red River formed a provisional government with Louis Riel playing the leading role.

1950 Canadian troops for the Korean War arrived at Fort Lewis, Washington, for training.

Charlottetown Looted, Governor Taken Prisoner

When the Revolutionary War broke out in 1775, the Americans invaded Canada, but very politely. General Philip Schuyler commanding troops from New York was ordered by Congress to "take possession of St. Jean, Montreal, and any other parts of the country . . . if General Schuyler finds that it is practicable and that it will not be disagreeable to the Canadians."

Later in the year, General George Washington heard that two ships had sailed from Britain with arms and supplies for Quebec. Two armed schooners, under Captains Broughton and Selman, were sent to patrol the Gulf of St. Lawrence. Their instructions were: "Should you meet with any vessel, the property of the inhabitants of Canada, not employed in any respect in the service of the ministerial army, you are to treat such vessel with all kindness, and by no means suffer them to be injured or molested."

Unfortunately Broughton and Selman were little better than pirates. Instead of patrolling the St. Lawrence, they spent three weeks capturing fishing vessels off the coast of Nova Scotia. Then they sailed for the Island of St. John (now Prince Edward Island) which they knew was unprotected. Arriving at Charlottetown on the morning of November 17, 1775, they rejected a friendly greeting by Acting Governor Phillips Callbeck, and took him prisoner. Then they looted stores and homes while searching for Mrs. Callbeck. She was the sister of a British admiral, and they were going to cut her throat. Fortunately Mrs. Callbeck had gone to a farm several miles inland.

The prisoners were eventually taken to Cambridge, Massachusetts, the headquarters of the American Army. General Washington was furious with Captains Broughton and Selman, and made arrangements for the Canadians to get back to the Island of St. John. Later, Callbeck wrote to Washington thanking him for his kindness, but he also wrote to General Howe, commanding the British forces in New York: "These monsters, bloodthirsty, sought out Mrs. Callbeck for the purpose of cutting her throat . . . these brutal violators of domestic felicity have left her without a single glass of wine, without a candle to burn, or a sufficiency of provisions of the bread kind, most of the furniture of her house taken away and, for what I know, all her clothes."

Other Events on November 17:

1623   A road to Upper Town was completed at Quebec.

1815   The Chippewa Indians ceded 250,000 acres, now part of Simcoe County, Ontario.

1856   The Grand Trunk Railway was completed between Guelph and Stratford, Ontario.

1874   The Carnarvon terms were announced for settling a dispute between British Columbia and the Federal Government.

1896   Sir Clifford Sifton was made Minister of the Department of the Interior (see November 27).

1903   The Northwest Mounted Police occupied Herschel Island and raised the British flag.
Silver was discovered at Cobalt, Ontario (see July 11).

1959   The Soviet bloc in the United Nations agreed to the Canadian proposal to study the effect of radiation from atomic explosions.

1960   The Honorable Lester B. Pearson was presented with the Medallion of Valour of the State of Israel for his "outstanding role in the deliberations of the United Nations which led to the judicious consideration of the differences between the State of Israel and the Arab nations."

Standard Time Adopted by Canada

One of the most remarkable men in Canadian history was Sir Sandford Fleming. His name has already been mentioned in connection with the good-will tour of the Maritimes which took place in 1864, before the Charlottetown meeting paved the way for Confederation (see August 2).

Sandford Fleming left Scotland for Canada as a young man and first came into the limelight by rushing into the burning Parliament Building in Montreal in 1849, and rescuing a portrait of Queen Victoria. The building had been set on fire by a mob protesting against the signing of the Rebellion Losses Bill (see April 25). He was in the news again two years later, when he designed the first Canadian stamp, the famous three-penny "Beaver" issued on April 23, 1851.

Fleming studied engineering and surveying in Toronto and became chief engineer of the Ontario, Simcoe and Huron Railway in 1857. Then the Government engaged him to survey the route of the Intercolonial Railway from Rivière du Loup to Quebec. This was a very important assignment because the agreement of the Maritimes to Confederation could only be won by a promise to build this railway. Sandford Fleming was chief engineer during its construction.

When British Columbia came into Confederation in 1871, one of the conditions was that a railway to the Pacific coast should be constructed. Once again, the task of finding the best route was entrusted to Fleming. Finding a way through the Rockies was the most difficult problem, and with 800 men working under him, Fleming surveyed Yellowhead Pass, now used by the C.N.R., and also Kicking Horse, Eagle, and Rogers Passes used by the C.P.R.

While all this was going on Fleming became an expert on time. Canadians are accustomed to hearing radio and television programs advertised in terms of "standard time." Canada is divided into seven time zones, beginning with Newfoundland Standard Time in the east. This is half an hour ahead of Atlantic Standard, and then the other zones are one hour apart: Eastern, Central, Mountain, Pacific and Yukon.

Standard time was the invention of Sandford Fleming and was adopted by Canada on November 18, 1883. The rest of the world adopted his system in 1884 at an international conference in Washington.

The birth of Standard Time

Other Events on November 18:

1678   La Salle sent a party which included La Motte and Father Hennepin to Niagara.

1791   The Constitutional Act, which divided Canada into Upper and Lower Canada, was proclaimed. It was to come into effect on December 26.

1929   A tidal wave struck south-west Newfoundland, killed twenty-seven people, and caused $1 million damage.

1936   The Toronto *Globe* bought the *Mail and Empire* and formed the present *Globe and Mail*.

B.C. Separate Colony

November 19 was an important day for British Columbia. On this date in 1858, the mainland was made a separate colony. James Douglas, who was already Governor of Vancouver Island, was sworn in as Governor of British Columbia at a ceremony at Fort Langley, which was intended to be the capital. The creation of the new colony was necessary because thousands of American gold miners were arriving, and there was a danger that the States might try to take over the territory unless it were governed by Britian.

One of the most remarkable figures in Canadian history presided at the swearing-in ceremony. He was Matthew Baillie Begbie, a giant of a man with a face like Mephistopheles. Bruce Hutchison in his book *The Fraser* wrote: "And in his thirty-six years of judging, riding, walking, feuding and praying he had more fun than any other man in British Columbia."

Douglas had asked the British Government to send him a judge to help keep order. Begbie proved to be the ideal man for the job, although he had no experience as a judge, and very little as a lawyer. At the time of his appointment he had no law practice but was a reporter for the *Law Times*. He wanted to leave Britain because his brother had stolen his fiancée!

Begbie, "a government on horseback," held courts everywhere. Although he was ruthless, he was known to be fair, and the miners understood his sense of justice. His *bête noire* was juries who failed to convict men of murder when Begbie felt they were guilty. On one occasion when a jury brought in a verdict of "not guilty" in the case of a man who had sandbagged a companion in a drunken brawl, Begbie said, "You can go, and I devoutly hope the next man you sandbag will be one of the jury." Actually his bark was worse than his bite. He disliked having to sentence men to death and had a chaplain at his side whenever he had to do so.

Sir Matthew Baillie Begbie (1819-1894)

November 19 was also chosen as the date when the colonies of British Columbia and Vancouver Island would be united in 1866. Historian Dr. Margaret Ormsby believes the choice of November 19 was sentimental rather than coincidental.

Other Events on November 19:

1775   Governor Carleton arrived at Quebec after eluding the Americans (see November 8).

1867   The British Government turned down a request that British Columbia be allowed to join Confederation.

1869   The body of Joseph Guibord was buried in Montreal under police protection. There had been riots in Montreal because he had criticized Roman Catholic clergy for banning certain books. Many Roman Catholics felt he should not be buried in consecrated ground.

1918   An Order-in-Council united government railways. This led to the creation of Canadian National Railways.

Oil well at Leduc

Oil Well Spudded In

If you would like to find an oil well (and who wouldn't!), a vast part of Canada is still waiting to be explored. Here's a tip to help you look for it. Petroleum is found in sedimentary rocks, underground, and Canada has about one million square miles of sedimentary basins, about one-quarter of the land area. Four-fifths of this is in western Canada, and includes the southwest corner of Manitoba, two-thirds of Saskatchewan, nearly all of Alberta, and a wide strip down the Mackenzie River to the Arctic. There is oil in British Columbia, Ontario (see February 28), and the Maritimes.

It might be said that Alberta's oil boom began on November 20, 1946, when the famous Leduc well was spudded in. It began producing on February 13, the following year. As early as June, 1892, however, the Edmonton *Bulletin* had reported indications of oil at St. Albert. The story said: "Whether or not the tar is a sure indication of a profitable petroleum field, there is no doubt of the genuineness of the find, and as little doubt that it is not confined to that single locality."

Alberta's first producing oil field was the Turner Valley, and one of its pioneers was W. S. Herron. He noticed gas seepage near Sheep Creek and bought 700 acres of land in the area. His attempts to raise development money from Calgary businessmen were unsuccessful until he devised a spectacular sales plan. He persuaded William Elder and A. W. Dingman to visit a place where there was gas seepage, touched a match to a rock fissure, and then pulled out a pan in which he fried eggs over the flame! Elder and Dingman were so impressed that they bought more than a half-interest in Herron's holdings and spudded in a well at Sheep Creek in January, 1913. Until this time, the Calgary Stock Exchange had occupied a corner in a local butcher shop. Now so many people wanted to buy shares that the cash drawers were not large enough, and the money had to be kept in wastepaper baskets! The boom lasted only a few months, owing to the outbreak of World War I, but fortunes were made and lost on the Calgary Stock Exchange.

Other Events on November 20:

1834   The Constitutional Society of Montreal drew up a list of ninety-two grievances which was sent to King William IV.

1877   Edmonton, Alberta, obtained its first telegraph service.

1880   The Federal Government and the C.P.R. signed the final agreement.

1893   The American Supreme Court held that the Great Lakes and connecting waters constituted "high seas." This led to a treaty in 1909, guaranteeing that the lakes would be open to citizens of Canada and the States on an equal basis.

1962   The United Nations approved the Canadian plan to measure worldwide atomic radiation.

X.Y. Company Formed

Fortitude in distress.

MOTTO OF THE BEAVER CLUB

The feudal state of Fort William is at an end; its council chamber is silent and deserted; its banquet-hall no longer echoes to the burst of loyalty, or the 'auld world' ditty; the lords of the lakes and forests have passed away.

WASHINGTON IRVING, 1836,
on the Nor'Westers

Even today a group of businessmen in Montreal, with distinguished guests from other places, meets occasionally to commemorate one of Canada's earliest social organizations, the *Beaver Club*. They appear in the costumes of the *coureurs de bois*, and the ceremonies always include an after-dinner "paddle"—the members and guests sit in a double line on the carpet, facing in the same direction, and use pokers, brooms, and walking sticks while they pretend to be paddling a war-canoe.

The original Beaver Club was founded by the aggressive members of the Northwest Company, mostly Scotsmen, who were determined to break the Hudson's Bay Company's fur-trading monopoly. While the H.B.C. (sometimes called "Here Before Christ") men waited at their posts for the Indians to bring their furs to them, the Nor'Westers sent their men all over western Canada to deal directly with the Indians. Some of the greatest explorers were Nor'Westers: Mackenzie, Fraser, Thompson, Henry, and others.

Competition was so keen that it almost became a civil war. The chief beneficiaries were the Indians, who learned to play off the rival fur traders to obtain higher prices for their furs. The Northwest Company not only competed with the Hudson's Bay Company, but some of its own men broke away and formed the X.Y. Company on November 21, 1795. John Jacob Astor's fur traders increased the competition, and Lord Selkirk's colonization of the Red River added further pressure. The Northwest Company's feud with Selkirk led to the battle of Seven Oaks (see June 19) and Selkirk's raiding of Northwest headquarters at Fort William. Although Selkirk lost a legal battle with the Northwest Company, as well as a large part of his fortune, and his life, his Red River colony did not fail. It was the beginning of the settlement of the Prairies, which were to become one of the greatest granaries of the world.

The fierce competition ended in 1821 when the Northwest Company merged with the Hudson's Bay Company, and surrendered its name and trading posts. The Hudson's Bay Company then reigned supreme from Labrador to the Pacific coast, and only the Beaver Club in Montreal remained as a memorial to the Nor'Westers.

Other Events on November 21:

1763   Benjamin Franklin established post offices at Montreal, Trois Rivières, and Quebec.

1817   St. John's, Newfoundland, was badly damaged by fire.

1829   Egerton Ryerson published the first issue of the *Christian Guardian* supporting Methodist interests in religion and politics.

1856   The Grand Trunk Railway was completed from St. Mary's to Sarnia, Ontario.

1890   The Indians of Ontario and Quebec petitioned to be able to elect their own chiefs as formerly, though still subject to the Queen.

1942   The Alaska Highway was opened.

1950   A collision between a troop train and the C.N. transcontinental at Canoe Lake, British Columbia, killed twenty-one, and injured fifty-three.

1954   H.M.C.S. *Labrador* completed an 18,-000 mile trip around the continent via the Northwest Passage and the Panama Canal.

French Ships Sighted Off Sillery, Near Quebec

After Wolfe's victory and death at Quebec in September, 1759, Brigadier Murray was left in command. The British fleet got away as quickly as possible; this was a calculated risk because Brigadier Lévis might have reorganized the French forces and tried to regain the city before winter. Fortunately for Quebec, Lévis had to stay in the Montreal area in case Amherst decided to attack from Lake Champlain, where he had a large army.

Murray had the difficult job of looking after his own troops and the people of Quebec during the long, cold winter ahead. The British soldiers had strict orders against harming the Canadians. Murray hanged one soldier who had robbed a citizen, and others were punished severely for lesser offences. For the most part, the soldiers got on well with the conquered people. Many of them shared their tobacco and rations with Quebec citizens.

Winter increased the problem of obtaining fuel. Men were always at work in the forest at Ste. Foy, strongly guarded against possible attacks by Indians. They dragged the logs on sleds for about 5 miles, each sled being pulled by eight men harnessed in pairs like horses. Quebec sentries were changed every hour to keep them from freezing.

Philip Durell (d. 1766)

There was some excitement on November 22, 1759, when a number of French ships appeared off Sillery, above Quebec. They were the supply ships Captain Durell had failed to intercept in May (see May 5), which had sheltered all summer in the Richelieu River. Now they intended to try to slip past Quebec and home to France. The attempt was made on the night of November 24, and seven or eight ships managed to get down the river safely, but four ran aground and were set on fire by their crews. One blew up, killing every man aboard, including the force of forty British soldiers that had stormed it.

As winter wore on, it became clear that Brigadier (now General) Lévis would attack when the river ice cleared. From February onwards, the Quebec garrison began to receive messages from Canadians and Indians, saying that a large company of "expert hairdressers" was ready to wait on them when required!

Other Events on November 22:

1612   Louis XIII granted the region from Florida to the St. Lawrence River to the Marchioness de Guercheville for Jesuit missions.

1784   Parrtown was made the capital of New Brunswick. The name was changed to Saint John the following year, and the capital was moved to Fredericton in 1786.

1806   The first issue of *Le Canadien* appeared. This was the first French-language newspaper in Canada.

1852   A submarine cable was laid from Carleton Head, Prince Edward Island, to Cape Tormentine, New Brunswick. It was the first in North America.

1915   Canada issued a War Loan of $50 million.

1957   The first ship passed through the Iroquois Lock, St. Lawrence Seaway.

Lighting Display (with Abraham Gesner, the discoverer of kerosene)

Street Lights Used in Montreal for First Time

Montreal's first street lights, using whale oil as fuel, were put up by private citizens on November 23, 1815. The occasion was reported by the Montreal *Herald*: "By the exertions of Mr. S. Dawson and other Gentlemen, that part of St. Paul Street west of the Old Market is now handsomely lighted by twenty-two lamps fixed at intervals of 54 feet. The novelty of the thing has a most pleasing effect which we hope will induce citizens in other parts of the city to follow the example. The cost of each lamp completely filled up is not quite seven dollars."

Three years later, whale oil lamps were supplied for the whole town, and were kept in use until 1836, when the latest European novelty was introduced. These were gas lamps supplied by the Montreal Gas Light Company. The chairman was John Molson who built an industrial empire including a bank, shipping company, and brewery. During the Rebellion of 1837, Robert Nelson's rebels planned to capture Molson and hold him for ransom (see November 9).

Policemen first came on the scene in Montreal in 1818. They were called "night watchmen" and carried long sticks, lanterns, rattles, and whistles. As they made their rounds they would shout "All's well" every half hour, which may not have been well for people trying to sleep.

The worst problem in Canada's fastest growing city was garbage disposal. People threw garbage and other refuse into open ditches which ran beside the streets. The result was a cholera epidemic in 1832 which took the lives of hundreds of people. Montreal (like Quebec) was incorporated in that same year. The mayor and sixteen councillors began working on the problem right away, and great improvements had been made by 1836. The first steam railway in Canada was also opened that year, at La Prairie across the river. It ran 15 miles to St. Jean, on the Richelieu River. This was the old portage route to Lake Champlain, where steamers completed the link to the Hudson Canal and New York. There is a plan today to build a canal like the St. Lawrence Seaway to provide a route for shipping between Montreal and New York.

Other Events on November 23:

1823 John Caldwell, Receiver-General of Lower Canada, was suspended from office for being £96,000 in arrears (see November 29).

1877 Canada was awarded $5.5 million from the United States for fishing rights and free navigation of the St. Lawrence (see February 27).

Lieutenant-Governor Bond Head Resigns

Many factors contributed to the outbreak of rebellion in Upper Canada in 1837. One was a clash of personalities. Lieutenant-Governor Sir Francis Bond Head and Reform Leader William Lyon Mackenzie (see January 2) just could not see eye to eye. Head was a veteran of Waterloo who looked down on Mackenzie. He described him as a tiny creature, restless like a squirrel in a cage, and not daring to look him in the face. Actually both men were emotional, wild in speech, and apt to stir up bitter, personal hatreds.

It is possible that Sir Francis Bond Head was never intended to be Lieutenant-Governor of Upper Canada. He received the appointment when he was living in Kent as a Commissioner of the Poor Law. It is said that Colonial Secretary Glenelg intended to appoint Sir Edmund Head, a competent man who later became Governor-General of Canada. The messenger went to Sir Francis Bond Head's home by mistake and asked him if he would be willing to become Lieutenant-Governor of Upper Canada. He accepted immediately, and it was too late for Glenelg to correct the mistake.

Head came to Canada as a liberal, claiming to be a reformer, although he had never even voted in Britain. For a time he was welcomed by leading Upper Canada reformers including Robert Baldwin, but the honeymoon ended quickly. Head insisted that he must make the decisions, and that the council was there only to serve him. He would not be controlled by the Assembly. The Assembly tried to curb Head by refusing to pay his personal supplies amounting to £7,000. Head retaliated by withholding his consent to the Assembly's money bills, amounting to £162,000! Payment could not be made for road-building and other public services, and the Assembly was blamed.

Head then dissolved the Assembly and called a general election which he won, and in which Mackenzie was defeated. He claimed that he had proved that the people of Canada detested democracy!

Although Head resigned on November 24, 1837, owing to a dispute with the British Government about an entirely different matter, he stayed long enough to repel Mackenzie's rebellion in December.

Other Events on November 24:

1648   The first white child was born in Montreal.

1784   A mail route was established between Montreal and Quebec. Fredericton, New Brunswick, was established by Loyalists.

1807   Joseph Brant, Chief of Six Nations Indians, died (see September 25).

1817   An award under the Treaty of Ghent gave the islands in Passamaquoddy Bay to Britain, except for Moose, Dudley and Frederick which became American. Grand Manan was included in the British award.

1845   Governor Metcalfe appointed a commission to determine losses suffered during the Upper and Lower Canada Rebellions (see April 25).

1852   The Normal School of Ontario was opened.

1888   William O'Connor of Toronto won the American rowing championship at Washington.

1890   The Cape Breton Railway was opened as part of the Intercolonial Railway.

1896   The Bering Sea Commission met at Victoria, British Columbia.

1905   Edmonton, Alberta, obtained its first direct transcontinental railway service when the Canadian Northern Railway was completed.

1956   The first Canadian contingent in the United Nations force arrived in Egypt.

Lower Canada Modifies British Criminal Law

The Quebec Act of 1774 retained French civil law in Canada, but introduced British criminal law because it was more merciful than that of France. British criminal law was cruel enough (see October 2) and a session of the Parliament of Lower Canada that opened on November 25, 1823, took steps to modify it. Among other things the penalties for petty theft were revised. Until then, for instance, a man could be hanged for stealing five shillings from a warehouse, shop, or stable, or for stealing forty shillings from a dwelling house or wharf.

One of the worst examples of capital punishment for petty theft occurred in Saint John, New Brunswick, in 1828. Patrick Burgan, a boy of eighteen years, was charged with entering the dwelling of John B. Smith, a manufacturer of ginger beer, and robbing the till of twenty-five cents. Young Burgan was tried by a jury of twelve members and pronounced guilty, with a recommendation for mercy. The judge sentenced the boy to be executed, said there was no hope of mercy, and advised him to lose no time in preparing for his death.

Despite the recommendation of the jury, and a petition sent to Lieutenant-Governor Sir Howard Douglas, the law was allowed to take its course. Patrick Burgan was hanged from the second storey of the old jail. The executioner was Blizard Baine, an Englishman who had been sentenced to two years for robbery. For acting as hangman, Baine was released from prison, given £10, and told to leave the city in a hurry. The difference in the currency (Burgan stole twenty-five cents but Baine was given £10) was that a number of currencies were circulating in the Maritimes until 1858.

Among the cruel spectacles of those days were public hangings. One of the last public hangings in Canada was in February, 1869, when James Patrick Whelan was executed in Ottawa for the murder of D'Arcy McGee (see April 7).

Other Events on November 25:

1657 Marguerite Bourgeoys opened a school for French and Indian children at Ville Marie (Montreal).

1758 General John Forbes captured Fort Duquesne and named it Fort Pitt, now Pittsburg. This marked the end of French rule in the Ohio Valley.

1783 Sir Guy Carleton sailed from New York. Britain retained Detroit and Niagara as hostages to see that the peace terms were carried out.

1837 William Lyon Mackenzie proclaimed the creation of a provisional government. This led to an armed clash in which he was defeated (see December 8).

1847 A railway was opened between Montreal and Lachine, Quebec.

1851 The Y.M.C.A. was organized at Montreal.

1857 Prime Minister Sir Etienne Taché resigned.

1878 Governor-General the Marquis of Lorne and his wife, Princess Louise, arrived at Halifax.

1885 Rocky Mountain Park was established at Banff, Alberta.

1892 Sir John Thompson became prime minister, succeeding Sir John Abbott who had resigned.

1919 Edward Prince of Wales sailed from Halifax after a visit to Canada which had begun on August 12.

Theodore Roosevelt (1858-1919)

Hamilton Greets "Teddy"

"Terrible Teddy" Roosevelt was the United States president who strong-armed Britain into voting against Canada on the Alaska boundary question (see March 25). His daughter Alice once said: "He has to be the bridegroom at every wedding and the corpse at every funeral!"

After depriving Canada of a seaport to the Yukon, it might be thought that Teddy Roosevelt would never dare cross the border, but "time heals all wounds." On November 26, 1917, he not only came to Canada but received a welcome usually reserved for royalty.

It was during the critical days of World War I, that Victory Bond rallies to raise money for the war effort were being organized everywhere, and the former American president had been invited to take part in one at Hamilton, Ontario. The slogan was "stand behind the men behind the guns."

Roosevelt was a glamorous figure, apart from having been a President of the United States. He had been colonel of the famous Rough Riders whom he led, dismounted, to the capture of San Juan Hill in Cuba. He always preserved an air of dash and vigor, and blew into Hamilton like an autumn hurricane. The city was never more decorated. Every downtown building displayed the Union Jack and Stars and Stripes entwined. Thousands of people jammed the streets as Roosevelt was driven from the railway station to the hotel, while guns boomed such a salute that many windows were broken from the concussion.

The big issue of the day was compulsory military service, and Roosevelt did not hesitate to express his opinion. In the fund-raising rally at the Lyric Theatre he said that people who would not back the war effort should lose the right to vote. As for conscientious objectors, he had Quaker friends who were lifelong objectors to fighting, but they did their best to help the war effort in other ways. All he could say to those who suddenly found themselves conscientious objectors overnight was "If a man's conscience makes him act like a fool, let him take it out and see what's wrong with it." Roosevelt aroused such enthusiasm that the people in the audience pledged themselves to buy $100,000 in Victory Bonds.

Other Events on November 26:

1843   The Lafontaine-Baldwin government resigned in a dispute with Governor Metcalfe (see March 29).

1857   The Macdonald-Cartier government was in power until July, 1858.

1892   The Canadian Privy Council denied the right of Roman Catholics in Manitoba to appeal to the Governor-General in the separate schools question.

1926   Vincent Massey was made the first Canadian minister to the United States.

I hear the tread of pioneers
Of nations yet to be,
The first low wash of waves
where soon
Shall roll a human sea.
JOHN G. WHITTIER, 1846

British settlers en route to Battleford, c. 1903

Sifton Plans World-Wide Immigration Campaign

Among the great promoters in Canadian public life was Sir Clifford Sifton who was made Minister of the Interior in the Laurier government on November 17, 1896.

Sir Clifford liked to get things done in a hurry, and by November 27, 1896, he was already making plans for the biggest immigration drive in Canadian history. First he compelled the railways to choose the millions of acres of land that had been allocated to them so that he would know what land could be made available to new settlers. Then he streamlined the process of land grants and put sub-agents in every district to cut red tape.

Those steps were the beginning of an almost world-wide campaign to bring new settlers to Canada, mostly from the United States and Britain. Thousands of pamphlets were sent out offering free land in western Canada. There were advertisements in 7,000 agricultural publications in the States alone. Editors of British and American papers were taken on tours of Canada. Agents were appointed in foreign lands and received $5 for every head of family sent to Canada, plus $2 for every member of the family.

There were results within the first year. In 1897, 32,000 settlers came to Canada, almost double the number who came in 1896. By 1911, when the Laurier government was defeated, more than 2,000,000 new citizens had come to Canada bringing the population to 7,206,643. If World War I had not broken out in 1914, the trend would have continued.

There were problems, of course. Many of the new settlers came from cities and were not suited for farming. One group from Britain had been advised to bring oxen which would provide milk as well as be used for ploughing!

Sifton, who has been described as a man of "chilled steel and flawless, machinelike competence," did not see the campaign through until 1911. When Prime Minister Laurier agreed to allow separate schools in Alberta and Saskatchewan when they became provinces in 1905, Sifton resigned from the cabinet. In 1911, he disagreed with Laurier's reciprocity deal with the United States and led a revolt within the Liberal party (see January 21).

Other Events on November 27:

1618   Marc Lescarbot was given permission to publish his *History of New France* (see May 11).

1783   The shipping service was restored between Halifax and New York.

1822   John McLeod of the Hudson's Bay Company began his journey through the Rockies and descended the Fraser River to the Strait of Georgia.

1829   The final section of the Welland Canal was opened.

1854   The Grand Trunk Railway was completed from Richmond to Lévis, Quebec.

1885   Eight Indians were hanged at Regina for murders in the Northwest Rebellion.

Count Frontenac Dies at Quebec

There are a number of stories about Count Frontenac in this book, but the time has come to tell the last. Frontenac had been asked to return to Canada in 1689 and serve as governor for the second time. His instructions were to regain the respect of the Indians and to drive the British from New England and New York. He succeeded with most of the Indians, but Frontenac was unable to take New England and New York for France.

After eight years of war, Britain and France signed the Treaty of Ryswick on September 20, 1697. Actually Ryswick meant little, and war resumed five years later. As there was supposed to be peace, however, Frontenac exchanged messages with the Governor of New York, and Captain John Schuyler arrived at Quebec as a peace emissary. He had led the raid on La Prairie, near Montreal, after the massacre at Schenectady (see February 9), but old wounds were forgotten. Schuyler was honored at a banquet in the chateau at which he proposed a toast to King Louis, while Frontenac toasted King William.

Not long afterwards winter began to close in, and the streets of Quebec were covered in snow. It was noticed that Frontenac seemed to be staying in his chateau. Then Bishop St. Vallier began paying visits there. This was strange because Frontenac and the Bishop had been at odds ever since the Gov-

ernor returned. Shortly after the candles were lighted in the late afternoon of November 28, 1698, the reason for the visits became known. The old soldier had died, eyes bright and mind alert to the last.

In his will he had asked that his heart be cut out, encased, and sent to his wife, who had never accompanied him to Canada. The casket containing the heart did not arrive in France until shipping opened in the spring, but Madame Frontenac, a proud and beautiful woman, would not accept it. She said that she did not want a heart in death that had not been hers in life. The heart was returned to Quebec and replaced in Frontenac's body, where it lay in a crypt in the church of the Récollets.

Other Events on November 28:

1797 The Northwest Company began building the Sault Ste. Marie Canal which was destroyed by Americans in 1812.

1822 The Mississauga Indians ceded 2,748,-000 acres, now parts of Hastings, Addington, Frontenac, Lanark, Carleton, and Renfrew counties, in Ontario.

1844 Parliament opened the session in Montreal that removed restrictions on the use of French.

1871 The Canada Post Office issued the first postcards.
A telegraph service opened between Winnipeg and Pembina, Manitoba.

1907 Dial telephones, believed to be the first in Canada, came into use in Sydney Mines, Nova Scotia. Edmonton, Alberta, received dial phones on April 5, 1908.

1950 Canada agreed to be one of the nations taking part in the Colombo plan.

1956 Canada granted one million dollars and free passage to victims of the revolution in Hungary.

Fort Frontenac

Officials Absent

One of the problems that hindered the development of Canada for many years was the absence of people appointed to do important jobs. On November 29, 1808, for instance, N. Francis Burton was appointed by the British Government to be Lieutenant-Governor of Lower Canada. He remained in Britain until 1822, but drew his salary. Then he came to Canada and stayed for ten years.

Many of the important positions in Canada were regarded as sinecures. General James Murray, who became Governor of Canada, after the fall of Quebec, until 1766, continued to draw pay as governor for eight years after he returned to Britain. When Sir Guy Carleton was Governor of Canada, his brother Thomas was made Lieutenant-Governor of the newly-created province of New Brunswick. He held the position for thirty-three years but was absent during the last fourteen of them. Yet, he was not without fortitude; on one occasion he traveled from Fredericton to Quebec on snowshoes to see his brother who was ill.

Many absentees were ministers of the church. The Rector of Sorel, an important military post, had a salary of £200 a year, but spent ten years of his term in England. Lord Plymouth said he was too charming a neighbor to be allowed to live in remote Canada!

The situation came to a head in 1823 when it was discovered that the Receiver-General of Lower Canada had stolen £96,000 of the provincial funds. French-speaking citizens of Lower Canada said this would not have happened if some of them had been given the responsible positions held by absentee British officials. Louis Joseph Papineau, who became one of the leaders of the 1837 rebellion, and John Neilson, editor of the Quebec *Gazette*, felt so strongly about this that they traveled to London to protest against a proposal to unite Upper and Lower Canada. They felt it would give English-speaking Canadians more power than ever. The union

Thomas Carleton (1735-1817)

was delayed until 1840 and this probably delayed Confederation.

Other Events on November 29:

1729 French settlers at Fort Rosalie (Natchez, U.S.A.) were massacred.

1745 A French and Indian force under Marin captured Saratoga.

1760 The French garrison at Detroit surrendered to the British. This final defeat led to Pontiac's attempt to wrest control from the new British rulers (see May 7).

1773 British citizens at Quebec petitioned for an Assembly.

1798 The Provincial Legislature of the Island of St. John changed the name to Prince Edward Island. The change received royal assent in 1799.

1855 The Grand Trunk Railway completed the line from Montreal to Brockville.

1918 The Canadian Council of Agriculture, meeting at Winnipeg, declared a national farmers' platform including reduced tariffs, free trade with Britain, and reciprocity with the United States.

1962 Public Works Minister Fulton resigned to become leader of the Conservatives in British Columbia.

Construction of Welland Canal Completed

Jean Talon, the great Intendant of Canada from 1665 to 1672, sent explorers as far west as Lakes Huron and Superior to find the copper which Indians said was there. They located huge supplies on the Island of Minong, which the French called Isle Royale, but the problem was how to get the copper to Quebec. Talon dreamed of the day when barges could be towed from the Great Lakes with supplies of copper to be used for the muzzles of King Louis' cannon.

His dream began to come true in 1798 when the Northwest Company built a small canal at Sault Ste. Marie. Then, on November 30, 1824, William H. Merritt of St. Catharines, Ontario, formed a company to build a canal that would by-pass Niagara Falls. It was completed on November 30, 1829. That was the first Welland Canal. Today, four canals later, the Welland Canal has the most spectacular task on the St. Lawrence Seaway system, of which it is an integral part. It lifts or lowers ships 139.5 feet between Lakes Ontario and Erie, a distance of 27 miles. Ships 730 feet long with a beam of 75 feet and drawing 25.5 feet of water can pass through. Lock Number 8 at Port Colborne is the longest in the world: 1,380 feet. More than 8,000 ships go through the Welland Canal every year.

Merritt's 1824 company soon ran out of money and had to borrow heavily from the Government of Upper Canada before the canal could be completed. The effort nearly made Upper Canada bankrupt and was one of the reasons why Lower Canada resisted the Act of Union in 1840.

In 1841, the new Province of Canada bought the canal and enlarged it so that ships drawing 9 feet of water could go through. The canal was enlarged again after Confederation, and the modern canal was built between 1913 and 1932 with subsequent improvements. Today the locks are "twinned", allowing two-way traffic. Bridges over the canal are being replaced by tunnels so that highway traffic will not be delayed.

William Hamilton Merritt (1855-1918)

Other Events on November 30:

1629　Charles La Tour was captured by the Kirke brothers and sent to England where King Charles I made him a Baronet of Nova Scotia (see October 18).

1696　St. John's, Newfoundland, surrendered to Iberville (see May 19).

1782　Britain and the United States agreed to peace terms (see May 8).

1852　Robert Campbell left Fort Simpson to snowshoe 3,000 miles to get married (see September 6).

1960　One hundred and ten Canadian trade commissioners met at Ottawa for a 15-day conference.

1962　Citizens of Cornwall, Ontario, were treated for chlorine gas poisoning.

Proclamation Forged

Colonization and the fur trade could not exist together.
—Sir George Cartier and
William McDougall, 1869

William McDougall, prospective Governor of the Northwest Territories, was prevented from entering his "kingdom" by Riel and his Métis (see October 31). He had to wait until December 1, the official date for the transfer.

There was a howling blizzard on the night of December 1, but McDougall and four companions saddled horses and rode 2 miles into the Northwest Territories. McDougall dismounted, fumbled in his pocket for a piece of paper, and tried to read it in the teeth of the howling gale: "Victoria, by the Grace of God, of the United Kingdom of Great Britain and Ireland, Queen, Defender of the Faith, to whom it may concern . . ." The proclamation said that the territory now belonged to Canada and that he, William McDougall, was its governor. Nobody could hear the words, and in any case the proclamation was forged. McDougall had written it himself!

Riel learned that the proclamation had been forged and declared that there was no legal government in the Northwest. His provisional government would negotiate with the Government of Canada. McDougall then attempted to raise a military force to quell the Métis. Colonel John Stoughton Dennis, an officer who had run away during the Fenian raid on Fort Erie three years before, was made commander (see June 1).

Dennis went to the Fort Garry area and obtained help from Dr. John Schultz, leader of the "Canadian" party. As they were not able to recruit enough men, Dennis tried to persuade the Indians to join his force. Riel then sent his Métis to attack Dennis, many of whose men deserted immediately. The others barricaded themselves in Dr. Schultz's home and surrendered a few days later without firing a shot. Dennis managed to escape across the border, disguised as a squaw.

Meanwhile the Americans were angry because McDougall and Dennis had been stirring up the Indians; they threatened to kill them if the Indians got out of hand. Sir John A. Macdonald had also written to McDougall and told him not to go to Fort Garry, and to make Riel an officer in the police. All this was too much for McDougall. He repacked his large train of wagons and headed back to St. Paul to board a train to Ottawa.

Other Events on December 1:

1680 The "Great Comet" appeared during the month, close to earth, causing considerable alarm. It was visible until February, 1681.

1775 General Montgomery joined General Arnold in an attack on Quebec.

1798 There was a public whipping and burning at York (Toronto).

1837 Louis Joseph Papineau was declared to be a rebel and £1,000 was offered for his capture. He escaped into the United States.

1841 The first copyright in Canada was the *Canadian Spelling Book*.

1855 The Post Office opened a money order branch.

1868 Baron Lisgar succeeded Viscount Monck as governor-general.

1899 Victoria Bridge, Montreal, was rebuilt for vehicles and pedestrians as well as trains.

1903 The central building, University of Ottawa, was destroyed by fire.

1919 Ambrose Small, Toronto millionaire, disappeared and was never seen again.

1952 A federal-provincial agricultural conference opened at Ottawa.

1960 Duty was increased on the importation of European automobiles.
The provincial premiers met at Ottawa.

The S.S. Selkirk *with its cargo, the* Countess of Dufferin

Railway Completion Marks End of Riverboat Era

December 2, 1878, marked the end of a colorful era in the West. A railway was completed from Winnipeg to the American border, where it connected with the St. Paul and Pacific. The sternwheelers were no longer needed on the Red River, with their bowmen shouting the depth of the water as they went along: "Mark One", Mark Three", "Mark Twain." It was this last cry which Samuel Clemens, author of *Tom Sawyer,* took as his pen name.

Although the riverboats (see April 15) had been carrying freight worth $10 million a year since 1870, they also carried the means of their own destruction. Beginning in 1875 every steamer sailing down the Red River to Winnipeg included in its cargo the rails and ties that would build the railway. Then in October, 1878, the S.S. *Selkirk* brought the locomotive *Countess of Dufferin* to Winnipeg, and the end was near (see September 27).

The opening of the railway line to the United States made a great difference to travelers from eastern Canada. Before the railways operated they had to find their way along the "Dawson route", which stretched for 450 miles from Dawson's (now Thunder Bay, Ontario) to Winnipeg. The trip involved seventeen changes from steamboats to wagons, and even to rowboats.

Pressure was already on for land in the West during these years. Crop failures in Europe had created a demand for North American wheat, and it rose in price to $1.25 a bushel for No. 1 Hard. People suddenly began to realize that one acre would produce about 40 bushels of wheat; so, in theory, it was possible to earn $8,000 from 160 acres, or $32,000 from 640 acres. Wheat farming would pay better than gold fields!

Unfortunately they forgot to take into consideration such natural hazards as grasshoppers and drought. What works out on paper does not always work out in practice, and this was especially true of farming.

Other Events on December 2:

1853　Governor Douglas established the Supreme Court of Vancouver Island.

1960　A nationwide rail strike was averted by an Act of Parliament.

Bowell Named Minister of Trade and Commerce

Among the most interesting jobs in the Canadian public service are those with the Department of Trade and Commerce, which now sends men and women to sixty-six offices in foreign nations.

Prime Minister Sir John A. Macdonald, who had the foresight to establish the department in 1887, said: "The rapidly and largely increasing trade of Canada has made it necessary, or at all events expedient, to appoint a Minister whose time and attention and energy should be applied to the important object of developing and maintaining everything connected with our trade and commerce, whether it be home or foreign trade."

Sir Mackenzie Bowell became the first Minister of Trade and Commerce on December 3, 1892. One of the first things he did after his appointment was to go on a one-man trade mission to Australia. Even though Prime Minister Macdonald spoke about Canada's largely increasing trade in 1887, the first Department of Trade and Commerce required only a staff of four in Ottawa and seven part-time commercial agents abroad. Now, in 1966, the department employs 4,000 people in Ottawa and abroad, including more than 200 trade commissioners at its sixty-six foreign offices.

The expansion is typical of Canada's growth. In 1892, total trade was $250 million. Today it is worth more than $14 billion. Canada now ranks as the world's fifth largest exporter, behind the United States, Germany, Britain, and France. The trade commissioners help Canadian businessmen in every way possible. They supply information and suggestions to increase the sale of Canadian products to other nations, and they also help Canadians buy products from those nations.

The work is far from routine and members of the Department of Trade and Commerce must be prepared to tackle the unusual. For instance, in 1963, Canada sponsored a large trade exhibit at the International Trade Fair at Sydney, Australia. It received wonderful publicity because it was learned that the only kangaroo in the Calgary Zoo needed a mate, and a red-headed one, at that! Australian newspapers put on a campaign to help, with the result that a giant female red kangaroo was located at Melbourne, and flown to Calgary. The marriage was completely successful, and both kangaroos have been living happily!

Other Events on December 3:

1653   Nicholas Denys was granted all the land between Cape Canso and Cape Rosier in Acadia.

1738   Pierre La Vérendrye and his sons entered the village of the Mandans in North Dakota where they hoped to obtain information about a route to the Pacific. They were disappointed (see March 30).

1827   Presbyterians in Montreal asked for a share of the clergy reserves.

1839   The Erie and Ontario Railroad, a horse tramway, was opened between Queenston and Chippewa, Ontario.

1855   The Great Western Railroad was opened between Toronto and Hamilton.

1861   Fourteen thousand British troops were sent to Canada on account of the *Trent* affair (see May 20).

1919   The Federal Government made $25 million available to enable tenants to purchase homes.

1951   The Federal and Ontario Governments agreed on the St. Lawrence power development.

1960   Edmonton Airport was opened. It was the largest civilian airport in Canada.

George Washington (1732-1799)

French Take Posts

George Washington is so revered as "the father of the United States" that it is difficult to remember that he was once Colonel George Washington, a British officer. Former officers like Sir Guy Carleton and John Graves Simcoe regarded him as a traitor.

Washington came into prominence when he was only twenty-one years old. In 1748, the Virginians had organized the Ohio Company to develop the interior, and in 1753, they were disturbed to hear stories that the French from Canada were developing trading posts there. Young Washington, whose career was being promoted by a wealthy British resident of Virginia, was sent to investigate.

On December 4, 1753, at a place called Venango, 60 miles north of the present city of Pittsburg, Washington and his companions noticed a French flag over a post which belonged to a British trader. Washington investigated, and found that it was occupied by Chabert de Joncaire, a French officer. Britain and France were not at war so Washington and Joncaire were able to meet sociably, and they engaged in some heavy drinking. Washington told Joncaire that he would have to get off British territory, but

Joncaire refused to move, and was incautious enough to disclose French plans to take possession of the Ohio Valley and link Canada with Louisiana.

When Washington reported the French plans to Governor Dinwiddie of Virginia, it was decided to build a fort where the Allegheny and Monongahela Rivers met, to block the entrance to the Ohio River. It was begun in the spring of 1754, but was quickly captured by the French even though there was supposed to be peace. Dinwiddie then sent out a force of 300 men led by Colonel Joshua Fry, with Major George Washington as second-in-command. There was fighting at Great Meadows and Fort Necessity, during which Washington took command. He was defeated and forced to retreat, having lost 100 men. Horace Walpole, British author, wrote later: "A volley fired by a young Virginian in the backwoods of America set the world on fire." The Seven Years' War, in which France lost Canada, was to follow. George Washington therefore helped Britain seize Canada from France, but soon needed the help of France to acquire the States from Britain!

Other Events on December 4:

1800 David Thompson crossed the Rocky Mountains.

1837 Eight hundred rebels gathered at Montgomery's Tavern, Yonge Street, Toronto.

1838 "General" Bierce of the Brotherhood of Hunters attacked Windsor from Detroit and was defeated.

1856 Bonding arrangements were made so that American goods could pass through Canada.

1866 The Confederation delegates began meetings with the British Government at the Westminster Palace Hotel, London, England.

1961 Dr. Marcel Chaput, Quebec separatist leader, resigned from the Defense Research Board.

"Horseless Carriages" Appear on Canadian Roads

Whenever a discussion arises about who had what first, there is seldom unanimous agreement. Just who did have Canada's first automobile? Perhaps the decision depends on the definition of an automobile. The distinction might belong to Father Belcourt who had a steam-propelled vehicle when he was serving in Prince Edward Island. It was demonstrated at a garden party in 1866 and the Charlottetown *Examiner* reported, "and with wonder and delight it was observed steaming away for half a mile on the road and back again at a fast speed."

Another "first" automobile was called a "horseless carriage." It was an electric car built for F. B. Fetherstonhaugh, K.C., by Dickson's of Toronto, and appeared on the streets on December 5, 1893. It could travel at a speed of 15 m.p.h. and go 15 miles before its batteries needed recharging.

It seems clear that the first Canadian-owned gasoline car was purchased by Colonel John Moodie of Hamilton, Ontario, on April 2, 1898. It was a "Winton" and looked like a horse-drawn buggy with the engine in the rear. There were spikes around the end of the car to keep people from climbing on board. Colonel Moodie liked to be first in everything. He owned the first bicycle in Canada, a Bayliff-Thomosin high-wheeler in 1878, and the first motorboat which he displayed on Hamilton Bay in 1895.

Cars in British Columbia and the Maritimes were driven on the left-hand side of the road until 1920-1922, as they are in Britain and parts of Europe. Then they fell in line with the other Canadian provinces which always drove on the right. The custom of driving on the left came from olden days when knights traveled the countryside on horseback. They wore their swords on the left, so they rode on the left side of the roads to be in a better position to draw their swords quickly with their right arms.

Driving on the right-hand side of the roads in North America evolved from the days of the covered wagons. The lead man walked to the left of the horses, holding the bridle with his right hand. Right-handers, then, set the traffic pattern of two continents.

Other Events on December 5:

1775 The Americans under General Arnold and Montgomery began the siege of Quebec.

1794 Lieutenant-Governor Simcoe of Upper Canada went from New York to Kingston in an open boat.

1821 The Hudson's Bay Company grant was renewed for twenty-one years with exclusive trade rights.

1837 Montreal was placed under martial law.

1869 The Métis published a list of rights as the Red River uprising developed.

1902 Marconi sent signals across the Atlantic from Glace Bay, Nova Scotia (see December 12).

1962 Mrs. Claire Kirkland-Casgrain became the first woman cabinet minister in the Province of Quebec.

First automobile in Sussex, N.B., 1903

Disaster at Halifax – *Mont Blanc* and *Imo* Collide

Canada's worst disaster took place at Halifax on December 6, 1917, when two ships collided in the harbour. One of them, *Mont Blanc,* was carrying explosives, and the collision set off a blast that killed 1,630 people, injured thousands more, and wrecked the north end of Halifax. The force of the explosion was strong enough to hurl a clock out of the tower at Truro, 60 miles away, and it was even felt at Sydney, a distance of 200 miles.

The inward-bound French freighter *Mont Blanc* was entering the narrows but was not flying a red flag warning other ships that there were explosives on board. It collided with the *Imo* in midstream, and the impact punctured some tins of highly inflammable benzine on the decks of the *Mont Blanc.* The benzine began to burn with a blue flame that crept along the decks. In the holds were 2,300 tons of picric acid, 500,000 pounds of T.N.T., and 61 tons of other explosives.

Captain Lemedie of the *Mont Blanc* ordered his crew to take to the lifeboats and they managed to reach shore, but he neglected to warn Halifax. Two British cruisers *Niobe* and *Highflyer* sent launches to put out the fire on the *Mont Blanc* but the explosion took place before they could get there. The smoke rose 5 miles into the sky, *Imo* and *Mont Blanc* sank, and a tidal wave drowned many people along the shore as it wrecked the waterfront. The tragedy was made worse by a blizzard when many people were living in tents, or homes without windows.

At an enquiry later, it was learned that the pilot of the *Mont Blanc* was English, while the ship's crew were French, so they could not conduct a conversation. The pilot was asked how he would instruct the French ship to reduce speed and he replied that he would shout "demi-tasse." Second Officer Leveque of the *Mont Blanc* was asked what he would do on hearing such an order, and he replied that he would go below for a cup of coffee!

Charges of manslaughter were dropped for lack of evidence but the judge recommended that licenses be cancelled for failure to warn the people of Halifax of the danger of an explosion.

Other Events on December 6:

1752 The Halifax *Gazette* published the first book in Canada, an eight-page pamphlet for the Government.

1880 The first issue of the Edmonton *Bulletin* was published.

1907 The first recorded flight in Canada took place when Thomas Selfridge rose 168 feet into the air in a kite designed by Alexander Graham Bell (see September 30).

1971 Prime Minister Trudeau and President Nixon met in Washington to discuss economic policy.

Devastation in the north end of Halifax after the explosion on Dec. 6, 1917

Hearne Begins Trip

Some of Canada's most famous explorers made incredible trips during the coldest winter weather. After his unsuccessful visit to the Mandans in 1738, Pierre La Vérendrye walked from the Missouri River to what is now Portage la Prairie, facing into the north wind, in January, 1739. David Thompson snowshoed through the Rocky Mountains in January, 1811, in 20 below zero weather (see July 15). Robert Campbell snowshoed 3,000 miles in 1852 to find a bride (see September 6). He liked to cut a hole in the ice and have a cold bath before setting out!

Young Samuel Hearne of the Hudson's Bay Company began an amazing trip from York Factory, Hudson Bay, on December 7, 1770, to see if there really was copper at the mouth of the Coppermine River, which flows into Coronation Gulf north of the Arctic Circle. Imagine beginning a trip from Hudson Bay in December! Hearne's company wanted more information about the interior, and he volunteered to go although he was only twenty-four years old. He tried first in 1769 with a small party of Indians as guides, and very little navigational equipment: only a compass, an old sea quadrant, a bottle of mercury, and a reflecting pan. After traveling about 200 miles the Indians stole his supplies, and left him to find his own way back to York Factory.

He made another effort in February, 1770, and had gone about 500 miles when he broke his quadrant and had to return. In December the same year, he began a trip that lasted two years and seven months. During this time he discovered Great Slave Lake, proved that there was no great river running through Canada to the Pacific, and also that there was no copper at the mouth of Coppermine River. It is possible that even today no white man has traversed the country covered by Hearne except from airplanes. He made another trip west in 1774 and founded Cumberland House on the Saskatchewan River.

Samuel Hearne (1745-1792)

The success of Hearne's trip to the Arctic was due in part to a remarkable Indian called Matonabbee, who brought along eight wives! They were big and strong, and carried the heavy loads. They did the work in the camps while Hearne and Matonabbee were hunting for food.

Other Events on December 7:

1649　The Iroquois took the Huron mission of St. Jean and murdered Fathers Garnier and Chabanel.

1729　The Mississauga Indians ceded 3 million acres comprising present-day Norfolk, Haldimand, and Wentworth counties of Ontario.

1899　Hugh John Macdonald, son of Sir John A. Macdonald, led the Conservatives to victory in the Manitoba election and became premier.

1941　Canada declared war on Japan, Finland, Hungary, and Roumania following the Japanese attack on Pearl Harbour, Hong Kong, and other bases. The United States and Britain did not declare war until the following day.

Rebels marching down Yonge Street

Rebellion Fails

William Lyon Mackenzie (see January 2) met his "Waterloo" on Yonge Street, Toronto, on December 8, 1837. The Upper Canada rebel leader had established his headquarters in Montgomery's Tavern. He intended to capture the city hall where the Government had stored several thousand muskets. When Mackenzie revealed that he was prepared to lead an armed rebellion, most responsible members of the Reform party would have nothing to do with what was, they realized, nothing less than treason.

Mackenzie had got out of hand by this time and was beginning to act like a demented man. For months he had gone through the countryside urging his followers to take up arms. They had trained in fields at night, armed with clubs, sticks, and old muskets. The only properly trained military man Mackenzie could rely on was Colonel Van Egmond, who had served in Napoleon's army as a young man. The colonel was supposed to meet Mackenzie at Montgomery's Tavern on December 7, but Mackenzie was too excited to wait for him. Mail intercepted at Peacock Inn had included information about government plans, and after reading them Mackenzie decided to lead a mob into the city right away. During the march his irresponsibility verged on madness as he

rushed into the home of a Toronto banker and set it on fire.

Mackenzie had some knowledge of government plans, but Lieutenant-Governor Bond Head knew all about Mackenzie's intentions —he had been informed by James Hogg of Hogg's Hollow. Sir Francis regarded Mackenzie almost as a joke, and sent most of his regular troops to Kingston so that they could help Sir John Colborne quell the rebellion in Lower Canada, if necessary. Mackenzie's march on city hall on December 5 was easily repelled by Sheriff Jarvis and twenty-six soldiers. Both sides fired a few shots and fled from each other! One man was killed.

When Colonel Van Egmond arrived at Montgomery's Tavern on December 7, as planned, most of Mackenzie's followers had fled. Nevertheless, he led a force down Yonge Street to Gallow's Hill, where they met a strong government force. Fighting lasted only a few minutes. The government forces blew up Montgomery's Tavern, and Mackenzie fled to the United States by way of Niagara. Later in the month he established a base on Navy Island and proclaimed a provisional government.

Other Events on December 8:

1764   The second registration of paper money took place.

1838   Von Schultz and nine other Hunters were hanged at Kingston (see November 13).

1852   Laval University, Quebec, received a royal charter.

1891   Canada put duty on fish from Newfoundland in retaliation for Newfoundland's having restricted bait for Canadian fishermen.

1897   Pope Leo XIV urged Catholics to accept the settlement proposed for Manitoba separate schools.

1913   An Order-in-Council prohibited the landing of skilled or unskilled labor at British Columbia ports.

Deportation of Acadians Completed

Many fascinating books, movies and television programs have been produced about the "Cajuns" who live in Louisiana. The "Cajuns" are really the "Acadians" who were expelled from Nova Scotia in 1755.

Nova Scotia had changed hands so often between Britain and France that the Acadians seldom knew where they stood. In 1749, when Halifax was founded, there were probably 10,000 Acadians in Nova Scotia. Governor Cornwallis had instructions to treat them justly and give them complete freedom, provided they took an oath of allegiance to the British Crown. The Acadians, however, insisted that they had taken an oath of allegiance in 1729 which exempted them from bearing arms or fighting against the French or Indians. They would not take another oath, in spite of repeated warnings that the British Government would take strong action if they continued to refuse.

On June 6, 1755, soldiers from Fort Edward at Windsor, Nova Scotia, arrived at Minas and took the Acadians' guns. The Acadians sent a petition to Governor Lawrence, who had succeeded Cornwallis, asking that their guns be returned because, they said, they were afraid of the Indians. After a second petition on July 5, Lawrence put the deputies in prison. Finally, on July 28, it was decided that as the Acadians were obdurate in their refusal to take the oath, the entire Acadian population must be deported (see February 11).

On September 5, 1755, Colonel John Winslow spoke to 418 Acadian representatives in a church at Grand Pré. He told them that their lands, homes, and livestock had been forfeited to the Crown, and that they were to be deported. Families were kept together as much as possible and they were allowed to take their money and household goods.

The deportation was completed by December 9, 1755, when the last ship sailed from Annapolis Royal. Colonel Winslow said, "It hurts me to hear their weeping and wailing. Thank God the transports are gone at last."

Gradually many of them, or their descendents, managed to return to their old holdings. There are more than 200,000 Acadians in Canada today. An Acadian, Louis J. Robichaud, was elected Premier of New Brunswick on July 12, 1960, the Orange anniversary!

Other Events on December 9:

1755 The first post office in Canada was opened at Halifax .

1843 Bishop's College, Lennoxville, was incorporated.

1878 The first train arrived at Winnipeg from Pembina, United States.

1926 The session of Parliament which introduced Old Age Pensions was opened.

1965 A power failure at Niagara Falls caused a serious blackout in a large part of Ontario and the northeast United States.

Evangeline Monument and Church, Grand Pré, N.S.

Saskatchewan Métis Elect Dumont President

The eventual fates of two rebel leaders, Louis Riel and Gabriel Dumont, form an extraordinary contrast. Riel was hanged at Regina in November, 1885, but Dumont became an honored citizen and lived to a ripe old age.

Dumont, a Métis, was far more warlike than Riel. During the rebellion of 1885, Riel would often go into battle carrying a crucifix, trying to stop the fighting. Dumont, on the other hand, wanted to incite the Indians to kill every white settler on the prairies so that General Middleton would be forced to scatter his forces to cope with the situation.

Dumont was only a young man during the Red River uprising in 1869-1870. When the provisional government collapsed in 1870, Dumont persuaded a number of Métis families to move with him to Batoche on the South Saskatchewan River. They were buffalo hunters and loved the free life of the open plains; they felt they would be safe from encroaching civilization at Batoche. Dumont was elected President of the Saskatchewan Valley Métis on December 10, 1873. He was a president who governed from the saddle of his horse, with his Winchester rifle always at hand. This was the type of government his people understood and respected.

When surveyors and settlers began to move into Saskatchewan a few years later, the buffalo were disappearing rapidly, and civilization was creeping nearer. Dumont knew that if his people were to resist this successfully they needed a leader who could make speeches and write letters, and he could not. He went to Montana, where Riel was a school teacher, and persuaded him to come back to Canada. The rebellion of 1885 was the result.

Riel surrendered on May 15 but Dumont escaped across the border. He was ready to return and accept the blame if the government would release Riel. Instead Riel went to the gallows. Dumont did not have to stay in Montana for long. He visited Batoche several times, and even Montreal, where he was received as a hero. He died in his own farmhouse on the South Saskatchewan in 1906, and the province has erected a cairn to honor his memory.

Gabriel Dumont (1838-1906)

Other Events on December 10:

1755   The ships, *Violet* and *Duke William*, sank during an Atlantic storm while carrying Acadians from Nova Scotia; 1,200 lives were lost.

1880   The contract to build the C.P.R. came before the House of Commons in Ottawa.

1894   The failure of a London firm caused a financial crisis in Newfoundland.

1949   The Supreme Court of Canada was made the final authority on judicial matters.

Father Lacombe Dies

December 11 was the last day of life on earth for one of Canada's most remarkable missionaries, Father Albert Lacombe, who died at the Lacombe Home in Alberta. Two towns in the province have been named after him.

Father Lacombe's story is beautifully told in Grant MacEwan's *Fifty Mighty Men*. He began his service in the West at Fort Edmonton in 1853, and won the hearts of the Crees and Blackfoot Indians although they were often at war with each other. Father Lacombe was cut down by a bullet during one of their fights.

One of the most delightful stories about him is how he became the president of the C.P.R. for one hour! When the railway tracks were being laid across the Prairies, the Indians sometimes tore them up during the night. Father Lacombe persuaded them to let the railway go through, and the C.P.R. was grateful. When the directors of the company made one of their first trips west in 1883, they stopped at Calgary, where they invited Father Lacombe to have lunch with them in their private car. As they sat down together President George Stephen (later Lord Mount Stephen) announced that he had resigned for one hour. Director R. B. Angus moved that Father Lacombe be elected to succeed him, and the motion was carried unanimously. During the lunch he was given $10,000 to help the work of his mission, and also a lifetime pass on the railway.

Father Lacombe made good use of the pass and did not hesitate to go to Ottawa to see the prime minister or a member of the cabinet whenever there was an important problem to be solved. He would not accept an evasive answer, or delay. On one occasion, when a cabinet minister told him that he would look into the situation, Father Lacombe replied, in effect, "Well now, that's very good of you. I am accustomed to sleeping on the ground, so I will just lie down on

Father Lacombe persuading the Indians

this nice carpet of yours and rest while you are attending to this matter!" He received his answer within an hour!

Other Events on December 11:

1687 A French and English commission, under a treaty of neutrality, gave Hudson Bay territory to France.

1753 George Washington claimed Ohio Valley for Virginia in opposition to the claims of Canada (see December 4).

1813 American General McClure burned Newark and Queenston on the Niagara Peninsula before retreating to the United States.

1916 Saskatchewan voted to abolish liquor stores.

1936 George VI became king on the abdication of Edward VIII, now the Duke of Windsor.

1948 Newfoundland and Canada signed an agreement for Newfoundland to join Confederation.

Guglielmo Marconi (1874-1937)

Marconi Hears Code

On December 12, 1901, at St. John's, Newfoundland, Marconi proved that wireless signals could be sent across the Atlantic. This was one of the most important developments in the world, and yet Marconi was almost run out of town!

In 1901, after important experiments in conjunction with the Royal Navy, Marconi built a transmitter at Poldhu, Cornwall. Then he established a receiving station at St. John's. His aerial was a 600-foot wire hoisted into the air by a kite. Poldhu had been instructed to transmit the letter "S" in Morse code (three dots) every day for three hours beginning at 3 p.m., G.M.T. The experiments began on December 10, 1901, but the kite blew away. Another aerial was lost the next day, but on December 12, at 12:30, Newfoundland time, a 400-foot aerial was flying. Suddenly the receiver began clicking. Marconi was listening with C. S. Kemp, P. W. Paget, and several fishermen from the neighborhood. He was so excited that he shouted in Italian, "Do you hear that?" They all listened carefully, and the three dots could be heard clearly. There was no doubt about it. The three dots being sent from Poldhu,

2,000 miles away, were being received at St. John's. They had cost about $200,000!

Marconi only had time to experiment for a few more days before he was told to leave St. John's as the Submarine Cable Company had exclusive communication rights from Newfoundland for fifty years. He went to Sydney, Nova Scotia, where he met Alex Johnson, a newspaper publisher, who introduced him to Prime Minister Laurier and Finance Minister Fielding. They gave him $80,000 to continue his experiments from Glace Bay.

Some scientists were claiming that the messages from Poldhu had been faked. Others said that although wireless signals had traveled from east to west, they would not go in the opposite direction against the movement of the earth. Marconi proved them wrong on December 5, 1902, when the signals he sent from Glace Bay were heard in Britain. On December 15, Governor-General Minto sent this message: "To His Majesty the King, London: May I be permitted by means of this first wireless message, to congratulate Your Majesty on the success of Marconi's great invention connecting England and Canada—Minto."

Other Events on December 12:

1813   Captain Black of the Royal Navy captured Fort Astoria (see October 6).

1831   W. L. Mackenzie was expelled from the Legislature of Upper Canada. He was expelled five times in three years (see January 2).

1837   Dr. Wolfred Nelson was captured and exiled during the Lower Canada Rebellion.

1885   The first freight train carrying Manitoba wheat left Portage for Montreal.

1949   Mrs. Nancy Hodges was appointed Speaker of the British Columbia Legislature. She was the first woman Speaker in the British Commonwealth.

1951   The St. Lawrence Seaway Authority was established.

Iroquois Sign Treaty, Impressed by French

France would have had a better chance of keeping Canada if it had been possible to secure the backing of the Iroquois. The Five Nations tribes eventually gave their full support to the British, whom they disliked—but they hated the French.

There was one period of peace between the Iroquois and the French and it lasted nearly twenty years. On December 13, 1667, representatives of the Oneidas, Onondagas, Cayugas, and Senecas signed a peace treaty at Quebec. They had been greatly impressed by the arrival of the Marquis de Tracy and the famous Carignan-Salières Regiment on June 30. The fifth Iroquois tribe, the fierce Mohawks, did not capitulate until Tracy captured Andaraqué (see October 15).

The peace between the French and the Iroquois was due in part to the efforts of a half-breed spokesman for the Indians who was known as the "Flemish Bastard." Although the "Flemish Bastard" helped to bring about peace, he was not popular with the French clergy. Father Ragueneau wrote in the *Jesuit Relations*: "This commander, the most prominent among the enemies of the Faith, was a Hollander—or rather, an execrable issue of sin, the monstrous offspring of a Dutch heretic father and a pagan woman." His mother was actually a Mohawk.

Although the peace was broken several times, it was feared by other Indian nations, in whose interest it was to keep the French and Iroquois at war with each other. Crafty Huron chief Kondiaronk, the Rat, governed his people in the Great Lakes area from Michilimackinac. After the incidents at Fort Frontenac and the massacre at Lachine (see August 5), he learned that the Iroquois were sending a delegation to Fort Frontenac to try to work out another peace treaty. Kondiaronk ambushed them, killed one of the chiefs, and took the others prisoner. Then he pretended that he had been acting under the orders of the French, and allowed them to "escape." When the Iroquois arrived back in their villages they described what they had been led to believe was the treachery of the French. That was the end of any possible peace between the Iroquois and Onontio, as the French governors were called.

Other Events on December 13:

1665   Intendant Talon built a ship of 120 tons at his own expense.
       The Dutch attacked St. John's, Newfoundland.

1783   It was estimated that there were 30,000 United Empire Loyalists in Nova Scotia.
       Penal laws against Roman Catholics were repealed in Nova Scotia.

1785   Loyalists petitioned Governor Carleton for an Academy of Arts and Science. This led to the creation of the University of New Brunswick.

1804   Joseph Howe was born in Halifax.

1837   W. L. Mackenzie occupied Navy Island above Niagara Falls (see December 7) and proclaimed a provisional government.

1893   Prince Edward Island voted for prohibition.

1907   The Women's Canadian Club was inaugurated at Montreal by Governor-General Earl Grey.

Earthquake Threatens Towns in British Columbia

One of Canada's most spectacular earthquakes, on February 5, 1663, has already been described. It helped Bishop Laval's campaign to stop his people from selling liquor to the Indians. They gave up the practice for a time, believing that the earthquake was punishment for their sins. The damage might have been worse except that the earthquake took place in the winter when there was a great deal of snow on the ground.

British Columbia, lying between California and Alaska which have both been badly damaged by earthquakes, had a narrow escape on December 14, 1872. A large part of the province was shaken by tremors which began shortly after 9.30 p.m., and continued for about forty seconds, especially in the inland areas. Usually an earthquake of ten seconds will cause a great deal of damage and loss of life, but there was little damage and no loss of life in British Columbia. Possibly the snow helped to cushion the effect.

In places like Clinton, Soda Creek, and Yale, the temperature was 20° below zero, but people ran out of their homes in the snow and bitterly cold weather. Buildings swayed and church bells rang. There was a general feeling of thanksgiving when the tremors stopped and so little damage was done.

The earthquake was also felt along the coast where there was no snow. It lasted for about ten seconds in Victoria where buildings might have collapsed. Miraculously, little damage was done. Vancouver did not exist in 1872 except for tiny communities like Hastings and Gastown in the general area.

Other Events on December 14:

1817 The Bank of Montreal was incorporated.

1837 Rebels at St. Eustache, Lower Canada, were defeated by Sir John Colborne.

1851 George Brown was elected to Parliament for the first time.

1885 Yoho National Park was established by Order-in-Council.

1929 The Federal Government transferred natural resources to Manitoba and Saskatchewan.

1951 Foreign exchange control regulations were abolished.

1956 John G. Diefenbaker was elected leader of the Conservative party.

1960 The University of Ottawa was given $35 million for expansion.

Legislation, which made the retirement of Superior and Supreme Court judges automatic at age seventy-five, was passed. It became effective in March, 1961.

Twenty nations, including Canada, signed a new trade agreement to set up the Organization for Economic Co-operation and Development. The purpose was to promote co-operation, more aid to underdeveloped countries, and to expand trade generally.

1963 A Canadian selection of prints, shown at the First American Biennial Exhibition of Engravings, at Santiago, Chile, won the Grand Award of Honor.

1964 Closure was imposed in the House of Commons to end the flag debate. One of the longest and most bitter debates in our history was concluded.

Beatty Arranges for Building of C.P.R. Ships

Some salt water sailors look down on the fresh water seamen, so captains of the Canadian Pacific Steamship Company may not like to be reminded that their service started on the Great Lakes. On the C.P.R. transcontinental, one of the most costly and difficult sections to build was along the north shore of Lake Superior. The directors decided to buy three ships which would operate from Owen Sound, Ontario, to Port Arthur's Landing, and transport supplies to the construction gangs.

The C.P.R. picked a good man for the job. He was Henry Beatty, an Ulster Scot, who had come to Canada as a young man and settled at Thorold, Ontario. Young Beatty went west in 1863 and made $40,000 in the Cariboo gold rush. Then he returned to Thorold and organized a steamship service that eventually became the Northwest Transportation Company of Sarnia.

In September 1883, it was settled that Beatty would organize a Great Lakes shipping service for the C.P.R. and on December 15, he was in Scotland arranging for the building of two ships. The *Alberta* and *Athabasca* were constructed in such a way that they could be cut in half after they sailed across the Atlantic. This enabled them to be brought through the relatively small canals, and then put together again for service on the Great Lakes. His third ship, the *Algoma,* was the former *City of Toronto* that had plied between Toronto and Hamilton.

The success of the three ships encouraged the C.P.R. to organize the transpacific and transatlantic steamship services that made the yellow funnels with red and white checkerboards, familiar sights in most harbors around the world. In fact it was as early as 1889 that the C.P.R. ordered three 6,000-ton liners: *Empress of India, Empress of Japan* and *Empress of China*. When the *Empress of India* made her trial runs in 1891, the company's red and white checkered house flag was unfurled for the first time.

The steamship service probably saved the C.P.R. from bankruptcy between 1893 and 1895. There was a depression which caused 156 American railroads to go out of business, but the C.P.R. made a profit, thanks to the business generated by the popular steamship service.

Other Events on December 15:

1818   The Provincial Agricultural Society was formed in Nova Scotia.

1858   A railway opened between Halifax and Truro, Nova Scotia.

1891   The first trainload of British sailors bound for China arrived at Halifax and crossed Canada by a train which was specially decorated. There were receptions at Montreal, Toronto, Winnipeg, and Calgary.

Premier Mercier of Quebec was dismissed because public contracts were used for campaign funds. He was acquitted of the charge in November 1892.

1896   The Canadian Northern Railway completed a line from Gladstone to Dauphin, Manitoba (see June 9).

1902   The first official wireless message was sent across the Atlantic.

1920   An Order-in-Council was passed so that no immigrant could enter Canada without having $250, $125 for every member of the family over eighteen, and $50 for each child.

1925   Canada and Britain signed an agreement reducing transportation rates for immigrants.

1960   Montreal's $30-million airport was officially opened.

A Habitant

Law Hits Profiteers

While the *habitants* of early Canada were said to be better off than they would have been had they remained as peasants in France, their lives were very restricted. Louis XIV liked to have a good time but he did not extend that privilege any further than the nobility of France. Louis was a very heavy eater, beginning dinner with at least three different soups, then several kinds of fish, meat dishes, poultry, and finishing with pastries and fruits. When dinner was over, he would become very melancholy and concoct further plans to order the lives of his people in Canada.

Clearing the new land was one of the biggest problems; so Louis ordered *habitants* to stay in the country and not move into towns. A farmer was not allowed to own more than two horses because he might neglect to raise cattle and sheep. Bakers were ordered to make brown bread although few people enjoyed eating it. Louis, who did not eat brown bread himself, said it was more nutritious. People were not allowed to sit on the benches in front of their homes after nine o'clock at night. Merchants could not hold meetings to discuss business matters. Women had to be home by nine o'clock. Unmarried girls were allowed to dance only with other girls, in their own homes, with their mothers present. Men were not allowed to use profanity. There were fines for the first four offences. If they were caught swearing five times, they were sent to the pillory. Their lips were branded for a sixth offence, and their tongues were cut out if they were caught eight times.

On December 16, 1663, a law was passed to reduce profiteering on goods imported from France. Merchants were permitted to mark up goods 65 per cent after paying 10 per cent duty. When ships arrived at Quebec, members of the Sovereign Council would go on board, inspect the goods for quality, and set the prices at which they must be sold. As in the case of the King's Girls (see April 5), the people of Quebec had a big advantage over those in Trois Rivières and Montreal because they had the first choice of imported products.

Other Events on December 16:

1674   The French West India Company's grant was revoked. It was supposed to develop Canada as well as other French colonies in the western hemisphere.

1901   Dawson City, Yukon, was incorporated.

1910   A delegation of 1,000 farmers marched on Ottawa demanding an increase in the preference for British goods and reciprocity with the United States.

1949   The British North America Act was amended, vesting the power to amend the constitution in Parliament.

1953   Royal assent was given for the formation of the Department of Northern Affairs and National Resources.

First Legislature of Lower Canada Opens

In 1791 the British parliament passed the Constitutional Act which created two Canadas. One was Lower Canada, predominantly French, and the other was Upper Canada, almost wholly English. Each province had its own legislature, with upper and lower chambers, and the system of laws it preferred. The lieutenant-governor of each province chose the members of the upper house, but the assembly was elected by the people.

The people of Upper Canada were accustomed to elections, because many of them came from the former British colonies in the United States. The French in Lower Canada had never known an election, except in the parishes where the people elected the church-wardens. There was some excitement in Lower Canada's first election campaign leading to the opening of the legislature on December 17, 1792. Even the *habitants* could vote, because they were landholders. Most of them were illiterate, but they returned one of the strongest assemblies in the history of Lower Canada. There were 50 members to represent 100,000 people, and they included merchants, lawyers, and seigniors. Montreal with 18,000, and Quebec with 14,000, had 4 members each.

When the legislature opened, the first question was which language would be used, English or French. One of the French members said that since they lived under the best of kings, gratitude and courtesy required that they should speak in English. However, few of the members knew any English at all, so it was decided that both languages would be used. The opening prayer would be in French one day, and English the next. The members were assured that God would understand both languages!

Other Events on December 17:

1867　British Columbia's legislature met for the first time at Victoria.

1893　The Canadian Bankers' Association was organized at Montreal.

1924　The Legislature of British Columbia adopted a resolution opposing further immigration of Orientals to Canada.

1939　The British Commonwealth Air Training Plan was signed in Ottawa by Canada, Britain, Australia and New Zealand.

First Parliament of Lower Canada

Canadian Overseas Generals, 1944

1st Div. Reaches U.K.

Although World War II began on September 1, 1939, when Germany attacked Poland, Canada did not declare war until Sunday, September 10, after a special session of Parliament had been called. There had been a general mobilization order on September 1, but Canadian forces were badly prepared. The full-time army had 4,000 officers and men, the non-permanent active militia ("Sunday soldiers") totaled 60,000; the R.C.A.F., 4,500; and the R.C.N., 1,800 men.

During the war years the strength of Canadian forces was increased many fold. In all, the army reached a peak strength of five divisions of nearly half a million men. The R.C.A.F. grew to nearly 250,000 men, including forty-eight fighter squadrons and a complete bomber group. The tiny navy of 1939 grew to 100,000 men operating more than 400 ships from cruisers to motor-torpedo boats. They played a vital part in keeping the lifeline to Britain open and winning the Battle of the Atlantic against the submarines.

In spite of its relatively small size in 1939, the 1st Canadian Division sailed from Halifax on December 10 in the liners *Aquitania*, *Empress of Britain*, *Empress of Australia*, *Duchess of Bedford*, and *Monarch of Bermuda*. They were escorted by R.C.N. destroyers part of the way, and the battleship *Resolution* all the way across the Atlantic. The skippers of the merchant ships did not like convoys (see October 3) and during a fog the *Empress of Australia* became "lost." Two days later, shortly after sunset, a British cruiser appeared on the horizon and made a lamp signal to the battleship "Luke 15: 6" which reads in part: "Rejoice with me; for I have found my sheep which was lost." The *Empress* rejoined the convoy the following morning!

When the Canadians reached the Clyde there was a great array of British sea power to welcome them. Winston Churchill, who was then First Lord of the Admiralty, broadcast the news of their safe arrival and said, "It has warmed the cockles of our hearts." The Division reached Aldershot on December 18, 1939. It was the beginning of a mighty effort by the army which was to include fighting in Sicily, France, Italy and Holland.

Other Events on December 18:

1963   Sieur de Monts was granted a monopoly of the fur trade for ten years. It was revoked later (see July 27).

1813   A British-Canadian force sacked Fort Niagara in the United States.

1889   The C.P.R. telegraph joined the Atlantic cable at Canso, Nova Scotia.

1897   An Order-in-Council changed the boundaries of Yukon, Franklin, and Ungava and established the Geographic Board of Canada.

1901   The Territorial Grain Growers' Association was organized at Indian Head, Manitoba.

Farmers vs. Protection

Protection is a monster when you come to look at it. It is the essence of injustice. It is the acme of human selfishness. It is one of the relics of barbarism.

—ALEXANDER MACKENZIE, 1876

I denounce the policy of protection as bondage — yea, bondage; and I refer to bondage in the same manner in which American slavery was bondage.

—SIR WILFRID LAURIER, 1894

Adequate protection is that which would at all times secure the Canadian market to Canadians in respect to all Canadian enterprises.

—SIR ROBERT BORDEN, 1904

When the workers of Canada wake up they will find that Protection is only one among the several economic fangs fastened in their "corpus vile" by the little group of railroad men, bankers, lumbermen and manufacturing monopolists who own their country.

—J. A. HOBSON, 1906

At the beginning of the twentieth century Canada began to change from an agricultural to an industrial nation. As a result, there was an increased demand for tariff protection for industry.

The tariff question was important in Canadian politics for many years. With a low tariff, Canadian wheat, pulp, timber and other raw products would flow across the border to the States; American cars, machinery, household articles, clothes, canned food and other products would pour into Canada because they could be made more cheaply in the States. With a high tariff, raw products would be harder to sell abroad. Manufactured products would rise in price, but more of them would be made at home and there would be more industry, and therefore more employment.

High tariffs were supposed to "protect" young Canadian industries until they were able to stand on their own feet. What actually happened was that they made big profits for eastern manufacturers and financiers, while Canadian consumers paid higher prices to keep sometimes inefficient manufacturers in business. McGill economist Stephen Leacock wrote: "the huge infants" of Canadian industry "rolled off their mother's lap" but still they continued to receive the benefit of high tariff protection.

Prime Minister Sir Wilfrid Laurier began to feel the resentment of Canadian farmers when he visited the West in 1910. He was met by rural delegations who urged him to reduce tariffs and make a reciprocal trade agreement with the States. John Evans, a pioneer in the Saskatchewan Farmers' movement, asked him, "Sir Wilfrid, in 1896 you said you would skin the Tory bear of protection—now we want to know what you did with the hide."

Farmers' organizations had been growing in strength since December 19, 1883, when a farmers' union met at Winnipeg and drafted a Bill of Rights. It sent a delegation of three members to Ottawa, without satisfactory results, but it marked the beginning of "farmers' marches on Ottawa." Prime Minister Laurier was undoubtedly influenced by a delegation of 1,000 farmers who went to Ottawa on December 16, 1910, and demanded a revision of tariffs. He made the reciprocal trade agreement with the States that led to his defeat in the election of 1911 (see September 21).

Other Events on December 19:

1813   James McGill died, leaving £10,000 for a university.

1846   A telegraph line was opened between Toronto and Hamilton. Railway service did not begin until December, 1855.

1854   Sir Edmund Walker Head was appointed Governor-General of Canada.

1960   Tunku Abdul Rahman Putra Al-Haj, Prime Minister of Malaya, visited Ottawa.

Government Begins Amalgamation of Railways

In many railway stations across Canada there is a bronze plaque commemorating Sir Henry Thornton, the first president of Canadian National Railways. When World War I ended, the privately-owned Grand Trunk and Canadian Northern Railways were bankrupt, and the Government decided to take them over. An Order-in-Council was passed on December 20, 1919, but the amalgamation was not completed until January, 1923. It included the Canadian Government Railways, the most important of which was the Intercolonial to the Maritimes.

Sir Henry Thornton was an American-born engineer who had gone to Britain in 1914 to become general manager of the Great Eastern Railway. During the war he served as Assistant Director-General of Transportation in France. Then a British subject, he was knighted for his services. Prime Minister Mackenzie King invited him to come to Canada to organize the Canadian National

Sir Henry Thornton (1871-1933)

Railways. Its 22,000 miles of track in Canada and 2,000 miles in the U.S.A. made it the longest in the world.

Sir Henry Thornton was a man of great drive and imagination. Before he resigned in 1932, it was said that he knew personally every member of the train crews. CN porters were proud that they had talked with him and shaken his hand. There was a great deal of criticism levelled at the railway with its annual deficits, but the morale of the CN employees was never shaken.

Sir Henry modernized railroading. He built hotels, acquired ships for coastal service, and Canadian National radio stations to provide entertainment for the passengers on the trains. The radio stations became the basis of the present Canadian Broadcasting Corporation. He even introduced two-way telephone service on trains like the International Limited between Montreal, Toronto, and Chicago. In all, Sir Henry Thornton spent about $400 million to make the CN one of the most modern railways in the world.

Sir Henry was heavily criticized because he built new hotels at Halifax, Saskatoon and Vancouver, and enlarged the Château Laurier in Ottawa. The C.P.R. had enough influence to prevent the Hotel Vancouver from being opened, and it stood empty for a number of years. When World War II began, conditions would have been chaotic if it had not been for Sir Henry Thornton's foresight. Yet criticism forced him to resign in 1932 and he died soon after.

Other Events on December 20:

1859   The first sod was turned for the Parliament Buildings in Ottawa. The cornerstone was not laid until September 1, 1860 when Edward Prince of Wales visited Canada (see January 27).

1929   Canada resumed diplomatic relations with Russia.

Canadian Force Fails to Reach Khartoum in Time

Canada's first contingent sent overseas to help Britain in a war was made up not of soldiers, but of canoemen. It lost a desperate race against tragedy by three days.

In 1884 Britain became involved in a Holy War in the Egyptian Sudan. General Charles Gordon was instructed to evacuate British citizens there, and managed to save 2,000 people before being besieged at Khartoum. General Lord Wolseley, who as Colonel Garnet Wolseley had put down the Red River uprising in 1870, was placed in command of a force to break the siege and get Gordon out. The best way to transport the force to Khartoum was up the Nile River, and General Wolseley remembered the *voyageurs* who had helped in the transportation of his 1,200 soldiers from Fort William to Fort Garry. They had built boats which they portaged on wooden rollers in a fantastic journey through the wilderness. They were the kind of men Wolseley wanted to take his men and supplies up the Nile.

A group of 386 lumbermen and Caughnawaga Indians was organized and sailed for Egypt on September 15, 1884. The men were under the command of Lieutenant-Colonel Fred C. Denison but did not wear uniforms as they had not been recruited as soldiers. Nevertheless, they were Canadians serving overseas in an Imperial war which was in no way even remotely connected with the defence of Canada. It was a precedent, although the men were paid by Britain, not Canada.

On December 21, 1884, Wolseley's force was battling the elements to reach Khartoum in time. General Gordon's garrison had been under siege since February and it was known that he could not hold out much longer. The lumbermen and Indians gave it everything they had, but Wolseley's force arrived at Khartoum three days too late. The entire garrison had been massacred.

Although Wolseley's rescue effort failed, he had high praise for the Canadians, and wrote: "I desire to place on record, not only my own opinion, but that of every officer connected with the direction and management of the boat columns, that the services of these *voyageurs* has been of the greatest possible value, and further, that their conduct throughout has been excellent. They have earned for themselves a high reputation among the troops up the Nile."

Other Events on December 21:

1620   *Mayflower* landed at Plymouth Rock. One of the ship's planks is included in the Peace Arch between British Columbia and the State of Washington.

1708   The French under St. Ovide captured St. John's, Newfoundland.

1814   Colonel Henry Procter was tried by court-martial at Montreal for his defeat at Moraviantown (see October 5).

1838   Joseph Cardinal and Joseph Duquette were executed for crimes during the Lower Canada Rebellion.

1865   George Brown withdrew from the coalition Government (see June 22).

1866   The Bytown and Prescott Railway became the St. Lawrence and Ottawa Railway.

1894   Sir Mackenzie Bowell became prime minister.

1942   Butter rationing began in Canada as a wartime measure. Gasoline had been rationed since April 1.

1956   Pandit Nehru, Prime Minister of India, visited Ottawa.

1962   Prime Minister Diefenbaker went to the Bahamas for talks with Prime Minister Macmillan of Britain, and President Kennedy of the United States.

Sir Charles Hibbert Tupper (1855-1927)

U.S. To Pay Damages

Canada and the United States have been remarkably good friends over the years. Although American armies invaded Canada in 1775 and again during the War of 1812, the bitterness was against Britain. Most of the disagreements between Canada and the United States have been over fishing rights along the Atlantic coast (see February 27 and May 16).

In 1885, the United States was annoyed because it had had to pay Canada a $5.5 million arbitration award for fishing rights obtained under the Washington Treaty, when Sir John A. Macdonald was forced to take a back seat in the British delegation. The States ended the fishing clause of the treaty, and took action against Canadian fishermen on the Pacific coast by declaring the Bering Sea to be an exclusive reserve for American fur-sealers. British Columbian ships were seized when they entered the area.

Once again there was a conference in Washington in 1887 and 1888. Canada was represented by Dr. Charles Tupper, former premier of Nova Scotia and a Father of Confederation. The Americans refused to discuss the Bering Sea situation, and a proposed fishing agreement was rejected by the American Senate. Canada, however, agreed to allow American fishing vessels to use Canadian ports on payment of a license fee, and the Bering Sea dispute was eventually submitted to arbitration in Paris.

The important thing about the Washington conference of 1887-1888 was that Canada's position had greatly strengthened since 1871 when Sir John A. Macdonald had only been allowed a minor role in the British delegation. Dr. Tupper dominated the British-Canadian delegation. His son, Charles Hibbert Tupper, acted as Britain's agent during the subsequent Bering Sea arbitration negotiations and was knighted for his service.

On December 22, 1896, the Paris arbitration tribunal announced that the States would pay Canada $463,000 compensation for British Columbian fishing vessels seized in the Bering Sea, and that the area could not be treated as an American reserve. Measures were taken to protect the fur-sealing industry by prohibiting sealing within 60 miles of the Pribilof Islands, the rookery of fur seals. All fur-sealing was prohibited in a wide area during May, June, and July.

Other Events on December 22:

1807 The American Congress placed an embargo on foreign ships entering American ports.

1856 The Buffalo and Lake Huron Railway was opened from Fort Erie to Stratford, Ontario. It later became the Grand Trunk.

1869 Pro-Confederation forces were defeated in Newfoundland.

1952 Prime Minister St. Laurent announced the construction of a National Library.

1961 Canada sold grain to China worth $71 million over a period of thirty months.

1962 Solon Low, former Leader of the Social Credit Party, died.

Arrival of Canadian Northern Railway at Dauphin, Man., Creates Problems and Prosperity

The railway building of Mackenzie and Mann has already been mentioned (see June 9). On December 23, 1896, their Canadian Northern Railway reached Dauphin, Manitoba.

The story of Dauphin is a good example of what a railway could do for progress. In September, 1896, Dauphin was a wheatfield. When it was announced that the Canadian Northern Railway would go through there, surveyors waited until the crop was harvested, and then laid out the townsite. Lots were offered for sale in October, and seventy buildings had been put up by the end of the year. Two years later the town had four hotels, a church, school, and a number of businesses. The population jumped from 2,500 to 12,000.

There were still not enough people to harvest the crops. One prairie farmer could seed half a section single-handed but ten more workers were needed to bring in the harvest. There was little help to be had from the Prairies themselves because every farmer was fully occupied with his own problems. Speed was essential if the grain was to be cut, stooked, threshed and taken to railway shipping points before it was spoiled by rain, frost and snow.

The problem was almost a national emergency. It was solved by running big advertisements in British Columbian and eastern newspapers urging able-bodied men to travel to prairie centres on special excursion trains provided by the Canadian Pacific and Grand Trunk Railways. The pay was $1.50 a day!

The first year of the harvest excursions was 1891, and 5,000 men answered the call. By 1929, the last year of the boom, as many as 75,000 workers were making the annual trip to harvest the wheatfields. The pay had risen to the highest in the land, $5 a day on the average, although it went as high as $8 in some localities. But men worked hard for their money, pitching stooks on wagons for 16 hours a day.

The harvest excursions were a feature of Canadian life until the stock market crash of 1929 (see October 29) led to the depression. By the time the depression had ended, giant combines had been invented. They threshed as they reaped, and manpower was no longer necessary. The colorful harvest excursions are now only memories.

Other Events on December 23:

1855 The Grand Trunk Railway was completed from Lévis to St. Thomas, Quebec.

1869 The Western extension of the European and North American Railroad opened from Fairville (Saint John), New Brunswick, to St. Croix on the American border.

1871 The Quebec Legislature revised municipal laws and established a code.

1872 Amor de Cosmos (lover of the world) became Premier of British Columbia (see February 7).

1963 The Federal Government approved, in principle, the establishment in Ottawa of a National Centre for the Performing Arts, and of an annual National Festival.

1964 Seven Christian Churches of Canada— Roman Catholic, United Church of Canada, Anglican, Presbyterian, Baptist, Greek Orthodox, and Lutheran— signed an undertaking to share a pavilion at Expo '67. The $3,500,000 building was to be financed by industry and business.

War of 1812 Ends

If this encroachment of Great Britain is not provided against, the United States have appealed in vain. If your efforts to accomplish it should fail, all further negotiations will cease, and you will return home without delay.

—SEC. OF STATE JAMES MONROE, 1813, *to the American Peace Commissioners before negotiations at Ghent, Belgium.*

Christmas Eve deserves a happy story, and there is one. A treaty to end the useless War of 1812 was signed at Ghent in Belgium, just as church bells were ringing the joyful advent of Christmas Day, 1814.

Negotiations to end the war had begun in June. The Americans, who had ended an armistice arranged by the British in August, 1812, were glad to seek peace now. Napoleon had been defeated in Europe and the Duke of Wellington was making crack troops available for the war against the States. Washington had been attacked and burned. The Americans decided that they had lost the war, but they could still try to win the peace. They sent Senator James Bayard, Jonathan Russell, John Quincy Adams (a future president), Albert Gallatin, and Henry Clay to Ghent to negotiate with the British. All were top-flight men.

The British delegation was weak. It was headed by Lord Gambier who had no experience in diplomacy. He had even been court-martialed for neglect of duty while serving with the navy. The second member of the delegation was Henry Goulburn, thirty-year-old Under-Secretary for War and the Colonies. William Adams was the third, a lawyer who took little part in the discussions. The Americans knew they could regain at the peace table what they had lost in battle.

The Treaty of Ghent ignored the issues that had led to the war, and no concessions were made by either side. Frontiers were almost unchanged, although Canada, where most of the fighting had taken place and the real objective of the Americans, might have obtained the west coast territory as far south as the Columbia River (see October 6).

At Ghent on Christmas Day, the British delegation entertained the Americans at dinner, at which roast beef and plum pudding were served. The orchestra played "God Save the King" and "Yankee Doodle." The Americans were the hosts a few days later and John Quincy Adams proposed the toast: "Ghent, the city of peace. May the gates of the temple of Janus, here closed, not be opened again for a century!" His wish has come true—and for more than a century.

Other Events on December 24:

1771 Samuel Hearne discovered Great Slave Lake.

1943 General Eisenhower was appointed Commander-in-Chief of the Allied Forces to invade France.

1960 Professor Frank Forward of the University of British Columbia was honored in the United States for his research in nickel.

Hong Kong Surrenders

We were greatly concerned to hear of the landings on Hong Kong Island which have been effected by the Japanese. We cannot judge from here the conditions which rendered these landings possible or prevented effective counter-attacks upon the intruders. There must however be no thought of surrender. Every part of the island must be fought and the enemy resisted with the utmost stubbornness.

The enemy should be compelled to expend the utmost life and equipment. There must be vigorous fighting in the inner defences, and, if the need be, from house to house. Every day that you are able to maintain your resistance you help the Allied cause all over the world, and by a prolonged resistance you and your men can win the lasting honour which we are sure will be your due.

—WINSTON CHURCHILL, 1941

Christmas Day is a time for remembrance as well as rejoicing. Perhaps the most tragic Christmas in Canadian history was in 1941 when the officers and men of the Royal Rifles of Canada and the Winnipeg Grenadiers had to surrender to the Japanese in Hong Kong during World War II. They were prisoners of war in the most gruesome surroundings until late in 1945. The fighting at Hong Kong and the prisoner-of-war camps took the lives of 550 of the 2,000 men sent from Canada. Many of those who returned to Canada had to be carried on stretchers; some were mere shadows, weighing less than 100 lbs. They suffered for years from the effects of the camps.

In September, 1941, it was decided to reinforce the British garrison at Hong Kong. The following December the Japanese made surprise attacks on British and American bases at Pearl Harbor, Northern Malaya, the Philippines, Guam, Wake Island, and Hong Kong. War was declared.

Canada agreed to send two battalions to Japan, and the Royal Rifles and Winnipeg Grenadiers were chosen. The Royal Rifles had been on coastal duty in Newfoundland and at Saint John, New Brunswick; the Winnipeg Grenadiers had been serving in the West Indies. After brief training at Valcartier, Quebec, and at Winnipeg, they were taken to Vancouver in special trains. Many of the men did not want to go and fifty of them deserted from the Winnipeg Grenadiers. On October 27, when the troops went on board the *Awatea,* the British ship that was to take them to Hong Kong, about forty men decided to get off and forced their way into a shed, where they remained for about twenty minutes until officers and N.C.O.s "persuaded" them to return to the ship.

Successful defense of Hong Kong was hopeless. The British commanding officer, Major-General C. M. Maltby, had a force of about 14,000 including the Canadians. They were overwhelmed by greatly superior Japanese forces in less than two weeks of fighting, with heavy casualties inflicted on both sides. The Japanese demanded the surrender of the Hong Kong garrison as early as December 13, but fighting continued until Christmas afternoon. By this time further opposition was impossible and the garrison surrendered.

Other Events on December 25:

1635   Samuel de Champlain died at Quebec.

1785   Christ Church opened at Sorel, Quebec. It is the oldest Protestant church in Quebec.

1898   It was announced that postage throughout the British Commonwealth would be one penny (two cents) for half ounce letters.

1971   Justin Pierre Trudeau born to Prime Minister and Mrs. Trudeau, becoming the second child born to a prime minister during his term of office. The first child born to a prime minister was Mary, daughter of Sir John A. Macdonald, in 1869.

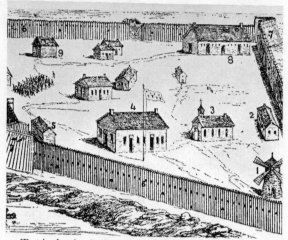

1. *Mill*
2. *Priest's house*
3. *Chapel*
4. *Seignior's house*
5. *Barn*
6. *Palisades*
7. *Bastions*

Typical seigniorial fort—Fort Rémy, Lachine, 1671

Christmas Celebrations Begin in Seigniory

In early Canada a good part of what is now the Province of Quebec was divided into seigniories. Every seignior was required to build a mill to which his tenants had to bring their grain to be ground into flour. The seignior was entitled to one-fourteenth of the grain. He could also claim one fish of every twelve caught by his habitants, and six days free labor every year.

The *habitants* also paid rent, but as they had very little money, payments were usually made in grain, chickens, or other farm produce. On Michaelmas Day, November 11, the rents were due. Then the road to the manor house was busy; perhaps one hundred tenants and members of their families brought their cackling poultry or bags of grain. They were received in the largest room of the mansion, knelt to ask the seignior's blessing, and then were treated to wine and other refreshments.

One of the most colorful days of the year was May Day. The tenants would place a gaily-decorated maypole in front of the mansion door. The seignior would make a ceremonial appearance, accept a glass of brandy, and blast the maypole with gunpowder! After that, the tenants danced around the maypole.

The happiest, gayest time was Christmas, and the celebrations lasted until Lent. It was almost the only time of year in which the *habitants* could relax, and they made the best of it. Preparations began in the spring when the mothers would set aside the best loaves of maple sugar, the jug of thickest syrup, and then as the year went on, the richest jams, clearest honey, and the prime cuts of meat and poultry.

On Christmas Eve the young people went to bed early, and were wakened for the drive through the snow to midnight Mass with sleighbells jingling. Heavy robes of buffalo or bearskin were spread over all to keep them warm. The seignior was the first to enter the church, and the first to leave. Christmas Day was spent quietly, perhaps singing old French carols. More lively festivities would begin on December 26 and continue until Lent, but gifts and good wishes were not exchanged until New Year's Day.

Other Events on December 26:

1791 The Canada Act, or Constitutional Act, went into effect. It divided Canada into Upper and Lower provinces.

1960 A federal-provincial conference opened in Ottawa.

John McDougall Born at Owen Sound, Ontario

Christmas dinner 1864, prairie style: buffalo boss and tongue, beaver tail, moose nose, wild cat, prairie chicken, rabbit, and pemmican. The menu was left in the writings of Methodist missionary, Reverend John Mc-Dougall, whose place in Canadian history ranks with the greatest of the western pioneers. He realized that the future of the western plains lay in agricultural development, not in fur-trapping.

John McDougall was born at Owen Sound, Ontario on December 27, 1842. He was educated at Cobourg, Ontario, until his missionary father, Reverend George McDougall, took over a post at Norway House at the north end of Lake Winnipeg. Young John spent a good deal of time teaching young Indians and learning their language. He was also a good athlete, and volunteered to paddle the canoe when his father decided to visit the missions which came under his charge. It meant a journey as far west as Fort Edmonton. When they arrived, John McDougall knew he had "come home." There could be no other place in the world for him but that region, and he established a mission at Victoria, 90 miles northeast of Fort Edmonton.

In order to obtain supplies it was necessary to journey to Fort Garry. On the trail, Mc-Dougall and his helpers camped one night with another group moving west. There was a good deal of banter about athletics, so it was decided to have a track meet the following day. John McDougall won all the races and the stone-throwing contest in what must have been the first athletic contest in Saskatchewan.

There are dozens of stories about the Mc-Dougalls in *Saddle, Sled and Snowshoe*, and in *Fifty Mighty Men* by Grant MacEwan. One of them is about John McDougall's toothache. It was torture but there was no dentist within 1,000 miles. Every possible remedy was tried, even applying a red hot iron, but there was no relief. Finally Reverend George McDougall made forceps from a pair of pincers and tried to pull out the tooth. After five attempts, it broke off at the gum, leaving painful roots still in the jaw. John Mc-Dougall's toothache lasted until he could get to a dentist while on a visit to eastern Canada, nine years later!

Other Events on December 27:

1610   Samuel de Champlain made a marriage contract with Hélène Boullé, who was twelve years old (see November 3).

1789   The first stage coach service in Upper Canada was inaugurated between Queenston and Fort Erie, 25 miles. The fare was one dollar.

1867   The Legislatures of Ontario and Quebec held their first meetings.

1869   Louis Riel was proclaimed president of the Red River settlement.
       The first issue of the Ottawa *Free Press* was released.

1960   The Federal and Quebec Governments agreed on the Quebec section of the Trans-Canada Highway.

Church constructed by George and John McDougall

John Christian Schultz Buys the *Nor'Wester*

Although Louis Riel always holds the spotlight of the Red River drama of 1870, Dr. John Christian Schultz also played a leading role. It is difficult to judge whether he was a villain or a hero. W. G. Hardy in *From Sea Unto Sea* wrote: "Wherever Schultz strode either the grass withered or the snow melted."

Schultz, like Clifford Sifton and John McDougall, was a student at Victoria College, Cobourg, Ontario. He went to Fort Garry in 1860 and bought the first newspaper, the *Nor'Wester,* which had first appeared on December 28 the previous year. It had been founded by two young Englishmen who had worked on newspapers in Toronto. They transported their printing press to Fort Garry in an oxcart with their wives sitting on top!

Schultz used the *Nor'Wester* to support his "Canadian Party" which opposed the Hudson's Bay Company control over the West, and favored annexation to Canada. He supplemented his income as a doctor by dealing in furs and land, and prospecting for gold along the North Saskatchewan River.

Dr. Schultz was largely responsible for Canada's sending surveyors to Red River before the official takeover from the Hudson's Bay Company. This action partly provoked the Red River uprising (see October 11). Later, Riel rounded up Dr. Schultz and other members of the Canadian Party and put them in jail in Fort Garry. The doctor's wife came to the rescue. She smuggled a knife to him in a plum pudding, and he pried his way through the window. Then he dropped to the ground by cutting his buffalo robe blanket into strips and making it into a rope.

When Riel finally fled from Red River, Dr. Schultz sought revenge on some of his followers. Elzear Goulet, who had taken part in the court-martial of Thomas Scott, was stoned to death as he tried to swim across a river. François Guilmette, who had fired the final shot into Scott's head, was killed. André Nault, on whose farm the survey had been stopped, was bayonetted and left for dead.

Yet Dr. Schultz went on to become a member of the House of Commons, then a senator, Lieutenant-Governor of Manitoba, and finally Sir John Schultz.

Sir John Christian Schultz (1840-1896)

Other Events on December 28:

1602   The Merchants of Rouen and St. Malo were summoned to form a company to colonize Canada.

1720   The British Lords of Trade proposed the removal of the Acadians.

1835   Britain withdrew assent to the New Brunswick-Maine border arbitration awarded by the King of the Netherlands. America had already rejected the award.

1858   Governor Douglas of British Columbia issued an edict that all gold found along the Fraser and Thompson Rivers belonged to the Crown. This meant that prospectors needed licences.

Marriage Law Changed

Jacob Mountain, First Anglican Bishop of Quebec

One of the most difficult problems in Canada as late as 1834 was how to get married. Until 1795, the Quebec Act seemed to invalidate marriages in Lower Canada which were not authorized by the Anglican or Roman Catholic Church. In Upper Canada one of the first things done by the Legislature after it was formed in 1792 was to pass a Marriage Act. However, Lieutenant-Governor Simcoe was determined that everyone should belong to the Church of England, and the Act allowed only Anglican ministers to perform marriage services.

Many of the United Empire Loyalists and other settlers belonged to "dissenting" faiths, chiefly Methodist, Presbyterian, Baptist, and Congregationalist and they wanted to be married by their own ministers. In many areas there was no clergy at all. Marriage services were often conducted by commanding officers of military posts or by civil magistrates. If the legality of these marriages was doubtful, the children were branded as illegitimate and prohibited from inheriting property.

The Marriage Act passed by the second session of the Legislature of Upper Canada in May, 1793, provided that marriages made in the past were legally binding, but stipulated that future marriages must follow the Church of England form. As there were now more "dissenters" than members of the Church of England in Upper Canada this aroused a great deal of criticism. In 1796 the magistrates of the eastern districts asked that ministers of all denominations be allowed to solemnize marriages, but Governor Simcoe would not hear of it. He said the idea was the product of a wicked head and disloyal heart!

Some order began to emerge from the confusion on December 29, 1798, when royal assent was given to an order validating marriages celebrated by other than Church of England clergy. By this time Simcoe had returned to Britain. It took until 1829 before a Dissenters' Marriage Bill finally became law in Upper Canada. There were similar problems in the other British North American colonies before Confederation.

Even today there are variations in marriage laws among the provinces. In Newfoundland, Prince Edward Island, Nova Scotia, New Brunswick and Quebec, marriages must be solemnized by persons in holy orders. In the other provinces, marriage services may be performed by civic officials.

Other Events on December 29:

1810 David Thompson began his journey from the Athabasca River to the Columbia River through the Rockies on snowshoes in 20 below zero weather.

1812 The Legislature of Lower Canada met to renew the Army Bill Act and voted £25,000 for the war against the United States.

1868 Lord Lisgar was appointed Governor-General.

1908 The first gold coin and sovereigns were minted in Canada.

1921 W. L. Mackenzie King formed his first government and served as prime minister for twenty-one years, five months, and five days (see April 21).

Chesapeake's *men attack Captain Broke*

Shannon Takes U.S. Ship

British prestige was greatly shaken soon after the outbreak of the War of 1812, when several warships of the proud Royal Navy were sunk or captured by the upstart Americans. On December 30, 1812, H.M.S. *Java* surrendered to the U.S. *Constitution*. In August the *Constitution* had captured H.M.S. *Guerrière,* whose captain was court-martialed although he had been wounded in the fight, and seventy-seven of his men killed.

Captain Broke of H.M.S. *Shannon* vowed to take revenge by capturing the *Constitution* and towing her into Halifax. Broke had one of the best-trained crews in the navy. He had a private fortune, and when the *Shannon* captured American merchant ships his share of the prize money was distributed among the sailors.

The *Shannon* sailed from Halifax on March 13, 1813, white sails billowing as it glided magnificently past George's Island. For two months Captain Broke searched for the *Constitution,* capturing twenty-five American ships during the chase. *Constitution* had

been in Boston for a refit, however, and escaped the British cruisers during a fog.

Broke learned that another outstanding American ship, *Chesapeake*, was in Boston, and he sent a message to its captain, Lawrence: "As the *Chesapeake* appears now ready for sea, I request you will do me the favour to meet the *Shannon* with her and try the fortune of our respective flags. Choose your terms but let us meet." Lawrence was one of the best American captains, a giant of a man, who had recently defeated another British ship, the *Peacock*, and he accepted the challenge immediately.

Chesapeake had heavier guns than *Shannon* so Captain Broke decided to try to maneuver close and get his men on board. The battle began at five minutes to six and was all over in fifteen minutes. Broke's men remained below decks until the two ships were close. Then there was an exchange of gunfire in which *Shannon's* crew got the upper hand. *Shannon* managed to clamp boarding hooks on *Chesapeake* and the men scrambled over. The Americans were killed or captured in a few minutes. *Shannon* lost 83 men killed or wounded, while *Chesapeake's* casualties were 146, including Captain Lawrence, who was killed. When he was dying he uttered a phrase now famous in the U.S. Navy: "Don't give up the ship."

Other Events on December 30:

1650 The Ursuline convent at Quebec was burned.

1813 British and Canadian troops raided Black Rock and Buffalo in retaliation for an American attack on Newark, Ontario.

1824 The Upper Canada Legislature at Toronto was destroyed by fire.

1861 The 62nd Wiltshire Regiment landed at St. Andrews, New Brunswick because of the danger of war with the United States.

1870 Manitoba held its first provincial election.

Montgomery Killed

The year 1775 was brought to a dramatic close in Canada when Generals Montgomery and Arnold launched an all-out attack on Quebec City. The combined American force was about 1,000 men, and their clothing, mainly uniforms captured from the British, was so like that of the British and Canadian defenders of Quebec that Montgomery had his men wear sprigs of hemlock in their caps to distinguish them.

Governor Carleton knew from experience what had happened to Generals Montcalm and Murray when they had tried to fight off invaders by battling on the Plains of Abraham. He resolved to sit tight in the city and force the enemy to do the attacking. If he could hold out until spring, the British navy would arrive and save the situation. This eventually did happen (see May 9).

Montgomery and Arnold saw their army melting away through disease and desertion, so they decided to try a surprise attack. It was carefully planned, preceded by a number of feints and diversionary moves around the city. The assault was launched at 2 a.m. on December 31, 1775. Arnold led one force from the east into Lower Town. Montgomery approached from the west along the river's edge.

The British sentries were alert, and the invading forces were met with heavy gunfire. Arnold was wounded, and Montgomery was killed as he led his men, waving his sword and shouting, "Come on, brave boys, Quebec is ours!" The bitterly fought battle lasted all night. When Arnold was wounded Daniel Morgan took over the leadership and his Virginian riflemen shot the gunners from the platforms. The Americans dragged ladders to the 12-foot walls and tried to climb over. One of the Canadian defenders was a giant named Charland. He would throw down the ladders or even drag them inside the fort.

When daylight came, the Americans were exposed, and Carleton finally drove them off

Death of General Montgomery

after more fierce fighting. The failure of the attack did not end Washington's resolve to take Quebec and he sent reinforcements. The Americans eventually had 3,000 men outside the walls, but they never launched another attack like the one on the last day of 1775. Soon after, they had to withdraw from Canada.

Other Events on December 31:

1814   General Pring was court-martialed for failures at Plattsburg and Lake Champlain.

1857   The decimal system of currency in public accounts came into effect at midnight.

Queen Victoria anounced the choice of Ottawa as the capital of Canada (see January 27).

1916   The immigration figure was surprising for a war year: 66,000, of whom 8,500 came from Britain and 52,000 from the United States.

1923   The wheat crop of 474 million bushels was the largest in history up to that time. Its value was $317 million, and the yield, 21 bushels per acre.

1954   Ottawa celebrated its centennial year.

INDEX

Dates printed in bold type denote a detailed story of the entry.